Lecture Notes in Artificial Intelligence 2056

Subseries of Lecture Notes in Computer Science
Edited by J. G. Carbonell and J. Siekmann

Lecture Notes in Computer Science

Edited by G. Goos, J. Hartmanis and J. van Leeuwen

T0223615

Springer
Berlin
Heidelberg
New York
Barcelona
Hong Kong
London
Milan
Paris
Singapore
Tokyo

Eleni Stroulia   Stan Matwin (Eds.)

Advances in Artificial Intelligence

14th Biennial Conference of the Canadian Society
for Computational Studies of Intelligence, AI 2001
Ottawa, Canada, June 7-9, 2001
Proceedings

 Springer

Series Editors

Jaime G. Carbonell, Carnegie Mellon University, Pittsburgh, PA, USA
Jörg Siekmann, University of Saarland, Saabrücken, Germany

Volume Editors

Eleni Stroulia
University of Alberta, Department of Computer Science
Edmonton, AB, Canada T6G 2E8
E-mail: stroulia@cs.ualberta.ca

Stan Matwin
University of Ottawa, School of Information Technology and Engineering
Ottawa, ON, Canada K1N 6N5
E-mail: stan@site.uottawa.ca

Cataloging-in-Publication Data applied for

Die Deutsche Bibliothek - CIP-Einheitsaufnahme

Advances in artificial intelligence : proceedings / AI 2001, Ottawa,
Canada, June 7 - 9, 2001. Eleni Stroulia ; Stan Matwin (ed.). - Berlin ;
Heidelberg ; New York ; Barcelona ; Hong Kong ; London ; Milan ;
Paris ; Singapore ; Tokyo : Springer, 2001
     (... biennial conference of the Canadian Society for Computational
     Studies of Intelligence ; 14)
     (Lecture notes in computer science ; Vol. 2056 : Lecture notes in
     artificial intelligence)
     ISBN 3-540-42144-0

CR Subject Classification (1998): I.2

ISBN 3-540-42144-0 Springer-Verlag Berlin Heidelberg New York

Springer-Verlag Berlin Heidelberg New York
a member of BertelsmannSpringer Science+Business Media GmbH

http://www.springer.de

© Springer-Verlag Berlin Heidelberg 2001
Printed in Germany

Typesetting: Camera-ready by author, data conversion by PTP-Berlin, Stefan Sossna
Printed on acid-free paper   SPIN: 10781551   06/3142   5 4 3 2 1 0

Preface

AI 2001 is the 14th in the series of Artificial Intelligence conferences sponsored by the Canadian Society for Computational Studies of Intelligence/Société canadienne pour l'étude de l'intelligence par ordinateur. As was the case last year too, the conference is being held in conjunction with the annual conferences of two other Canadian societies, Graphics Interface (GI 2001) and Vision Interface (VI 2001). We believe that the overall experience will be enriched by this conjunction of conferences.

This year is the "silver anniversary" of the conference: the first Canadian AI conference was held in 1976 at UBC. During its lifetime, it has attracted Canadian and international papers of high quality from a variety of AI research areas. All papers submitted to the conference received at least three independent reviews. Approximately one third were accepted for plenary presentation at the conference. The best paper of the conference will be invited to appear in Computational Intelligence.

This year, we have some innovations in the format of the conference. In addition to the plenary presentations of the 24 accepted papers, organized in topical sessions, we have a session devoted to short presentations of the accepted posters, and a graduate symposium session. With this format, we hope to increase the level of interaction and to make the experience even more interesting and enjoyable to all the participants. The graduate symposium is sponsored by AAAI, who provided funds to partially cover the expenses of the participating students.

Many people contributed to the success of this conference. The members of the program committee coordinated the refereeing of all submitted papers. They also made several recommendations that contributed to other aspects of the program. The referees provided reviews of the submitted technical papers; their efforts were irreplaceable in ensuring the quality of the accepted papers. Our thanks also go to Howard Hamilton and Bob Mercer for their invaluable help in organizing the conference. We also acknowledge the help we received from Alfred Hofmann and others at Springer-Verlag.

Lastly, we are pleased to thank all participants. You are the ones who make all this effort worthwhile!

June 2001   Eleni Stroulia, Stan Matwin

Organization

AI 2001 is organized by the Canadian Society for Computational Studies of Intelligence (Société canadienne pour l'étude de l'intelligence par ordinateur).

Program Committee

Program Co-chairs: Stan Matwin (University of Ottawa)
    Eleni Stroulia (University of Alberta)

Committee Members: Irene Abi-Zeid (Defence Research Establishment Valcartier)
Fahiem Bacchus (University of Toronto)
Ken Barker (University of Texas at Austin)
Sabine Bergler (Concordia University)
Nick Cercone (University of Waterloo)
Michael Cox (Wright State University)
Chrysanne DiMarco (University of Waterloo)
Toby Donaldson (TechBC)
Renee Elio (University of Alberta)
Ali Ghorbani (University of New Brunswick)
Jim Greer (University of Saskatchewan)
Howard Hamilton (University of Regina)
Graeme Hirst (University of Toronto)
Robert Holte (Univesity of Ottawa)
Nathalie Japkowicz (Univesity of Ottawa)
Guy LaPalme (Université de Montréal)
Dekang Lin (University of Alberta)
André Trudel (Acadia University)
Joel Martin (National Research Council)
Gord McCalla (University of Saskatchewan)
Robert Mercer (University of Western Ontario)
John Mylopoulos (University of Toronto)
Witold Pedrycz (University of Alberta)
Fred Popowich (Simon Fraser University)
Yang Qiang (Simon Fraser University)
Bruce Spencer (University of New Brunswick)
Ahmed Tawfik (University of Windsor)
Afzal Upal (Daltech / Dalhousie University)
Peter van Beek (University of Waterloo)
Kay Wiese (TechBC)

Referees

Irene Abi-Zeid
Fahiem Bacchus
Ken Barker
Sabine Bergler
Nick Cercone
Michael Cox
Toby Donaldson
Renee Elio
Dan Fass
Ali Ghorbani
Paolo Giorgini

Jim Greer
Howard Hamilton
Graeme Hirst
Robert Holte
Nathalie Japkowicz
Guy LaPalme
Dekang Lin
André Trudel
Joel Martin
Gord McCalla
Tim Menzies

Robert Mercer
John Mylopoulos
Witold Pedrycz
Fred Popowich
Bruce Spencer
Ahmed Tawfik
Afzal Upal
Peter van Beek
Kay Wiese

Sponsoring Institutions

AAAI, American Association for Artificial Intelligence

Table of Contents

Posters

Graduate Symposium Contributions

A Case Study for Learning from Imbalanced Data Sets

Aijun An, Nick Cercone, and Xiangji Huang

Department of Computer Science, University of Waterloo
Waterloo, Ontario N2L 3G1 Canada
{aan, ncercone, jhuang}@uwaterloo.ca

Abstract. We present our experience in applying a rule induction technique to an extremely imbalanced pharmaceutical data set. We focus on using a variety of performance measures to evaluate a number of rule quality measures. We also investigate whether simply changing the distribution skew in the training data can improve predictive performance. Finally, we propose a method for adjusting the learning algorithm for learning in an extremely imbalanced environment. Our experimental results show that this adjustment improves predictive performance for rule quality formulas in which rule coverage makes positive contributions to the rule quality value.

Keywords: Machine learning, Imbalanced data sets, Rule quality.

1 Introduction

Many real-world data sets exhibit skewed class distributions in which almost all cases are allotted to one or more larger classes and far fewer cases allotted for a smaller, usually more interesting class. For example, a medical diagnosis data set used in [1] contains cases that correspond to diagnoses for a rare disease. In that data set, only 5% of the cases correspond to "positive" diagnoses; the remaining majority of the cases belong to the "no disease" category. Learning with this kind of imbalanced data set presents problems to machine learning systems, problems which are not revealed when the systems work on relatively balanced data sets. One problem occurs since most inductive learning algorithms assume that maximizing accuracy on a full range of cases is the goal [12] and, therefore, these systems exhibit accurate prediction for the majority class cases, but very poor performance for cases associated with the low frequency class. Some solutions to this problem have been suggested. For example, Cardie and Howe [5] proposed a method that uses case-specific feature weights in a case-based learning framework to improve minority class prediction. Some studies focus on reducing the imbalance in the data set by using different sampling techniques, such as data reduction techniques that remove only majority class examples [9] and "up-sampling" techniques that duplicate the training examples of the minority class or create new examples by corrupting existing ones with artificial noise

E. Stroulia and S. Matwin (Eds.): AI 2001, LNAI 2056, pp. 1–15, 2001.

[6]. An alternative to balancing the classes is to develop a learning algorithm that is intrinsically insensitive to class distribution in the training set [11]. An example of this kind of algorithm is the SHRINK algorithm [10] that finds only rules that best summarizes the positive examples (of the small class), but makes use of the information from the negative examples. Another approach to learning from imbalanced data sets, proposed by Provost and Fawcett [13], is to build a hybrid classifier that uses ROC analysis for comparison of classifier performance that is robust to imprecise class distributions and misclassification costs. Provost and Fawcett argued that optimal performance for continuous-output classifiers in terms of expected cost can be obtained by adjusting the output threshold according to the class distributions and misclassification costs. Although many methods for coping with imbalanced data sets have been proposed, there remain open questions. According to [12], one open question is whether simply changing the distribution skew can improve predictive performance systematically. Another question is whether we can tailor the learning algorithm to this special learning environment so that the accuracy for the extreme class values can be improved.

Another important issue in learning from imbalanced data sets is how to evaluate the learning result. Clearly, the standard performance measure used in machine learning - predictive accuracy over the entire region of the test cases is not appropriate for applications where classes are unequally distributed. Several measures have been proposed. Kubat *et al* [11] proposed to use the geometric mean of the accuracy on the positive examples and the accuracy on the negative examples as one of their performance measures. Provost and Fawcette [13] made use of ROC curves that visualize the trade-off between the false positive rate and the true positive rate to compare classifiers. In information retrieval, where relevant and irrelevant documents are extremely imbalanced, recall and precision are used as standard performance measures.

We present our experience in applying rule induction techniques to an extremely imbalanced data set. The task of this application is to identify promising compounds from a large chemical inventory for drug discovery. The data set contains nearly 30,000 cases, only 2% of which are labeled as potent molecules. To learn decision rules from this data set, we applied the ELEM2 rule induction system [2]. The learning strategies used in ELEM2 include sequential covering and post-pruning. A number of rule quality formulas are incorporated in ELEM2 for use in the post-pruning and classification processes. Different rule quality formulas may lead to generation of different sets of rules, which in turn results in different predictions for the new cases. We have previously evaluated the rule quality formulas on a number of benchmark datasets [3], but none of them is extremely imbalanced. Our objective in this paper is to provide answers to the following questions. First, we would like to determine how each of these rule quality formulas reacts to the extremely imbalanced class distribution and which of the rule quality formulas is most appropriate in this kind of environment. Second, we would like to know whether reducing the imbalance in the data set can improve predictive performance. Third, we would like to compare different measures of performance to discover whether there is correlation between them. Finally, we would like to know whether a special adjustment of the learning algorithm can improve predictive performance in an extremely imbalanced environment. The paper is organized as follows. In Section 2, we describe our data set and the application tasks related to the data set. We then briefly describe the learning and classification algorithms used in our experiment. In Section 6 we present our experiments and experimental results. We conclude the paper with a summary of our findings from the experiments.

2   Domain of the Case Study

The data set we used was obtained from the National Cancer Institute through our colleagues in the Statistics Department at the University of Waterloo. It concerns the prediction of biological potency of chemical compounds for possible use in the pharmaceutical industry. Highly potent compounds have great potential to be used in new medical drugs. In the pharmaceutical industry, screening every available compound against every biological target through biological tests is impossible due to the expense and work involved. Therefore, it is highly desirable to develop methods that, on the basis of relatively few tested compounds, can identify promising compounds from a relatively large chemical inventory.

2.1   The Data Set

Our data set contains $29,812$ tested compounds. Each compound is described by a set of descriptors that characterize the chemical structure of the molecule and a binary response variable that indicates whether the compound is active or not. 2.04% of these compounds are labeled as active and the remaining ones as inactive. The data set has been randomly split into two equal-sized subsets, each of which contains the same number of active compounds so that the class distribution in either of the subsets remain the same as in the original data set. We use one subset as the training set and the other as the testing test in our experiments.

2.2   Tasks and Performance Measures

One obvious task is to learn classification rules from the training data set and use these rules to classify the compounds in the test set. Since it is the active compounds that are of interest, appropriate measures of classification performance are not the accuracy on the entire test set, but the precision and recall on the active compounds. *Precision* is the proportion of true active compounds among the compounds predicted as active. *Recall* is proportion of the predicted active compounds among the active compounds in the test set.

However, simply classifying compounds is not sufficient. The domain experts would like identified compounds to be presented to them in decreasing order of a prediction score with the highest prediction indicating the most probably active compound so that identified compounds can be tested in biological systems one by one starting with the compound with the highest prediction. Therefore, in addition to classification, the other task is to rank the compounds in the test set according to a prediction score. To be cost effective, it is preferred that a high proportion of the proposed lead compounds actually exhibit biological activity.

3   The Learning Algorithm

ELEM2 [2] is used to learn rules from the above bio-chemistry data set. Given a set of training data, ELEM2 learns a set of rules for each of the classes in the data set. For a class C, ELEM2 generates a disjunctive set of conjunctive rules by the *sequential covering* learning strategy, which sequentially learns a single conjunctive rule, removes the examples covered by the rule, then iterates the process until all examples of class C is covered or until no rule can be generated. The learning of a single conjunctive rule begins by considering the most general rule precondition, then greedily searching for an attribute-value pair that is most relevant to class C according to the following attribute-value pair evaluation function: $SIG_C(av) = P(av)(P(C|av) - P(C))$, where av is an attribute-value pair and P denotes probability. The selected attribute-value pair is then added to the rule precondition as a conjunct. The process is repeated by greedily adding a second attribute-value pair, and so on, until the hypothesis reaches an acceptable level of performance. In ELEM2, the acceptable level is based on the consistency of the rule: it forms a rule that is as consistent with the training data as possible. Since this "consistent" rule may overfit the data, ELEM2 then "post-prunes" the rule after the initial search for this rule is complete.

To post-prune a rule, ELEM2 computes a rule quality value according to one of the 11 statistical or empirical formulas. The formulas include *a weighted sum of rule consistency and coverage (WS), a product of rule consistency and coverage (Prod), the χ^2 statistic (Chi), the G2 likelihood ratio statistic (G2), a measure of rule logical sufficiency (LS), a measure of discrimination between positive and negative examples (MD), information score (IS), Cohen's formula (Cohen), Coleman's formula (Coleman), the C1 and C2 formulas*. These formulas are described in [3,4]. In post-pruning, ELEM2 checks each attribute-value pair in the rule in the reverse order in which they were selected to determine if removal of the attribute-value pair will decrease the rule quality value. If not, the attribute-value pair is removed and the procedure checks all the other pairs in the same order again using the new rule quality value resulting from the removal of that attribute-value pair to discover whether another attribute-value pair can be removed. This procedure continues until no pair can be removed.

4   The Classification Method

The classification procedure in ELEM2 considers three possible cases when a new example matches a set of rules. (1)*Single match*. The new example satisfies one or more rules of the same class. In this case, the example is classified to the class indicated by the rule(s). (2)*Multiple match*. The new example satisfies more than one rule that indicates different classes. In this case, ELEM2 activates a conflict resolution scheme for the best decision. The conflict resolution scheme computes a decision score for each of the matched classes as follows: $DS(C) = \sum_{i=1}^{k} Q(r_i)$, where r_i is a matched rule that indicates C, k is the number of this kind of rules, and $Q(r_i)$ is the rule quality of r_i. The new example is then classified into the class with the highest decision score. (3)*No match*. The new example e is not covered by any rule. Partial matching is considered where some attribute-value pairs of a rule match the values of corresponding attributes in e. If the partially-matched rules do not agree on the classes, a partial matching score between e and a partially-matched rule r_i with n attribute-value pairs, m of which match the corresponding attributes of e, is computed as $PMS(r_i) = \frac{m}{n} \times Q(r_i)$. A decision score for a class C is computed as $DS(C) = \sum_{i=0}^{k} PMS(r_i)$, where k is the number of partially-matched rules indicating class C. In decision making, e is classified into the class with the highest decision score.

5   Ranking the Test Examples

The classification procedure of ELEM2 produces a class label for each test example. To meet the requirement of our particular application, we design another prediction procedure which outputs a numerical score for each test example. The score is used to compare examples as to whether an example more likely belongs to a class than another example. Intuitively, we could use the decision score computed in the classification procedure to rank the examples. However, that decision score was designed to distinguish between classes for a given example. It consists of either *full*-matching scores (when the example fully matches a rule) or *partial*-matching scores (when no rule is fully matched with the example, but partial matching exists). It is possible that an example that only partially matches some rules of class C obtains a higher decision score than an example that fully matches one rule of C, even though the fully matched example is more likely to belong to C than the partially matched example.

In order to rank examples according to their likelihood of belonging to a class we need to design a criterion that can distinguish between examples given the class. To do so, we simply adjust the calculation of the decision score in the classification procedure to consider both kinds of matches (full and partial matches) in calculating a score for an example. The score is called the *ranking score* of an example with respect to a class. For class C and example e, we first compute a *matching score* between e and a rule r of C using $MS(e,r) = \frac{m}{n} \times Q(r)$, where n is the number of attribute-value pairs that r contains and m is the number of attribute-value pairs in r that are matched with e. Note that this calculation covers a full match when $m = n$, a partial match when $< m < n$, and no match when $m = 0$. The ranking score of e with respect to C is defined as $RS(e, C) = \sum_{i=0}^{k} MS(e, r_i)$, where r_i is a rule of C and k is the number of rules of C.

The ranking algorithm of ELEM2 ranks the test examples according to both the predicted class label (produced by ELEM2's classification program) for the example and the ranking score of that example with respect to a specified class C, e.g., the minority class for an imbalanced data set. It places test examples that are classified into the specified class C in front of other test examples and ranks the examples in each group in decreasing order of the ranking score with respect to C.

6   Experiments with the Pharmaceutical Data Set

6.1   Comparison on Rule Quality Formulas

Our first objective is to determine how each of the rule quality formulas incorporated in ELEM2 reacts to the imbalance in our data set. To achieve this goal, we run ELEM2 with different rule quality formulas on our training data set. For each formula, a set of rules is generated. We then test these rules by running the classification program of ELEM2 to classify the examples in the test set. This program generates a discrete output for each test example, which is the predicted class label for that example. The performance of this classifier is measured by *precision* and *recall* (defined in Section 2.2) on the smaller class that corresponds to the active compounds. We also combine precision and recall by way of a geometric mean (g-mean) defined as $\sqrt{precision * recall}$. Figure 1 shows the precision, recall and g-mean of ELEM2's classification program using different rule quality formulas. Generally, formulas that produce higher recalls give lower precisions and formulas that give lower recalls produce higher precisions. In terms of g-mean, the G2 (*the G2 likelihood ratio statistic*) formula produces the best result, while the WS (a weighted sum of rule consistency and rule coverage) and Prod (a product of rule consistency and rule coverage) formulas have the worst performance.

We then run the ranking program of ELEM2 to rank the test examples according to the ranking score defined in Section 5. The performance of this program is measured by recall-level precisions, case-level precisions and an average precision.[1] *Recall-level precisions* are the precisions at a list of recall cutoff

---

[1] These measures are used in the TREC competitions of the information retrieval community [8]. We adopt these measures for use in our application because the requirement for our application (presenting predicted active compounds in an order in which the most probably active compounds are ranked first) is similar to the requirement in information retrieval, which ranks the retrieved documents according to the degree of relevance.

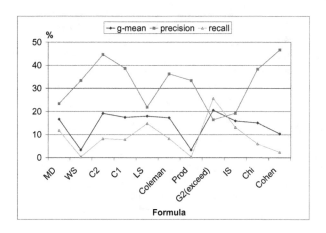

Fig. 1. Classification Performance of the Formulas

values. The recall cutoff values used are 0.1, 0.2, 0.3, 0.4, 0.5, 0.6, 0.7, 0.8, 0.9 and 1. A graph on recall-level precisions depicts tradeoffs between precision and recall. *Case-level precisions* are the precisions at a list of *case* cutoff values. A case cutoff value is a number of cases being "retrieved". A precision at a case cutoff value n is the precision of the first n examples in the ranked list of test examples. The case cutoff values we used are 5, 10, 20, 30, 50, 100, 200, 400, 800, and 1000. Compared to recall-level precisions, case-level precisions give a better picture on the precisions at the top ranked cases. *Average precision* is the average of the precision values at the points where active compounds were correctly recognized in the run.

Figure 2 illustrates recall-level precisions and case-level precisions of the results generated by the ranking program using different formulas. In the figure, we only show the results for 7 formulas; the curves for our remaining 4 formulas (whose performance ranked medium) were deleted for graph clarity. The average precisions from each of the 11 formulas are shown in Figure 3. From recall-precision curves, we observe that formula G2 takes the lead generally, especially in the small to middle recall cutoff region. However, at the recall cutoff value of 0.1, formula LS (*measure of logical sufficiency*) takes the lead, followed by formula MD (*measure of discrimination*). The right graph of Figure 2 presents a clearer picture on the top ranked cases, which shows that LS is the "winner" for the top 50 cases and the χ^2 statistic (Chi) also performs well within this top region. In terms of average precision, Figure 3 shows that G2 takes the lead, followed by LS and then MD.

We also evaluate the result of each run using the ROC convex hull method proposed by Provost and Fawcett [13]. A ROC curve shows how the percentage of

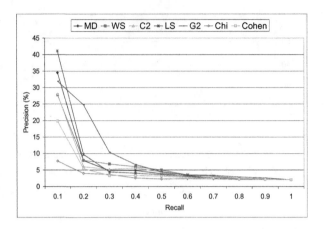

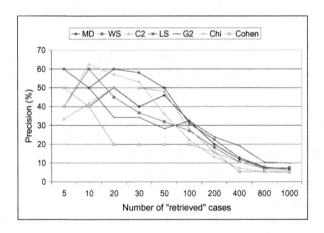

Fig. 2. Recall-level Precisions (top) and Case-level Precisions (bot)

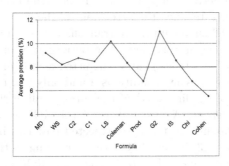

Fig. 3. Average Precisions

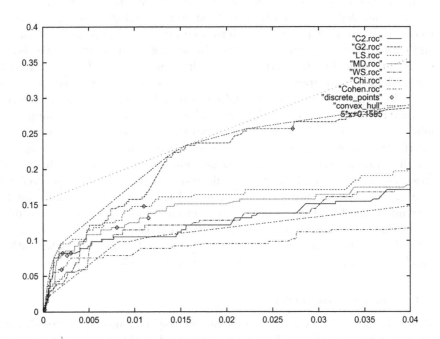

Fig. 4. ROC curves and the ROC convex hull from 7 Formulas

correctly recognized active compounds (recall or "true positive rate") depends on the "false positive rate", i.e., the percentage of the incorrectly classified inactive compounds. ROC curves illustrate tradeoffs between recall and false alarm rate for continuous output classifiers. The performance of a discrete classifier (which outputs only class labels) can be depicted as a point in the ROC space. A classifier is optimal for some conditions if and only if it lies on the northwest boundary (i.e., above the line y=x) of the convex hull of the set of points and curves in the ROC space. A nice feature of the ROC convex hull method is that the optimal classifier in terms of expected cost can be determined using *iso-performance lines* [13] in the ROC space according to the class distribution and the misclassification costs. Figure 4 depicts the ROC curves generated from the results of 7 formulas. Again the curves for the 4 other formulas were deleted for clarity. Figure 4 also shows the points corresponding to the performance of ELEM2's "discrete" classifier. Each point in the graph corresponds to a rule quality formula that was used to generate the classifier. The convex hull of these 7 curves and 11 points is shown in the picture. We notice that none of the discrete classifiers is optimal because their corresponding points are not on the convex hull curve. An optimal performance in terms of misclassification costs and class distribution can be obtained by setting a threshold for the continuous output value for the continuous "classifier" whose curve intersects with the convex hull. In our application, the cost of missing an active compound (cost of a false negative error) is potentially much higher than the cost of screening an inactive compound in the lab (cost of a false positive error). Suppose the false negative cost is 10 times higher than the false positive cost and the true distribution of the data is the same as the distribution in the training data. We can draw an *iso-performance line* (the straight line of $5x + 0.1555$) in the ROC space in Figure 4 based on the formula provided in [13], which intersects the convex hull. The intersection of this line and the convex hull is the point that determines the threshold value for the continuous-output classifier in order to obtain the optimal performance. These ROC curves also clearly show that G2 is the leading formula, followed by LS and then MD, which correlates with the conclusion obtained from average precisions in Figure 3.

6.2   Balancing the Data

We would like to discover whether decreasing the imbalance in the training data set would improve the predictive performance. For this purpose, we created 6 additional training sets by duplicating the examples of active compounds to increase the prevalence of active compounds in the training data. Distributions of active compounds in these 6 training sets are 4%, 8%, 14%, 25%, 40% and 50%, respectively.

We picked three formulas (G2, MD, Cohen) ranging from good to poor based on the above results for use in this experiment. Figure 5, illustrates the results of increasing the minority class prevalence in terms of g-mean, precision, recall and average precision for the three formulas, respectively. All the three graphs

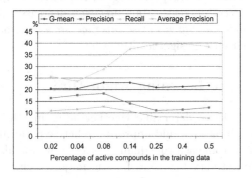

a

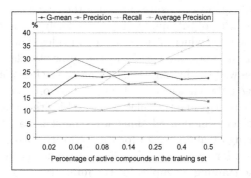

b

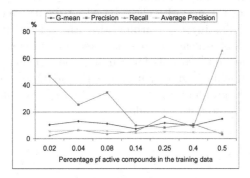

c

Fig. 5. Results of Increasing Prevalence for the G2 (**a**), MD (**b**) and Cohen's (**c**) Formulas

indicate that, generally, as the percentage of the active compounds in the training set increases, *recall* increases, but *precision* decreases. As a result, *g-mean* does not have significant changes. Also, *average precision* (for continuous output classifiers) does not change significantly either.

7 Adjusting the Learning Algorithm

Finally, we would like to determine whether adjusting the learning algorithm for an imbalanced data set would improve predictive performance. By analyzing the rules generated from each rule quality formula, we found that some formulas lead to generation of very few rules for the majority class. This is due to the fact that, when post-pruning a rule, removing an attribute-value pair from a rule for the majority class can greatly increase the coverage of the rule. In this case, for some rule quality measures in which the rule coverage makes a positive contribution, the value of rule quality is mostly likely to increase when removing an attribute-value pair, which results in general rules that cover a large number of cases of both the majority class and the minority class. This kind of rule does not describe well the instances in the majority class and has limited power in discriminating between the two classes. Therefore, we adjust the learning algorithm to only post-prune the rules generated for the minority class when the data set is extremely imbalanced. This adjustment is based on the assumption that we have enough training cases for the majority class and there is no noise in the training set for this class. We still post-prune the rules for the minority class because the training examples for the minority class is relatively rare and we do not want the rules to overfit the minority class examples.

We use five rule quality formulas that led to generation of a relatively small number of rules for the majority class, based on the above experiments, to test our strategy for adjusting the learning algorithm. The left graph of Figure 6 compares, in terms of g-mean and average precision, the results for pruning only minority class rules to the results for pruning rules for both classes. The results show that this adjustment greatly improves the predictive performance of these formulas. The right graph of Figure 6 shows the improvement on the recall-level precisions for the χ^2 statistic formula.

8 Conclusions

We have compared a number of rule quality formulas on an extremely imbalanced data set for identifying active chemical compounds. The rule quality formulas are used in ELEM2's rule induction and classification processes. Among the 11 tested statistical and empirical formulas, the G2 likelihood ratio statistic outperforms others in terms of g-mean, average precision and recall-level precisions. The ROC analysis also shows that G2 gives the best results. Other formulas that perform relatively well on this data set include the measure of logical sufficiency (LS) and the measure of discrimination (MD). In evaluating these formulas, we

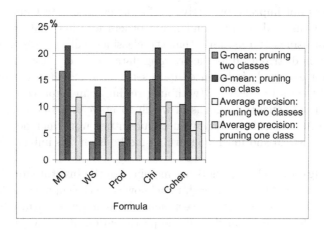

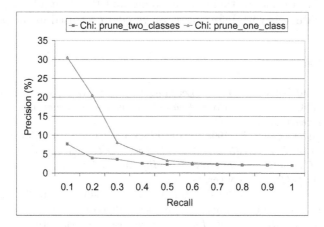

Fig. 6. Differences between pruning rules for 2 classes and pruning rules for the minority class

observed that ROC curves give a clearer picture than recall-precision curves on the overall performance of continuous output classifiers. Case-level precision curves produce a better picture on precisions at the top ranked cases. Another good measure of performance is average precision, which is good at ranking the evaluated continuous output classifiers. In our evaluation of rule quality formulas, the conclusion drawn from average precisions correlates well with the observation on ROC curves.

We also observed that increasing prevalence of the minority class in the training data does not improve predictive performance on our test data. This is because our learning algorithm (and many others for that matter) is based on statistical measures and assumes that the classifier will operate on data drawn from the same distribution as the training data. In terms of adjusting learning algorithm for extremely imbalanced data sets, we found that allowing rules for the majority class to "overfit" (without pruning) can improve predictive performance for rule quality formulas in which coverage of a rule makes a positive contribution to the rule quality value. Our future work includes evaluating a variety of statistical and machine learning methods on this imbalanced data set.

Acknowledgment. The authors are members of the Institute for Robotics and Intelligent Systems (IRIS) and wish to acknowledge the support of the Networks of Centres of Excellence of the Government of Canada, the Natural Sciences and Engineering Research Council, and the participation of PRECARN Associates Inc. We would like to thank Ms. Yuanyuan Wang and Professor Will Welch of the Statistics Department at University of Waterloo for passing the data set to us. We would also like to thank Stan Young and Ray Lam of Glaxo Wellcome Inc. for providing us with information on the data set used in the paper.

References

1. Aha, D. and Kibler, D. 1987. "Learning Representative Exemplars of Concepts: An Initial Case Study." *Proceedings of the Fourth International Conference on Machine Learning*, Irvine, CA.
2. An, A. and Cercone, N. 1998. "ELEM2: A Learning System for More Accurate Classifications." *Proceedings of the 12th Biennial Conference of the Canadian Society for Computational Studies of Intelligence, AI'98 (Lecture Notes in Artificial Intelligence 1418)*, Vancouver, Canada.
3. An, A. and Cercone, N. 2000. "Rule Quality Measures Improve the Accuracy of Rule Induction: An Experimental Approach", *Proceedings of the 12th International Symposium on Methodologies for Intelligent Systems*, Charlotte, NC. pp.119-129.
4. Bruha, I. 1996. "Quality of Decision Rules: Definitions and Classification Schemes for Multiple Rules", in Nakhaeizadeh, G. and Taylor, C. C. (eds.): Machine Learning and Statistics, The Interface. Jone Wiley & Sons Inc.
5. Cardie, C and Howe, N. 1997. "Improving Minority Class Prediction Using Case-Specific Feature Weights", *Proceedings of the Fourteenth International Confernece on Machine Learning*, Morgan Kaufmann. pp.57-65.
6. DeRouin, E., Brown, J., Beck, H., Fausett, L. and Schneider, M. 1991. "Neural Network Training on Unequally Represented Classes", In Dagli, C.H., Kumara, S.R.T. and Shin, Y.C. (eds.), *Intelligent Engineering Systems Through Artifical Neural Networks*, ASME Press. pp.135-145.
7. Duda, R., Gaschnig, J. and Hart, P. 1979. "Model Design in the Prospector Consultant System for Mineral Exploration". In D. Michie (ed.), *Expert Systems in the Micro-electronic Age*. Edinburgh University Press, Edinburgh, UK.
8. Harman, D.K. (ed.) 1995. *Overview of the Third Text REtrieval Conference (TREC-3)*, NIST Special Publication. pp. A5-A13.

9. Kubat, M. and Matwin, S. 1997. "Addressing the Curse of Imbalanced Training Sets: One-Sided Sampling". *Proceedings of the Fourteenth International Conference on Machine Learning*, Morgan Kaufmann. pp.179-186.

10. Kubat, M., Holte, R. and Matwin, S. 1997. "Learning when Negative Examples Abound," *Proceedings of ECML-97*, Springer. pp.146-153.

11. Kubat, M., Holte, R. and Matwin, S. 1998. "Machine Learning for the Detection of Oil Spills in Satellite Radar Images", *Machine Learning*, 30, pp.195-215.

12. Provost, F. 2000 "Machine Learning from Imbalanced Data Sets", *Invited paper for the AAAI'2000 Workshop on Imbalanced Data Sets, http://www.stern.nyu.edu/~fprovost/home.html#Publications* .

13. Provost, F. and Fawcett, T. 2000. "Robust Classification for Imprecise Environments", to appear in *Machine Learning*.

A Holonic Multi-agent Infrastructure for Electronic Procurement

Andreas Gerber and Christian Russ

German Research Centre for Artificial Intelligence (DFKI)
Stuhlsatzenhausweg 3, 66123 Saarbrücken
{agerber, russ}@dfki.de

Abstract. This paper presents a holonic co-ordination infrastructure for electronic procurement. The agent-based infrastructure consists of two components which are holonicly made up of a recursive hierarchy of three different agent types: a co-ordination server and a set of co-ordination assistant agents. The co-ordination server represents a platform through which buyers and sellers can interact, provides matchmaking services, and is equipped with co-ordination mechanisms such as auctions, negotiations and coalition formation mechanisms. The co-ordination assistant agents support their users, i.e. buyers and sellers, in their market interactions on the server. Particularly, they support their users in purchasing and selling of product bundles because adopting optimal bidding and pricing strategies while taking part in many auctions simultaneously is a task too complex for humans to solve optimally. The holonic structure of the co-ordination assistant agents and the co-ordination server helps to reduce complexity while allowing a high grade of adaptability and flexibility.

Keywords. Agent-based Co-ordination, Intelligent Agents, Holonic Multi-agent Systems, Auctions, Agent-based E-Commerce, Supply Chain Management. Motivation

1 Motivation

In today's markets, business entities are forced to interact with other market participants flexibly in order to stay competitive. The trend towards virtual enterprises [14] and supply webs [12] shows that market participants are forced to form flexible business partnerships that require more interactions with more autonomous business entities than ever before.

Agents offer the advantage that they can automatically and flexibly react to changes in the environment since they can autonomously perform tasks on behalf of their users. Since the interactions between business partners in virtual enterprises or in electronic markets together with their interrelations can get too complex for humans to

E. Stroulia and S. Matwin (Eds.): AI 2001, LNAI 2056, pp. 16-25, 2001.

handle efficiently encapsulating business entities (e.g. buyers/sellers, suppliers/producers/retailers) within agents has been suggested.

For handling the interactions efficiently, an agent-based co-ordination infrastructure is needed that provides a set of co-ordination services (e.g. matchmaking services) as well as co-ordination mechanisms (e.g. auctions, coalition formation mechanisms, profit division mechanisms). It brings together potential partners with common, or complementing, goals and enables them to co-ordinate their activities by using the provided co-ordination mechanisms.

In this paper, we will describe the structure of a holonic co-ordination server that fulfils these requirements.

2 Holonic Multi-agent Systems

In many domains a task that is to be accomplished by an agent can be hierarchically decomposed into particular subtasks. Thus, the task's completion may require the distribution of the subtasks to some subagents as well as the combination of their results. To model this combined activity the concept of *holonic agent* or *holon* has been introduced [7].

The concept is inspired by the idea of recursive or self-similar structures in biological systems. Analogous to this, a holonic agent consists of parts which in turn are agents (and maybe holonic agents). The holonic agent himself is part of a whole and contributes to achieve the goals of this superior whole. Along with agents, holonic agents share the properties of autonomy, goal-directed behavior and communication. But a holonic agent possesses capabilities that emerge from the interaction of subagents. A holon may have actions at its disposal that none of its subagents could perform alone.

Three forms of association are possible for a holon: first, subagents can build a loose federation sharing a common goal for some time before separating to regulate their own objectives. Second, subagents can give up their autonomy and merge into a new agent. Third, a holon can be organized by a *head* which moderates the activities of the subagents and represents the holon to the agent society for all kinds of interaction processes.

Multi-Agent Systems (MAS) are well suited for dealing with complex tasks (e.g. planning tasks) that can be divided into several subtasks. Each subtask is then represented by an agent that autonomously solves the task. MAS exhibit the features of stability and robustness since one agent can often take the role of an other agent that has been delayed or suspended for some reason. Furthermore, agents in MAS are characterized by their capability of exchanging messages to achieve coordination and cooperation.

MAS consisting of holonic agents are called *holonic multi-agent system (H-MAS)* [2]. In a H-MAS, autonomous agents may join others and form holons. But they are also free to reconfigure the holon, to leave the holon and act autonomously, or to form new holons with other agents. Holonic MAS share the advantages of MAS, but also provide additional advantages. Holonic agents are highly flexible at solving their tasks, having the ability to deal with inevitable change, since they are self-organizing and decentralized. Finally, as an advantage of analysis and building a system, holonically structured MAS exhibit a mapping of conceptual view and operational implementation. The implementation reflects the conceptual structure.

Therefore, it seems to be a natural way to represent many organization forms in e-commerce (e.g. virtual enterprises, supply webs) by a H-MAS because the holonic agent-based structuring supports their flexible and fluid formation as well as their dissolving. Furthermore, as the partners of a supply web or a virtual enterprise the sub-agents of a holon have to pursuit at least one common goal and thus show a common goal-directed behavior.

Holonic agents as well as atomic sub-agents and operative supply chain units can be represented by Java agents furnished with a high level control architecture, called Procedural Reasoning System (PRS) [11]. This PRS control architecture has the advantage that the Java PRS agents can behave goal-directed while staying responsive. They execute predefined procedures and plans that lie on a plan stack but are able to replan the course of their actions when an unforeseen event occurs. The *agent control unit (ACU)* of our agents executes according to the PRS model the following main steps: Situation Recognition, Goal Activation, Planning, and Plan Execution.

3 A Holonic Co-ordination Infrastructure

In the following, we will describe a holonic coordination infrastructure which we have implemented at the German Research Center for Artificial Intelligence (DFKI). The infrastructure is made up of three parts that all are holonicly structured. Two of them, namely the user-supporting *co-ordination assistant agent (CA)* and the auction-performing *auction matchmaker agent (AMM)* are holonic agents that are hierarchically structured. The requests of the CAs in the market environments are brought together with the services offered by several AMMs by the matching services of *facilitator (FA)* and *domain matchmaker agents (DMM)*. FAs and DMMs integrate CAs and AMMs in a mediation holon which is organized as a networked federation of trusted agents. In the next three sections we will illustrate the holonic structure of the three parts of our infrastructure in detail.

3.1 The Holonic Co-ordination Assistant Agent

Since most products consist of many parts, a single producer has to be present in a great number of auctions (maybe several auctions for one part or raw material). This setting is an ideal application scenario for agents and especially multi-agents. An agent can be used as an auction assistant, furnished with some authority to participate in an auction, making bids until a specified amount. Furthermore, since the number of auctions increases, many auctions have to be co-ordinated. It may be interesting to use one single agent to manage all different auctions by one agent, if the same product part is provided by several auctions. If there are many auctions for different parts, the bids that can be made in different auctions put constraints on each other in a complex, reciprocal way. To deal with this constraints, multi-agents for different auctions can be used. The flexibility of multi-agents systems, their ability to deal with online decisions in decentralized domains, pays attention to the dynamic changes of situation in auction-oriented marketplaces.

The *Co-ordination assistant agent* is in charge of fulfilling all the procurement tasks of an user which can be a private person or company. The agent communicates with its user through an user interface and represents the user to the external market entities as e.g. facilitators, auction houses and other market participants. It has a certain set of constrained resources, e.g. an amount of money, on its disposal.

3.1.1 Holonic Structuring for Reducing Complexity

An approach to overcome this complexity problem is to structure the co-ordination assistant agent as an hierarchical holon as shown in figure 1. This means, the co-ordination assistant agent is made up of a recursive hierarchy of agents being in charge of achieving the procurement tasks and subtasks of the co-ordination assistant agent. Since each task consists in purchasing or selling a bundle of items, the co-ordination assistant agent spawns *bundle agents* for non-basic bundles of tasks (e.g. a bundle of a product purchase task and a corresponding task for transporting the purchased product) which again recursively spawn both other bundle agents for non-basic sub-tasks as buying and selling sub-bundles and *executor agents* for performing basic tasks as buying and selling basic items (e.g. products or services) or monitoring ongoing auctions. All the agents of the holon have one common goal since they are all striving for fulfilling the assigned tasks while expending as few resources as possible.

3.1.2 Functionality of the Agents

Each bundle agent that wants to perform a basic task, has to gather information about appropriate auction houses at first. Subsequently, it has to select an auction house together with an advantageous auction mechanism whose rules give him a strategic advantage. After that, the bundle agent registers at the auction house server. While spawned *sell executor agents* monitor the course of an auction, *buy executor agents* also are endowed with bidding strategies for making bidding decisions depending on the auction mechanism they are taking part in.

3.1.3 Bottom-Up Information Flow

All the communication of the bundle and executor agents with external market entities is propagated upwards and finally routed over the co-ordination assistant agent if authentication mechanisms are required. Otherwise, in order to avoid communication bottlenecks, also direct communication to market entities may be allowed but since the co-ordination assistant agent acts as the head of the holon he is generally supposed to be the holon's communication interface. Information collected by monitor actions is also propagated upwards. The information propagated upwards in the holon is needed by the bundle agents in order to dynamically adapt their resource allocation decisions.

3.1.4 Top-Down Resource Allocation

The resource allocation decisions are made top-down by the superior agents. The co-ordination assistant agent possesses a priority relation over the set of tasks it strives to accomplish and allocates resources to the corresponding subordinated bundle agents according to the priorities of the tasks they are striving to accomplish. They again allocate resources to their subordinated agents and so on. All the buy and sell tasks a superior agent delegates to its subordinated agents are interrelated with each other with respect to the resource money. Successful sell tasks increase the amount of money the bundle agents can allocate to their spawned agents while buy tasks decrease this amount. Since the assignment of priorities to procurement tasks as well as auction prices change very dynamically, superior agents within the holon are forced to adapt dynamically the assignment of resources to their subordinated agents.

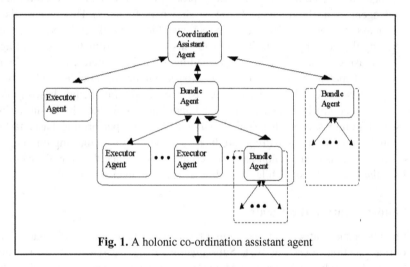

Fig. 1. A holonic co-ordination assistant agent

In order to calculate the highest possible bid in a given situation, a holon has to take several constraints into account. Addition of the prices of the other components, in-cluding stock and transportation costs, production and distribution costs result in the minimum price for the whole product the holon wants to achieve. Since in a given situation it is not clear whether a subagent gets a component for the price he is willing to pay, this fact affects the chances of reaching the highest gain. In many domains (e.g. the production of computers) there is the possibility (and the need) to decide between alternatives. In order to do this, it is necessary to weight the chance of getting a component at a specified cost level and in time.

Further research is dedicated to the specification of holonic agent based decision algorithms for highly flexible and dynamic auction domains. It is not to be expected that these algorithms provide the best solution (this is only realistic when we have total information which is not the case), but lead to a solution which is close to the maxi-mum.

3.2 A Holonic Co-ordination Server

The co-ordination server is included in our co-ordination infrastructure in order to provide to the business agents in a supply web or electronic marketplace a generic platform with services, such as auction mechanisms, that enable them to co-ordinate their interrelated activities in a decentral fashion.

Our co-ordination server is designed as an agent that can be easily accessed by other agents for registration, requests, etc..

3.2.1 The CMM Agent

The *co-ordination matchmaker agent (CMM)* constitutes the top of our hierarchy. It represents the co-ordination server to the agents in the external market environment. The CMM agent holds up-to-date data of all co-ordinations run by subordinated agents and thus can match requests about what service/item can be offered by using which co-ordination mechanisms. To get the information about the co-ordination processes it stands in contact with its subordinated *co-ordination mechanism agents (CMech)*.

The co-ordination mechanism agents are a meta-control authority for all running,

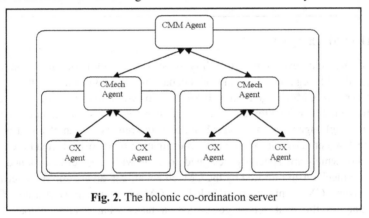

Fig. 2. The holonic co-ordination server

and planned, co-ordination processes which are performed by so-called service providing *co-ordination execution agents (CX)*. The CMech agents get the current information about the running co-ordination processes (start, termination, variations, etc.) from the CXs and propagate this information together with the information about the planned co-ordination processes upwards to the CMM agent.

The CMM agent couples requesting agents (which want to find or start an co-ordination for a given item) with the CX agents. It stores the information about the CX agents in a database and updates the information depending on the status reports of the CMech agents. After it has matched the request with its current database, the CMM agent simply returns a ranked list of relevant CX or CMech agents to the requesting agent. The requesting agent then has to contact and negotiate with the relevant CX or CMech agents to get the services/items it desires.

This direct interaction between the requesting agent and selected CX or CMech agents is performed independently from the CMM agent (see figure 3). This avoids data transmission bottlenecks, and even if a failure of the CMM agent does occur, running co-ordinations would still work [12]. Furthermore, the CMM agent has additional functionalities, e.g. to build a history about co-ordinations, their results and the satisfaction of customers over time and goods.

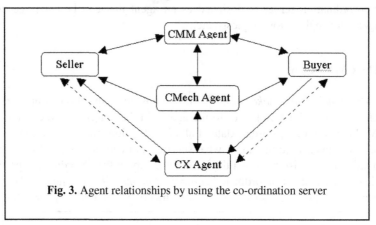

Fig. 3. Agent relationships by using the co-ordination server

3.2.2 The CMech Agent

The next hierarchy level of our co-ordination server is built up of CMech agents which are created with regard to the kind of mechanisms the co-ordination house wants to offer. There are CMech agents for all kind of co-ordination mechanisms, e.g. for the English-, Dutch- or Vickrey-auction [3]. If many auctions are running at the same time, one single agent can no longer handle all the requests in an efficient way. Thus, the CMech agent does not execute any co-ordination on its own. Instead it creates new CX agents which are specially designed to deal with a specific instance of a co-ordination mechanism imposed by the CMech agent, e.g. an auction for a certain good. If the existing CX agents are overloaded the CMech agent can start a new CX agent which handles the next set of co-ordination tasks what results in load balancing through agent networks [9]. Each of the CMech agents administrates a variable number of CX agents which perform the same co-ordination mechanism. Thus, these agents can be bundled into one holon per mechanism. The holon is represented by an CMech agent which is the head of the holon and co-ordinates the distribution of the co-ordination tasks to its subagents.

3.2.3 The CX Agents

The third level of the hierarchy contains CX agents which are able to execute multiple co-ordinations of the same mechanism. Only if such an agent is overloaded, another agent of this type is created and may be started at/on another place/computer in the co-ordination server network, guaranteeing a good performance. If a co-ordination task has ended the CX agent having performed the task will push the information about that co-ordination task to the CMech agent and to all participants of that co-ordination task. The CMech agent forwards this information to the CMM which stores the information for later use, e.g. statistic computations. After all co-ordinations of the CX agent have ended this agent might be terminated if it is not needed anymore.

3.2.4   Interactions between the Agents of the Three Levels of the Co-ordination Server

We will describe the interactions between the agents by taking a look at an auction that could be executed by the co-ordination server (see figures 3 and 4):

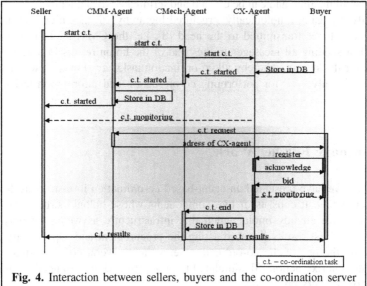

Fig. 4. Interaction between sellers, buyers and the co-ordination server agents

A seller wants to start an auction and sends an appropriate message to the CMM agent in which the item to be auctioned off as well as the seller's preferences concerning the co-ordination/auction mechanism to be used and the auction monitoring services are specified. Then the CMM agent triggers an appropriate CMech agent which spawns a CX agent for executing the auction. After that the CMech agent transmits the address of the spawned CX agent back to the superior CMM agent.

The CMM stores the information about the started auction in its database and sends the address of the CX agent executing the auction to the seller, if the seller wants to have auction monitoring (see the dotted line in figure 3) access to the CX agent. Otherwise the CX agent automatically sends information about the auction state in intervals to the seller.

While executing an co-ordination task, CX agents forget that they are part of a holon and act as single agents. Thus it is possible for co-ordination participants to contact them directly, this avoids the need to parse all messages from the head of the holon (CMM) down to the CX agents. Therefore, the CX agents do not only have to push the results of executed co-ordination tasks to their upper CMech agent but also to all participants in that co-ordination.

Hence a buyer that is by chance interested in buying this specific item asks the CMM agent if such an item is currently auctioned off. The CMM agent says yes to this question and sends the address of the corresponding CX agent stored in its database to the buyer. After that the buyer registers at the CX agent and monitors as well as bids in the auction. After the auction has finished the CX agent reports its outcome to the superior CMech agent that informs the bidders about it.

The upper two levels of the hierarchy consist of holonic agents whose lifecycles are not limited to any point of time. The lowest level includes only agents which do not have to exist all the time and can be created and terminated dynamically.

Generally, by using a holonically structured hierarchy, all incoming and outgoing messages have to be transmitted to the head [8], i.e. the CMM agent in our server structure. But sending all messages to the head of the holon results in a very narrow bottleneck for the system, whereby all co-ordination tasks are slowed down. Thus our CMM agent is only used for performing co-ordination and information tasks within the holon.

4 Conclusion & Further Work

In this paper, we have presented an agent-based co-ordination infrastructure for electronic procurement. It consists of two components whose holonic structure is three-layered. We have already implemented this infrastructure as well as supply chain agents in Java. First results in coordinating the procurement and supply activities of the agents by the use of the co-ordination server and several co-ordination mechanisms, as the matrix auction [3], simulated trading [16] and the extended contract net protocol [16], are very promising.

Our main goal is to extend the developed infrastructure by integrating more co-ordination mechanisms such that the agents can co-ordinate their activities more efficiently by using them. Therefore, our future activities will mainly consist in the development of a set of agent-based co-ordination and negotiation mechanisms as well as their integration in the co-ordination infrastructure. The developed mechanisms are intended to support the configuration and co-ordination of distributed business processes as well as the (re)allocation of resources and tasks within supply webs. Moreover, we will investigate their effects on supply chain execution by applying them to simulation scenarios.

The developed agent technology could be directly applied in related areas, e.g. for implementing electronic markets and virtual enterprises. Our work has been supported by the European Union and the SAP subsidiary SAP Retail Solutions.

5 References

1. Bachem, W. Hochstättler, and M. Malich. Simulated Trading: A New Approach For Solving Vehicle Routing Problems. Technical Report 92.125, Mathematisches Institut der Universität zu Köln, Dezember 1992.
2. H.-J. Bürckert, K. Fischer, and G. Vierke. Transportation Scheduling with Holonic MAS — The TeleTruck Approach. In: Proceedings of the Third International Conference on Practical Applications of Intelligent Agents and Multiagents (PAAM'98), 1998.
3. K. Fischer, C. Russ, and G. Vierke. Decision Theory and Coordination in Multi-agent Systems. Research Report RR-98-02, DFKI, 1998.
4. K. Fischer, J. P. Müller, and M. Pischel. Cooperative transportation scheduling: an application domain for DAI. Journal of Applied Artificial Intelligence. Special issue on Intelligent Agents, 10(1), 1996.
5. C. Gerber, C. Russ, and G. Vierke. An empirical evaluation on the suitability of market-based mechanisms for telematics applications. Technical Report TM-98-02, German Research Center for Artificial Intelligence, 1998.
6. C. Gerber, C. Ruß, and G. Vierke. On the Suitability of Market-Based Mechanisms for Telematics Applications. In Proceedings of the International Conference on Autonomous Agents (Agents'99), 1999.
7. C. Gerber, J. Siekmann, and G. Vierke. Flexible Autonomy in Holonic Agent Systems. In Proceedings of the 1999 AAAI Spring Symposium on Agents with Adjustable Autonomy, 1999.
8. C. Gerber, J. Siekmann, G. Vierke. Holonic Multi-Agent Systems, DFKI Research Report RR-99-03, ISSN 0946-008X, Kaiserslautern 1999.
9. C. Gerber. Self-Adaptation and Scalability in Multi-Agent Societies, PhD Thesis, Universität des Saarlandes, Saarbrücken, 2000.
10. P. Gomber, C. Schmidt, and C. Weinhardt. Efficiency incentives and computational tractability in the coordination of multi-agent systems. In Proceedings of the Workshop Kooperationsnetze und Elektronische Koordination, 1998.
11. F. F. Ingrand, R. Chatila, R. Alami, F. Robert. PRS: A High Level Supervision and Control Language for Autonomous Mobile Robots. In Proceedings of the 1996 IEEE International Conference on Robotics and Automation (Minneapolis, USA).
12. M. Klusch, K. Sycara. Brokering and Matchmaking for Coordination of Agent Societies: A Survey. In: A. Omicini et al. (eds.) Coordination of Internet Agents, Springer 2001, Upcoming.
13. T. M. Laseter. Balanced Sourcing: Cooperation and Competition in Supplier Relationships. Jossey-Bass, ISBN: 0787944432, October 1998.
14. W. H. Davidow and M. S. Malone. The Virtual Corporation: Structuring and revitalizing the corporation for the 21st century. New York: Harper Business, 1992.
15. W. Vickrey. Counterspeculation, Auctions, and Competitive Sealed Tenders. In: Journal of Finance 16: 8- 37, 1961.
16. G. Vierke. TELETRUCK - A Holonic Multi-Agent System for Telematics. PhD Thesis, Universität des Saarlandes, Saarbrücken, 2000.

A Low-Scan Incremental Association Rule Maintenance Method Based on the Apriori Property

Zequn Zhou and C.I. Ezeife⋆

School of Computer Science University of Windsor,
Windsor, Ontario, Canada N9B 3P4
cezeife@uwindsor.ca
http://www.cs.uwindsor.ca/users/c/cezeife

Abstract. As new transactions update data sources and subsequently the data warehouse, the previously discovered association rules in the old database may no longer be interesting rules in the new database. Furthermore, some new interesting rules may appear in the new database. This paper presents a new algorithm for efficiently maintaining discovered association rules in the updated database, which starts by computing the high n level large itemsets in the new database using the available high n level large itemsets in the old database. Some parts of the $n-1, n-2, \ldots, 1$ level large itemsets can then be quickly generated by applying the apriori property, thereby avoiding the overhead of calculating many lower level large itemsets that involve huge table scans.

Keywords: Maintaining Mining Asociation Rules, High Level Large Itemsets, Low Level Large Itemsets, Apriori Property

1 Introduction

Data mining is a rapidly evolving area of data analysis that attempts to identify trends or unexpected patterns in large pools of data using mathematical tools. It could help end users extract useful business information from large databases and warehouses.

Association rule mining is a data mining technique which discovers strong associations or correlation relationships among data. Given a set of transactions (similar to database records in this context), where each transaction consists of items (or attributes), an association rule is an implication of the form $X \rightarrow Y$, where X and Y are sets of items and $X \cap Y = \emptyset$. The support of this rule is defined as the percentage of transactions that contain the set X, while its confidence is the percentage of these "X" transactions that also contain Y. In association rule mining, all items with support higher than a specified minimum

---

⋆ This research was supported by the Natural Science and Engineering Research Council (NSERC) of Canada under an operating grant (OGP-0194134) and a University of Windsor grant.

E. Stroulia and S. Matwin (Eds.): AI 2001, LNAI 2056, pp. 26–35, 2001.

support are called large or frequent itemsets. An itemset X is called an i-itemset if it contains i items. The Apriori property states that an n-large itemset must have all its subsets also large.

Agrawal *et al.* [1] presents the concept of association rule mining and an example of a simple rule is "98% of customers who purchase milk and bread also buy eggs". Since discovering all such rules may help market baskets or cross-sales analysis, decision making, and business management, algorithms presented in this research area include [1,6,4]. These algorithms mainly focus on how to efficiently generate association rules and how to discover the most interesting rules. However, data stored in the database are often updated making association rules discovered in the previous database possibly no longer interesting rules in the new database. Furthermore, some new interesting rules may have developed in the new database which were not in the old database. Thus, work on incremental maintenance of association rules include [3,2].

In this paper, we present a new algorithm that efficiently generates incremental association rules in the updated database by applying the Apriori property [1]. The new algorithm first computes the high level n-large itemsets. Then, it starts by generating all lower level $n - 1, n - 2, \ldots, 1$ large itemsets. This approach cuts down the overhead of generating some low level large itemsets that have no chance of being large in the updated database, there by reducing the number of database table scans needed to compute large itemsets.

1.1   Related Work

The problem of mining association rules is decomposed into two subproblems, namely (1) generating all large itemsets in the database and (2) generating association rules in the database according to the large itemsets generated in the first step. Apriori algorithm [1] is designed for generating association rules. The basic idea of this algorithm is to find all the large itemsets iteratively. In the first iteration, it finds the large 1-itemsets L_1 (each large 1-itemset contains only one item). To obtain L_1, it first generates candidate set C_1 which contains all 1-itemsets of basket data, then the database is scanned for each itemset in the set C_1 to compute its support. The items with support greater than or equal to minimum support (minsupport) are chosen as large items L_1. The minsupport is provided by the user before mining. In the next iteration, apriori_gen function [1] is used to generate candidate set C_2 by joining L_1 and L_1 and keeping all unique itemsets with 2 items in each. The large itemsets L_2 is again computed from the set C_2 by selecting items that meet the minsupport requirement. The iterations go on by applying apriori_gen function until L_i or C_i is empty. Finally, the large itemsets L is obtained as the union of all L_1 to L_{i-1}. FUP2 algorithm is proposed by [3] to address the maintenance problem for association rule mining. Assume that D denotes the old database, D' denotes the new database, D^- denotes the deleted part of the old database, D^+ denotes the newly inserted part to the old database, D^* denotes unchanged part in the old database. S^+ denotes the support count of itemset X in D^+, S^- denotes the support count of itemset X in D^-, S denotes the support count of itemset X in D, S' denotes the support count of itemset X in D'. Obviously, $D^* = D - D^- = D' - D^+$. This algorithm utilizes the idea of Apriori algorithm, to find the large itemsets iteratively. The difference between FUP2 and Apriori is that FUP2 separates the candidate itemsets in the new database into two subsets in each iteration. That is, in kth iteration, candidate itemsets C_k is divided into P_k and Q_k, where P_k is the intersection of C_k and L_k, L_k is the the previous large itemsets of size k in the old database. Q_k is the remaining part of C_k not included in the set L_k, that is, $Q_k = C_k - (C_k \cap L_k)$. For all itemsets x in P_k, the support S of x in the old database is known. Thus, in order to compute the new support S' for each itemsets in P_k, it only scans D^+, D^-, to get S^+, S^- and compute S' as $S' = S + S^+ - S^-$. For each itemset x in Q_k, which represents the new candidate sets that are not part of the old large itemsets, since the support of x in the old database is unknown, the new database D' is scanned to decide if x should be added to the new large itemset L_k'. DELI algorithm [5] applies a sampling technique to estimate the support counts using an approximate upper/lower bounds on the amount of changes in the set of newly introduced association rules. A low bound would mean that changes in association rules is small and there should be no maintenance.

1.2   Contributions

This paper contributes by proposing a new algorithm called MAAP (maintaining association rules with apriori property) for incremental maintenance of association rules in the updated database. The algorithm utilizes an Apriori property, and starting with the high level large itemsets in the previous mining result, it computes the equivalent high level large itemsets in the new database as well as infers some low level large itemsets in the new database. Thus, this algorithm eliminates the need to compute some low level large itemsets and save on rule maintenance time. It yields more benefit when high level large itemsets generate a high percentage of low level large itemsets.

1.3   Outline of the Paper

The organization of the rest of the paper is shown as follows: section 2 presents an example; section 3 presents a detailed formal algorithm; section 4 presents performance analysis of the algorithm; and finally, section 5 presents conclusions and future work.

2   An Example

Since MAAP algorithm being proposed in this paper is related to both the Apriori and FUP2 algorithms, we first apply both of these algorithms to an example in section 2.1 before applying MAAP to the same example in section 2.2.

2.1   Apriori and FUP2 on Sample Database

Suppose we have a database DB with set of items, I=A, B, C, D, E, F and MinSupport=3 transactions. A simple database transaction table for illustrating the idea is given as Table 1.

Table 1. The Example Database Transaction table

TID	Items				
100	A	B	C	D	F
200	A	B	C	D	E
300	B	C	D		
400	A	D	E		
500	A	C	D		
600	A	B	C	E	

If we delete transacion 400, and add new transaction 700 B D E, we can get an updated database DB', which is suitable for FUP2.

To compute the large itemsets in the old database (Table 1), Apriori algorithm first generates the candidate set C_1={A, B, C, D, E, F}, then scans the database to obtain the support of each itemset in C_1. Then, it throws away the item F which has a support that is lower than 3. So, $L_1 = \{A, B, C, D, E\}$. In the second iteration, Apriori computes $C_2 =$ apriori_gen(L_1)={AB, AC, AD, AE, BC, BD, BE, CD, CE, DE}. Then, it scans DB to obtain the support of each itemset in C_2. This results in an $L_2 = \{AB, AC, AD, AE, BC, BD, CD\}$. During the third iteration, $C_3 =$ apriori_gen(L_2)={ABC, ABD, ACD, BCD}. Apriori scans database and gets the support of these itemsets to generate $L_3 = \{ABC, ACD, BCD \}$. Next step computes $C_3 =$ Apriori_gen(L_3)= {}, causing the algorithm to terminate and resulting in an overall Large itemsets $L = L_1 \cup L_2 \cup L_3$, which is, {A, B, C, D, E, AB, AC, AD, AE, BC, BD, CD, ABC, ACD, BCD}. The generated L above will represent the old association large items sets from the old database DB. In order to update the large itemsets L to L' for the newly updated database DB', the Apriori algorithm would go through all C_1', L_1', ..., L_3' to produce an L' of {A, B, C, D, E, AB, AC, AD, BC, BD, BE, CD, ABC, ACD, BCD}.

Applying the FUP2 algorithm on the same updated database DB' with I=A,B,C,D,E,F and minsupport of 3 transactions will proceed as follows. In the first step, we get the new C_1' as the previous C_1 in the old database. That is, $C_1 = \{A, B, C, D, E, F\}$. Then comparing C_1 with L_1 (as computed with the Apriori above), would lead to breaking C_1 into two parts, (1) the set of elements common to both C_1' and L_1, called set P_1={A, B, C, D, E } and (2) the set of elements in C_1', which are not in the first set P_1, called set Q_1={F}. FUP2 proceeds to compute the support of each itemset in P_1, to obtain all large itemsets in P_1 that are still large itemsets in the new database in order to include them to the new large itemset L'_1. It further computes the support of each itemset in Q_1 in the new database to see if these previous small items are now large. With this example, F is still a small itemset in the new database. Thus, the updated new level 1 large itemset, $L'_1 = \{A, B, C, D, E\}$. The next step applies apriori_gen function to generate candidate itemsets C'_2, then goes on with the rest of the iterations to compute $L'_2, \ldots, L'_k$ when L'_{k+1} is empty. The result of each step is shown below. The C_2 generated from L'_1 is $C'_2 = \{AB, AC, AD, AE, BC, BD, BE, CD, CE, DE\}$, which is broken into P_2 and Q_2, $P_2 = \{AB, AC, AD, AE, BC, BD, CD\}$, $Q_2=\{BE, CE, DE\}$. $L'_2=\{AB, AC, AD, BC, BD, BE, CD\}$ is computed from P_2 and Q_2. C'_3 is generated from L'_2, $C'_3=\{ABC, ABD, ACD, BCD, BCE, BDE\}$ and when broken into P_3 and Q_3 gives $P_3 = \{ABC, ACD, BCD\}$, $Q_3 = \{ABD\}$. The new level 3 large itemsets, $L'_3 = \{ABC, ACD, BCD\}$.

2.2   The Proposed MAAP Algorithm on Example Database

Agrawal [1] proposes an Apriori property, which states that "All non-empty subsets of a large itemset must be large". For example, if a large 3-itemset is $L_3=\{123\}$, we can immediately infer that the following itemsets are large as well: $\{12\}, \{13\}, \{23\}, \{1\}, \{2\}, \{3\}$. Based on this principle, when association rules are to be maintained in the updated database, the large itemsets can be computed from the highest level large itemsets, that is, from L_k. If any itemset in L_k is still large in the new database, its lower level subset itemsets are included to their appropriate level large itemsets in $L_{k-1}, L_{k-2}, \ldots, L_1$. For example, since $L_3 = \{123\}$ is confirmed to be still large in the new database, MAAP includes $\{12\}, \{13\}, \{23\}$ to L_2 and $\{1\}, \{2\}, \{3\}$ to L_1. By so doing, some computation time is saved. Utilizing the large itemsets computed in section 2.1 as the result in the old database, the MAAP algorithm proceeds by checking if each itemset in $L_3 = \{ABC, ACD, BCD\}$ is still large in the new database. Since ABC is large in the new database, AB, AC, BC, A, B, C are also large itemsets. Thus, ABC is added to L'_3 (L'_i denotes the large i-itemsets in the new database), add AB, AC, BC to L'_2, add A, B, C to L'_1. It continues to test the next itemset in L_3 which is ACD and since ACD is large, AC, AD, CD, A, C, D are also large itemsets. MAAP adds ACD to L'_3, if not already a member of this large itemset. After testing ACD, L'_3 has elements ABC, ACD; L'_2 has AB, AC, BC, AD, CD; L'_1 has A, B, C, D. Next, the last itemset in L_3 is tested, which is BCD. BC, CD, BD, B, C, D are large itemsets since BCD is a large itemset. These itemsets are included to L'_3, L'_2 and L'_1 respectively. The temporary results at this stage are: $L'_3 = \{ABC, ACD, BCD\}$, $L'_2 = \{AB, AC, BC, AD, CD, BD\}$, $L1' = \{A, B, C, D\}$. These are not yet the final updated large itemsets in the new database. These large itemsets are only some large itemsets in the old database that remain large itemsets in the new database.

The next step checks the itemsets in each of the old L_1 to L_{k-1} large itemsets not yet in the corresponding new L'_1 to L'_{k-1} large itemsets to see if they are still large in the new database. Continuing with the running example, $L_1 - L'_1 = \{E\}$

represents large 1-itemsets in the old database not yet in the so far computed $L'_1 = \{A, B, C, D\}$. There is need to scan the new database to obtain the support of item E which is included in the new large itemset if this support is greater than or equal to minimum support. Since E is large, the algorithm adds E to L'_1. The same way L_2 - $L'_2 = \{AE\}$ is also used to compute additional elements of L'_2 as $\{\}$ since AE is not large. To complete the computation of large itemsets, the algorithm finally checks all previous small itemsets in the old database to see if they are now large in the new database. For 1-itemset, to compute the old small itemsets, e.g. S_1, MAAP subtracts the large 1-itemsets from its candidate set, C_1. Thus, $S_1 = C_1$ - $L_1 = \{F\}$. The algorithm scans the new database for the support of F. Since this support does not meet the minsupport requirement, then F is still not a large itemset. For 2-itemsets, $S_2 = C_2$ - $L_2 = \{BE, CE, DE\}$. After scanning the new database, only BE is a large itemset and this is included in the L'_2 to make $L'_2 = \{AB, AC, AD, BC, BD, BE, CD\}$. Since these itemsets were small in the old database, they are not part of the old candidate itemset and thus, we need to modify the new candidate itemset one level higher than the computed large itemset. Here, additional $C'_3 = L'_2 \bowtie \{BE\} = \{BDE\}$, those new candidate itemsets are added to S_3. And $C'_3 = C'_3 \cup additional C'_3 = \{ABC, ABD, ACD, BCD, BDE\}$. For each itemset in the additional C'_3, MAAP checks the new database for support and if item is large, it is included in the new large 3-itemset L'_3. Since none of the elements in the additional C'_3 is large, final $L'_3 = \{ABC, ACD, BCD\}$. The final large itemsets for all levels is now $L' = \{A, B, C, D, E, AB, AC, AD, BC, BD, BE, CD, ABC, ACD, BCD\}$.

3   The Proposed Association Rule Maintenance Algorithm

The steps in the MAAP algorithm being proposed in this paper are discussed below.

- Step 1: Compute Parts of New large itemsets using only itemsets that were large in the old database, and are guaranteed to still be large in the new database because of a superset itemset in a higher level new large itemset. Assume for each iteration in the old database, we divide the candidate itemsets into two parts. One part consists of the large itemsets, another part is the small itemsets. For instance, C_1 is divided into L_1 and S_1, C_2 is divided into L_2 and S_2, and so on.

  Starting with highest level large itemsets in the old database, such as L_k, we test each itemset of L_k in the new database, by computing their support scanning only the changed part of the database, to identify any large itemsets in the new database, which are added to L'_k. L'_k denotes large k-itemsets in the new database and for each element in this new large itemsets, the algorithm computes the union of all its non-empty subsets, which are included in the appropriate level new large itemsets $L'_{k-1}, \ldots, L'_1$ respectively. Continue to test next itemsets in L_k and include in L'_k if it is still a large itemset in the new database, until all itemsets in L_k have been tested. This step has computed only part of new large itemsets L'_k, $L_{k-1'}$, ..., L'_1, which come from large itemsets in the old database that continue to be large itemsets in the new database. If there are no large itemsets in the new database, the next lower level large itemset k=k-1 in the old database is used to do the computation.

- Step 2: Compute for each new large itemset, additional large itemsets that were large in the old database but not computed in the first step because their superset higher level itemset is small in the new database, but these old lower level large itemsets may still be large in the new database.
- Step 3: Compute the rest of the itemsets in the candidate itemsets that may be large itemsets in the new database. Since by the end of step 2 above, we reduced the sizes of all level small itemsets and candidate sets, the algorithm now takes each small itemset $S_i = C_i - L'_i$ and scans the new database to determine if these itemsets are large in the new database. If they are large, they are included in the appropriate level new large itemset L'_i.
- Step 4: Adjusting all level i candidate sets to include the new large itemsets previously small in the old database at level (i-1). This accommodates the set computed above in Step 3 by including all candidate sets that arise from these new large itemsets.

4   Performance Analysis

Comparing the MAAP algorithm with FUP2 algorithm [3], the most important benefit is that MAAP avoids computing some parts of large itemsets from the database, especially, when generating L'_1 and L'_2, which have the longest lists of candidate itemsets for which the database is scanned to compute their supports. If a lot of low level large itemsets whch are still large itemsets in the new database are generated from step 1 of the MAAP algorithm, there is a huge performance gain in terms of reduced computation time achieved by using the MAAP algorithm. In the best case, all large itemsets in the old database remain large itemsets in the new database and all large itemsets can be computed from the old high level large itemsets, and the only database scan performed by MAAP in this case, is equivalent to the number of large itemsets at the highest level, each of which needs only a scan of the changed part of the database. In the worst case, all the large itemsets in the old database are no longer large itemsets in the new database. In this case, time is spent applying step 2 of MAAP algorithm.

Two experiments were conducted comparing the performance of both FUP2 and MAAP.

- Experiment 1: Given a fixed size dataset (inserted and deleted parts of the dataset are also fixed), we test CPU execution time at different thresholds of support for MAAP, FUP2 and Apriori algorithms. The aim of this experiment is to show that performance of MAAP algorithm is better than that of FUP2 and Apriori algorithms at different levels of support using the same dataset size. We choose a synthetic dataset generated with a program given in [1] with the following parameters. The number of transactions (D) is one hundred thousand records, that is $|D| = 100,000$ records, the average size of transactions (T) (that is, average number of items in transactions) is 5, $|T| = 5$, average size of the maximal potentially large itemsets (I) (that is, average number of items in the possibly longest large itemsets) is 2, or $|I| = 2$, number of itemsets in the longest large itemsets (L) (that is, the total number of maximal potentially large itemsets) is two thousand or $|L| = 2000$, number of items (N) (the total number of attributes) is one thousand that N=1000. Assume the size of updated (inserted) dataset is 15,000 records, the size of updated (deleted) dataset is 15,000 records (these parameters are abbreviated as T5.I2.D100K-15K+15K, the support thresholds are varied between 1.4% and 1.9% meaning that for a support level of 1.4%, an itemset has to appear in 1400 (fourteen hundred) or more transactions to be taken as a large itemset. An experimental results is shown in Table 2.

Table 2. CPU Execution Times for Dataset: T5.I2.D100K-15K+15K at Different Supports

Algorithms	CPU Time (in secs) at Supports of					
	1.4	1.5	1.6	1.7	1.8	1.9
Apriori	13451.99	3716.02	2041.77	1268.18	856.88	625.77
FUP2	7807.21	2208.75	954.10	596.04	408.66	312.89
MAAP	4955.29	1608.67	700.98	436.68	302.82	235.61

From the observation of the experimental result, we can see that (i) as the size of the support increases, the execution time of all the algorithms (FUP2 and MAAP) decreases because of decrease in the total number of candidate and large itemsets during each iteration. (ii) for the same support, the execution time of MAAP algorithm is less than that of FUP2 and Apriori algorithm. (iii) as the size of support increases, the difference in execution times of MAAP algorithm and FUP2 diminishes. This is because as the support increases, the total number of large itemsets and candidate itemsets decreases reducing the need to spend time searching huge database for support of large itemsets.

– Experiment 2: Given a fixed size dataset (including inserted and deleted datasets) and a fixed support, we test CPU execution times when different numbers of old large itemsets are allowed to change in the new database. Since the number of large itemsets changed may affect CPU time of MAAP algorithm, this experiment is conducted to observe the performance of both MAAP and FUP2 algorithms. The dataset used for this experiment is the same as for experiment 1 above except that the size of updated (inserted) database is 1.5K records, the size of updated (deleted) database is 1.5K records (these parameters are abbreviated as T5.I2.D100K-1.5K+1.5K). Assume x represents the percentage of old large itemsets that changed in the new database and x is varied between 10% and 50%, the result of this experiment is shown in Table 3.

Table 3. CPU Execution Times for Dataset: T5.I2.D10K-1.5K+1.5K at Different Percentage Changes in Old Large Itemsets

Algorithms	Percentage changes in Old Large Itemsets			
(times in secs)	12.3	25.1	37.8	49.6
FUP2	1426.26	1567.33	1623.52	1765.59
MAAP	1059.71	1348.54	1546.93	1837.32

It can be concluded that (i) as the change of old large itemsets increases, the CPU execution time of MAAP and FUP2 algorithms increase because of increase in the total number of large itemsets that need to be computed. (ii) as the change of old large itemsets increases, the difference in CPU execution times between MAAP and FUP2 algorithms decreases, when the change of old large itemsets is around 45%, CPU execution times for MAAP algorithm is higher than that of FUP2 algorithm. The reason is that if the percentage change in old large itemsets is over 45%, MAAP algorithm will test many large itemsets that are no longer large in the new database, incurring the overhead of CPU computation time for obtaining their support. In such circumstances, it is more beneficial to start computing large itemsets from level 1 and upward as FUP2 would do.

5   Conclusions and Future Work

This paper presents a new algorithm MAAP, for incrementally maintaining association rules in the updated database. This algorithm applies an Apriori property to the set of large itemsets in the old database, generates some parts of the lower level large itemsets in the new database using all previous old large itemsets that are confirmed to be still large in the new database. Thus, it eliminates the need to compute parts of lower level large itemsets and saves rule maintenance time by reducing the number of times the database is scanned. It achieves more benefit when high level large itemsets can be used to generate a lot of low level large itemsets in the first step of applying the Apriori property.

Future work may consider at what kth highest level it is most beneficial to start applying this technique. The highest level that yields most low level large itemsets when the Apriori property is applied is the needed level. For example, if the total number of large itemsets in L'_3 is 5, and the total number of large itemsets in L'_4 is 1, comparing numbers 3,5 with 4, 1, may tell us to begin from L'_3, since L'_3 may cover more lower level large itemsets than L'_4.

References

[1] Agrawal, R. and Skrikant, R.: Fast Algorithms for Mining Association Rules in Large Databases, In Proceedings of the 20th International Conference on very Large Databases, Santiago, Chile, 1994, pp. 487-499.

[2] Cheung, D.W., Han, J., Ng, V.T., Wong, C.Y.: Maintenance of Discovered Association Rules in Large Database: An I ncremental Updating Technique, In Proceedings of the 12th International Conference on Data Engineering, New Orleans, Louisiana, 1996.

[3] Cheung, D.W., Lee, S.D., Kao, B.: A General Incremental Technique for Maintaining Discovered Association Rules, In Proceedings of the Fifth International Conference on Database Systems for Advanced Applications, Melbourne, Australia, jan, 1997.

[4] Holsheimer, M., Kersten, H., Mannila, M., Toivonen, H.: A Perspective on Databases and Data Mining. First International conference on Knowledge, Discovery and data Mining, Montreal, canada, AAAI Press, 1995, pp. 150-155.

[5] Lee, S.D., Cheung, D.W., Kao, B.: Is sampling Useful in Data Mining? A Case in the Maintenance of Discovered Association Rules, Data Mining and Knowledge Discovery, 1998, pp. 233-262.

[6] Park, J.S., Chen, M.S., Yu, P.S., An Effective Hashed Based Algorithm for Mining Association Rules, In Proceedings of the ACM SIGMOD Conference on Management of Data, San Jose, California, may, 1995.

A Statistical Corpus-Based Term Extractor

Patrick Pantel and Dekang Lin

Department of Computing Science
University of Alberta
Edmonton, Alberta T6G 2H1 Canada
{ppantel, lindek}@cs.ualberta.ca

Abstract. Term extraction is an important problem in natural language processing. In this paper, we propose a language independent statistical corpus-based term extraction algorithm. In previous approaches, evaluation has been subjective, at best relying on a lexicographer's judgement. We evaluate the quality of our term extractor by assessing its predictiveness on an unseen corpus using perplexity. Second, we evaluate the precision and recall of our extractor by comparing the Chinese words in a segmented corpus with the words extracted by our system.

1   Introduction

Term extraction is an important problem in natural language processing. The goal is to extract sets of words with exact meaning in a collection of text. Several linguists have argued that the base semantic unit of language are these terms. Applications of automatic term extraction include machine translation, automatic indexing, building lexical knowledge bases, and information retrieval.

In previous systems, evaluation has relied mostly on human assessments of the quality of extracted terms. This is problematic since experts often disagree on the correctness of a term list for a corpus. Consequently, it is difficult to replicate the evaluation procedure to compare different systems. Furthermore, experts normally evaluate only a few hundred terms. These tend to be the highest-ranking ones, those most easily recognizable by lexicographers. A term extraction tool that assists humans would be more useful if it were able to extract those terms less obvious to humans. This is difficult to evaluate.

In this paper, we present a language independent statistical corpus-based term extraction algorithm. First, we collect bigram frequencies from a corpus and extract two-word candidates. After collecting features for each two-word candidate, we use mutual information and log-likelihood ratios to extend them to multi-word terms. We experiment with both English and Chinese corpora. Using perplexity, we quantify the definition of a term and we obtain a comparative evaluation of term extraction algorithms. Furthermore, we evaluate the precision and recall of our term extractor by comparing the words in a segmented Chinese corpus with the words extracted by our system. Our evaluation methodology circumvents the problems encountered by previously used human evaluations. It also provides a basis for comparing term extraction systems.

E. Stroulia and S. Matwin (Eds.): AI 2001, LNAI 2056, pp. 36–46, 2001.

2   Previous Work

There have been several approaches to automatic term extraction mostly for technical terminology and noun phrases. Many successful algorithms are statistical corpus-based approaches [2], [5], [10].

Several term extraction tools have been developed. Dagan and Church [4] proposed a tool that assists terminologists in identifying and translating technical terms. Smadja [19] developed a lexicographic tool, *Xtract*, which extracts collocations from English. Fung [11] later extended this model to extract words from Chinese corpora. The latter work was the first to attempt an automatic evaluation of term extraction. Previous methods used human experts to evaluate their extracted term lists. Fung first uses a tagger to retrieve Chinese words. Then, the extraction system is evaluated by counting the number of these words retrieved by the term extractor.

More recently, Eklund and Wille [8] describe an algorithm that utilizes discourse theory to extract terms from single-subject texts. Hybrid approaches combining statistical techniques with linguistic knowledge (syntax and morphology) have also emerged [14], [17], [18].

3   Term Extraction Algorithm

Our term extractor is a two-phase statistical corpus-based algorithm that extracts multi-word terms from corpora of any language (we experiment with English and Chinese corpora in this paper).

Our algorithm uses two metrics to measure the information between terms (or words): *mutual-information* (*mi*) and *log-likelihood* (*logL*) [7]. Mutual information is defined as:

$$mi(x, y) = \frac{P(x, y)}{P(x)P(y)} \tag{1}$$

where x and y are words or terms. Mutual information is highest when all occurrences of x and y are adjacent to each other and deteriorates with low frequency counts. To alleviate this problem, we use a second measure, log-likelihood, which is more robust to low frequency events. Let $C(x, y)$ be the frequency of two terms, x and y, occurring adjacent in some corpus (where the asterix (*) represents a wildcard). Then, the log-likelihood ratio of x and y is defined as:

$$logL(x, y) = ll\left(\frac{k_1}{n_1}, k_1, n_1\right) + ll\left(\frac{k_2}{n_2}, k_2, n_2\right)$$
$$- ll\left(\frac{k_1+k_2}{n_1+n_2}, k_1, n_1\right) - ll\left(\frac{k_1+k_2}{n_1+n_2}, k_2, n_2\right) \tag{2}$$

where $k_1 = C(x, y)$, $n_1 = C(x, *)$, $k_2 = C(\neg x, y)$, $n_2 = C(\neg x, *)$,   and:

$$ll(p, k, n) = k \log(p) + (n - k)\log(1 - p) \tag{3}$$

Input: A corpus L in any language.

Step 1: Collect bigram frequencies for L in a proximity database DB.

Step 2: For all 4-grams $w\,x\,y\,z$ in L, remove one count for $x\,y$ in DB if
- $mi(x, y) < mi(w, x) - k$ or
- $mi(x, y) < mi(y, z) - k$.

Step 3: For all entries (x, y) in DB, add (x, y) to a list T if:
- $C(x, y) > minCount$
- $S(x, y) > minLogL$

Output: The list T of candidate multi-word terms.

Fig. 1. Candidate extraction algorithm.

The log-likelihood ratio is highest when all occurrences of x and y are adjacent to each other (as in mutual information). However, the ratio is also high for two frequent terms that are rarely adjacent. For example, the word pair (*the, the*) has a very high log-likelihood ratio in English even though it rarely occurs (mostly as a typographical error).

To overcome the shortcomings of mutual information and log-likelihood, we propose a hybrid metric. The score S for a pair (x, y) is defined as:

$$S(x, y) = \begin{cases} logL(x, y) & if \ \ mi(x, y) \geq minMutInfo \\ 0 & otherwise \end{cases} \tag{4}$$

We use the mutual information as an initial filter to eliminate term pairs such as (*the, the*). Below, we describe each phase of our term extraction algorithm.

3.1   Candidate Extraction

Figure 1 outlines the first phase of our term extraction algorithm. It extracts a list of two-word candidate terms from a corpus of any language. Optimally, this list contains all two-word terms as well as fragments of all multi-word terms.

In Step 1, we construct a proximity database consisting of the frequency counts for each adjacent pair of words in the corpus [16].

The purpose of Step 2 is to eliminate frequency counts for those adjacent words that are separated by a phrasal (word) boundary [1], [20]. A phrasal boundary separates words that are not part of a same term. Given a 4-gram (w, x, y, z), we assume there is a phrasal boundary between x and y if $mi(x, y) < mi(w, x) - k$ or $mi(x, y) < mi(y, z) - k$, for some fixed constant k.

Step 3 performs the selection of two-word candidates. An adjacent pair of words is selected if its frequency and score surpasses a fixed threshold. We experimentally set $minCount$ to 3, $minLogL$ to 5, and $minMutInfo$ to 2.5.

Input: A list T of two-word candidates for a corpus L in any language and a proximity
database DB consisting of bigram frequencies for L.

Step 1: Accumulate features for candidate terms
For each candidate c in T
For each $w_1\ w_2\ ...\ c\ ...\ w_{2k-1}\ w_{2k}$ in L
Add all possible substrings involving c in DB.

Step 2: Update the proximity database
Remove each entry in DB that has frequency $< minFreq$.

Step 3: Extend two-word candidates into an initially empty list E
For each candidate c in T
$extend(c, E, DB)$ – see Figure 3
if most occurrences of c in the corpus have not been extended then add c to E.

Output: The list E of extracted multi-word terms.

Fig. 2. Multi-word term extraction algorithm.

3.2   Multi-word Term Extraction

The input to the second phase of the term extraction algorithm is the proximity database and the list of two-word candidates extracted from phase one. The goal is to
extend each candidate to multi-word terms (two words or more up to a fixed size).
Below we describe the multi-word term extraction algorithm in two parts: the main
extraction driver and the recursive term extension algorithm.

3.2.1 Extraction Driver

Figure 2 outlines the main driver for the multi-word term extraction algorithm.

The input proximity database consists of the bigram frequencies of a corpus. In the
first step of the algorithm, we update this database with new features. Given a two-
word candidate c, we consider all possible expansions e of c containing no more than
k words on each side. We then count the frequency between e and all its adjacent
words. Later, in our expansion algorithm, we will use these frequencies to determine
whether e should expand to any of these adjacent words.

For example, suppose $k = 2$ and we have a candidate *drop-down* that occurred in a
corpus in the following contexts:

- ...from the drop-down list in...
- ...Network Logon drop-down list when...

The features extracted for the first context are: (*drop down, list*), (*drop down list,
in*), (*the, drop down*), (*the drop down, list*), (*the drop down list, in*), (*from, the drop
down*), (*from the drop down, list*), and (*from the drop down list, in*).

In Step 2 of the algorithm, we remove those features that occurred only a fixed
small number of times. In our experiments, we found that most extracted features
occurred only once. This step significantly reduces the size of the proximity database
and removes spurious features.

Input: A multi-word term c to extend into a list E and a proximity database DB consisting of bigram frequencies of a corpus L and features extracted from Step 2 of Figure 2. Let c_1 and c_2 be the terms merged to create c.

Step 1: For each word w adjacent to c in L
   If $S(w, c) > S(c_1, c_2) - k$, add w to a list G sorted in decreasing order of $S(w, c)$.

Step 2: For each possible extension g in G
   Let p be the extended phrase $(c\ g)$ or $(g\ c)$
   If p is not a substring of a term in E
      If (not extend(p) and filter(p)) add p to E

Step 3: If any p's were extended or added to E then return *true*, otherwise return *false*.

Output: The list of extracted multi-word terms is appended to E and a boolean value indicating whether or not at least one extension was made is returned.

Fig. 3. Recursive algorithm that extends a given multi-word term to larger terms.

Table 1. 10-fold cross-validation evaluation of the perplexity of our term extraction system.

CORPUS	UNIGRAM PERPLEXITY	SP PERPLEXITY	SP WITH MUT-INFO
UNTS	647.01	523.93	547.94
NAG	706.54	605.59	654.94

Step 3 of Figure 2 uses the added features in the proximity database to extend candidate terms (see the next section for a description of the extension algorithm). We are then left only with deciding whether or not a two-word candidate c is a term. We verify this by obtaining the ratio of the frequencies of extended terms containing c as a substring to the frequency of c. If it is large, then this indicates that most occurrences of c in the corpus were also occurrences of an extended phrase of c. So, we only extract c if the ratio is small.

3.2.2 Term Extension Algorithm

Figure 3 describes the recursive term extension algorithm. The goal is to extend an input term c using the updated proximity database from Section 3.2.1.

In the first step of the algorithm, we build a sorted list G of all *good* extensions of c (the best extensions are first in the list). Let (c_1, c_2) be the two terms that compose c. For a two-word candidate, the first and second words are c_1 and c_2, respectively. A word w is a *good* extension of c if $S(w, c) > S(c_1, c_2) - k$, for some fixed threshold k. The frequency counts required to compute S are stored in the proximity database. The list G then contains all 1-word extensions from c. But, these might still be term fragments.

Step 2 is the recursive step of the algorithm. We loop through each good extension g in G. Let p be the extension of c with g (i.e. either $c\ g$ or $g\ c$). Before processing p, we require that p is not a substring of an extracted term (i.e. g has not been previously extended). For example, suppose that *Jones Computer* and *Computer Publishing* are both two-word candidates and that the former is extended to *Jones Computer Publishing*. Now, suppose that we are attempting to extend *Computer Publishing* with $g = Jones$. Since *Jones Computer Publishing* has already been extracted, we do not want to extend *Computer Publishing* with $g = Jones$.

If p is not a substring of an extracted phrase, then we try to extend p recursively. If p is successfully extended to an even larger term, then we do not add p to E. However, if p is not extended then p is classified as a term and added to E.

So far, the algorithm is purely statistical. However, the final part of Step 2 provides the option of using linguistic knowledge to filter the extracted terms. For example, if the statistical processor treats punctuation marks as words, it is probable that some extended features will contain punctuation marks. This filter allows for easy removal of such erroneous terms.

The final step of the extension algorithm simply determines and returns whether or not c was extracted in whole or in part as a term.

4   Experimental Results

Below, we evaluate our term extractor using perplexity, precision and recall.

4.1   Perplexity

Perplexity measures how well a model predicts some data. In natural language, we often use perplexity to compare the predictiveness of different language models over a corpus. Let W be a random variable describing words with an unknown probability mass function $p(w)$ and let $C(w)$ be the frequency count of a word or term w in a language. Also, let $m(w) = C(w) / C(*)$ be an approximation of $p(w)$ (a unigram model), where $*$ represents a wildcard. Since W is stationary and ergodic, the cross-entropy of W, $H(p, m)$, is defined as [3]:

$$H(p,m) = \lim_{n \to \infty} -\frac{1}{n}\log_2 m(w_1 w_2 w_3 ... w_n) \tag{5}$$

Cross-entropy gives us an upper bound on the true entropy of W, $H(p, m) \geq H(W)$. Standard unigram models approximate the probability of a sequence of words by computing the product of the word probabilities (i.e. assume words are independent). We augment this model to also describe terms by computing the probability of a sequence of words as the joint probability of the terms and words in the sequence.

Using our term extractor, we extract a list of terms from a training corpus. To compute m, we require the frequency counts of all words and terms. We obtain these frequencies by counting all terms and words that are not terms in the training corpus. Using a testing corpus L with a finite number of words n, we approximate the cross-entropy $H(p, m)$ from formula (5) with:

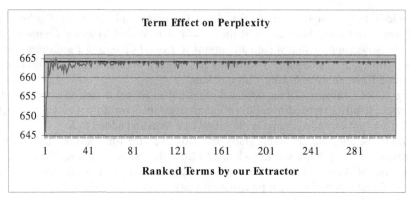

Fig. 4. The effect on perplexity when each ranked term is added individually. The left-most points represent the highest ranked terms.

$$H(p,m) = -\frac{1}{n}\sum_{t \in L} \log_2 m(t) \qquad (6)$$

where t is a term or a word in L. The better the list of extracted terms, the more predictive the model will be of the testing corpus (i.e. the lower $H(p, m)$ will be). Hence, this model can serve to perform a comparative evaluation of different term extraction algorithms. A related measure, *perplexity*, is defined as:

$$perplexity(p,m) = 2^{H(p,m)} \qquad (7)$$

4.1.1 Analysis

We used two corpora for evaluating the perplexity of our system: UNTS [12] consisting of 439,053 words and NAG [15] consisting of 117,582 words. We divided each corpus into 10 equal parts and performed ten-fold cross validation to test our system's perplexity. We used Witten-Bell discounting [21] to estimate the probability of unseen events. Table 1 presents a comparison between our system's perplexity (*SP*) and the perplexity of a unigram model (i.e. with an empty term list). On both corpora, the term list generated by our system significantly reduces perplexity.

We also experimented with a different expansion function for our term extraction algorithm. Instead of using the log-likelihood ratio as in Step 1 of the algorithm presented in Figure 3, we used the mutual information metric. The third column of Table 1 shows the result. This metric performs much worse on the smaller NAG corpus. This supports the claim from Section 3 that mutual information deteriorates with sparse data.

Finally, we divided the UNTS corpus in two equal parts (even vs. odd numbered chapters) and used one for training and the other for testing. We evaluated the effect that specific phrases had on the perplexity of our system. Figure 4 shows the variation in perplexity when each phrase extracted by our system is individually extracted. The horizontal line represents the perplexity of the standard unigram model on this test

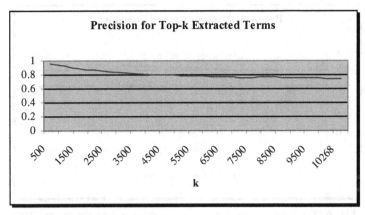

Fig. 5. The precision of the top-k words extracted by our term extractor.

corpus, which is 664.1. The highest spike is caused by the term *boot record*. This is because almost all of its occurrences were in chapters 9 and 29 (part of the training corpus). Finally, we manually created a list of 5 bad terms from a training corpus for UNTS. As expected the perplexity on the test set increased to 664.3.

4.2 Precision and Recall

Making use of a segmented Chinese corpus, we compute the precision and recall of our term extractor. Chinese text does not contain word boundaries and most Chinese words are one or two characters long. In fact, since Chinese characters carry a lot more information than English characters, the average length of a Chinese word contains 1.533 characters [12].

The task of identifying words in Chinese text is very similar to identifying phrasal words in English if one treats each Chinese character as a word. In fact, our term extractor can be applied straightforwardly to Chinese text.

Our extractor can be evaluated as retrieving multi-character words from a segmented Chinese corpus. The target words for the retrieval task are multi-character words in the segmented corpus with a frequency above a certain threshold. The percentage of words in the target set that are extracted by the term extractor is the recall. We measure the precision of the extractor by computing the percentage of the extracted words among the words in the segmented corpus (including those with frequency lower than the threshold).

4.2.1 Analysis
The test data is a cleaned up version of a segmented Chinese corpus [12]. It contains about 10MB of Chinese news text. We extracted 10,268 words from the corpus. Among them, 6,541 are words in the segmented corpus. A further 1,096 of our extracted words are found in HowNet, a Chinese lexical knowledge base [6]. This gives an overall precision of 74.4% for our extraction algorithm. This is a significant improvement over the precision of 59.3% given by Fung's extractor [11]. We also

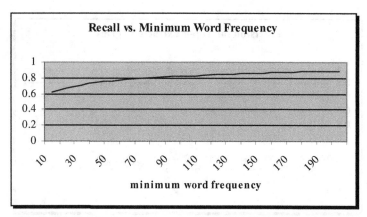

Fig. 6. The recall of our term extractor on words in the corpus that occurred a minimum number of times.

evaluated the precision of the top-k extracted words sorted by their log-likelihood ratio. Figure 5 shows the result.

Since the segmented corpus is generated automatically and is only lightly cleaned up, it contains many errors. The segmentor tends to break words aggressively. Upon inspection of the remaining 2,631 words not found in the corpus nor HowNet, we found many correct terms such as those shown in Table 2. Many of these words are names of persons and organizations, which are not readily found in lexicons such as HowNet.

There are 8,582 words in the segmented corpus that occurred at least 10 times. We extracted 5,349 of these, which gives an overall recall of 62.3%. Again, this is a significant improvement over the recall of 14% given by Fung's extractor [11]. Figure 6 shows the result of evaluating recall for sets with a fixed minimum frequency.

5   Conclusion and Future Work

In this paper, we presented a language independent statistical corpus-based term extractor. It improved the perplexity of a testing corpus by 16-23% and achieved 74.4% precision and 62.3% recall. Of the top 1000 terms retrieved by our system, we achieved 92.6% precision. Also, we recalled 89.1% of the terms that occurred at least 200 times in a corpus.

Our evaluation methodology provides a significant improvement over the current dependence on human evaluators for evaluating systems. It allows for easy comparison of extraction systems and it measures the precision and recall of a system at different word frequency levels.

A promising extension to our algorithm is to apply similar methods to non-linear structures such as dependency structures of sentences. The result would be collocational dependency structures.

Table 2. Some terms extracted by our system that are not found in the lexicon nor in the segmented Chinese corpus.

CHINESE TERM	ENGLISH TRANSLATION	CHINESE TERM	ENGLISH TRANSLATION
冀朝铸	person name	股票指数	stock index
经济特区	special economic zone	国际公约	international treaty
技术革新	technological innovation	国际足联	FIFA
集贸市场	farmer's market	国际奥委会	IOC
姜春云	person name	国际红十字会	International Red Cross
加勒比地区	Caribbean region	国家教委	State Education Commission
贾志杰	person name	国家科委	State Science Commission
军事演习	military exercise	美国国务卿贝克	US State Secretary Baker
单桂芳	person name	马克思主义哲学	Marxist philosophy
艰苦朴素	hard work and plain living (Chinese idiom)	联合国安理会	United Nation Security Council

References

1. Ando, R. K. and Lee, L. 2000. Mostly-unsupervised statistical segmentation of Japanese: Application to Kanji. In *Proceedings of NAACL-2000*. pp. 241-248. Seattle, WA.
2. Bourigault, D. 1992. Surface grammatical analysis for the extraction of terminological noun phrases. In *Proceedings of COLING-92*. pp. 977-981. Nates, France.
3. Cover, T. M., Thomas, J. A. 1991. *Elements of Information Theory*. Wiley, New York.
4. Dagan, I. and Church, K. 1994. Termight: identifying and translating technical terminology. In *Proceedings of Applied Language Processing*. pp. 34-40. Stuttgart, Germany.
5. Daille, B., Gaussier, E., and Langé, J.M. 1994. Towards automatic extraction of monolingual and bilingual terminology. In *Proceedings of COLING-94*. pp. 515-521. Kyoto, Japan.
6. Dong, Z. 1999. Bigger context and better understanding - Expectation on future MT technology. In *Proceedings of ICMT&CLIP-99*. pp.17-25.
7. Dunning, T. 1993. Accurate methods for the statistics of surprise and coincidence. *Computational Linguistics*, 19(1):61-74.
8. Eklund, P. and Wille, R. 1998. A multimodal approach to term extraction using a rhetorical structure theory tagger and formal concept analysis. In *Proceedings of Conference on Cooperative Multimodal Communication: Theory and Applications*. pp. 171-175. Tilburg, Netherlands.
9. FDMC. 1986. *Xiandai Hanyu Pinlu Cidian*(Modern Chinese Frequency Dictionary). Beijing Language Institute Press.
10. Frantzi, K.T. and Ananiadou, S. 1999. The C-Value/NC-Value domain independent method for multi-word term extraction. *Natural Language Processing*, 6(3):145-179.
11. Fung, P. 1998. Extracting key terms from Chinese and Japanese texts. *The International Journal on Computer Processing of Oriental Language*. Special Issue on Information Retrieval on Oriental Languages, pp. 99-121.
12. Guo, J. 1998. Segmented Chinese corpus. ftp://ftp.cogsci.ed.ac.uk/pub/chinese/.
13. Jennings, R., Benage D. B., Crandall, S. and Gregory K. 1997. *Special Edition Using Windows NT Server 4: The Most Complete Reference*. Macmillan Computer Publishing.

14. Justeson, J.S. and Katz, S.L. 1996. Technical terminology: some linguistic properties and an algorithm for identification in text. *Natural Language Engineering*, 3(2):259-289.
15. Kirch, O. 1995. *LINUX: Network Administrator's Guide*. O'Reilly.
16. Lin, D. 1998a. Extracting collocations from text corpora. In *Proceedings of COLING/ACL-98 Workshop on Computational Terminology*. Montreal, Canada.
17. Maynard, A. and Ananiadou, S. 2000. Identifying terms by their Family and friends. In *Proceedings of COLING-2000*. pp. 530-536. Saarbrucken, Germany.
18. Maynard, A. and Ananiadou, S. 1999. Identifying contextual information for multi-word term extraction. In *Proceedings of Terminology and Knowledge Engineering Conference-99*. pp. 212-221. Innsbruck, Austria.
19. Smadja, F. 1993. Retrieving collocations from text: Xtract. *Computational Linguistics*, 19(1):143-177.
20. Sun, M., Shen, D. and Tsou B. K. 1998. Chinese word segmentation without using lexicon and hand-crafted training data. In *Proceedings of COLING-ACL-98*. pp. 1265-1271. Montreal, Canada.
21. Witten, I. H. and Bell, T. C. 1991. The zero-frequency problem: Estimating the probabilities of novel events in adaptive text compression. IEEE Transactions on Information Theory, 37(4).

Body-Based Reasoning Using a Feeling-Based Lexicon, Mental Imagery, and an Object-Oriented Metaphor Hierarchy

Eric G. Berkowitz[1] and Peter H. Greene[2]

[1] Roosevelt University, Chicago IL 60605, USA
eberkowi@roosevelt.edu
[2] Illinois Institute of Technology, Chicago IL 60616, USA
greene@iit.edu

Abstract. Our computer reasoning system uses a set of memory networks, a spatial simulator and an object-oriented hierarchy of body-based spatial metaphors to reason about abstract concepts. The metaphor hierarchy is based on the hierarchical nature of embodied actions, and the simulator is designed to model these actions. The system maps its input to a set of spatial metaphors at the most detailed level possible, and then uses modeling of the metaphorical concepts to reason about the original input.

1 Introduction

This paper describes a system that uses body-based metaphor interpretation and the hierarchical nature of embodied metaphor to perform metaphor-based reasoning on abstract concepts. The system, named MIND (Metaphor-based Interpretation and Natural Discourse), is built from (a) a spatial simulator where physical events are modeled and body-based feelings are generated; (b) a set of integrated networks representing a metaphor hierarchy, a semantic network, a feeling based lexicon, and feelings and imagery from remembered scenes and episodes; and (c) a pattern and sequence matcher. MIND creates feeling-based mappings of events into its restricted set of metaphors producing a mental image that can be manipulated in the spatial processor. Objects (nouns), actions (verbs), and relationships (prepositions) in the actual event are mapped to metaphorical prototypes. Using an image created from the prototypes, MIND can expand upon the spatial interpretation finding other relationships and possible continuations. MIND also models the spatial mappings of events or actions. Using this modeling of events, MIND can determine possible continuations of the metaphorical scene that can be mapped back into the original domain. MIND also determines satisfaction or failure of expectations emanating from the physical imagery, and uses these determinations to perform deductions that can also be mapped back into the domain of the original event.

Our approach stemmed from studies of how the brain controls movement without being overwhelmed by the many degrees of freedom of the body (Greene

E. Stroulia and S. Matwin (Eds.): AI 2001, LNAI 2056, pp. 47–56, 2001.

[1971], [1972], [1982]), which led us to study an object-oriented organization of movement (Solomon [1989]; Greene and Solomon [1991]). We also developed our first model of object-oriented action in general (Greene [1987], [1988]), having a general class DO-SOMETHING (with methods such as START and STOP), a subclass DO-SOMETHING-QUANTITATIVE (with methods for concepts such as such as MORE and LESS, and for adjustment strategies), in turn having a subclass DO-SOMETHING-WITH-EFFORT (for ideas such as TRY, PRE-VENT, and OVERCOME). Combining these models provided connections between movement and language. Thus, we do not focus on the general use of metaphorical natural language, but rather on metaphorlike schemas used as *ideas that organize families of other ideas*, and as feeling-based guides and aids (Damasio [1999]) to reasoning and making choices.

2   The Model of Mind

2.1   Reasoning

MIND processes inputs and attempts to create a spatial portrayal of appropriate metaphors. Processing the statement "I will leave that assertion out of the argument," MIND first determines that the base of its interpretation is the *out* relationship, that is, its top level memory of an *out* situation. MIND's memory of *outside* consists of a container, and a set of feelings. The feelings serve a dual purpose. By being matched against a stream of input feelings, they let MIND know when it encounters an *out* situation. They also tell MIND what a speaker is trying to convey when the speaker uses the word "out."

After recognizing that the reference is to an *out* situation, MIND maps the entities in the input to the entities in the memory of *out*, which includes an *object*, a *container*, and an *outside*. MIND matches up the physical entities and then the feeling set that is appropriate for what is being described. Not all the objects in the memory are mapped to entities in the input. In fact, no mappings are required at all. Mappings merely give the ability to draw more domain specific inferences; they are not required for MIND to process the input. MIND can reason using only the high level metaphorical forms stored in the memory. In this case MIND, knowing nothing about the situation being described except what it is told and what it knows via the fact that it is an outside situation, proceeds to form a spatial perception by creating the appropriate mental imagery.

MIND starts to use its prototypical image of a container to represent the argument. MIND then deduces that existence of an unmentioned "conclusion" or point to the argument, and that this unmentioned object is in fact to be the focal object of the imagery produced. The key to determining the existence of an unmentioned conclusion is in how MIND creates its imagery. Before settling on using as a representation an image mentioned in a memory, MIND constantly attempts to find more specific image classifications by examining new information provided in the input and specific knowledge about objects mapped to general categories.

When MIND processes "...the assertion out of the argument," its first choice of an image for argument is that of a container. Before settling on this image, MIND checks whether it knows anything about arguments that will allow it to use a more detailed image.

MIND knows that an argument has implications. If it knows nothing else (and at this point it in fact knows little else about arguments except a few inherited attributes), MIND knows that the existence of an argument implies the existence of a conclusion that is the focus of the argument. After processing this information, MIND has knowledge of the existence of an entity not mentioned in the input. MIND then checks its memory of the current mapping of argument, a *container*, to see if a more detailed type of container can incorporate this new information. In fact, a more detailed type of container is the *container-with-contents*.

This entry in the memory contains very little information. All it states, is that a container with content has a focal object that must be able to be imparted physical characteristics and that there is a remembered image of a container with content. The actual physical relationship of the content to the container is implicitly found in the image. Although the imagery MIND creates will now have another object, which will, in fact, become the focal object, there is no mention of this object in the text, and MIND has no situational entity to which it can map this object.

There is a major difference between the manner in which MIND determines where to draw the conclusion in the image, and how it determines where to draw the assertion. The location of the conclusion is predetermined by a remembered image of a container with content. Thus, MIND places the conclusion in the location of the content in the memorized image. It is important to remember that its existence and location in the memorized images inherently represent all that MIND needs to know, and their presence in the mental imagery will affect MIND's reasoning process. The location of the spatial representation of the conclusion is determined from the input. The assertion is said to be "out of the argument." MIND knows where to place the assertion because it knows the spatial interpretation of "out." MIND knows what "out" feels like, and what are the elements required to have "out." MIND also knows what "out" looks like, and how to create an image of "out" using objects it can portray in a mental space.

MIND also has some knowledge about the assertion that is not mentioned in the input. MIND knows that assertions are considered to be able to exert a force in contexts in which they are mentioned. MIND therefore refines the image used to represent the assertion from an image of an object to an image of an object with a force. An object with a force exerts, by default, a force that expands in all directions, and causes an expectation that this force will, in some way, affect the focal object of the context in which it is mentioned. MIND, therefore, not only places a representation of the assertion in space, but also places a representation of a force. MIND's spatial processor has a sufficient understanding of the laws of physics to know how a force propagates and what happens when it encounters another entity. As the scenario is played out in the processor, feelings are generated, including a sense of expectation, satisfaction, or failure.

2.2   Finding Expected Continuations

In our examples, once MIND determines a spatial understanding of a situation, it can also find expected and/or possible continuations by processing remembered sequences of feelings and events at the level of the memories it is using to portray the current situation. A small example will demonstrate this point.

MIND finds a probable antecedent (presequence) for events and scenarios with which it is presented. MIND then uses the antecedent as its own input, causing the generation of the same results as if this sequence of events were actually fed into the system as input. MIND has the ability to reinterpret its own output as input and feed it back into itself. Using this new "input," MIND determines what is being described. MIND then determines a set of possible continuations by determining which memorized sequences actually begin with the sequence of feelings generated in the processor by processing the supplied information along with the antecedent MIND has assumed.

2.3   System Components

The model of MIND consists of a set of integrated networks functioning as the following five components: a semantic network, a feeling based lexicon (Berkowitz and Greene [2000]), a memory network, a spatial processor, and a memory matcher (Berkowitz [2000]). The following will describe how the semantic network fits into the overall component structure of MIND. The semantic network consists of links between the nodes in the networks. Each link has an activation coefficient quantifying the relative strength of the relationship between the two connected nodes. Nodes in the semantic network can be activated, causing the activation to propagate. The resultant set of activated nodes and their corresponding activation levels can then be used as an input set to other components in the system.

"On," "out," "inside," "stumble," and "fall" are lexemes, connected to nodes of the semantic net via links with varying activation levels. When a lexeme is activated, its activation is multiplied by the activation levels of the links along which it travels. Since the activation levels are slightly less than 1.0, the activation will slowly dissipate as it spreads throughout the network until it finally drops below a threshold value and propagation stops. Only a subset of the nodes in the networks are actually linked into the semantic network. Each of the connected nodes represents either, one of the basic feelings that are used to create the entries in the feeling-based lexicon, or a named aggregate feeling representing a combination of basic feelings.

The feeling-based lexicon provides direct links between lexemes and nodes in the semantic network. It is via the lexicon that complete feeling sets can be created from external textual information. Each entry in the lexicon is linked to its direct entry points in the semantic network. These links make up its basic feeling-based definition. Activation of a lexical entry causes activation of its direct entry points, that in turn causes propagation of the activation throughout the network, yielding a complete feeling set. Although it may appear as though the lexicon exists as a separate entity, and indeed in its earliest incarnations it was one, it currently exists as another subset of the overall memory network. The lexicon represents those nodes in the network to which a natural language word or phrase can be associated. The nodes form the basic building block of recognizable natural language sequences.

The memory network forms the linkage between the components of the system. It is actually not a single network, but the collection of interconnected networks that share a common node structure but have different sets of links. The component networks are not subnetworks; they are not severable, and any attempt to separate them will necessarily result in duplicated data. They represent different perspectives on the same data, represented by the different sets of links forming different organizational structures. The metaphor network views the nodes as a hierarchical structure representing levels of abstractions, while the semantic network has no form of hierarchical structure at all. This network structure allows the various components of MIND to look at exactly the same data but to interpret it in different ways. The node for "in" can be part of the feeling-based lexicon representing a lexeme. To the semantic network, the same node is linked via activation coefficients to the rest of the semantic network, allowing propagated activations. To the spatial processor, the same node represents the prototypical spatial representation of "in."

The metaphor hierarchy is based upon the levels of abstraction that can be used in perceiving situations. The most generalized perceptions form the top of the metaphor hierarchy. Lower nodes in the tree represent metaphors with added detail. This added detail is not domain detail, but spatial detail that can be exploited should it be alluded to, or should there be domain-specific detail to which it can be mapped. The top level abstraction for all verbs in the hierarchy is the metaphor named *Do*, representing movement of an actor along a path (Greene [1987,1988]). The basic abstraction *Do* would be a superclass of the representation for "I think." Although represented by a path, it lacks landmarks required for measurement of distance and, therefore, proportions. Without any additional information, one can not measure how much one has "thought," or divide thinking into units—how many thinks in a thought? Thus, reasoning is limited to a sense of progress or forward motion but is prevented from quantifying that motion. The first level of specialization is *Do-Quantifiable*, representing acts in which the amount of the act performed can be measured and divided into discrete countable units. For example, in the statement "I run," one can quantify how far I have run. In this case, the only available landmarks are current and previous positions. One can measure in terms of units, the distance that has been traveled. The next level of specialization is *Do-with-Objective*. Here, there is a goal or objective to be reached; not only can the amount of the act performed be quantified, but so can the distance to the goal. Given a current position on a path and a goal, one can measure the distance between them, determining how much of the act needs to be performed, and measuring progress in units not just based on a feeling of unquantifiable forward motion.

The metaphor hierarchy exists as its own network within the memory network. It links those nodes in the memory network that represent metaphorical prototypes. These prototypes contain imagery allowing them to be recreated as mental images in the spatial processor leading to the ability to perform spatial reasoning. The links that make up this part of the memory form a structure representing levels of abstraction in metaphorical detail.

MIND's ability to produce spatial abstractions and mappings from natural language derives, in part, from the lexical sequence network. As it reads input, it attempts to turn the text into a specific instance of a known generalized memory. It utilizes the semantic network to derive feelings and feeling sequences. Utilizing these feelings, it determines an appropriate metaphorical prototype to be used to create a feeling-based abstraction of the text. Based on the metaphorical abstraction, it determines which mappings can be made for elements of the abstraction, and which elements of the abstraction will remain in their generalized form. It constantly attempts to create mappings for generalized forms utilizing new information from the text and searching the memory for implied mappings based on elements of the text. It also maintains a record of the activated memories.

The lexical sequence network is made up of ordered sequences of high level lexical classifications linked to memories of generalized situations to which the sequences can be mapped. When a match is made between a segment of text and a sequence, the feelings activated in the semantic network, the number of mappings that can be made, and the inferences that can be drawn, all serve to determine the correct metaphorical prototype, and the level of metaphorical abstraction from the metaphor tree that will be used as the spatial representation for reasoning. The sequences are made up of the highest possible lexical classifications in order to allow maximum freedom in matching actual sequences to those in the network. Where possible, general categories such as verb or noun are used to designate what form of lexical entry should appear at a given point in a sequence. At other times, a specific lexeme may be the clue to matching the rest of the sequence and the mapping of entities. In this case, the sequence will contain the needed lexeme at the correct position. Completely unrecognized elements of an actual sequence that can not be mapped into the network are ignored, in the hope that utilizing those elements that are recognized, will yield a correct interpretation.

Lexical sequences can be as short as *"noun verb,"* matching any noun followed by a verb. This basic type of sequence will be associated with the highest level abstractions since, without additional information, no mappings can be created beyond the existence of a noun mapped to an object and a verb mapped to "Do." More complex sequences such as *"noun verb toward noun"* would match an actor performing an act toward a goal or objective. All components of MIND are designed to support future handling of much more complex lexical sequences. Sentences such as "I ran toward Sara inside the room under the broken ceiling" could be matched by creating spatial representation for all of the clauses, and combining them as subspaces represented as entities in a meta-representation of the entire sequence. Such subspace/meta-space representation is supported although the current implementation does not exploit it. The sequence recognizer is also designed to recognize subsequences and combine them into larger sequences of sequences.

As a feeling based reasoning system, MIND needs to be able to match concepts not only to textual clues from discourse, but also to feelings generated either by the system's interaction with its environment or as a result of manipulations in its spatial processor. If MIND is trapped in a container, it must realize this via a sequence of feelings common to *trapped* situations. It does not determine *trapped* via a set of rules defining tests for *trapped*, nor even actively test to see if it is trapped. The sequence matcher is watching the generated feelings, and when that sequence indicative of *trapped* is noticed, the appropriate nodes in the memory network are triggered, causing MIND to know it is trapped. The feeling sequence network is made up of ordered collections of feelings linked to an aggregate feeling or to a concept. In MIND, the aggregate feeling *stuck* can be triggered by matching the following sequence of feelings: *internal-force counterforce disappointment null-movement.* The feeling of *stuck* represents a situation in which the application of force does not yield change. This is more primitive than the feeling of *blocked*, as *blocked* implies the existence of some obstacle or impediment. One can be stuck for any number of reasons, including being held back or a lack of adequate traction.

The scenario *blocked* is typified by the sequence: *internal-force counterforce obstructed stuck pressed.* If such a sequence is recognized then it can be called "blocked," and the word "blocked" indicates the existence of these feelings. The possible responses, in general categorical form, for *blocked* are *try-harder*, *go-around*, and *give-up*. The feeling sequence network utilizes the same sequence matcher as the lexical sequence network allowing for equally complex sequences.

The memory sequence network combines sets of memory nodes into a sequence constituting a complete memory. The sequences constitute a "script" or "movie" representing a remembered flow of events (Greene and Chien [1993]). These sequences would allow MIND to have presuppositions about what preceded a recognized scenario and what might follow it. These sequences would also allow MIND to conceive rational responses to situations. MIND's first response, based on a memory sequence, to feeling stuck is to try harder, by applying increased force. This response is not an arbitrary phrase produced by rules. It is a representation of memories in the memory network that allow MIND not only to know that trying harder is an appropriate response, but also to reason about trying harder. It can remember through added sequences what might happen when it tries harder. It would model trying harder in its spatial processor and come up with possible outcomes without reliance on remembered events, but only on its spatial abstraction of the current scenario and associated feelings.

Using MIND as a reasoning engine and building on our prior systems we are now enlarging the feeling-based lexicon and developing control structures and choice strategies for reasoning in real-world scenarios. Although we currently use symbolic techniques, we are researching the application of various forms of reduced representations of sequences proposed in the connectionist literature as representations of bodily "feelings" or "somatic markers" (Damasio [1999]) associated with our "scripts" or "movies" in MIND's memory, and their use in guiding choices that would then be confirmed and refined through symbolic reasoning.

3   Origins of This Work

Relying on our previous work developing a conceptual hierarchy for action and the works of Talmy ([1985]), Lakoff ([1987]), Johnson ([1987]), and Langacker ([1987], [1991]) who developed an extensive theory of how metaphor based on bodily feelings of space and force organizes our ideas and speech, Greene and Chien ([1993]) presented an unsupervised neural network that classified clusters of feelings generated when a simple simulated creature collided with a physical obstacle, one class turning out to be the feelings at the moment of impact; this paper speculated on mapping instances of abstractly "running into an obstacle" into such a simulation, allowing retrieval of the fact that it had three options, *push hard*, *go around*, or *give up*, to be converted by a suitable object-oriented organization of domain knowledge into the particular forms of these options appropriate to the current situation. We hoped that, through similar feelings, abstract instances of body-based concepts might evoke concrete physical "scripts" of feeling clusters, that could be used as abstract "diagrams" of a situation, from which useful information could be read. Kozak ([1994], [1995]) presented a program demonstrating this form of body-based abstraction but without organizing actions into an object-oriented structure. Berkowitz ([2000]) presented the first fully integrated system, using feeling-based definitions, and exploiting hierarchical metaphors.

4   Conclusion

Using a minimal set of body-based metaphors, MIND can demonstrate reasoning about abstract concepts such as leaving an assertion out of an argument. Elevating reasoning to the level of body based metaphors can facilitate the general application of basic reasoning mechanisms as well as modeling of human communication through the use of simulated human reasoning.

We believe our work is compatible with other schools of work often regarded as mutually incompatible. For example, reactive creatures, such as those of Brooks, who avoids a cognitive level (Brooks [1990]), should be good substrates for our body-based concepts. Furthermore, the physical knowledge in the motor schemas might be expected to fit nicely into both Pinker's ([1989]) work on verb structure, and the cognitive approach of Langacker([1987], [1991]), Lakoff

([1987]), Johnson ([1987], Bailey ([1997]) and Narayanan ([1997]). The possibility of using our work as a method bringing together these currently separate research pursuits creates fascinating prospects for future work.

References

[1997] Bailey, D.: A Computational Model of Embodiment in the Acquisition of Action verbs. Ph.D. dissertation, Computer Science Division, EECS Dept., University of California at Berkeley. Berkeley, CA. (1997)

[2000] Berkowitz, E. G.: Metaphor-Based Reasoning for Software Agents and Heterogeneous Robots Using Body-Based Feeling Sequences. Ph. D. dissertation, Illinois Institute of Technology, Chicago IL. (2000)

[2000] Berkowitz, E. G. and Greene, P. H.: Using a Feeling Based Lexicon to Integrate Language and Reasoning. Preceedings of KBCS 2000. Mumbai, India. (2000) 355–364

[1990] Brooks, R.: Elephants Don't Play Chess. Robotics and Autonomous Systems. **6**(1990) 3–15

[1999] Damasio, A. R.: The Feeling of What Happens: Body and Emotion in the Making of Consciousness. New York: Harcourt Brace. (1999)

[1971] Greene, P. H.: Introduction to I. M. Gelfand, (Ed.-in-Chief), with V. S. Gurfinkel, S. V. Fomin, and M. I. Tsetlin (Assoc. Eds.). Models of the Structural-Functional Organization of Certain Biological Systems, (Translated by C. R. Beard). Cambridge, MA: MIT Press. (1971)

[1972] Greene, P. H.: Problems of Organizaton of Motor Systems. In R. Rosen and F. M. Snell (Eds.), Progress In Theoretical Biology. **2** New York: Academic Press. (1972)

[1982] Greene, P. H.: Why Is It Easy to Control Your Arms? Journal of Motor Behavior. **14** (1982) 260–286.

[1987] Greene, P. H.: Cognitive Structures in Movement: Cahiers de Psychologie Cognitive. **7** (1987) 163–166

[1988] Greene, P. H.: The Organization of Natural Movement. Journal of Motor Behavior. **20** (1988) 180–185.

[1993] Greene, P. H. and Chien, G. H.: Feeling-Based Schemas, Neural Architectures, and Distributed AI: From Schema Assemblage to Neural Networks. Proceedings of the 1993 Workshop On Neural Architecture and AI. Univ. of Southern California, Los Angeles, CA. (1993) 112–115

[1991] Greene P. H. and Solomon D.: A Computer System for Movement Schemas. In Badler, N. I., Barsky, B. A., and Zeltzer, D., Making It Move: Mechanics and Animation of Articulated Figures. Palo Alto, CA: Morgan Kaufmann. (1991) 193–205

[1987] Johnson, M.: The Body in the Mind: The Bodily Basis of Meaning, Imagination, and Reason. Chicago: University of Chicago Press. (1987)

[1994] Kozak, M. M.: Body-Based Cognition: Reasoning Guided by Feeling, Emotion, and Metaphor. Ph. D. Dissertation, Illinois Institute of Technology, Chicago, IL. (1994)

[1995] Kozak, M. M.: Reasoning Based on Feelings and Metaphor, Sixth Midwest Artificial Intelligence and Cognitive Science Conference, Carbondale, IL. (1995) 132–137

[1987] Lakoff, G.: Women, Fire, and Dangerous Things. University of Chicago Press. Chicago, IL.(1987)

[1987] Langacker R. W.: Foundations of Cognitive Grammar, Vol. I, Stanford, CA.: Stanford Univ. Press. (1987)

[1991] Langacker R. W.: Foundations of Cognitive Grammar, Vol. II, Stanford, CA.: Stanford Univ. Press. (1991)

[1997] Narayanan S.: Knowledge-Based Action Representation For Metaphor and Aspect. Dissertation in Engineering and Compuer Science, University of California at Berkeley. Berkeley, CA. (1997)

[1989] Pinker, S.: Learnability and Cognition. Cambridge, MA: MIT Press. (1989)

[1989] Riesbeck, C. and Schank, R.: Inside Case Based Reasoning. NY, NY: Lawrence Elbaum Associates. (1989)

[1989] Solomon, D.: An Object-Oriented Representation for Motor Schemas. Ph. D. Dissertation, Illinois Institute of Technology. Chicago, IL. (1989)

[1985] Talmy, L.: Force Dynamics in Language and Thought. In Papers from the Parasession on Causatives and Agentivity. Chicago, Chicago Linguistic Society (1985)

Combinatorial Auctions, Knapsack Problems, and Hill-Climbing Search

Robert C. Holte

School of Information Technology and Engineering,
University of Ottawa, Ottawa, Ontario, Canada, K1N 6N5
holte@site.uottawa.ca

Abstract. This paper examines the performance of hill-climbing algorithms on standard test problems for combinatorial auctions (CAs). On single-unit CAs, deterministic hill-climbers are found to perform well, and their performance can be improved significantly by randomizing them and restarting them several times, or by using them collectively. For some problems this good performance is shown to be no better than chancel; on others it is due to a well-chosen scoring function. The paper draws attention to the fact that multi-unit CAs have been studied widely under a different name: multidimensional knapsack problems (MDKP). On standard test problems for MDKP, one of the deterministic hill-climbers generates solutions that are on average 99% of the best known solutions.

1   Introduction

Suppose there are three items for auction, X, Y, and Z, and three bidders, B1, B2, and B3. B1 wants any one of the items and will pay \$5, B2 wants two items – X and one of Y or Z – and will pay \$9, and B3 wants all three items and will pay \$12. In a normal auction items are sold one at a time. This suits buyers like B1, but not B2 and B3: they cannot outbid B1 on every individual item they require and stay within their budget. If X is auctioned first it will likely be won by B1, and the seller's revenue (\$5) will be much worse than optimal (\$14). In a combinatorial auction (CA) each bid offers a price for a set of items (goods). Thus, bidders can state their precise requirements and the seller can choose the winners to optimize total revenue (sum of the selected bids' prices).

Combinatorial auctions have been studied since at least 1982[32], when they were proposed as a mechanism for selling time-slots at airports in order to permit airlines to bid simultaneously for takeoff and landing time-slots for a given flight. Fuelled by the FCC's interest [13] and potential e-commerce [22] and other applications [21,25], interest in combinatorial auctions has increased rapidly in recent years. Among the many research issues raised, of main interest to AI is the fact that "winner determination" - selecting the set of winning bids to optimize revenue - is a challenging search problem. A recent survey of CA research is given in [10]. Previous research has mainly focused on single-unit CAs, in which there is exactly one copy of each item. Multi-unit CAs, in which there can be any number of identical copies of each item, were introduced to the AI

E. Stroulia and S. Matwin (Eds.): AI 2001, LNAI 2056, pp. 57–66, 2001.

community in [27], which claimed the problem was new. One contribution of the present paper is to point out that multi-unit CAs have been studied extensively in the Operations Research literature, where they are called multidimensional knapsack problems (MDKP).

This paper examines the performance of hill-climbing algorithms on standard test problems for CAs. Theoretical analysis shows that greedy algorithms cannot guarantee finding near-optimal solutions for winner determination [1,7,9,12,15, 17,18,29,33,34]. But these are mostly worst-case results, and in some cases apply only to specific types of greedy algorithm and not to the type of hill-climbing algorithm considered here. The main finding of this paper is that on the standard CA and MDKP test sets, hill-climbers perform very well.

2   The Hill-Climbing Algorithms

The hill-climbing algorithms compared in this paper are identical except for the criterion used to select which successor to move to. Search begins with the empty set of bids and adds one bid at a time. Because bids have positive prices and search can only add bids to the current bid-set, the total revenue for the current bid-set must increase as search proceeds. Search terminates when a bid-set is reached that has no successors. The solution reported is the bid-set seen during search that maximizes revenue, which may be different than the local maximum at which the search terminated.

Each different way of adding one bid to the current bid-set creates a potential successor. A potential successor is eliminated if it is infeasible or if it can be shown that no extension of it can possibly yield a greater revenue than the best solution seen so far. For this purpose Sandholm & Suri's "admissible heuristic" (p.96, [35]) is used. Of the remaining successors the one that adds the bid with the maximum "score" is selected to be the current bid-set and and the process is repeated. Three different ways of computing a bid's score are considered:

Price: the bid's price

N2norm: the bid's price divided by its "size", where the size of bid j is the 2-norm (square root of the sum of squares) of the $f_{i,j}$, the fraction of the remaining quantity of item i that bid j requires.

KO: the bid's price divided by its "knockout cost", where a bid's knockout cost is the sum of the prices of the available bids that are eliminated if this bid is chosen. KO is the only novel scoring function; the others, and many variations of them, have been studied previously [5,17,23,28,39,40].

Also included in the experiments is a form of randomized hill-climbing in which, after pruning, a successor is chosen randomly: the probability of choosing each successor is proportional to its score. Such hill-climbers can produce different solutions each time they are run. In the experiments each is restarted from the empty bid-set 20 times and the best solution on any of the runs is recorded. In the tables these are identified by appending ×20 to the scoring function. For example, **Price**×20 is the randomized hill-climber that makes its probabilistic selection based on Price.

Table 1. Percentage of problems on which the heuristic solution is optimal

heuristic	arb	match	path	r75P	r90P	r90N	sched
1. Price	3	39	4	0	10	8	14
2. N2norm	4	39	11	0	11	9	14
3. KO	4	25	14	1	10	8	15
best of 1-3	5	54	28	1	11	9	27
4. Price×20	12	39	4	1	19	15	22
5. N2norm×20	9	39	11	0	15	13	19
6. KO×20	13	25	14	1	18	16	22
best of 4-6	19	54	28	2	26	22	37

3   The Test Problems

Test problems were generated using the CATS suite of problem generators version 1.0 [26]. Each problem generator in CATS models a particular realistic scenario in which combinatorial auctions might arise. For example, matching.c models the sale of airport time-slots. The experiments use each of CATS's five generators for single-unit CAs, one with 3 different parameter settings, for a total of seven different types of test problem. The abbreviations used to identify the type of test problem in the tables of results and the corresponding CATS program and parameter settings are as follows (default parameter settings were used except as noted): **arb** (arbitrary.c), **match** (matching.c), **path** (paths.c with NUMBIDS=150), **r90P** (regions.c), **r90N** (regions.c with ADDITIVITY= -0.2), **r75P** (regions.c with ADDITIONAL LOCATION= 0.75), **sched** (scheduling.c with NUMGOODS=20 and NUMBIDS=200).

100 instances of each problem type are generated. In addition to the hill-climbers, a systematic search algorithm is run in order to determine the optimal solution. This is a relatively unsophisticated branch-and-bound search. There were a handful of instances that it could not solve within a 1 million node limit; these are excluded from the results.

4   Heuristic Hill-Climbing Experimental Results

Tables 1-3 have a column for each type of test problem and a row for each of the hill-climbers. There are also two "best of" rows. "Best of 1-3" refers to the best solution found by the deterministic hill-climbers on each individual test problem. "Best of 4-6" is the same but for the randomized hill-climbers. Because hill-climbing is so fast, these represent realistic systems which run a set of hill-climbers on a given problem and report the best of their solutions.

Table 1 shows the percentage of test problems of a given type that are solved optimally by a given hill-climber. On the **r75P** problems the hill-climbers almost never find the optimal solution. On **match**, **path**, and **sched** problems, the deterministic hill-climbers collectively (best of 1-3) find the optimal solution on

Table 2. Suboptimality decile of the worst heuristic solutions

heuristic	arb	match	path	r75P	r90P	r90N	sched
1. Price	60-69 (1)	80-89 (8)	70-79 (2)	50-59 (3)	70-79 (7)	60-69 (1)	60-69 (1)
2. N2norm	70-79 (22)	80-89 (8)	80-89 (4)	60-69 (7)	70-79 (8)	60-69 (1)	70-79 (8)
3. KO	60-69 (1)	80-89 (3)	80-89 (3)	60-69 (16)	70-79 (7)	60-69 (1)	70-79 (2)
best of 1-3	70-79 (14)	90-99 (46)	80-89 (1)	60-69 (2)	70-79 (4)	70-79 (5)	80-89 (9)
4. Price×20	80-89 (23)	80-89 (7)	80-89 (28)	70-79 (2)	70-79 (1)	80-89 (18)	80-89 (11)
5. N2norm×20	70-79 (1)	80-89 (7)	80-89 (3)	70-79 (1)	80-89 (11)	80-89 (21)	80-89 (13)
6. KO×20	80-89 (29)	80-89 (1)	80-89 (3)	70-79 (2)	80-89 (13)	80-89 (16)	70-79 (1)
best of 4-6	80-89 (10)	90-99 (46)	90-99 (72)	80-89 (29)	80-89 (3)	80-89 (4)	80-89 (1)

over a quarter of the problems, and on all types of problem except **r75P** the randomized hill-climbers collectively find the optimal solution on between 19% and 54% of the problems.

Table 2 summarizes the worst solutions found by each heuristic on each type of problem. The heuristic's solution, as a percentage of the optimal solution, is put into a 10-point bin, or decile (e.g. 63% falls in the 60-69% decile). The worst non-empty decile is reported in the table; in brackets beside the decile is the percentage of test problems that fell into that decile. For example, the $60 - 69(1)$ entry in the upper left indicates that on 1% of the **arb** problems, the solutions found by the Price hill-climber were 60-69% of optimal, and on none of the **arb** problems were this hill-climber's solutions worse than 60% of optimal. On all the problems all the hill-climbers find solutions that are 50% of optimal or better, and only very rarely do any of them find solutions worse than 70% of optimal. The solutions found by the randomized hill-climbers are very rarely worse than 80% of optimal.

Table 3 gives the average percentage of optimal of the solutions found by each heuristic on each type of problem. The first row is for the "blind" hill-climber discussed in the next section and will be ignored until then. **r75P** is clearly the most difficult type of problem for the hill-climbers. **arb**, **r90P** and **r90N** are moderately difficult for the deterministic hill-climbers. On all problem types other than **r75P** the randomized hill-climbers find solutions that are more than 90% of optimal on average (95% if taken collectively).

The differences between the solutions found by the different hill-climbers are not large in most cases, but paired t-tests indicate that some of the differences are significant ($p < 0.05$). On all types of problem except **match**, where the difference was not significant, a randomized hill-climber is significantly better than the deterministic version with the same scoring function and the randomized hill-climbers collectively ("best of 4-6") are significantly better than the deterministic hill-climbers collectively. The Price scoring function is never superior to others. For deterministic hill-climbing KO is significantly better than N2norm on **sched** problems, but the opposite is true on **arb**, **path** and **r75P** problems. For randomized hill-climbing N2norm is significantly better than KO on **path** problems; on all other types of problem either the difference is not significant or KO is better.

Table 3. Average solution value as a percentage of optimal

heuristic	arb	match	path	r75P	r90P	r90N	sched
blind	84	63	52	73	90	88	65
1. Price	85	97	91	75	90	89	92
2. N2norm	87	97	97	81	90	89	92
3. KO	86	97	96	79	90	89	94
best of 1-3	87	99	98	83	90	89	96
4. Price×20	94	97	92	88	95	94	95
5. N2norm×20	93	97	97	89	94	94	95
6. KO×20	93	97	96	90	95	94	96
best of 4-6	95	99	98	92	96	96	98

The overall conclusion of this experiment is that hill-climbing always finds acceptable solutions, usually very good ones, for the problem types studied. **r75P** is the most challenging problem type. On it the hill-climbers rarely find an optimal solution, but the randomized hill-climbers collectively find a solution that is at least 90% of optimal more than 60% of the time. Thus, very good solutions are found most of the time even on the most challenging type of problem. Problem types **match**, **path**, and **sched** are the easiest. For them very good solutions can almost always be found even by the deterministic hill-climbers (collectively).

5 Blind Hill-Climbing

The experiment in this section was suggested by the unexpectedly strong performance of Monte Carlo search on some of the standard test problems for the multidimensional knapsack problem [4]. The previous section has shown that the scoring mechanisms used by the hill-climbers, especially KO and N2norm, lead to good solutions. But perhaps a blind hill-climber, which, after pruning, selects among successors randomly with uniform probability, would do equally well. To examine this, 100 instances of each problem type were generated, as above, and solved by the deterministic hill-climbers. In addition, each instance was solved 200 times by the blind hill-climber.

Table 4 gives the percentage of the blind hill-climber's solutions that are strictly worse than the solution found by a particular deterministic hill-climber on each problem type. On **match**, **path** and **sched** problems the deterministic hill-climbers virtually always outperformed the blind hill-climber. On these types of problem a well-chosen scoring function is essential for good performance. On the other types of problem the scoring functions were no better than chance. This may also be seen by comparing the blind hill-climber's average solution quality – the first row in Table 3 – with the averages for the deterministic hill-climbers.

Each column in Table 5 is a histogram. Each of the blind hill-climber's solutions is expressed as a percentage of the optimal solution and put into the appropriate decile. The table shows what percentage of the solutions fall into

Table 4. Percentage of blind solutions worse than heuristic solutions

heuristic	arb	match	path	r75P	r90P	r90N	sched
1. Price	20	100	100	53	7	6	98
2. N2norm	40	100	100	76	16	23	99
3. KO	20	100	100	63	7	6	99

Table 5. Percentage of blind solutions in each suboptimality decile

% of optimal	arb	match	path	r75P	r90P	r90N	sched
10 − 19			0.01				
20 − 29		0.005	2				
30 − 39		1	13				0.05
40 − 49		8	29	0.12			6
50 − 59		29	32*	4			30
60 − 69	2	38*	19	30		0.56	33*
70 − 79	21	20	5	48*	9	13	20
80 − 89	63*	4	0.7	16	46*	45*	8
90 − 99	13	0.1	0.03	2	34	33	1.5
100	1				11	9	0.075

each decile for each type of problem. For example, the 0.01 at the top of the **path** column means that on problems of type **path** 0.01% of the blind hill-climber's solutions were 10-19% of optimal (i.e. extremely poor). A blank entry represents 0. In each column an asterisk indicates the median decile. On **match**, **path** and **sched** problems blind hill-climbing sometimes produces very poor solutions and has a poor median. The opposite is true of **arb**, **r90P** and **r90N**. On these types of problems no blind hill-climbing solution is worse than 60% of optimal and the median decile is 80-89%. **r75P** is of medium difficulty. The bottom row gives the percentage of blind hill-climbing runs which find the optimal solution. Comparing this to the deterministic hill-climbing rows in Table 1, it is apparent that on **arb**, **r90P** and **r90N** problems the ability of the scoring functions to guide the hill-climber to optimal solutions is no better than chance, whereas on **match**, **path** and **sched** problems they are far better than chance.

Table 6. Average solution value as a percentage of optimal

hill-climber	mknap1	mknap2	mknapcb1	mknapcb2	mknapcb3	mknapcb7
1. Price	90	94	89	89	89	93
2. N2norm	98.99	99.00	98.94	99.03	99.21	98.35
3. KO	83	79	85	85	85	85
blind	84	58	82	83	83	81

Two overall conclusions follow from the experiments in this and the preceding section. In problems of type **match,** **path** and **sched** good solutions are relatively rare, but the scoring functions are very effective for these problems and deterministic hill-climbing performs very well on them. If suboptimal solutions are acceptable, problems of these types (with the parameter settings used in this study) are not especially promising as testbeds for comparing search strategies. By contrast, for problems of type **arb, r90P, r90N** and **r75P** the guidance of the scoring functions is no better than chance. These types of problems are therefore good choices for evaluating search strategies, but in using them it is crucial to take into account the high baseline performance of blind hill-climbing.

6   Multidimensional Knapsack Experimental Results

A multi-unit combinatorial auction is precisely a multidimensional knapsack problem (MDKP): each item in the auction is a "dimension" and including a bid in the solution bid-set corresponds to putting the bid into the knapsack. MDKP has been the subject of several theoretical analyses [6,9,12,15,29,38] and experimental investigations involving all manner of search methods, including genetic algorithms[8,20,24], TABU search [2,19], local search [5,11,30] and classical complete algorithms such as branch-and-bound [16,37] and dynamic programming [41]. A good review of previous work is given in [8].

A standard set of test problems for the MDKP is available through J. Beasley's ORLIB[3]. Files mknap1 [31] and mknap2 [14,36,37,41] contain real-world test problems widely used in the literature. The others were generated with the aim of creating more difficult problems[8]. Each problem has an associated best known solution, which in some cases is known to be optimal, and in all cases is extremely close to optimal.

The hill-climbing algorithms were run on the six test sets indicated in the column headings of Table 6. N2norm performs extremely well. Its average solution is 99% of the best known solution on all the test sets except mknapcb7, where its average is 98.35%. Only on two problems in mknap2 is its solution worse than 90% of the best known (those solutions are in the 80-89% range). On more than 25% of the problems in mknap1 and mknap2 its solution is equal to the best known (this virtually never happens for the other test sets). N2norm is competitive with all previously reported systems on these datasets, and superior to previous "greedy" approaches. The blind hill-climber's median decile is 50-59% for mknap2, but it is 80-89% for the other test sets, indicating that very good solutions are abundant. KO performs poorly in the multi-unit setting.

7   Conclusions

The primary aim of this paper has been to examine the performance of hill-climbing algorithms on standard test problems for combinatorial auctions (CAs). On the CATS suite of test problems for single-unit CAs deterministic hill-climbers perform well, and their performance can be improved significantly by randomizing them and restarting them several times, or by using them collectively. For some types of problem their performance, although good, is no better than chance: these types of problems therefore have an abundance of high-quality solutions. Providing the chance performance baseline is taken into account these problems are good testbeds for comparative studies. On the other types of CATS problems the good performance is due to the scoring function that guides the hill-climbing. Unless parameter settings can be found which result in poor performance by the hill-climbers, these problems are not especially good choices for testbeds in experiments where suboptimal solutions are permitted. On the standard test problems for multi-unit CAs (also known as multidimensional knapsack problems) deterministic hill-climbing using N2norm as a scoring function generates solutions that are on average 99% of the best known solutions; it is therefore competitive with all previously reported systems on these problems.

Acknowledgements. I am grateful to the maintainers of the compendium of NP optimization problems [9], and to J. Beasley and the authors of CATS for creating and distributing their tests suites. ORLIB is available at http://mscmga.ms.ic.ac.uk/info.html. CATS is available at http://robotics.stanford.edu/CATS/. This research was supported in part by an operating grant from the Natural Sciences and Engineering Research Council of Canada.

References

[1] E. M. Arkin and R. Hassin. On local search for weighted packing problems. *Mathematics of Operations Research*, 23:640–648, 1998.

[2] R. Battiti and G. Tecchiolli. Local search with memory: Benchmarking RTS. *Operations Research Spectrum*, 17(2/3):67–86, 1995.

[3] J. E. Beasley. OR-library: distributing test problems by electronic mail. *Journal of the Operational Research Society*, 41(11):1069–1072, 1990.

[4] M. Bertocchi, I. Brandolini, L. Slominski, and J. Sobczynska. A monte-carlo approach for 0-1 programming problems. *Computing*, 48:259–274, 1992.

[5] M. Bertocchi, A. Butti, L. Slominski, and J. Sobczynska. Probabilistic and deterministic local search for solving the binary multiknapsack problem. *Optimization*, 33:155–166, 1995.

[6] A. Caprara, H. Kellerer, U. Pferschy, and D. Pisinger. Approximation algorithms for knapsack problems with cardinality constraints. *European Journal of Operational Research*, 123:333–345, 2000.

[7] Barun Chandra and Magnus M. Halldorsson. Greedy local improvement and weighted set packing approximation. *Proceedings of the tenth annual ACM-SIAM Symposium on Discrete Algorithms*, pages 169–176, 1999.

[8] P.C. Chu and J.E. Beasley. A genetic algorithm for the multidimensional knapsack problem. *Journal of Heuristics*, 4:63–86, 1998.

[9] Pierluigi Crescenzi and Viggo Kann. A compendium of NP optimization problems. http://www.nada.kth.se/~viggo/wwwcompendium.

[10] Sven de Vries and R. Vohra. Combinatorial auctions: A survey. Technical Report (discussion paper) no. 1296, The Center for Mathematical Studies in Economics and Management Science, Northwestern University, 2000.

[11] A. Drexl. A simulated annealing approach to the multiconstraint zero-one knap-sack problem. *Computing*, 40:1–8, 1988.

[12] M.E. Dyer and A. M. Frieze. Probabilistic analysis of the multidimensional knap-sack problem. *Maths. of Operations Research*, 14(1):162–176, 1989.

[13] FCC. Public notice DA00-1075: Auction of licenses in the 747-762 and 777-792 MHZ bands scheduled for September 6, 2000: Comment sought on modifying the simultaneous multiple round auction design to allow combinatorial (package) bidding.

[14] A. Freville and G. Plateau. Hard 0-1 multiknapsack test problems for size reduc-tion methods. *Investigation Operativa*, 1:251–270, 1990.

[15] A. M. Frieze and M. R. B. Clarke. Approximation algorithms for the m-dimensional 0-1 knapsack problem: worst-case and probabilistic analyses. *European Journal of Operational Research*, 15:100–109, 1984.

[16] B. Gavish and H. Pirkul. Efficient algorithms for solving multiconstraint zero-one knapsack problems to optimality. *Mathematical Programming*, 31:78–105, 1985.

[17] Rica Gonen and Daniel Lehmann. Optimal solutions for multi-unit combinatorial auctions: Branch and bound heuristics. *Proceedings of the Second ACM Confer-ence on Electronic Commerce (EC-00)*, pages 13–20, 2000.

[18] M. M. Halldorsson. Approximations of weighted independent set and hereditary subset problems. *J. Graph Algorithms and Applications*, 4(1):1–16, 2000.

[19] S. Hanafi and A. Freville. An efficient tabu search approach for the 0–1 multidi-mensional knapsack problem. *European Journal of Operational Research*, 106(2-3):663–697, 1998.

[20] Christian Haul and Stefan Voss. Using surrogate constraints in genetic algorithms for solving multidimensional knapsack problems. In David L. Woodruff, editor, *Advances in Computational and Stochastic Optimization, Logic Programming, and Heuristic Search: Interfaces in Computer Science and Operations Research*, chap-ter 9, pages 235–251. 1998.

[21] Luke Hunsberger and Barbara J. Grosz. A combinatorial auction for collaborative planning. *Proceedings of the Fourth International Conference on Multi-Agent Systems (ICMAS-2000)*, pages 151–158, 2000.

[22] Joni L. Jones. Incompletely specified combinatorial auction: An alternative allo-cation mechanism for business-to-business negotiations (Ph.D. thesis).

[23] A. H. G. Rinnooy Kan, L. Stougie, and C. Vercellis. A class of generalized greedy algorithms for the multi-knapsack problem. *Discrete Applied Mathematics*, 42:279–290, 1993.

[24] S. Khuri, T. Back, and J. Heitkotter. The zero/one multiple knapsack problem and genetic algorithms. *Proceedings of the ACM Symposium of Applied Computation*, pages 188–193, 1993.

[25] Erhan Kutanoglu and S. David Wu. On combinatorial auction and Lagrangean relaxation for distributed resource scheduling. Technical report, Lehigh University, April, 1998.

[26] K. Leyton-Brown, M. Pearson, and Y. Shoham. Towards a universal test suite for combinatorial auctions algorithms. *Proceedings of the Second ACM Conference on Electronic Commerce (EC-00)*, pages 66–76, 2000.

[27] K. Leyton-Brown, Y. Shoham, and M. Tennenholtz. An algorithm for multi-unit combinatorial auctions. *Proceedings of the Seventeenth National Conference on Artificial Intelligence (AAAI-2000)*, pages 56–61, 2000.

[28] R. Loulou and E. Michaelides. New greedy-like heuristics for the multidimensional 0-1 knapsack problem. *Operations Research*, 27:1101–1114, 1979.

[29] Michael J. Magazine and Maw-Sheng Chern. A note on approximation schemes for multidimensional knapsack problems. *Mathematics of Operations Research*, 9(2):244–247, 1984.

[30] M. Ohlsson, C. Peterson, and B. Soderberg. Neural networks for optimization problems with inequality constraints - the knapsack problem. Technical Report LU TP 92-11, Dept. of Theoretical Physics, Univ. of Lund, 1992.

[31] C. C. Petersen. Computational experience with variants of the Balas algorithm applied to the selection of R&D projects. *Management Science*, 13(9):736–750, 1967.

[32] S. J. Rassenti, V. L. Smith, and R. L. Bulfin. A combinatorial auction mechanism for airport time slot allocation. *Bell Journal of Economics*, 13:402–417, 1982.

[33] M. H. Rothkopf, A. Pekec, and R. M. Harstad. Computationally manageable combinatorial auctions. *Management Science*, 44(8):1131–1147, 1998.

[34] Shuichi Sakai, Mitsunori Togasaki, and Koichi Yamazaki. A note on greedy algorithms for maximum weighted independent set problem.
http://minnie.comp.cs.gunma-u.ac.jp/ koichi/TecRep/gamis.ps.

[35] Tuomas Sandholm and Subhash Suri. Improved algorithms for optimal winner determination in combinatorial auctions and generalizations. *Proceedings of the Seventeenth National Conference on Artificial Intelligence (AAAI-2000)*, pages 90–97, 2000.

[36] S. Senju and Y. Toyoda. An approach to linear programming with 0-1 variables. *Management Science*, 11:B196–B207, 1967.

[37] Wei Shih. A branch and bound method for the multiconstraint zero one knapsack problem. *J. Operational Research Society*, 30(4):369–378, 1979.

[38] Krzysztof Szkatula. On the growth of multi-constraint random knapsacks with various right-hand sides of the constraints. *European Journal of Operational Research*, 73:199–204, 1994.

[39] J. Thiel and S. Voss. Some experiences on solving multiconstraint zero-one knapsack problems with genetic algorithms. *INFOR*, 32(4):226–242, 1994.

[40] Y. Toyoda. A simplified algorithm for obtaining approximate solution to zero-one programming problems. *Management Science*, 21:1417–1427, 1975.

[41] H. M. Weingartner and D. N. Ness. Methods for the solution of the multidimensional 0/1 knapsack problem. *Operations Research*, 15:83–103, 1967.

Concept-Learning in the Presence of *Between-Class* and *Within-Class* Imbalances

Nathalie Japkowicz[*]

School of Information Technology and Engineering
University of Ottawa
150 Louis Pasteur, P.O. Box 450 Stn. A
Ottawa, Ontario, Canada K1N 6N5
nat@site.uottawa.ca

Abstract. In a concept learning problem, imbalances in the distribution of the data can occur either *between* the two classes or *within* a single class. Yet, although both types of imbalances are known to affect negatively the performance of standard classifiers, methods for dealing with the class imbalance problem usually focus on rectifying the between-class imbalance problem, neglecting to address the imbalance occuring within each class. The purpose of this paper is to extend the simplest proposed approach for dealing with the between-class imbalance problem—random re-sampling—in order to deal simultaneously with the two problems. Although re-sampling is not necessarily the best way to deal with problems of imbalance, the results reported in this paper suggest that addressing both problems simultaneously is beneficial and should be done by more sophisticated techniques as well.

1   Introduction

Imbalanced data sets are inductive learning domains in which one class is represented by a greater number of examples than the other. [1] Several methods have previously been proposed to deal with this problem including stratification (re-sampling or down-sizing approaches), cost-based learning, and one-sided learning. In this paper, we will only focus on stratification methods, though the close relationship between cost-based and stratification based learning makes the observations made in this paper applicable to cost-based learning as well.

Although stratification approaches have previously been shown to increase classification accuracy [Kubat and Matwin1997, Ling and Li1998], none of these studies took into consideration the fact that both *between-class* and *within-class* imbalances may occur. In the context of this study, a between-class imbalance corresponds to the case where the number of examples representing the positive class differs from the number of examples representing the negative class;

---

[*] This research was supported by an NSERC Research Grant.

[1] Throughout this paper, we focus on concept-learning problems in which one class represents the concept while the other represents counter-examples of the concept.

E. Stroulia and S. Matwin (Eds.): AI 2001, LNAI 2056, pp. 67–77, 2001.

and a within-class imbalance corresponds to the case where a class is composed of a number of different subclusters and these subclusters do not contain the same number of examples. The within-class imbalance problem along with the between-class imbalance problem are instances of the general problem known as the *problem of small disjuncts* Holte *et al.*1989 which can be stated as follows: Since classification methods are typically biased towards classifying large disjuncts (disjuncts that cover a large number of examples) accurately, they have a tendency to overfit and misclassify the examples represented by small disjuncts.

The purpose of this paper is to show that the within-class imbalance problem and the between-class imbalance problem both contribute to increasing the misclassification rate of multi-layer perceptrons. More specifically, the study distinguishes between different types of imbalances and observes their effects on classification accuracy with respect to perfectly balanced situations or rebalanced ones in artificial domains. It then derives an optimal re-balancing strategy which it tests on a real-world domain.

2   Experiments on Artificial Domains

This section presents a systematic study of the generalized imbalance problem in two cases. The first case, the symmetrical case, involves data sets that have as many subclusters in each class. The second case, the asymmetrical case, involves data sets that have more subclusters in one class than in the other.

2.1   The Symmetric Case

In order to study the effect of between-class and within-class imbalances as well as to choose an appropriate solution to these problems in the case of a symmetrical domain, we generated a series of variations of the X-OR problem in which the data distribution differed from one experiment to the other. We then tested the relative accuracy performance of a standard Multi-Layer Perceptron with fixed parameters. These experiments gave a sense of which tasks are more or less difficult to learn by this standard classifier.

Task. The X-OR domain used in this experiment is depicted in Figure 1(a). Each class is composed of two subclusters located at the bottom left and top right corner in the case of the positive class (positive instances are represented by '$\star$') and at the top left and bottom right corners in the case of the negative class (negative instances are represented by 'o'). The subclusters are non-overlapping and, in the original domain, each subcluster contains 1,500 training examples. The testing set is distributed in the same way, except for the size of each subcluster which is of 500 examples. Unlike for the training set, the size of the testing set remains fixed for all the experiments. This means that even if the training set contains less data in one subcluster than in the other, we consider the small subcluster to be as important to classify accurately as the larger one. In other words, the cost of misclassifying the small subcluster is considered to be as high as the cost of misclassifying the larger one.

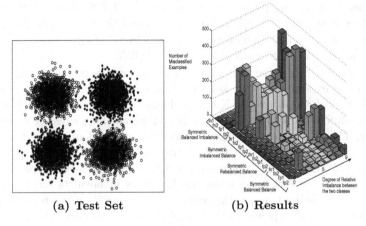

(a) **Test Set**   (b) **Results**

Fig. 1. Experiment on a Symmetric Artificial Domain

Experiments. Starting from the original domain, four series of experiments were conducted which changed the between-class balance or the within-class balance of the negative class by modifying the size of the negative subclusters either at the same rate or at a different one while the size of the positive subclusters was either kept fixed or modified simultaneously. These experiments were named: 1) Symmetric Balanced Balance (SBB), 2) Symmetric Balanced Imbalance (SBI), 3) Symmetric Imbalanced Balance (SIB), and 4) Symmetric Rebalanced Balance (SRB), where the first term indicates that there are as many subclusters in the positive and negative class, the second one represents the status of the *within-class* cluster relation and the third one represents the status of the *between-class* cluster relation.

In other words, SBB corresponds to the experiment in which the four subclusters (positive or negative) are of the same size; SBI corresponds to the case where although there are as many examples in the two positive subclusters and the two negative subclusters respectively, there are overall more positive examples than negative ones; SIB corresponds to the case where the size of the overall positive set equals that of the negative one, but although the two positive subclusters are of the same size, the two negative ones are of different sizes; finally, SRB corresponds to the case where the SIB data set has been re-balanced by resampling each subcluster (positive and negative) to make it match the size of the largest subcluster present in the training set (this largest subcluster is necessarily one of the negative subclusters).

Within each experiment set, 10 different degrees of between-class or within-class imbalance were considered, following an exponential rate of size decrease. More specifically, the imbalance was created by decreasing the size of the subcluster(s) targetted by the particular approach at hand at a rate of $\frac{original\_subcluster\_size}{2^i}$ with $i = 0..9$. For example, when $i = 5$, the SBB set is composed of two positive and two negative subclusters of size $ceiling(\frac{1,500}{2^5}) = 47$;

the SBI set contains two positive subclusters of size $1,500$ each and two negative subclusters of size $ceiling(\frac{1,500}{2^5}) = 47$, each; The SIB set contains two positive subclusters of size $1,500$ each one negative subcluster of size $ceiling(\frac{1,500}{2^5}) = 47$ and one negative cluster of size $3,000 - 47 = 2,953$.

As mentioned previously, the size of the parameters of the neural networks used for these experiments were kept fixed since we are not interested in whether a neural network can solve the X-OR problem (which we know is always possible given sufficient ressources), but rather in which tasks cause it more or less difficulty. The parameters we chose—since they were adequate for the original domain—were of 4 hidden units and 200 training epochs. The training procedure used was Matlab's default optimization algorithm: the Levenberg-Marquardt procedure. The network used sigmoidal functions in both its hidden and output layer. After being trained, the networks were tested on the testing set. The experiments were all repeated 5 times and the results of each trial averaged.

Results. The results of all the experiments in this section are reported in Figure 1(b). In this figure, the results are reported in terms of four quantities: number of false negatives for positive subcluster 1 (fn1), number of false negatives for positive subcluster 2 (fn2), number of false positives for positive subcluster 1 (fp1), number of false positives for positive subcluster 2 (fp2). The results are also reported for each level of imbalance starting at level 0 (no imbalance) reported in the front row to level 9 (largest imbalance) reported in the back row. The results are reported in terms of number of misclassified examples in each subcluster. In each case, the maximum possible number of misclassified examples is 500, the size of each testing subcluster. The results were reported in the following order: SBI, SIB, SRBand SBB. This order corresponds to the least accurate to the most accurate strategy and was chosen to allow for the best perspective on a single graph.

In more detail, the results indicate that the results on the SBI strategy are the least accurate because it causes both negative subclusters a high degree of misclassification. The positive class, on the other hand, is generally well classified. This can be explained by the fact that, in this experiment, both negative subclusters have smaller sizes than the positive ones.The degree of imbalance observed between the two classes, however, does not appear to be an important factor in the misclassification rates observed (remember, however, that the imbalance level grows exponentially which means that the absolute difference between two consecutive levels is greater at the begining than it is at the end). The results on the SIB domain are a little more accurate than those on the SBI domain since this time, only one of the two negative subclusters—the one represented by the smallest number of examples—suffers from some misclassification error. The third set of results, the set of results obtained when using a rebalancing sampling strategy so as to rectify the SIB problem is shown to be effective although, as the degree of within-class imbalance in the negative class increases, the re-sampling strategy is shown to loose some accuracy in the originally small but re-sampled subcluster, though this loss is much smaller than the loss incurred when no re-sampling is used.[2] This result can be explained by the fact that re-sampling the same data over and over is not as useful as having individual data points belonging to the same distribution (as shown by the fourth set of results on the SBB domain). Indeed, a re-sampling strategy may rectify the imbalance problem but it does not introduce all the information necessary to prevent the inductive learner to overfit the training examples. On the contrary, it probably encourages some amount of overfitting in the originally small negative subcluster.

These results, thus, suggest that balancing a domain with respect to the between-class problem is not sufficient since, if within-class imbalances are present, the classifier will not be very accurate.

2.2   The Asymmetric Case

Although the experiments of the previous section gave us an idea of the effect of between-class and within class imbalances on the classification accuracy of a multi-layer perceptron, they only considered the case where there are as many subclusters in the positive and the negative class. The question asked in this section is how to handle the case of within-class and between-class imbalance when the number of subclusters in each class is different. In particular, we are interested in finding out whether, in such cases, better classification can be expected when all the subclusters (independently of their class) are of the same size and, thus, the two classes are represented by different numbers of examples or when all the subclusters within the same class are of the same size, but altogether, the class sizes are the same.

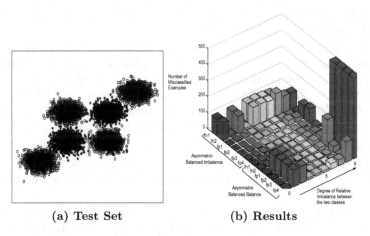

(a) Test Set	(b) Results

Fig. 2. Experiment on an Asymmetric Artificial Domain

---

[2] In a couple of isolated cases, one of the positive subclusters also seems to be affected, but the significance of this observation is unclear.

Task. In order to answer this question, we generated a new test set closely related to the X-OR problem of the previous section. As a matter of fact, the test set represents the X-OR problem plus two new negative subclusters, both located on the same diagonal as the two positive subclusters, but just outside the square formed by linking the four subclusters of the X-OR problem. This new problem is depicted in Figure 2(a) with '$\star$' representing positive examples and 'o"s representing negative ones.

Once again, each subcluster of the training set is originally represented by 1,500 examples, independently of its class. Like in the previous section, the testing set is distributed in the same way, except for the size of each subcluster which is of 500 examples.

Experiments. In this section, two series of experiments were conducted that only changed the between-class balance. The within-class balance was untouched (since its effect was already tested in the previous section) although the size of the subclusters belonging to each class, respectively, was allowed to differ. These experiments were named: Asymetric Balanced Balance (ABB) and Asymetric Balanced Imbalance (ABI), where the first term indicates that there are different numbers of subclusters per class, the second term represents the status of the within-class cluster relation and the third one represents the status of the between-class cluster relation. In other words, ABB corresponds to the experiment in which the two positive subclusters are of the same size and the four negative subclusters are of the same size, but the negative subclusters are half the size of the positive ones so that, altogether, the two classes have the same number of training instances; ABI corresponds to the case where all the positive and negative subclusters are of the same size and, thus, the two classes have different numbers of training instances.

Again within each experiment set, 10 different degrees of between-class or within-class imbalance were considered, following an exponential rate of size decrease. As before, the imbalance was created by decreasing the size of the subcluster(s) targetted by the particular approach at hand at a rate of $\frac{original\_subcluster\_size}{2^i}$ with $i = 0..9$. For example, when $i = 5$, the ABB Set has two positive subclusters of size $ceiling(\frac{1,500}{2^5}) = 47$ and four negative subclusters of size $floor(\frac{1,500}{2 \times 2^5}) = 23$, with no between-class imbalance; Similarly, the ABI set is composed of two positive and four negative subclusters of size $ceiling(\frac{1,500}{2^5}) = 47$, each, thus creating a between-class imbalance of 94 examples.

Like previously and for the same reasons, the size of the parameters of the neural networks used for these experiments were kept fixed, though, due to the increased difficulty of the test domain, we increased the number of hidden units to 8. All the other parameters remained the same. These parameters were adequate for the original domain of Figure 2(a). After being trained, the networks were again tested on a testing set. The experiments were all repeated 5 times and the results of each trial averaged.

Results. The results of all the experiments in this section are reported in Figure 2(b). In this figure, the results are reported in terms of six quantities: number of false negatives for positive subcluster 1 (fn1) and positive subcluster 2 (fn2), number of false positives for positive subcluster 1 (fp1), positive subcluster 2 (fp2), positive subcluster 3 (fp3) and positive subcluster 4 (fp4). The results are also reported for each level of imbalance starting at level 0 (no imbalance) reported in the front row to level 9 (largest imbalance) reported in the back row. The results are reported in terms of number of misclassified examples in each subcluster. In each case, the maximum number of misclassified examples is 500, the size of each testing subcluster. The results were reported in the following order: ABI and ABB since this order corresponds to the least accurate to the most accurate strategy and was, again, chosen to allow for the best perspective on a single graph.

In more detail, the results indicate that the results on the ABI domain are less accurate than those obtained on the ABB domain because they suggest that the two positive subclusters are prone to misclassification errors whereas they are generally not in the case of the ABB domain. This can be explained by the fact that in the ABI domain, the size of the positive class is half that of the negative one. In most cases, it thus, appears that it is generally better to be in a situation where the two classes are balanced (with no between- nor within-class imbalance), even if that means that the size of the subclusters of the class composed of the greater number of subcluster is smaller than that of its counterparts in the other class.[3]

3   An Optimal Re-balancing Strategy

Based on the results obtained in the symmetrical and asymmetrical domains of section 2, we can now hypothesize on an optimal re-balancing strategy for the cases where both within-class and between-class imbalances are present in a domain. The benefits of this strategy is then tested in a grouped-letter recognition problem.

3.1   Formulation of the Strategy

Let L be a concept-learning problem with two classes A and B each composed of N_A and N_B subclusters respectively. Class A is composed of subclusters a_i of size n_a^i, respectively (with $i \in \{1, 2, ...N_A\}$) and class B is composed of subclusters b_j of size n_b^j, respectively (with $j \in \{1, 2, ...N_B\}$). Let $maxcluster_A = max(n_a^1, n_a^2, ...n_a^{N_A})$ and $maxcluster_B = max(n_b^1, n_b^2, ..., n_b^{N_B})$. Let, further, $maxclasssize = max(maxcluster_A \times N_A, maxcluster_B \times N_B)$ and $maxclass$ be the class corresponding to maxclasssize (i.e., class A in case

---

[3] Note, however, that the graph shows several cases where the ABB strategy causes misclassification to the negative class. These cases, however, are rarer than the cases where the positive class is negatively affected in the ABI situation.

$maxcluster_A \times N_A \geq maxcluster_B \times N_B$ and class B, otherwise. Let $altclass$ be the class *not* corresponding to maxclass (i.e., altclass=A if maxclass=B and vice-versa). According to the results of Section 2, L will be learned more accurately by multi-layer perceptrons if the training set is transformed as follows:

> Each subcluster of class *maxclass* is re-sampled until it reaches size $maxcluster_{maxclass}$. At this point, the overall size of *maxclass* will be *maxclasssize* and there will be no within-class imbalance in class *maxclass*. In order to prevent a between-class imbalance as well as within-class imbalances in altclass, each subcluster of altclass is re-sampled until it reaches size $maxclasssize/N_{altclass}$.

This procedure will guarantee no between-class imbalance and no within-class imbalance although, like in the asymmetrical case above, the size of A's subclusters may differ from that of B's.

3.2   Testing the Stategy

In order to determine whether the strategy just derived is practical, we tested our approach on a real world-domain. In particuliar, we tested the multi-layer perceptron on the letter recognition problem consisting of discriminating between a certain number of vowels and consonnants.

More specifically, we used the letter recognition data set available from the UC Irvine Repository. However, we defined a subtask which consisted of recognizing vowels from consonnants and, in order to make our task more tractable, we reduced the vowel set to the letters a, e, and u and the consonnant set to the letters m, s, t and w. In addition, rather than assuming the same number of examples per letter in the training set, we constructed the training data in a way that reflects the letter frequency in English text.[4] The testing set was always fixed and consisted of 250 data points per letter. The reason why the distribution of the testing set differs from that of the training set is because the cost of misclassifying a letter is independent of its frequency of occurence. For example, confusing "war" for "car" is as detrimental as confusing "pet" for "pat" even though "w" is much more infrequently used than "e".

In the experiments we conducted on these data, the performance of the multi-layer perceptron was compared to its performance in three different training-set situations: Imbalance, Naive Re-Balance, Informed Re-Balance, and Uninformed Re-Balance. The purpose of the Imbalance, Naive Re-Balance, and Informed-Rebalance experiments is simply to verify whether our optimal-resampling strategy also helps on a real-world domain. The Imbalance experiment consisted of running the multi-layer perceptron on the letter recognition domain without

---

[4] In particular, we relied on the following frequencies: a: .0856, e: .1304, u: .0249, m: .0249, s: .0607, t: .1045, w: .0017 and consequently built a training set containing the following corresponding number of training examples per letter: a= 335 points, e= 510 points, u= 97 points, m= 97 points, s= 237 points, t= 409 points, w= 7 points. These letters were chosen because of their interesting differing frequencies.

practicing any type of re-balancing. The Naive Re-Balance strategy consisted of re-sampling from the negative class (containing 750 training data), ignoring its internal distribution, until its size reached that of the positive class (containing 942 training data). The Informed-Rebalance experiment assumes that the subcluster division of each class is fully known and the data sets are rebalanced according to our optimal re-balancing strategy.[5] In the Uninformed Re-Balance strategy, no prior knowledge about the data is assumed. In this case, the k-means unsupervised learning algorithm is used to determine the inner-distribution of each class, followed by our optimal re-balancing method.[6]

In all three experiments, the neural networks were optimized using Matlab's default optimization algorithm: Levenberg-Marquardt, and the network used sigmoidal units in both their hidden and output layers. In each experiment, four different networks were ran five times each with 2, 4, 8 and 16 hidden units. The results were averaged over the five runs and the best results were reported.

The results obtained on these experiments are reported in Figure 3. In particular, Figure 3 is composed of 8 clusters of 4 columns each. Within each cluster, each column corresponds to the performance of each of our 4 strategies. The leftmost column of each cluster represents the results obtained on the Imbalance experiment; next are the results obtained with the Naive Re-Balance Strategy; this is followed with the Informed Re-Balance strategy; and the last column was obtained using the Uninformed Re-Balance strategy. The rightmost cluster represents the cumulative results obtained on the overall testing set, while each of the preceeding cluster represents the results on particular subclusters.

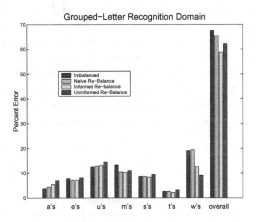

Fig. 3. Results

---

[5] Although this situation is unrealistic, this case is considered since it represents a lower bound on the results that can be obtained using our re-sampling strategy.

[6] An estimate of the number of clusters per class was determined prior to running the k-means algorithm. Our estimation procedure, however, is sub-optimal and will be refined in future work, using cross-validation experiments.

The results shown in Figure 3 suggest that, overall, as can be expected the Imbalance experiment shows a slightly larger error rate than the Naive Re-Balance experiment. The Informed Re-balance experiment shows a lower error rate than the Naive Re-Balance experiment and the Uninformed Re-Balance experiment falls in-between the two results, helping to improve on the imbalanced results, but not performing quite as well as in the case where the composition of each class is fully known. In more detail, the results show that the Informed and Uninformed Re-Balance strategies are particularly effective in the case of a very small subcluster (w), but that the Uninformed strategy causes a slight decrease in accuracy in the other subclusters. This is usually not the case for the Informed strategy and we hope that improving our clustering approach in the Uninformed strategy will help in reducing this problem.

4   Conclusion and Future Work

It is not uncommon for classification problems to suffer from the problem of class imbalances. In particular, these imbalances can come in two forms: *between-class* and *within-class* imbalances. Though both problems are well-known and have been previously considered in the machine learning literature, they have not been previously considered simultaneously. The purpose of this paper was to derive a re-sampling strategy that considers both imbalances simultaneously and demonstrate that even a very simple method for dealing with the problem can be helpful in the case of drastically imbalanced subclusters.

There are many extensions of this work. First, the experiments on artificial domains were conducted on *unnaturally* imbalanced data sets. It would be useful to repeat these experiments on *naturally* imbalanced ones. Second, rather than testing our re-balancing strategy on a balanced domain, it would be more representative to test it on a range of class distributions using ROC Hulls or Cost Curves [Provost and Fawcett2001, Drummond and Holte2000]. Third, it would be interesting to test our strategy on other classifiers and other domains.[7] Finally, we should try to adapt our strategy to cost-based algorithms that usually perform more accurately on imbalanced data sets than stratification methods.

References

[Drummond and Holte2000] Chris Drummond and Robert Holte. Explicitly representing expected cost: An alternative to roc representation. In *Proceedings of the sixth ACM SIGKDD International Conference on Knowledge Discovery and Data Mining*, pages 198–207, 2000.

[Holte *et al.*1989] R. C. Holte, Acker L. E., and B. W. Porter. Concept learning and the problem of small disjuncts. In *IJCAI-89*, 1989.

[Kubat and Matwin1997] Miroslav Kubat and Stan Matwin. Addressing the curse of imbalanced data sets: One-sided sampling. In *ICML-97*, 1997.

---

[7] Some preliminary work in this area can be found in Nickerson *et al.*2001.

[Ling and Li1998] Charles X. Ling and Chenghui Li. Data mining for direct marketing: Problems and solutions. In *KDD-98*, 1998.

[Nickerson *et al.*2001] Adam Nickerson, Nathalie Japkowicz, and Evangelos Milios. Using unsupervised learning to guide resampling in imbalanced data sets. In *AISTATS-01 (to appear)*, 2001.

[Provost and Fawcett2001] Foster Provost and Tom E. Fawcett. Robust classification for imprecise environments. *Machine Learning*, 42:203–231, 2001.

Constraint Programming Lessons Learned from Crossword Puzzles

Adam Beacham, Xinguang Chen, Jonathan Sillito, and Peter van Beek

Department of Computing Science
University of Alberta
Edmonton, Alberta, Canada T6G 2H1
{abeacham,xinguang,sillito,vanbeek}@cs.ualberta.ca

Abstract. Constraint programming is a methodology for solving difficult combinatorial problems. In the methodology, one makes three design decisions: the constraint model, the search algorithm for solving the model, and the heuristic for guiding the search. Previous work has shown that the three design decisions can greatly influence the efficiency of a constraint programming approach. However, what has not been explicitly addressed in previous work is to what level, if any, the three design decisions can be made independently. In this paper we use crossword puzzle generation as a case study to examine this question. We draw the following general lessons from our study. First, that the three design decisions—model, algorithm, and heuristic—are mutually dependent. As a consequence, in order to solve a problem using constraint programming most efficiently, one must exhaustively explore the space of possible models, algorithms, and heuristics. Second, that if we do assume some form of independence when making our decisions, the resulting decisions can be sub-optimal by orders of magnitude.

1   Introduction

Constraint programming is a methodology for solving difficult combinatorial problems. A problem is modeled by specifying constraints on an acceptable solution, where a constraint is simply a relation among several unknowns or variables, each taking a value in a given domain. Such a model is often referred to as a constraint satisfaction problem or CSP model. A CSP model is solved by choosing or designing an algorithm that will search for an instantiation of the variables that satisfies the constraints, and choosing or designing a heuristic that will help guide the search for a solution.

As previous work has shown, the three design decisions—model, algorithm, and heuristic—can greatly influence the efficiency of a constraint programming approach. For example, Nadel [13] uses the n-queens problem to show that there are always alternative CSP models of a problem and that, given the naive chronological backtracking algorithm, these models can result in different problem solving performances. Ginsberg et al. [9] use one possible model of crossword puzzle generation (model m_2 in our notation) to study the effect on performance of various backtracking algorithms and variable ordering heuristics. Smith et al. [17]

E. Stroulia and S. Matwin (Eds.): AI 2001, LNAI 2056, pp. 78–87, 2001.

use Golomb rulers to study the effect on performance of alternative models, algorithms and heuristics. Finally, a variety of studies have shown how the relative performance of various search methods and heuristics vary with properties of a random binary CSP instance such as domain sizes, tightness of the constraints, and sparseness of the underlying constraint graph (e.g., [2,6,8,10,18]).

However, what has not been explicitly addressed in previous work is to what level, if any, the three design decisions can be made independently. There are three possible levels of independence in the design decisions: complete independence, one-factor independence, and conditional independence (see, e.g., [4]). Suppose that there are four choices each for the model, the algorithm, and the heuristic. Complete independence would mean that choosing the best model, the best algorithm, and the best heuristic could all be done independently and a total of $4 + 4 + 4 = 12$ tests would need to be performed to choose the best overall combination. One-factor independence would mean that, while two of the design decisions might depend on each other, the third could be made independently and a total of $4 + (4 \times 4) = 20$ tests would need to be performed to choose the best overall combination. Conditional independence would mean that two of the design decisions could be made independently, given the third design decision and a total of $4 \times (4 + 4) = 32$ tests would need to be performed to choose the best overall combination. Finally, if none of the independence conditions hold and the design decisions are mutually dependent a total of $4 \times 4 \times 4 = 64$ tests would need to be performed to choose the best overall combination. Thus, it is clear that the level of independence of the design decisions can have a large impact if we seek the best overall combination of decisions.

In this paper we use crossword puzzle generation as a case study to examine the interdependence of the choice of model, backtracking search algorithm, and variable ordering heuristic on the efficiency of a constraint programming approach. We perform an extensive empirical study, using seven models, eight backtracking algorithms, and three variable ordering heuristics for a total of 34 different combinations (not all algorithms can be applied on all models). The goal of our study is to examine to what extent the design decisions can be made independently. We draw the following general lessons from our study. First, that the three design decisions—model, algorithm, and heuristic—are mutually dependent. In other words, neither complete independence, one-factor independence, nor conditional independence hold. As a consequence, in order to solve a problem using constraint programming most efficiently, one must exhaustively explore the space of possible models, algorithms, and heuristics. Second, that if we do assume some form of independence when making our decisions, the resulting decisions can be sub-optimal. As one example, if the model is chosen independently of the algorithm and the heuristic, the result can be orders of magnitude less effective as the best algorithm and heuristic cannot overcome a poor choice of model.

2   CSP Models for Crossword Puzzles

In crossword puzzle generation, one is required to fill in a crossword puzzle grid with words from a pre-defined dictionary such that no word appears more than once. An example grid is shown in Figure 1. In this section, we present the seven different CSP models of the crossword puzzle problem that we used in our experiments. A constraint satisfaction problem (CSP) consists of a set of variables, a domain of possible values for each variable, and a collection of constraints. Each constraint is over some subset of the variables called the scheme of the constraint. The size of this set is known as the arity of the constraint.

1	2	3		
4	5	6	7	8
9	10	11	12	13
14	15	16	17	18
		19	20	21

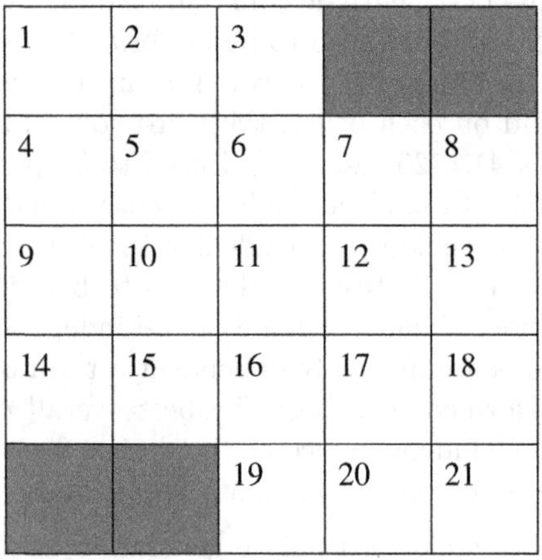

Fig. 1. A crossword puzzle grid.

Model m_1. In model m_1 there is a variable for each unknown letter in the grid. Each variable takes a value from the domain $\{a, \ldots, z\}$. The constraints are of two types: word constraints and not-equals constraints. There is a word constraint over each maximally contiguous sequence of letters. A word constraint ensures that the sequence of letters forms a word that is in the dictionary. The arity of a word constraint reflects the length of the word that the constraint represents. For example, the word at "1 Across" in Figure 1 has three letters and will result in a 3-ary constraint over those letter variables. The tuples in the word constraints represent the words that are of the same length as the arity of the constraint in the pre-defined dictionary. There is a not-equals constraint over pairs of maximally contiguous sequences of letters of the same length. A not-equals constraint ensures that no word appears more than once in the puzzle. The arity of a not-equals constraint depends on whether the corresponding words intersect. For example, the words at "9 Across" and "3 Down" will result in a 9-ary constraint over those letter variables.

Model m_1^+. Model m_1^+ is model m_1 with additional, redundant constraints. One technique to improve the performance of the forward checking algorithm is to add redundant constraints in the form of projections of the existing constraints. (Projection constraints are not as effective for algorithms that maintain generalized arc consistency.) In model m_1^+, for each word constraint C and for each proper subset S of the variables in the scheme of C in which the variables are consecutive in the word, we add a redundant constraint which is the projection of C onto S. For example, for the constraint over the three letter variables x_1, x_2, and x_3 which form the word at "1 Across" in Figure 1, projection constraints would be added over x_1 and x_2, and over x_2 and x_3. The tuples in these constraints would represent the valid prefixes and valid suffixes, respectively, of the three-letter words in the dictionary.

Model m_2. In model m_2 there is a variable for each unknown word in the grid. Each variable takes a value from the set of words in the dictionary that are of the right length. The constraints are of two types: intersection constraints and not-equals constraints. There is an intersection constraint over a pair of distinct variables if their corresponding words intersect. An intersection constraint ensures that two words which intersect agree on their intersecting letter. There is a not-equals constraint over a pair of distinct variables if their corresponding words are of the same length. A not-equals constraint ensures that no word appears more than once in the puzzle. All of the constraints in model m_2 are binary. Although a natural model, model m_2 can be viewed as a transformation of model m_1 in which the constraints in m_1 become the variables in m_2. The transformation, known as the dual transformation in the literature, is general and can convert any non-binary model into a binary model [16].

Model m_3. In model m_3 there is a variable for each unknown letter in the grid and a variable for each unknown word in the grid. Each letter variable takes a value from the domain $\{a, \ldots, z\}$ and each word variable takes a value from the set of words in the dictionary that are of the right length. The constraints are of two types: intersection constraints and not-equals constraints. There is an intersection constraint over a letter variable and a word variable if the letter variable is part of the word. An intersection constraint ensures that the letter variable agrees with the corresponding character in the word variable. There is a not-equals constraint over a pair of distinct word variables if their corresponding words are of the same length. All of the constraints in model m_3 are binary. Model m_3 can be viewed as a transformation of model m_1 which retains the variables in the original problem plus a new set of variables which represent the constraints. The transformation, known as the hidden transformation in the literature, is general and can convert any non-binary model into a binary model [16].

A CSP problem can be encoded as a satisfiability (SAT) problem (see, e.g., [19]). To illustrate the encoding we use in this paper, consider the CSP with three variables x, y, and z, all with domains $\{a, b, c\}$, and constraints $x \neq y$, $x \neq z$, and $y \neq z$. In the SAT encoding a proposition is introduced for every variable in the CSP and every value in the domain of that variable: x_a, x_b, x_c, y_a,

y_b, y_c, and z_a, z_b, z_c. The intended meaning of the proposition x_a, for example, is that variable x is assigned the value a. Clauses (or constraints) are introduced to enforce that each variable must be assigned a *unique* value. For example, for the variable x, the following clauses are introduced: $x_a \vee x_b \vee x_c$, $x_a \Rightarrow \neg x_b$, $x_a \Rightarrow \neg x_c$, and $x_b \Rightarrow \neg x_c$. Clauses are introduced to specify the illegal tuples in the constraints. For example, for the constraint $x \neq y$, the following clauses are introduced: $x_a \Rightarrow \neg y_a$, $x_b \Rightarrow \neg y_b$, and $x_c \Rightarrow \neg y_c$.

Model s_1. Model s_1 is the SAT encoding of model m_1 with the following improvements designed to reduce the amount of space required. In the generic encoding, clauses are introduced to rule out the tuples that are not allowed by a constraint. For the word constraints in m_1, the illegal tuples represent sequences of letters that are not words in the dictionary. In s_1, not all illegal words are translated to clauses. Instead, we translate all invalid prefixes. For example, "aa" is not a valid prefix for words of length 4. Instead of recording all of the illegal tuples "aaaa" ... "aazz", just "aa" is recorded. For not-equals constraints in m_1, only the tuples that form a word are translated into clauses in s_1. For example, we do not say that "aaaa" $\neq$ "aaaa" because "aaaa" is not a valid word.

Model s_2. Model s_2 is the SAT encoding of model m_2. In particular, for each pair of propositions that represents intersecting words in the puzzle and words from the dictionary that do not agree, we introduce a negative binary clause ruling out the pair.

Model s_3. Model s_3 is the SAT encoding of model m_3 with the following improvements. The clauses for the domains of the hidden variables that ensure that each word must get a unique value are dropped as they are redundant (the clauses for the domains of the letter variables and the clauses for the intersection constraints together entail that a hidden variable can take only one value).

3   Backtracking Algorithms

In this section, we present the eight different backtracking algorithms we used in our experiments. At every stage of backtracking search, there is some current partial solution which the algorithm attempts to extend to a full solution by assigning a value to an uninstantiated variable. The idea behind some of the most successful backtracking algorithms is to look forward to the variables that have not yet been given values to determine whether a current partial solution can be extended towards a full solution. In this forward looking phase, the domains of the uninstantiated variables are filtered based on the values of the instantiated variables. The filtering, often called constraint propagation, is usually based on a consistency technique called arc consistency or on a truncated form of arc consistency called forward checking (e.g., [7,10]). If the domain of some variable is empty as a result of constraint propagation, the partial solution cannot be part of a full solution, and backtracking is initiated. A further improvement can be made to backtracking algorithms by improving the backward looking phase when the algorithm reaches a dead-end and must backtrack or uninstantiate some of the variables. The idea is to analyze the reasons for the dead-end and to backtrack or backjump enough to prevent the conflict from reoccurring (e.g., [7,14]). All of the algorithms we implemented used some form of constraint propagation and all were augmented with conflict-directed backjumping [14].

Algorithm FC. Algorithm FC performs forward checking [10].

Algorithm GAC. Algorithm GAC performs generalized arc consistency propagation in the manner described in [12].

Algorithm EAC. Algorithm EAC performs generalized arc consistency propagation in the manner described in [3]. In the implementation of EAC used in the experiments the constraints were stored extensionally and advantage was taken of this fact to improve overall performance.

Algorithms PAC(m_1), PAC(m_2), and PAC(m_3). A technique for improving the efficiency of generic constraint propagation is to design special purpose propagators where constraints have methods attached to them for propagating the constraint if the domain of one of its variables changes (see, e.g., [1]). Propagators provide a principled way to integrate a model and an algorithm [15]. We designed and implemented propagators which enforce arc consistency for each of the constraints in models m_1, m_2, and m_3.

Algorithms ntab_back, ntab_back2. These algorithms are the implementations of the TABLEAU algorithm described in [5]. Algorithm ntab_back uses backjumping and algorithm ntab_back2 uses relevance bounded learning[1].

4   Experimental Results

We tested a total of 34 different combinations of seven models, eight backtracking algorithms, and three variable ordering heuristics (not all algorithms can be applied on all models; e.g., the algorithms based on TABLEAU are applicable only to SAT problems and each propagator-based algorithm is designed for a particular model). The three dynamic variable orderings heuristics used were the popular *dom+deg* heuristic [10] which chooses the next variable with the minimal domain size and breaks ties by choosing the variable with the maximum degree (the number of the constraints that constrain that variable, excluding the not-equals constraints), the *dom/deg* heuristic proposed by Bessière and Régin [2] which chooses the next variable with the minimal value of the domain size divided by its degree, and a variant of the MOM heuristic [5] which is geared to SAT problems and chooses the next variable with the Maximum Occurrences in clauses of Minimum size.

In the experiments we used a test suite of 50 crossword puzzle grids and two dictionaries for a total of 100 instances of the problem that ranged from easy to hard. For the grids, we used 10 instances at each of the following sizes: 5×5,

---

[1] Available at: http://www.cirl.uoregon.edu/crawford

Table 1. Effect of model, algorithm, and heuristic on number of instances (out of a total of 100) that could be solved given a limit of 228 Mb of memory and ten hours of CPU time per instance; (a) dom+deg heuristic; (b) dom/deg heuristic; (c) variant of the MOM heuristic. The absence of an entry means the combination was not tested.

algorithm	model					algorithm	model					algorithm	model		
	m_1	m_1^+	m_2	m_3			m_1	m_1^+	m_2	m_3			s_1	s_2	s_3
FC	20	59	61	48		FC	20	50	63	55		ntab_back	10	0	20
GAC	20	10	50	83		GAC	20	10	50	81		ntab_back2	11	0	20
EAC	89		0	0		EAC	92		0	0					
PAC	88		80	84		PAC	91		85	84					

(a)   (b)   (c)

15×15, 19×19, 21×21, and 23×23^2. For the dictionaries, we used Version 1.5 of the UK cryptics dictionary[3], which collects about 220,000 words and in which the largest domain for a word variable contains about 30,000 values, and the Linux /usr/dict/words dictionary, which collects 45,000 words and in which the largest domain for a word variable has about 5,000 values. Although use of a smaller dictionary decreases the size of search space, the number of solutions also decreases and, in this case, made the problems harder to solve.

All the experiments except those for EAC were run on a 300 MHz Pentium II with 228 Megabytes of memory. The experiments on EAC were run on a 450 MHz Pentium II and the CPU times were converted to get approximately equivalent timings. A combination of model, algorithm, and variable ordering heuristic was applied to each of the 100 instances in the test suite. A limit of ten hours of CPU time and 228 Megabytes of memory was given in which to solve an instance. If a solution was not found within the resource limits, the execution of the backtracking algorithm was terminated.

Table 1 summarizes the number of instances solved by each combination. The low numbers of instances solved by the SAT-based models are due to both the time and the space resource limits being exceeded (as can be seen in Table 2, the SAT models are large even for small instances and storing them requires a lot of memory). The EAC algorithm also consumes large amounts of memory for its data structures and ran out of this resource before solving any instances from models m_2 and m_3. In all other cases, if an instance was not solved it was because the CPU time limit was exceeded.

Because the number of instances solved is a coarse measure, Figure 2 shows approximate cumulative frequency curves for some of the timing results. We can read from the curves the $0, \ldots, 100$ percentiles of the data sets (where the value of the median is the $50th$ percentile or the value of the $50th$ test). The curves are truncated at time $= 36000$ seconds (ten hours), as a backtracking search was aborted when this time limit was exceeded.

---

[2] The ten 5×5 puzzles are all of the *legal* puzzles of that size; the other puzzles were taken from the Herald Tribune Crosswords, Spring and Summer editions, 1999.

[3] Available at: http://www.bryson.demon.co.uk/wordlist.html

Table 2. Size of an instance of a model given a dictionary and the grid shown in Figure 1, where n is the number of variables, d is the maximum domain size, r is the maximum constraint arity, and m is the number of constraints.

model	dictionary	n	d	r	m
m_1	UK	21	26	10	23
m_1^+	UK	21	26	10	83
m_2	UK	10	10,935	2	34
m_3	UK	31	10,935	2	55
s_1	UK	546	2	26	1,336,044
s_2	UK	65,901	2	10,935	$\approx 8 \times 10^8$
s_3	UK	66,447	2	10,935	408,302
m_1	words	21	26	10	23
m_1^+	words	21	26	10	83
m_2	words	10	4,174	2	34
m_3	words	31	4,174	2	55
s_1	words	546	2	26	684,464
s_2	words	26,715	2	4,174	$\approx 2 \times 10^8$
s_3	words	27,261	2	4,174	168,339

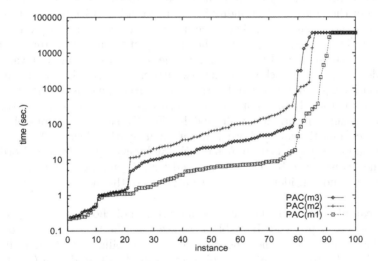

Fig. 2. Effect of model on time (sec.) of backtracking algorithms, given the dom/deg dynamic variable ordering heuristic. Each curve represents the result of applying the given backtracking algorithm to the 100 instances in the test suite, where the instances are ordered by time taken to solve it (or to timeout at 36,000 seconds).

5   Analysis

In this section, we use the experimental results to show that the design decisions are not completely independent, one-factor independent, nor conditionally independent. Hence, the design decisions are mutually dependent.

Complete independence. For the choice of the best model, algorithm, and heuristic to be completely independent decisions *all* of the following must hold: (i) the ordering of the models, such as by number of problems solved, must be roughly invariant for all algorithms and heuristics, (ii) the ordering of the algorithms must be roughly invariant for all models and heuristics, and (iii) the ordering of the heuristics must be roughly invariant for all models and algorithms. However, none of these conditions hold. For (i), consider the different orderings of the models given by FC and GAC using the dom+deg heuristic in Table 1; for (ii), consider the relative orderings of the FC and GAC algorithms given by the different models; and for (iii), consider the reversed orderings of the heuristics given by FC on m_1^+ and m_3.

One-factor independence. One-factor independence can occur in three ways, corresponding to the three conditions given under complete independence. As shown there, none of these conditions hold.

Conditional independence. Conditional independence of the decisions can occur in three ways: (i) the choice of the best algorithm and heuristic can be independent decisions, given a choice of model (i.e., given a model, the ordering of the algorithms is roughly invariant for all heuristics, and, by symmetry, the ordering of the heuristics is roughly invariant for all algorithms); (ii) the choice of the best model and heuristic can be independent decisions, given a choice of algorithm (i.e., given an algorithm, the ordering of the models is roughly invariant for all heuristics, and the ordering of the heuristics is roughly invariant for all models); and (iii) the choice of the best model and algorithm can be independent decisions, given a choice of heuristic (i.e., given a heuristic, the ordering of the models is roughly invariant for all algorithms, and the ordering of the algorithms is roughly invariant for all models). For (i), suppose the model given is m_3 and consider the reversed orderings of the heuristics given by FC and GAC; for (ii), suppose the algorithm given is FC and consider the reversed orderings of the heuristics given by m_1^+ and m_3; and for (iii), suppose the heuristic given is dom+deg and consider the different orderings of the models given by FC and GAC.

We can also see from the data the importance of choosing or formulating a good model of a problem. In Table 1 we see that the best algorithm or set of algorithms cannot overcome a poor model and compiling a CSP to an instance of SAT in order to take advantage of progress in algorithm design (cf. [11]) can be a disastrous approach. In Figure 2 we see that even when our models are all relatively good models (such as m_1, m_2, and m_3), and much effort is put into correspondingly good algorithms, the form of the model can have a large effect—ranging from one order of magnitude on the instances of intermediate difficulty to two and three orders of magnitude on harder instances.

6   Conclusions

We draw the following three general lessons from our study: (i) the form of the CSP model is important; (ii) the choices of model, algorithm, and heuristic are interdependent and making these choices sequentially or assuming a level of independence can lead to non-optimal choices; and (iii) to solve a problem using constraint programming most efficiently, one must simultaneously explore the space of models, algorithms, and heuristics.

References

1. P. Baptiste and C. Le Pape. A theoretical and experimental comparison of constraint propagation techniques for disjunctive scheduling. In *Proc. of IJCAI-95*, pp. 600–606.
2. C. Bessière and J.-C. Régin. MAC and combined heuristics: Two reasons to forsake FC (and CBJ?) on hard problems. In *Proc. of CP-96*, pp. 61–75.
3. C. Bessière and J.-C. Régin. Arc consistency for general constraint networks: Preliminary results. In *Proc. of IJCAI-97*, pp. 398–404.
4. P. R. Cohen. *Empirical Methods for Artificial Intelligence*. The MIT Press, 1995.
5. J. M. Crawford and L. D. Auton. Experimental results on the crossover point in random 3-SAT. *Artif. Intell.*, 81:31–57, 1996.
6. D. Frost and R. Dechter. In search of the best search: An empirical evaluation. In *Proc. of AAAI-94*, pp. 301–306.
7. J. Gaschnig. Experimental case studies of backtrack vs. Waltz-type vs. new algorithms for satisficing assignment problems. In *Proc. of the 2nd Canadian Conf. on AI*, pp. 268–277, 1978.
8. I. P. Gent, E. MacIntyre, P. Prosser, B. M. Smith, and T. Walsh. An empirical study of dynamic variable ordering heuristics for the constraint satisfaction problem. In *Proc. of CP-96*, pp. 179–193.
9. M. L. Ginsberg, M. Frank, M. P. Halpin, and M. C. Torrance. Search lessons learned from crossword puzzles. In *Proc. of AAAI-90*, pp. 210–215.
10. R. M. Haralick and G. L. Elliott. Increasing tree search efficiency for constraint satisfaction problems. *Artif. Intell.*, 14:263–313, 1980.
11. H. Kautz and B. Selman. Planning as satisfiability. In *Proc. of ECAI-92*, pp. 359–363.
12. A. K. Mackworth. On reading sketch maps. In *Proc. of IJCAI-77*, pp. 598–606.
13. B. A. Nadel. Representation selection for constraint satisfaction: A case study using n-queens. *IEEE Expert*, 5:16–23, 1990.
14. P. Prosser. Hybrid algorithms for the constraint satisfaction problem. *Comput. Intell.*, 9:268–299, 1993.
15. J.-F. Puget and M. Leconte. Beyond the glass box: Constraints as objects. In *Proc. of ISLP-95*, pp. 513–527.
16. F. Rossi, C. Petrie, and V. Dhar. On the equivalence of constraint satisfaction problems. In *Proc. of ECAI-90*, pp. 550-556.
17. B. Smith, K. Stergiou, and T. Walsh. Using auxilliary variables and implied constraints to model non-binary problems. In *Proc. of AAAI-00*.
18. E. P. K. Tsang, J. E. Borrett, and A. C. M. Kwan. An attempt to map the performance of a range of algorithm and heuristic combinations. In *Proc. of the AI and Simulated Behaviour Conf.*, pp. 203–216, 1995.
19. T. Walsh. SAT v CSP. In *Proc. of CP-00*.

Constraint-Based Vehicle Assembly Line Sequencing

Michael E. Bergen[1], Peter van Beek[1], and Tom Carchrae[2]

[1] Department of Computing Science, University of Alberta
Edmonton, Alberta, Canada T6G 2H1
{bergen,vanbeek}@cs.ualberta.ca
[2] TigrSoft Inc., Edmonton, Alberta, Canada T5J 3G2
carchrae@tigrsoft.com

Abstract. In this paper, we consider the optimal sequencing of vehicles along multiple assembly lines. We present a constraint-based model of the problem with hard and soft constraints. An advantage of a constraint-based approach is that the model is declarative and there is a separation between the model and an algorithm for solving the model. As a result, once the model had been defined, we could experiment with different algorithms for solving the model, with few or no changes to the model itself. We present three approximation algorithms for solving the model— a local search algorithm, a backtracking algorithm with a constraint relaxation and restart scheme, and a branch and bound algorithm—and we compare the quality of the solutions and the computational performance of these methods on six real-world problem instances. For our best method, a branch and bound algorithm with a decomposition into smaller sub-problems, we obtained improvements ranging between 2% and 16% over an existing system based on greedy search.

1 Introduction

The vehicle assembly line sequencing problem is to determine the order in which a given list of vehicles should be produced on one or more assembly lines subject to a set of constraints. Determining a good sequence is important as the sequence chosen affects the cost of production, the quality of the vehicles produced, and even employee satisfaction.

The particular problem that we study comes from a North American manufacturing plant that produces approximately 36,000 vehicles in a month on two assembly lines and the sequencing is done once per month. A system developed by TigrSoft Inc., an Edmonton company that specializes in planning and scheduling software, currently schedules the production of vehicles. While our motivating application is quite specific, the constraints which define the quality of a sequence are shared with other sequencing and scheduling problems. For example, one important constraint on an acceptable sequence in our problem is that each day a worker on an assembly line should see as much diversity as the current orders permit, including making economy and luxury models, four and

E. Stroulia and S. Matwin (Eds.): AI 2001, LNAI 2056, pp. 88–99, 2001.

five door models, and so on. This "distribution" constraint allows the assembly line workers to maintain their skill set as well as ensuring that at least a certain amount of every order is produced prior to any unexpected line shutdowns. Similar distribution constraints arise in diverse scheduling problems from scheduling sports teams, where the issue of a fair distribution of rest and travel days arises, to other manufacturing problems where a robust schedule is desired in the face of possible machine breakdowns. A second example of important constraints on acceptable sequences are "change-over" constraints that prohibit undersirable transitions such as sequencing white vehicles immediately after red vehicles (the vehicles could come out an undesirable pink colour). Similar change-over constraints also arise in other manufacturing scheduling problems.

In this paper, we describe how we modeled and solved this real-world vehicle assembly line sequencing problem using a constraint-based approach. In a constraint-based approach to problem solving, a problem is modeled by specifying constraints on an acceptable solution, where a constraint is simply a relation among several unknowns or variables, each taking a value from a given domain (see [4] for an introduction). Our model contains both hard constraints (must be satisfied) and soft constraints (can be violated at a cost). Each soft constraint is associated with a penalty value that is incurred every time it is violated. Thus the problem is one of optimization on these penalty values.

An advantage of a constraint-based approach is that the model is declarative and there is a separation between the model and an algorithm for solving the model. As a result, once the model had been defined, we could experiment with different search algorithms for solving the model, with few or no changes to the model itself. We present three approximation algorithms for solving the model: a local search algorithm, a backtracking algorithm with a constraint relaxation and restart scheme, and a branch and bound algorithm. We also demonstrate the importance of decomposing the problem into one-day sub-problems. We compare the quality of the solutions and the computational performance of these methods on six real-world problem instances. For our best method, a branch and bound algorithm with a decomposition into smaller sub-problems, we obtained improvements ranging between 2% and 16% over the existing system developed by TigrSoft, which is based on greedy search.

The software we have developed is in a stand-alone prototype form. We are currently integrating our work into TigrSoft's deployed system and hope in the near future to perform user trials in a production environment.

Related work. Assembly lines are process-oriented and are arranged according to the sequence of operations needed to manufacture a product. This is in contrast to job shops which are job-oriented and machines which perform similar operations are spatially grouped together. While there has been an extensive amount of work on job shop scheduling (see [11] for an overview of constraint-based approaches), in spite of its importance, there has been little work reported specifically on the vehicle assembly line sequencing problem in the literature.

Of the work that has been reported, most has focused on the specification of the vehicle assembly line sequencing problem introduced by Parrello *et al.*

[6]. Van Hentenryck *et al.* [10] and Régin and Puget [7] solve this version of the problem using backtracking search with specialized propagators to maintain arc consistency during the search. Local search techniques have also been developed for this version of the problem including a hill-climbing approach [3] and a simulated annealing approach [9]. However, while this specification has demand and capacity constraints, it omits time-window, change-over, and balancing constraints important in our version of the problem.

More directly related is the work done by ILOG on the vehicle sequencing problem for Chrysler. Unfortunately, there is no published information about this research beyond a press release [8] and a set of presentation slides [2]. The problem they address also has distribution and change-over constraints similar the problem addressed in this paper. Their solution decomposes the problem into smaller sub-problems on which it performs backtracking search, attempting to satisfy constraints with the highest priorities first.

2   The Problem Domain

The manufacturing plant that we study produces approximately 36,000 vehicles in a month on two assembly lines and the sequencing is done once per month. The input to the problem is a list of orders (an order is a quantity of identical vehicles) that need to be produced during that month, capacity values that specify how many vehicles can be produced on each day on each assembly line, and the user-specified constraints. As a first step, each order is split into several smaller quantities of vehicles called *lots* such that the size of each lot is less than or equal to 60 vehicles, called the batch size. The lots are then grouped together into *batches* by putting together similar lots with sizes that add up to the batch size (see Table 1(a) for an example). Each batch is assumed to take one hour of time to produce on an assembly line. A typical problem instance has lots with between one and 60 vehicles, and batches with between one and ten lots, with the majority of batches having only one lot. It is important to note that after batching, the lots are not sequenced in a batch and thus sequencing actually occurs at the lot level.

The lots and batches have attributes. Some attributes are common to all problem instances and others are user-definable and thus specific to a problem instance. Common attributes include the assembly lines that a lot can be produced on, the date a lot must be produced after (line-on date), and the date a lot must be produced by (line-off date). User definable attributes are either selected from a set of basic attributes such as vehicle model, exterior colour, type of engine, and type of transmission; or are constructed from these basic attributes by Cartesian-product. A batch's attribute values are taken from the attribute values of its lots. Each attribute has a different method for deriving the batch attribute value from the lot values when the lot values differ.

The capacity values specify the number of batches that can be produced on each assembly line on each day. If no vehicle production is desired on a particular day, then the capacities for that day are zero. The capacities are assigned such that the sum of all the capacities for each day and assembly line equals the total number of batches that need to be produced for the month. Hence, there is no excess capacity. A day's production on an assembly line is sub-divided into consecutive intervals of time called slots which have a fixed start time and a duration of one hour (since each batch is assumed to take one hour of time to produce). In a final sequence, every slot is assigned one and only one unique batch. A typical problem instance consists of two assembly lines each with 20 days of non-zero capacities. Each of these daily capacities is approximately fifteen batches, which gives a total capacity of 600 batches or 36,000 vehicles.

Each problem contains constraints that restricts which sequences are acceptable. Each constraint is over one or more slots, each slot taking a value from the set of all batches. The constraints can be classified as either a batch constraint or a lot constraint. Lot constraints rely on lot attributes, and influence the sequencing of lots and hence the sequencing of batches. Batch constraints rely on batch attributes and influence the sequencing of batches with no concern for the sequencing of lots within a batch. Constraints can also be classified as either soft or hard. A hard constraint cannot be violated, while a soft constraint can be violated but imposes a penalty value for each violation. Each soft constraint has a penalty value that is given as part of the input of the problem; the higher the penalty value, the more undesirable the violation.

There are eight constraint types. Six of the constraint types—the assembly line, line-on and line-off, even distribution, distribution exception, batting order, and all-different—define hard, batch constraints. The remaining two constraint types—the run-length and change-over—define soft, lot constraints. We now describe these constraints types in detail.

Assembly Line. The manufacturing plant contains two assembly lines. Because of unique equipment, some vehicles can only be assembled on one of the lines, while others can be assembled on either line. If a batch contains a lot that can only be assembled on one of the assembly lines, then the batch must be assembled on that assembly line. There is an assembly line constraint over each slot. Since each slot belongs to an assembly line, only batches that can be made on that assembly line can be assigned to the slot.

Line-On and Line-Off. Each vehicle that is ordered must be produced sometime during the month. However, because of part availability or shipping deadlines, some orders have more stringent scheduling requirements. For this reason, each lot has a line-on and line-off day. A lot must be produced on or after its line-on day, and on or before its line-off day. A batch's line-on day is the maximum line-on day of its lots and its line-off day is the minimum line-off day of its lots. There is a line-on and line-off constraint over each slot.

Even Distribution. An assembly line should produce a variety of different types of vehicles each day and the production of similar types of vehicles should be spread evenly over the month. Reasons for this include maintaining workers skills for making all types of vehicles, part availability, and producing certain amounts of each type of vehicle prior to any unexpected assembly line shutdown.

Table 1. (a) Example lots and their attributes. Lots are grouped together into batches of size 60. The attributes of a single-lot batch are the same as those of its lot. The derived attributes of the multi-lot batches are shown underlined. (b) Example even distribution values. (c) One possible sequencing of the batches and lots over two days.

(a)

Lot	Batch	Lot Size	Line On	Line Off	Model	Exterior Colour	Sun Roof
L01	B01	60	1	2	M1	Blue	Y
L02	B02	20	1	2	M1	Red	Y
L03	B02	40	_1_	_1_	_M1_	_Red_	_N_
L04	B03	10	1	2	M2	Green	Y
L05	B03	20	_2_	2	_M2_	Red	N
L06	B03	30	1	2	M2	_Blue_	_Y_
L07	B04	10	1	2	M3	Red	N
L08	B04	10	_1_	_2_	_M3_	Green	Y
L09	B04	10	1	2	M3	Red	Y
L10	B04	30	1	2	M3	_Green_	_N_
L11	B05	60	1	2	M1	Green	N
L12	B06	60	1	2	M1	Blue	Y
L13	B07	60	2	2	M1	Blue	Y
L14	B08	60	1	1	M1	Blue	N
L15	B09	60	2	2	M1	Green	N
L16	B10	60	1	2	M2	Red	Y
L17	B11	60	1	1	M2	Red	Y
L18	B12	60	1	2	M2	Green	N
L19	B13	60	1	2	M3	Red	N
L20	B14	60	1	2	M3	Green	Y

(b)

Attribute	Day 1	Day 2
M1-Y	2	1
M1-N	2	2
M2-Y	1	2
M2-N	1	0
M3-Y	0	1
M3-N	1	1

(c)

Day	Slot	Batch	Lots
1	1	B06	L12
	2	B08	L14
	3	B01	L01
	4	B02	L02, L03
	5	B11	L17
	6	B12	L18
	7	B04	L08, L07, L09, L10
2	1	B05	L11
	2	B09	L15
	3	B07	L13
	4	B10	L16
	5	B03	L05, L04, L06
	6	B14	L20
	7	B13	L19

The even distribution constraint spreads the batches by specifying the number of batches with a particular attribute value that must be produced on each day. There is an even distribution constraint for each production day and the constraint is over all of the slots that belong to that day.

Distribution Exception. Sometimes an even distribution is inappropriate. For example, when a new model year is introduced, production teams need time to learn new procedures and the distribution of new models should be restricted so that fewer are produced early in the month. To do this, a distribution exception constraint specifies a minimum and maximum number of batches with a particular attribute value that can be produced on each day during a specified period of days in the month. There is a distribution exception constraint for each production day and the constraint is over all of the slots that belong to that day.

Batting Order. Each day, a similar sequencing pattern should be followed on each assembly line. One reason for this is to sequence simple vehicles at the beginning of the day and gradually progress to more difficult vehicles. This allows the production teams to warm up before building more complicated vehicles. To do this, batting order constraints are defined on user-specified attributes and on user-specified orderings of those attributes' values. Specifically, on each day, a batch must be produced before another batch if its attribute value is ordered before the attribute value of the other batch. There is a batting order constraint between each pair of consecutive slots that are on the same day.

All-Different. A constraint is needed to ensure that every batch appears exactly once in any sequence. The all-different constraint is defined over all the slots.

Run-Length. Each day, it is desirable that certain attribute values are not repeated too often. Avoiding monotony of an attribute value can improve the effectiveness of production and quality inspection teams, and avoid part supply problems. A run-length constraint is a soft constraint that incurs a penalty whenever the number of consecutive vehicles with a particular attribute value exceeds a specified limit called the run-length. The run-length constraint is applied to consecutive slots. One penalty value is counted for each lot that exceeds the run-length value. Typical instances have around five different run-length constraints defined and the penalty values for these constraints range between ten and 300.

Change-Over. In a sequence, transitions from one lot attribute value to another lot attribute value may be undesirable. For instance, painting a white vehicle immediately after a red one is undesirable because the vehicle may turn out pink. A change-over constraint is a soft constraint that incurs a penalty value whenever an undesirable transition occurs. The change-over constraint is applied to consecutive slots. It relies on two user-specified attributes, called the former and the latter attributes, to evaluate a transition between two sequenced lots. Typical instances have around forty different change-over constraints defined and the penalty values for these constraints range between one and 100.

A solution to the vehicle assembly line sequencing problem consists of an assignment of batches to slots and a sequencing of the lots within batches such that all the hard constraints are satisfied. The quality of a solution is measured by the total penalty values that are incurred by violations of the soft constraints. The lower the total penalty values, the higher the quality of the solution.

Example 1. Table 1(a) shows an example set of lots and their grouping into batches. The batches are to be sequenced on one assembly line over two days, where each day has a capacity of seven batches. Suppose we define the following constraints. An even distribution constraint is defined on the Cartesian-product of the model and sun-roof attributes and the distribution values are as listed in Table 1(b). To illustrate, there are three batches with attribute values Model "M1" and Sun-roof "Yes" and the distribution values specify that two of these batches must be sequenced on the first day and one batch must be sequenced on the second day. A distribution exception constraint is defined on the Exterior Colour attribute value "Green" for the first of the two days with a minimum value of one batch and a maximum value of two batches. A batting order constraint is defined on the attribute Model specifying that on each day, M1 batches should be produced first, followed by M2 batches, and then M3 batches. A run-length constraint is defined on the Exterior Colour attribute value "Red" with a run-length value of 120 vehicles and a penalty value of 200. Thus, sequencing lots L16, L17, and L19 consecutively would incur a penalty value of 200. A change-over constraint is defined on the Exterior Colour attribute with a penalty value of 100. The former attribute value is "Red" and the latter attribute value is "NOT Red", where "NOT Red" means any colour except "Red". Thus, sequencing lot L17 followed by L18 would incur a penalty value of 100. Table 1(c) gives one possible sequencing of the batches and lots. The change-over constraint is violated three times (L17 → L18, L09 → L10, and L05 → L04) and the run-length constraint is not violated at all for a total penalty value of 300.

3   Solution Techniques

Since the problem is large, we solved the constraint-based model approximately rather than optimally. We describe three algorithms for solving the vehicle sequencing problem: a local search method, a backtracking method, and a branch and bound method. All of the algorithms used the following two techniques for simplifying the problem. First, the overall problem was split into equal sized sub-problems by placing, for a particular assembly line, a specified number of consecutive production days in each sub-problem. To determine which batches should go with which sub-problem, we used the solution found by the greedy search algorithm and assigned a batch to a sub-problem if its placement within the solution fell on one of those days. The sub-problems were then solved in order of the days they contain. Since soft constraint violations can occur between sub-problems, after a sub-problem is solved, the batch that was sequenced last is added to the beginning of the next sub-problem. Second, the sequencing of batches and the sequencing of the lots within batches were decoupled and done in stages rather than simultaneously. In stage one, the lots within each batch were sequenced without consideration of the other batches and then in stage two, the batches were sequenced with the lots considered fixed. The sequencing of the lots was done either by using the solution provided by the greedy search algorithm, or by optimizing the lot sequence according to the soft constraints using a simple generate and test procedure.

Local search. Local search is a general approach to solving combinatorial optimization problems (see [1] for an overview). To apply local search to the vehicle assembly line sequencing problem, we need to define a cost function and a neighborhood function. The cost function takes as its input a solution to the hard constraints and returns the total number of penalty values incurred by the soft constraints. Thus, all the soft constraints are moved into or are represented by the cost function. There are many possible ways to define a neighborhood function. In general, the way that the neighborhood function is defined influences the quality of the solutions that a local search algorithm finds and the cost of searching the solution space. In our experiments, we define the neighborhood of a solution to consist of any solution where two variables' values have been swapped and no hard constraint is violated.

The local search algorithm we devised is a simple hill-climbing algorithm. Our algorithm begins with an initial solution that satisfies all of the hard constraints. The default initial solution is the solution provided by the greedy search algorithm. Of the solutions in the neighborhood, the solution that reduces the total penalty value the most is selected. This process is repeated until no solution can be found in the current neighborhood that improves on the quality of the current solution.

Backtracking with relaxation and restart. Standard backtracking requires the satisfaction of all constraints. However, in a problem that contains soft constraints, it is common that some of the soft constraints are not satisfied. Two modifications to make backtracking applicable are possible (see [12] for an overview). The optimistic approach first searches for a solution satisfying all of the constraint and then iteratively removes or relaxes constraints—the weakest first—until a solution is found. The pessimistic approach first searches for a solution satisfying the strongest constraints and then iteratively adds more constraints—the strongest first—until no solution is found. We chose to pursue an optimistic or relaxation approach.

For our relaxation approach, each soft constraint's instances that belong to the same day and assembly line are grouped together into a parameterized hard constraint. Since soft constraint violations can occur between lots that are sequenced on different days, the last slot of the previous day is included in each of these parameterized constraints. Let p represent the parameter for an instance of a parameterized constraint. For a run-length constraint p represents the maximum run-length that can occur on the day. For a change-over constraint p represents the maximum number of change-over violations that can occur. If more than p violations occur, then the parameterized change-over constraint is not satisfied. This method has advantages over simply removing selected soft constraints from the problem as it decreases the number of possible selections that need to be made and leaves more decision power to the search algorithm.

The backtracking algorithm begins with each parameterized change-over constraint initialized with a value of zero and each parameterized run-length constraint initialized with the run-length value of the constraint. As the backtracking algorithm attempts to solve the problem a count is kept of how many times each parameterized constraint fails. Associated with each parameterized constraint is a failure limit that is proportional to its penalty value. If any parameterized constraint fails more often than its failure limit the search stops. If the search stopped without finding a solution, a parameterized constraint is chosen to be relaxed by selecting a constraint with the smallest penalty value that failed at least once. The chosen constraint is relaxed by adding a value to its parameter. For a change-over constraint, its parameter is incremented by one. For a run-length constraint, its parameter is incremented by the batch size, increasing the run-length by sixty vehicles. The backtracking algorithm is then restarted, and the relaxation and restart processes is continued until a solution is found.

The efficiency of the backtracking algorithm was improved by using variable and value ordering heuristics and by reducing the search space by constraint propagation (see [4] for an overview). The variable ordering selects the variable belonging to the earliest day with ties broken by smallest domain size. The value ordering is based on the greedy search solution. For each variable, the value assigned in the greedy search solution is placed first in the variable's domain. To achieve a high level of propagation with limited computation, specialized propagators, which take advantage of the constraint's structure, were devised for the all-different constraint and the distribution constraints.

Branch and bound. To apply branch and bound search to the vehicle assembly line sequencing problem, we need to define a cost function and a function to provide a lower bound on the cost of any partial solution (see [5] for an overview). As with the local search approach, the cost function takes as its input a solution to the hard constraints and returns the total number of penalty values incurred by the soft constraints. The lower bound function takes as its input a partial solution to the hard constraints and returns the total number of penalty values incurred by the batches that have been sequenced so far.

The algorithm begins with an upper bound on the cost of an optimal solution and tightens the bound until no solution is found. The upper bound is initialized to be the cost of the solution returned by the greedy search algorithm. After backtracking finds a solution, we take the total penalty value for the solution, reduce it by the smallest constraint penalty value in the problem instance (a value of one for the problem instances we examine), and set this as the new bound value. The branch and bound algorithm then continues, and backtracks whenever the lower bound on the cost of a partial solution exceeds the current bound. If it finds a solution with the current bound value, we reduce the bound value again. This process is continued until no solution can be found. In this case, the last solution found is an optimal solution.

For the branch and bound algorithm, the variable ordering was fixed to be the ordering of the slots in time. This was chosen to simplify the way the lower bound function was implemented. The value ordering and constraint propagation techniques were the same as described for the relaxation approach.

4   Evaluation

In this section, we present the results of applying the three solution methods to six real-world problem instances. Each problem instance represents a month's worth of orders for a vehicle manufacturing plant with two assembly lines. We use the quality of the solutions produced by the existing system developed by Tigr-Soft as our base of comparison. The existing system, which is based on greedy search, took about 15 seconds to solve each of the instances (all experiments were run on 450 MHz Pentium III's with 256 Megabytes of memory).

Table 2 summarizes the results for the three methods. In all of the reported results, each problem instance was divided into one day sub-problems. We also examined the effect of dividing into two and three day sub-problems and found

Table 2. (a) Total penalties and (b) percentage improvement over greedy search of hill climbing methods, backtracking methods, and branch and bound methods with a decomposition into sub-problems of a single day. For branch and bound a time limit per sub-problem of either 2 hours or 1 minute was used.

(a)

| | Greedy | Hill climbing | | | Backtracking | | | Branch and bound | | | |
| | | | | | | | | 2 hours | | 1 minute | |
#	GS	HC	HC-R	HC-O	RR	RR-N	RR-O	BB	BB-O	BB	BB-O
1	8,018	7,036	7,623	7,055	7,337	8,718	7,721	7,002	6,925	7,002	6,925
2	5,042	4,579	5,059	4,470	4,640	5,353	4,549	4,528	4,403	4,528	4,399
3	3,412	3,347	3,543	3,409	3,357	3,441	3,443	3,306	3,348	3,306	3,348
4	2,498	2,233	2,269	2,174	2,308	2,532	2,265	2,206	2,137	2,218	2,145
5	2,956	2,885	2,996	2,605	2,883	3,069	2,618	2,762	2,479	2,762	2,485
6	2,818	2,560	2,605	2,577	2,602	3,028	2,625	2,489	2,500	2,489	2,500

(b)

| | Hill climbing | | | Backtracking | | | Branch and bound | | | |
| | | | | | | | 2 hours | | 1 minute | |
#	HC	HC-R	HC-O	RR	RR-N	RR-O	BB	BB-O	BB	BB-O
1	12	5	12	8	-9	4	13	13	14	14
2	9	0	11	8	-6	10	10	10	13	13
3	2	-4	0	2	-1	-1	3	3	2	2
4	11	9	13	8	-1	9	12	11	14	14
5	2	-1	12	2	-4	11	7	7	16	16
6	9	8	9	8	-7	7	12	12	11	11

that for each of the three methods, the CPU time increased (sometimes dramatically) but the quality of the solutions did not change significantly. It appears that the even distribution constraint significantly reduces the possibility of improving the solution by solving multiple days at a time. For all of the problem instances examined, the even distribution constraint was defined on an attribute that contained more than 200 attribute values and many attribute values only had one or two batches associated with them. Since the even distribution constraint defines for each day and attribute value the number of batches with the attribute value that can be assigned to the day, many days did not share batches. Thus when solving multi-day problems of two or three days, it was unlikely that the days within a sub-problem would share batches.

For the local search algorithms, the sequencing of lots within a batch was fixed to be the sequence of the lots within the solution determined by the greedy search (HC and HC-R) or was fixed to be the optimized sequence of the lots (HC-O). The initial solution given to the hill-climbing algorithm to improve upon was either the sequencing of the batches provided by the greedy search algorithm (HC and HC-O) or a random sequencing of the batches (HC-R). The HC and HC-O hill climbing algorithms took between two and three minutes to solve each of the instances; the HC-R algorithm took on average double the CPU time. We note that when a random initial solution was used, the results were poorer. These results indicate the importance of a good initial solution when using a hill-climbing method on the problem.

For the backtracking algorithms that used a relaxation and restart approach, the failure limits for each soft constraint were set by multiplying each constraint's penalty value by 200 (the value chosen is somewhat arbitrary; we have verified that choosing a different multiplicative value does not materially change the conclusions that we draw from our study). The sequencing of lots within a batch was fixed to be the sequence of the lots within the solution determined by the greedy search (RR and RR-N) or was fixed to be the optimized sequence of the lots (RR-O). The approaches RR and RR-O used a value ordering that was based on the greedy search solution. Each slot's domain values were ordered by placing the batch that was assigned to the slot in the greedy search solution first in the slot's domain. As well, since the choice of which constraint to relax next may not be perfect, after a sub-problem was solved with the backtracking algorithm, the sub-problem solution was compared with the greedy search solution and the sub-problem solution with the lowest total penalty value was selected. The algorithms took between five and fifteen minutes to solve each of the instances. We note that when the value ordering and the best solution selection process was removed (RR-N) the quality of the solutions decreased significantly. The value ordering appears to give the backtracking algorithm a good solution to build on.

For the branch and bound algorithms, the sequencing of lots within a batch was fixed to be the sequence of the lots within the solution determined by the greedy search (BB) or was fixed to be the optimized sequence of the lots (BB-O). Time limits were set on how much CPU time could be spent on each sub-problem. If the algorithm had not completed within the time limit, the best solution found so far was used. We report the results for time limits of two hours and of one minute. When the time limit per sub-problem was two hours, four of the six instances had all of their sub-problem solutions proven optimal. The other two instances had in total only five sub-problems with potentially sub-optimal solutions. These five sub-problem solutions may in fact be optimal, but they were not proven so within the time limit. The total CPU time required to solve an instance when the time limit per sub-problem was two hours varied significantly, ranging between five minutes and fourteen hours. When the time limit per sub-problem was reduced from two hours down to one minute, only one problem instance's total penalty values slightly increased. However, although almost all of the solutions found were of the same quality, few of these solutions were proven optimal within the reduced time limit. On these instances finding an optimal solution to a sub-problem was relatively easy, but proving its optimality was often hard. The total CPU time required to solve an instance when the time limit per sub-problem was one minute varied between five and 25 minutes.

5   Conclusion

We introduced a real-world optimization problem that we modeled and solved using constraint-based approaches. We also demonstrated the importance of decomposing the problem into one-day sub-problems. We argued that because of the tightness of the even distribution constraint such a decomposition had little effect on the quality of the overall solution. For nearly all of these one-day sub-problems, we proved optimal solutions within a reasonable amount of time using the branch and bound technique. In even less time, the branch and bound method was able to find nearly identical results without proving optimality for many sub-problems. The local search method was also able to find relatively good solutions. Given the simplicity of this algorithm, it is likely that even better results could be found with a local search approach. The relaxation approach was the least successful of the three algorithms. Improving this approach is likely possible, but the usefulness of such an improvement is questionable due to the quality of the solutions obtained by the other two simpler algorithms.

In the preliminary stages of this research, we established with TigrSoft the criteria by which our results would be judged a "real-world" success. It was determined that solutions with a 5% reduction in penalty values that could be found in less than 30 minutes would be considered significant. All three algorithms were capable of finding solutions to the six problem instances within 30 minutes. For four of the six problem instances we were able to obtain more than a 5% improvement with any of the three solution methods. For the best method, a branch and bound algorithm with a decomposition into one-day sub-problems and a one minute time limit on each sub-problem, we obtained improvements ranging between 2% and 16% and averaging 11.6% over the existing system.

References

1. E. Aarts and Lenstra J. K., editors, *Local Search in Combinatorial Optimization*, John Wiley & Sons Ltd., 1997.
2. T. Chase *et al.* Centralized vehicle scheduler: An application of constraint technology. http://www.ilog.com/products/optimization/tech/research/cvs.pdf, 1998.
3. A. Davenport and E. Tsang. Solving constraint satisfaction sequencing problems by iterative repair. In *Proc. of PACLP-99*, pages 345–357, 1999.
4. K. Marriott and P. J. Stuckey. *Programming with Constraints*. MIT Press, 1998.
5. C. H. Papadimitriou and K. Steiglitz. *Combinatorial Optimization: Algorithms and Complexity*. Prentice-Hall, 1982.
6. B. D. Parrello *et al.* Job-shop scheduling using automated reasoning: A case study of the car-sequencing problem. *J. of Automated Reasoning*, 2:1–42, 1986.
7. J-C. Régin and J-F. Puget. A filtering algorithm for global sequencing constraints. In *Proc. of CP-97*, pages 32–46. Springer-Verlag, 1997.
8. ILOG Press Release. ILOG drives productivity improvements at Chrysler. http://www.ilog.com/success/chrysler/index.cfm, 1997.
9. K. Smith *et al.* Optimal sequencing of car models along an assembly line. In *Proc. 12th Nat'l Australian Society for Operations Research*, pages 580–603, 1993.
10. P. Van Hentenryck, H. Simonis, and M. Dincbas. Constraint satisfaction using constraint logic programming. *Artificial Intelligence*, 58:113–159, 1992.
11. M. Wallace. Applying constraints for scheduling. In B. Mayoh and J. Penjaam, editors, *Constraint Programming*. Springer-Verlag, 1994.
12. M. Wallace. Practical applications of constraint programming. *Constraints*, 1:139–168, 1996.

How AI Can Help SE; or: Randomized Search Not Considered Harmful

Tim Menzies[1] and Harhsinder Singh[2]

[1] Dept. Electrical & Computer Eng. University of British Columbia, 2356 Main Mall, Vancouver, B.C. Canada, V6T 1Z4 tim@menzies.com; http://tim.menzies.com
[2] Department of Statistics, West Virginia University, Morgantown, West Virginia, hsingh@stat.wvu.edu

Abstract. In fast-paced software projects, engineers don't have the time or the resources to build heavyweight complete descriptions of their software. The best they can do is lightweight incomplete descriptions which may contain missing and contradictory information. Reasoning about incomplete and contradictory knowledge is notoriously difficult. However, recent results from the empirical AI community suggest that *randomized search* can tame this difficult problem. In this article we demonstrate the the *relevance* and the *predictability* of randomized search for reasoning about lightweight models.

1 Introduction

Software engineering (SE) faces a dilemma which might be resolved by artificial intelligence (AI) research. However, before SE practitioners accept AI methods, they must be satisfied as to the *relevance* and the *predictability* of AI solutions.

The dilemma of current SE research is that much of that research is out of step with much of current industrial practice. At the recent International Symposium on Software Predictability (San Jose, California, 2000), a keynote address from Sun Microsystems shocked the researchers in the audience: few of the techniques endorsed by the SE research community are being used in fast-moving dot-com software companies. For such projects, developers and managers lack the resources to conduct *heavyweight software modeling*; e.g. the construction of complete descriptions of the business model[1] or the user requirements. Yet such heavyweight software modeling is very useful. Complete models of (e.g.) specifications can be used for a variety of tasks. For example, test cases could be auto-generated from the specification. Also, the consequences of conflicts between the requirements of different stakeholders could be studied. Further, we can automatically test that important temporal constraints hold over the lifetime of the execution of the specification. Lastly, model-based diagnosis could be used to localize errors.

---

[1] For the the purposes of explaining this work to an SE audience, we will adopt widely used terminology. Hence, we will say business "model" when, strictly speaking, we should say business "theory".

E. Stroulia and S. Matwin (Eds.): AI 2001, LNAI 2056, pp. 100–110, 2001.

To better support the fast pace of modern software, we need a new generation of *lightweight software modeling* tools. Lightweight software models can be built in a hurry and so are more suitable for the fast-moving software companies. However, software models built in a hurry can contain incomplete and contradictory knowledge. The presence of contradictions in the lightweight theories complicates the above useful tasks. Suppose some inference engine is trying to build a proof tree across a lightweight software model containing contradictions. Gabow et.al. [4] showed that building pathways across programs with contradictions is *NP-complete* for all but the simplest software models (a software model is very simple if it is very small, or it is a simple tree, or it has a dependency networks with out-degree ≤ 1). No fast and complete algorithm for NP-complete tasks has been discovered, despite decades of research.

Empirical results from AI offers new hope for the practicality of NP-complete tasks such as reasoning about lightweight software models. A repeated and robust empirical result (e.g. [14, 1]) is that theoretically slow NP-complete tasks are only truly slow in a narrow *phase transition* zone between under-constrained and over-constrained problems. Further, it has been shown empirically that in both the under/over-constrained zones, seemingly naive *randomized search algorithms* execute faster than, and nearly as completely, as traditional, slower, complete algorithms. Much of that research is based on conjunctive normal forms (e.g. [14]) but some evidence exists that the result holds also for horn-clause representations [10, 9]. These empirical results suggest that we might be able to implement the processing of lightweight software models using randomized search.

SE practitioners may well rebel at the prospect of applying randomized search to their applications. One issue is the *relevance problem*. With the exception of database programmers, it is not usual practice to view a (e.g.) "C" program as a declarative search space that can be explored this way or that way. Another issue is the *predictability problem*. Nondeterministic programs are usually not acceptable to an SE audience. For example, the SE guru Nancy Leveson clearly states "Nondeterminism is the enemy of reliability" [6]. If random search algorithms generate significantly different conclusions each time they run, then they would be unpredictable, uncertifiable, and unacceptable to the general SE community.

The goal of this article is to solve the relevance and predictability problems. §2 discusses the relevance problem and argues that declarative representations are common in SE, even when dealing with procedural programs. We will further argue that these declarative representations are compatible with *NAYO graphs*: a directed, possibly cycle graph containing No-edges, And-nodes, Yes-edges, and Or-nodes. §3 discusses the predictability problem in the context of NAYO graphs. That discussion formalizes the predictability problem in terms of multiple world reasoning. If very different conclusions are found in the worlds of belief extracted from NAYO graphs, then we cannot predictably assert what conclusions hold. §4 builds and explores a mathematical model that predicts the likelihood of multiple worlds. This section concludes that randomized set-covering abduction, the odds of multiple worlds are very small. Hence, predictability is not a major concern.

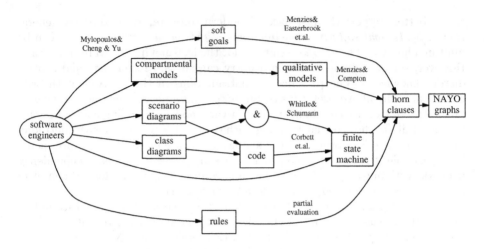

Fig. 1. Methods of generating NAYO graphs.

2   The Relevance Problem

Figure 1 shows a variety of commonly used representations in SE. AI search is relevant to SE if these representations can be mapped into declarative representations. There are many examples of such a mapping in the literature, a sample of which is offered in this section.

Before beginning, we note that each of the mappings described potentially confound the predictability problem. Some information is lost when mapping down into low-level declarative representations. Typically, the information lose removes certain constraints which means that more inferences are possible in the abstracted form than in the non-abstracted form. Fortunately, in the next section, we show that the predictability problem is less of an issue that we might expect.

Common representations used in SE are object-oriented specification documents and procedural code. Whittle and Schumann have shown that specifications containing class diagrams and scenario diagrams can be automatically converted to finite state machines [15]. Also, Corbett et.al have shown that code written in some languages can be converted into finite state machines [3]. For example, the BANDERA system automatically extracts (slices) the minimum portions of a JAVA program's bytecodes which are relevant to proving particular properties models. These minimal portions are then converted into the finite state machine required for automatic formal analysis.

Before generating procedural code, software engineers may build requirement documents. Mylopoulos, Chung, and Yu express system requirements using an and-or structure called "soft goals" [12]. "Soft goals" have been mapped into horn-clause form by Menzies, Easterbrook, et.al. [9]. Horn clauses are a declarative representation that take the form

Goal if SubGoal1 and SubGoal2 and ...

which, in a Prolog notation, we would write as `goal :- subGoal1, subGoal2,...` If there exists more than one method of demonstrating some *Goal*, then each method is a separate clause.

Sometimes software engineers describe business rules in some rule-based language. These rules can be mapped into horn-clauses using standard partial evaluation techniques [13]. At other times, software engineers build discrete event simulations of their systems in some sort of compartmental modeling framework[2]. Menzies and Compton offered an declarative (abductive) semantics for executing incomplete compartmental models [8].

Finite state machines are a commonly used representation, particularly for real-time systems. Finite-state diagrams contain transitions between states. Transitions may be conditional on some guard. States may contain nested states. To translate state machines to horn-clauses, we create one variable for each state, then create one clause for each transition from state $S1$ to $S2$. Each clause will take the form `s2 :- s1, guard` where *guard* comes from the conditional tests that activate that transition. If a state $S1$ contains sub-states $S1.a, S1.b,...$ then create clauses of the form `s1a :- s1` and `s1b :- s1`, etc.

Horn-clauses can be easily reduced to NAYO graphs. A NAYO graph is a finite directed graph containing two types of edges and two types of nodes. *Or-nodes* store assignments of a single value to a variable. Only one of the parents of an or-node need be reached before we visit the or-node. *And-nodes* model multiple pre-conditions. All the parents of an and-node must be reached before this node is visited. *No-edges* represent illegal pairs of inferences; i.e. things we can't believe at the same time. For example, we would connect `diet(light)` and `diet(fatty)` with a no-edge. *Yes-edges* represent legal inferences between or-nodes and and-nodes. Figure 2 shows some sample horn clauses and its associated NAYO graph.

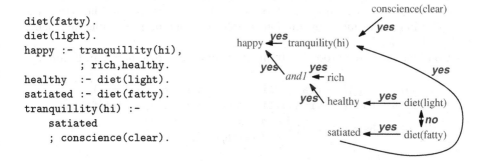

```
diet(fatty).
diet(light).
happy :- tranquillity(hi),
         ; rich,healthy.
healthy :- diet(light).
satiated :- diet(fatty).
tranquillity(hi) :-
    satiated
    ; conscience(clear).
```

Fig. 2. Some ground horn clauses (left) converted to a NAYO graph (right).

[2] Compartmental models utilize the principal of conservation of mass and assume that the sum of flows of substance in and out of a compartment must equal zero. Flows are typically modeled using a time-dependant exponential function since the rate of flow is often proportional to the amount of stuff in the compartment [7].

We focus on NAYOs for three reasons. Firstly, it is merely a graphical form a common representation: negation-free horn clauses. Secondly, and related to the first point, a range of representations can be expressed as NAYOs. Thirdly, there exist average case search results for NAYO graphs (see below). Any other representation with these three properties might be a suitable alternative framework for our analysis.

At first glance, it might appear that we can simply emulate the execution of a program by building proof trees across the NAYO graph. For example, we could mark some nodes as "inputs" then grow trees across the NAYO graph whose leaves are the inputs and whose root is some reached part of the program. However, we can't reckless grow proof trees across a NAYO: as a proof tree grows it should remain consistent (i.e. must not contain two nodes connected by a no-edge).

Proving a goal in a NAYO graph means recursively exploring all edges that arrive at that node. A randomized search would explore these edges in an order chosen randomly. HT0 is such a random search algorithm for NAYO graphs [10]. When HT0 reaches a literal, it retracts all other literals that might contradict this literal. The algorithm is very fast since it removes the Gabow et.al precondition for NP-completeness (any node that contradicts the nodes already in the proof tree). The random order in which HT0 explores the NAYO graphs selects which literals will be explored. Hence, HT0 repeats its processing several times. After trying to prove all it's goals in this random way, HT0 re-asserts the retracted literals and executes another "try" to prove all its goals. This process terminates when algorithm detects a plateau in the largest percentage of reachable goals found in any "try".

3   NAYO Graphs and Predictability

NAYO graphs offer a common declarative reading for a range of representations (e.g. those shown in Figure 1). At the NAYO level it is easy to show that the heuristic inferences made by random search may not be repeatable and hence not predictable.

Consider the three proofs HT0 might generate to prove happy in Figure 2.

$Proof_1$: happy ← tranquility(hi) ← conscience(clear)
$Proof_2$: happy ← tranquility(hi) ← satieted ← diet(fatty)
$Proof_3$: happy ← and1 $\begin{cases} \leftarrow \texttt{rich} \\ \leftarrow \texttt{healthy} \leftarrow \texttt{diet(light)} \end{cases}$

Some of these conclusions made by these proofs are not categorical conclusions. For example, our belief in healthy is contingent on accepting $Proof_3$ and not $Proof_2$ ($Proof_3$ is incompatible with $Proof_2$ since these two proofs require different diets). In the general case, a random search engine like HT0 will find only some subset of the possible proofs, particularly if it is run for a heuristically selected time interval. That is, a random search engine may not repeatedly realize that (e.g.) healthy is an uncertain conclusion.

Clearly for tiny systems like Figure 2 generating only a handful of proofs, the conclusions from random search are unpredictable and our SE colleagues are wise to reject it. However, for such tiny systems, manual analysis will suffice. The automatic processing of NAYO graphs only gets interesting for larger systems. In such large systems, the goal nodes are a small subset of the total nodes. Further, as we show below, there emerges average case properties relating to our ability to quickly probe all the possible contingencies from a system. The sequel present these average case properties using the terminology of Menzies' prior work on set-covering abduction [8] (for notes on other abductive frameworks, see [2,5]).

Given a model such as Figure 2 and a goal such as happy, HT0 builds proof trees to those goals; e.g. $Proof_1...Proof_3$. Anything that has not been asserted as a fact is an assumption. No proof can contain mutually exclusive assumptions or contradict the goal; i.e. assuming ¬happy is illegal. The generated proofs should be grouped together into maximal consistent subsets called *worlds*. Our example generates two worlds: $World_1 = \{Proof_1, Proof_3\}$ and $World_2 = \{Proof_1, Proof_2\}$.

A world contains what we can conclude from NAYO inference. A goal is proved if it can be found in a world. In terms of multiple world reasoning, the predictability problem can be formalized as follows:

Random search is unpredictable when it does not generate enough worlds to cover the range of possible conclusions.

Note that this is a weak objection if it can be shown that the number of generated worlds is not large. This will be our argument below.

4   Average Number of Generated Worlds

Assumptions can be categorized into three important groups, only one of which determines how many worlds are generated. Some assumptions are *dependant* on other assumptions. For example, in $Proof_3$, the healthy assumptions depends fully on diet(light). In terms of exploring all the effects of different assumptions, we can ignore the dependant assumptions. Another important category of assumptions are the assumptions that contradict no other assumptions. These *non-controversial* assumptions are never at odds with other assumptions and so do not effect the number of worlds generated. In our example, the non-controversial assumptions are everything except diet(light) and diet(healthy). Hence, like the dependant assumptions, we will ignore these non-controversial assumptions. The remaining assumptions are the *controversial, non-dependant* assumptions or *funnel* assumptions. These funnel assumptions control how all the other assumptions are grouped into worlds of belief. DeKleer's key insight in the ATMS research was that a multi-world reasoning device need only focus on the funnel[3] When switching between worlds, all we

---

[3] DeKleer called the funnel assumptions the *minimal environments*. We do not adopt that terminology here since DeKleer used consistency-based abduction while we are exploring set-covering abduction here. For an excellent discussion that defines and distinguishes set-covering from consistency-based methods, see [2].

need to resolve is which funnel assumptions we endorse. Continuing our example, if we endorse diet(light) then all the conclusions in $World_2$ follow and if we endorse diet(healthy) then all the conclusions in $World_1$ follow.

Proofs meet and clash in the funnel. If the size of the funnel is very small, then the number of possible clashes is very small and the number of possible resolutions to those clashes is very small. When the number of possible resolutions is very small, the number of possible worlds is very small and random search can quickly probe the different worlds of beliefs (since there are so few of them). Hence, if we can show that the average size of the funnel is small, then we can quickly poll the range of possible conclusions from our NAYO graphs.

There are numerous case studies suggesting that generating a few worlds (picked at random) adequately samples the space of possibilities that would be found after sampling a much larger number of worlds. Williams and Nayak found that a locally guides conflict resolution algorithm performed as well as the best available ATMS algorithm [16]. Menzies, Easterbrook et.al. report experiments comparing random world generation with full world generation. After millions of runs, they concluded that the random world generator found almost as many goals in less time as full world generation [9]. In other work, Menzies and Michael showed that the maximum percentage of reachable goals found by HT0 plateaus after a small number of tries [10]. These case studies are consistent with the claim that (1) the total number of worlds is usually very small, hence (2) average funnel size is not large. In order to test if this claim generalizes beyond these isolated case studies, we developed the following mathematical model [11]. Suppose some goal can be reached by a narrow funnel M or a wide funnel N as follows:

$$
\left.\begin{array}{r} \xrightarrow{a_1} M_1 \\ \xrightarrow{a_2} M_2 \\ \cdots \\ \xrightarrow{a_m} M_m \end{array}\right\} \xrightarrow{c} goal_i \xleftarrow{d} \left\{\begin{array}{l} N_1 \xleftarrow{b_1} \\ N_2 \xleftarrow{b_2} \\ N_3 \xleftarrow{b_2} \\ N_4 \xleftarrow{b_2} \\ \cdots \\ N_n \xleftarrow{b_n} \end{array}\right.
$$

Under what circumstances will the narrow funnel be favored over the wide funnel? More precisely, when are the odds of reaching $goal_i$ via the narrow funnel much greater than the odds of reaching $goal_i$ via the wide funnel? To answer this question, we begin with the following definitions. Let the M funnel use m variables and the N funnel use n variables. For comparison purposes, we express the size of the wider funnel as a ratio α of the narrower funnel; i.e. $n = \alpha m$. Each member of M is reached via a path with probability a_i while each member of N is reached via a path with probability b_i. Two paths exist from the funnels to this goal: one from the narrow neck with probability c and one from the wide neck with probability d. The probability of reaching the goal via the narrow pathway is $narrow = c\prod_{i=1}^{m} a_i$ while the probability of reaching the goal via the wide pathway is $wide = d\prod_{i=1}^{n} b_i$.

Assuming that the goal is reached, then there are three ways to do so. Firstly, we can reach the goal using both funnels with probability $narrow.wide$. Secondly, we can reach the goal using the narrow funnel and not the wider funnel with probability $narrow(1 - wide)$. Thirdly, we can reach the goal using the wider funnel and not the narrow funnel with probability $(1 - narrow)wide$. Let g be probability of reaching $goal_i$ which is the sum of the three probabilities; i.e. $g = narrow + wide - narrow.wide$.

Given the goal is reached, then the conditional probabilities of reaching the $goal_i$ via two our funnels is:

$$P(narrow|g) = \frac{narrow}{narrow + wide - narrow.wide}$$

$$P(wide|g) = \frac{wide}{narrow + wide - narrow.wide}$$

Let R be the ratio of the odds[4] of these conditional probabilities. Our precondition for use of the narrow funnel is $R > 1$. More generally, using the narrow funnel is much more likely if R is bigger than some threshold value t:

$$\left(R = \frac{(narrow)^2 (1 - wide)}{(wide)^2 (1 - narrow)} \right) > t \tag{1}$$

4.1   Assuming Uniform Distributions

Assuming that a_i and b_i come from uniform probability distributions, then $\sum_{i=1}^{m} a_i = 1$ and $a_i = \frac{1}{m}$, so $narrow = c\left(\frac{1}{m}\right)^m$. Similarly, under the same assumptions, $wide = d\left(\frac{1}{n}\right)^n$. Thus, by Equation 1 when $t = 1$, narrow funnels are more likely when:

$$narrow^2(1 - wide) > wide^2(1 - narrow)$$

which we can rearrange to: $(narrow - wide)(narrow + wide - narrow.wide) > 0$. This expression contains two terms, the second of which is always positive. Hence, this expression is positive when $\frac{narrow}{wide} > 1$. We can expand this expression to:

$$\frac{narrow}{wide} = \frac{c\left(\frac{1}{m}\right)^m}{d\left(\frac{1}{n}\right)^n}$$

Recalling that $n = \alpha m$, this expression becomes $(\alpha m)^{\alpha m} m^{-m} > \frac{d}{c}$

Consider the case of two funnels, one twice as big as the other; i.e. $\alpha = 2$. This expression can then be rearranged to show that $\frac{narrow}{wide} > 1$ is true when

$$(4m)^m > \frac{d}{c} \tag{2}$$

At $m = 2$, Equation 2 becomes $d < 64c$. That is, to access $goal_i$ from the wider funnel, the pathway d must be 64 times more likely than the pathway c. This

---

[4] The odds of an event with probability $P(x)$ is the ratio of the probability that the event does/does not happen; i.e. $\frac{P(X)}{1-P(X)}$

is not highly likely and this becomes less likely as the narrower funnel grows. By the same reasoning, at $m = 3$, to access $goal_i$ from the wider funnel, the pathway d must be 1728 times more likely than the narrower pathway c. That is, under the assumptions of this uniform case, as the wide funnel gets wider, it becomes less and less likely that it will be used.

4.2 Assuming Non-uniform Distributions

To explore the case where $\sum_{i=1}^{m} a_i \neq 1$ and $\sum_{i=1}^{m} b_i \neq 1$ (i.e. the non-uniform probability distribution case), we created and executed a small simulator many times. The mean μ and standard deviation σ^2 of the logarithm of the variables a_i, b_i, c, d were picked at random from the following ranges: $\mu \in \{1, 2, \ldots 10\}$; $spread \in \{0.05, 0.1, 0.2, 0.4, 0.8\}$. μ and $spread$ where then converted into probability as follows: $\sigma^2 = spread * \mu$; $probability = 10^{-1*normDist(\mu,\sigma^2)}$. Next, m and α were picked at random from the ranges: $m \in \{1, 2, \ldots 10\}$; $\alpha \in \{1, 1.25, 1.5, \ldots 10\}$. R was then calculated and the number of times R exceeded different values for t is shown in Figure 3. As might be expected, at $t = 1, \alpha = 1$ the funnels are the same size and the odds of using one of them is 50%. As α increases, then increasingly Equation 1 is satisfied and the narrower funnel will be preferred to the wider funnel. The effect is quite pronounced. For example, at $\alpha = 3$, 82% of our simulated runs, random search will be 10,000,000,000 times more likely to favor narrow funnels $\frac{1}{3}$ the size of alternative funnels.

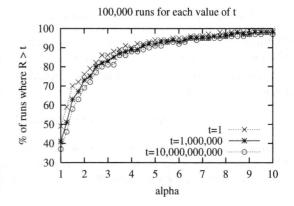

100,000 runs for each value of t

Y-axis: % of runs where R > t

legend: t=1, t=1,000,000, t=10,000,000,000

x-axis: alpha

Fig. 3. 100000 runs of the funnel simulator. Y-axis shows what percentage of the runs satisfies Equation 1.

In summary, in both the uniform and non-uniform case, random search engines such as HT0 will favor worlds with narrow funnels. Since narrow funnels mean fewer worlds, we can now assure our SE colleagues that it is highly likely that random search will sample the entire space of possible conclusions.

5   Conclusion

Modern SE research urgently needs to address the issue of lightweight modeling in order to support current industrial practices. A central problem with the processing of lightweight models is that they are incomplete and contain contradictions. AI research has been exploring theories containing contradictions for decades. Random search is an AI technique that can explore very large models, even when they contain contradictions.

Before the SE community accepts random search, it must be shown that these techniques are relevant and predictable. We have shown that a wide range of SE artifacts can be mapped into a declarative representation called NAYO graphs. We have also shown that after the randomized generation of a small number of worlds from the NAYO graphs, it is unlikely that very different goals will be reachable if we randomly generated many more worlds. Hence, we assert that (1) random search is both relevant and surprisingly predictable; and (2) SE can use random search to support the lightweight modeling tools needed for the current fast pace of software development.

References

1. P. Cheeseman, B. Kanefsky, and W. Taylor. Where the really hard problems are. In *Proceedings of IJCAI-91*, pages 331–337, 1991.
2. L. Console and P. Torasso. A Spectrum of Definitions of Model-Based Diagnosis. *Computational Intelligence*, 7:133–141, 3 1991.
3. J. Corbett, M. Dwyer, J. Hatcliff, S. Laubach, C. Pasarenu, Robby, and H. Zheng. Bandera: Extracting finite-state models from java source code. In *Proceedings ICSE2000, Limerick, Ireland*, pages 439–448, 2000.
4. H. Gabow, S. Maheshwari, and L. Osterweil. On two problems in the generation of program test paths. *IEEE Trans. Software Engrg*, SE-2:227–231, 1976.
5. A. Kakas, R. Kowalski, and F. Toni. The role of abduction in logic programming. In C. H. D.M. Gabbay and J. Robinson, editors, *Handbook of Logic in Artificial Intelligence and Logic Programming 5*, pages 235–324. Oxford University Press, 1998.
6. N. Leveson. *Safeware System Safety And Computers*. Addison-Wesley, 1995.
7. J. McIntosh and R. McIntosh. *Mathematical Modeling and Computers in Endocrinology*. Springer-Verlag, 1980.
8. T. Menzies and P. Compton. Applications of abduction: Hypothesis testing of neuroendocrinological qualitative compartmental models. *Artificial Intelligence in Medicine*, 10:145–175, 1997. Available from http://tim.menzies.com/pdf/96aim.pdf.
9. T. Menzies, S. Easterbrook, B. Nuseibeh, and S. Waugh. An empirical investigation of multiple viewpoint reasoning in requirements engineering. In *RE '99*, 1999. Available from http://tim.menzies.com/pdf/99re.pdf.
10. T. Menzies and C. Michael. Fewer slices of pie: Optimising mutation testing via abduction. In *SEKE '99*, June 17-19, Kaiserslautern, Germany. Available from http://tim.menzies.com/pdf/99seke.pdf, 1999.
11. T. Menzies and H. Singh. Many maybes mean (mostly) the same thing. In *2nd International Workshop on Soft Computing applied to Software Engineering (Netherlands), February*, 2001. Available from http://tim.menzies.com/pdf/00maybe.pdf.
12. J. Mylopoulos, L. Cheng, and E. Yu. From object-oriented to goal-oriented requirements analysis. *Communications of the ACM*, 42(1):31–37, January 1999.

13. D. Sahlin. *An Automatic Partial Evaluator for Full Prolog.* PhD thesis, The Royal Institute of Technology (KTH), Stockholm, Sweden, May 1991. Available from `file://sics.se/pub/isl/papers/dan-sahlin-thesis.ps.gz`.

14. B. Selman, H. Levesque, and D. Mitchell. A new method for solving hard satisfiability problems. In *AAAI '92*, pages 440–446, 1992.

15. J. Whittle and J. Schumann. Generating statechart designs from scenarios. In *Proceedings of the 22nd International Conference on Software Engineering (ICSE). Limerick, Ireland,* June 2000. Available from `http://www.riacs.edu/research/detail/ase/icse2000.ps.gz`.

16. B. Williams and P. Nayak. A model-based approach to reactive self-configuring systems. In *Proceedings, AAAI '96*, pages 971–978, 1996.

Imitation and Reinforcement Learning in Agents with Heterogeneous Actions

Bob Price[1] and Craig Boutilier[2]

[1] Department of Computer Science, University of British Columbia, Vancouver, B.C.,
Canada V6T 1Z4 price@cs.ubc.ca
[2] Department of Computer Science, University of Toronto, Toronto, ON, Canada
M5S 3H5 cebly@cs.toronto.edu

Abstract. Reinforcement learning techniques are increasingly being used to solve difficult problems in control and combinatorial optimization with promising results. *Implicit imitation* can accelerate reinforcement learning (RL) by augmenting the Bellman equations with information from the observation of expert agents (mentors). We propose two extensions that permit imitation of agents with heterogeneous actions: feasibility testing, which detects infeasible mentor actions, and k-step repair, which searches for plans that approximate infeasible actions. We demonstrate empirically that both of these extensions allow imitation agents to converge more quickly in the presence of heterogeneous actions.

1 Introduction

Traditional methods for solving difficult control and combinatorial optimization problems have made frequent recourse to heuristics to improve performance. Increasingly, adaptive methods such as reinforcement learning have been used to allow programs to learn their own heuristic or "value" functions to guide search. The results in such diverse areas as job-shop scheduling [1] and global optimization problems [2] have been quite promising. Typically, however, the types of problems we would like to solve are similar to problems already solved or to problems being pursued by others. We have therefore argued [3], as have others, for a broader, sociologically inspired model of reinforcement learning which can incorporate the knowledge of multiple agents solving multiple related problems in a loosely coupled way.

Coupling between agents is typically achieved through communication, however, the lack of a common communication protocol or the presence of a competitive situation can often make explicit communication infeasible. We have demonstrated, using simple domains, that it is possible to overcome communication barriers by equipping agents with imitation-like behaviors [3]. Using imitation, agents can learn from others without communicating an explicit context for the applicability of a behavior [4]; without the need for an existing communication protocol; in competitive situations where agents are unwilling to share information; and even when other agents are unwilling to fulfill a teacher role. The ability of imitation to effect skill transfer between agents has also

E. Stroulia and S. Matwin (Eds.): AI 2001, LNAI 2056, pp. 111–120, 2001.

been demonstrated in a range of domains [5,6,7,8,9,10]. These domains, however, have dealt with agents imitating other agents with similar actions. Our goal is to extend imitation to allow agents to learn from expert agents (mentors) with different action capabilities or inhabiting different environments. For example, an agent learning to control a newly upgraded elevator group in a large building could benefit from the adaptive learning of a prior controller on the previous elevator system of that building.

Previously, we have showed that *implicit imitation* can accelerate reinforcement learning (RL) by allowing agents to take advantage of the knowledge implicit in observations of more skilled agents [3]. Though we did not assume that the learner shared the same objectives as the mentors, we did rely on the fact that actions were *homogeneous*: every action taken by a mentor corresponded to some action of the learner. In this work, we relax this assumption and introduce two mechanisms that allow acceleration of RL in presence of *heterogeneous actions*: *action feasibility testing*, which allows the learner to determine whether a specific mentor action can be duplicated; and *k-step repair*, in which a learner attempts to determine whether it can approximate the mentor's trajectory.

Our work can be viewed loosely as falling within the framework proposed by Nehaniv and Dautenhahn [11], who view imitation as the process of constructing mappings between states, actions, and goals of different agents (see also the abstraction model of Kuniyoshi at al. [8]). Unlike their model, we assume that state-space mappings are given, the mentor's actions are not directly observable, the goals of the mentor and learner may differ, and that environments are stochastic. Furthermore, we do not require that the learner explicitly duplicate the behavior of the mentor. Our model is also related to behavioral cloning, but again we do not share the goal of behavioral cloning which aims to reproduce an observed behavior by inducing an objective function from observed behavior [12]. As in [5], our model incorporates an independent learning and optimization component that differs from "following" and "demonstration" models often used in robotics [7,13], though the repair strategies we invoke do bear some relation to "following" models.

2   Imitation with Homogeneous Actions

In this section we summarize the implicit imitation model developed in [3]. Further details and motivation can be found in this paper. In *implicit imitation* [3], we assume two agents, a *mentor m* and an *observer o*, acting in a fixed environment.[1] We assume the observer (or learner) is learning to control a Markov decision process (MDP) with states S, actions A_o and reward function R_o. We use $\Pr_o(t|s, a)$ to denote the probability of transition from state s to t when action a is taken. The mentor too is controlling an MDP with the same underlying state space (we use A_m, R_m and $\Pr_m$ to denote this MDP).

---

[1] The extension to multiple mentors with varying expertise is straightforward [3].

We make two assumptions: the mentor implements a deterministic stationary policy π_m, which induces a Markov chain $\Pr_m(t|s) = \Pr_m(t|s, \pi_m(s))$ over S;[2] and for each action $\pi_m(s)$ taken by the mentor, there exists an action $a \in A_o$ such that the distributions $\Pr_o(\cdot|s, a)$ and $\Pr_m(\cdot|s)$ are the same. This latter assumption is the *homogeneous action assumption* and implies that the learner can duplicate the mentor's policy. We do not assume that the learner knows *a priori* the identity of the mentor's action $\pi_m(s)$ (for any given state s), nor that the learner *wants* to duplicate this policy (the agents may have different reward functions). Since the learner can observe the mentor's transitions (though not its actions directly), it can form estimates of the mentor's Markov chain, along with estimates of its own MDP (transition probabilities and reward function). We define the *augmented Bellman equation* as follows:

$$V(s) = R_o(s) + \gamma \max \left\{ \max_{a \in A_o} \left\{ \sum_{t \in S} \Pr_o(t|s, a) V(t) \right\}, \sum_{t \in S} \Pr_m(t|s) V(t) \right\}. \quad (1)$$

This is the usual Bellman equation with an extra term added, namely, the second summation, denoting the expected value of duplicating the mentor's action $\pi_m(s)$. Since this (unknown) action is identical to one of the observer's actions, the term is redundant and the augmented value equation is valid. Furthermore, under certain (standard) assumptions, we can show that the estimates of the model quantities will converge to their true values; and an *implicit imitation learner* acting in accordance with these value estimates will converge optimally under standard RL assumptions.[3] More interesting is the fact that by acting in accordance with value estimates produced by augmented Bellman backups, an observer generally converges much more quickly than a learner not using the guidance of a mentor. As demonstrated in [3], implicit imitators typically accumulate reward at a higher rate earlier than standard (model-based) RL-agents, even when the mentor's reward function is not identical to the observer's.

At states the mentor visits infrequently (because they are rarely traversed by its optimal policy), the learner's estimates of the mentor's Markov chain may be poor compared to the learner's own estimated action models. In such cases, we would like to suppress the mentor's influence. We do this by using model confidence in augmented backups. For the mentor's Markov chain and the observer's action transitions, we assume a Dirichlet prior over the parameters of each of these multinomial distributions. From sample counts of mentor and observer transitions, the learner updates these distributions. Using a technique inspired by Kaelbling's [15] interval estimation method, we use the variance in our estimated Dirichlet distributions for the model parameters to construct crude lower bounds on both the augmented value function incorporating the mentor model and an unaugmented value function based strictly on the observer's own experience. If the lower bound on the augmented value function is less than

---

[2] Generalization to stochastic policies can easily be handled.

[3] We assume a model-based RL algorithm (e.g., prioritized sweeping [14] and an exploration model which is influenced by state values (e.g. ϵ greedy).

Table 1. Augmented Backup

FUNCTION augmentedBackup($V^+, Pr_o, \sigma_o^2, Pr_m, \sigma_m^2, s$)
$a^* = \text{argmax}_{a \in \mathcal{A}_o} \sum_{t \in \mathcal{S}} Pr(s, a, t) V^+(t)$

$V_o(s) = R_o(s) + \gamma \sum_{t \in \mathcal{S}} Pr(s, a^*, t) V(t); \quad V_m(s) = R_o(s) + \gamma \sum_{t \in \mathcal{S}} Pr_m(s, t) V(t)$

$\sigma_o(s) = \gamma^2 \sum_{t \in \mathcal{S}} \sigma(s, a^*, t) V^+(t)^2; \quad \sigma_m(s) = \gamma^2 \sum_{t \in \mathcal{S}} \sigma_m(s, t) V^+(t)^2$

$V_o^-(s) = V_o(s) - \sigma_o(s); \quad V_m^-(s) = V_m(s) - \sigma_m(s)$

IF $V_o > V_m$ THEN $V^+(s) = V_o(s)$
ELSE $V^+(s) = V_m(s)$
RETURN $V^+(s)$

the lower bound on the unaugmented value function, then either the augmented value is in fact lower, or it is highly variable. Using lower bounds ensures that uncertainty about an action model makes it look worse. In either circumstance, suppression of the mentor's influence is appropriate and we use an unaugmented Bellman backup.

In the algorithm shown in Table 1, the inputs are the observer's augmented value function V^+, its action model and variance PR_o, σ_o^2, the action model and variance for mentor observations Pr_m, σ_m^2 and the current state s. The output is a new augmented value for state s. The program variable $V_o(s)$ represents the best value the observer can obtain in state s using its own experience-based action models and $V_m(s)$ represents the value the agent could obtain if it employed the same action as the mentor. The term $\sigma_o^2(s)$ represents a conservative overestimate of the variance in the estimate of the value of state s, $V(s)$, due to the *local* model uncertainty in the observer's own action models and $\sigma_m^2(s)$ represents a similar uncertainty in the estimate derived from the mentor action model. The uncertainty is used to construct loose lower bounds on the value estimates denoted V_o^- and V_m^-. These bounds are crude but sufficient to suppress mentor influence at appropriate states.

3   Imitation with Heterogeneous Actions

When the homogeneity assumption is violated, the implicit imitation framework described above can cause the learner to perform very poorly. In particular, if the learner is unable to make the same state transition (with the same probability) as the mentor at a state s, it may drastically overestimate the value of s.[4] The inflated value estimate may cause the learner to return repeatedly to this (potentially undesirable) state with a potentially drastic impact on convergence time

---

[4] Augmented backups cannot cause underestimation of the value function.

(see Section 4). Implicit imitation has no mechanism to remove the unwanted influence of the mentor's model (confidence estimates play no role here). What is needed is the ability to identify when the key assumption justifying augmented backups—that the observer can duplicate *every* mentor action—is violated.

In such heterogeneous settings, this issue can be resolved by the use of an explicit *action feasibility test*: before an augmented backup is performed at s, the observer tests whether the mentor's action a_m "differs" from each of its actions at s, given its current estimated models. If so, the augmented backup is suppressed and a standard Bellman backup is used to update the value function. By default, mentor actions are assumed to be feasible for the observer; however, once the observer is reasonably confident that a_m is infeasible at state s, augmented backups are suppressed at s.

Recall that action models are estimated from data with the learner's uncertainty about the true transition probabilities reflected in a Dirichlet distribution. Comparing a_m with a_o is effected by a difference of means test w.r.t. the corresponding Dirichlets. This is complicated by the fact that Dirichlets are highly non-normal for small sample counts. We deal with the non-normality by requiring a minimum number of samples and using robust Chebyshev bounds on the pooled variance of the distributions to be compared. When we have few samples, we persist with augmented backups (embodying our default assumption of homogeneity). If the value estimate is inflated by these backups, the agent will be biased to obtain additional samples which will then allow the agent to perform the required feasibility test. We deal with the multivariate complications by performing the *Bonferroni test* [16] which has been shown to give good results in practice [17], is efficient to compute, and is known to be robust to dependence between variables. A Bonferroni hypothesis test is obtained by conjoining several single variable tests. Suppose the actions a_o and a_m result in r possible outcomes, $s_1, \cdots, s_r$, at s (i.e., r transition probabilities to compare). For each s_i, hypothesis E_i denotes that a_o and a_m have the same transition probability $\Pr(s_i|s)$, and $\bar{E}_i$ the complementary hypothesis. The Bonferroni inequality states:

$$\Pr\left[\bigcap_{i=1}^{r} E_i\right] \geq 1 - \sum_{i=1}^{r} \Pr\left[\bar{E}_i\right].$$

Thus we can test the joint hypothesis $\bigcap_{i=1}^{r} E_i$—the two action models are the same—by testing each of the r complementary hypotheses $\bar{E}_i$—transition probability for outcome i is the same— at confidence level α/r. If we reject any of the complementary hypotheses we reject the notion that the two actions are equal with confidence α. The mentor action a_m is deemed infeasible if for every observer action a_o, the multivariate Bonferroni test, just described, rejects the hypothesis that the action is the same as the mentor's.

The feasibility test is summarized in Table 2. The feasibility test tests whether the action demonstrated by mentor m in state s, is likely to be feasible for the observing agent in state s. The parameters of the observer's own Dirichlet distributions are denoted $n_o(s, a, t)$ which denotes the number of times the observer observes itself making the transition from state s to state t when it executes action a in state s. The parameters for the mentor action model are denoted $n_m(s,t)$ which gives the number of times the observer observes the mentor making the transition from state s to state t. The difference of means is denoted μ_Δ and the test statistic z_Δ.

Table 2. Action Feasibility Testing

```
FUNCTION feasible(m,s) : Boolean
    FOR each aᵢ in 𝒜ₒ DO
        allSuccessorProbsSimilar = true
        FOR each t in successors(s) DO
```
$$\mu_\Delta = Pr_o(s,a,t) - Pr_m(s,t)$$
$$z_\Delta = \mu_\Delta \sqrt{\frac{n_o(s,a,t)*var_o(s,a,t)+n_m(s,t)var_m(s,t)}{n_o(s,a,t)+n_m(s,t)}}$$
```
            IF zΔ > zα/r
                allSuccessorProbsSimilar = false
        END FOR
        IF allSuccessorProbsSimilar THEN return true
    END FOR
    RETURN false
```

Action feasibility testing has some unintended effects. Suppose an observer has previously constructed an estimated value function using augmented backups. Subsequently, the mentor's action a_m is judged to be infeasible at s. If the augmented backup is suppressed, the value of $V(s)$ and all of its preceding states will drop as value backups propagate the change through the state space. As a result, the bias of the observer toward s will be eliminated. However, imitation is motivated by the fact that the observer and mentor are similar is some respects. We might hope, therefore, that there exists a short path or a *repair* around the infeasible transition. The observer's ability to "duplicate" a_m might take the form of local policy rather than a single action.

To encourage the learner to explore the vicinity of an infeasible action, we will sometimes consider retaining the mentor's influence through augmented backups and then use the notion of k-*step repair* to search for a local policy. Specifically, when a_m is discovered to be infeasible at state s, the learner undertakes a k-step reachability analysis (w.r.t. its current model Pr_o) to determine if it can "workaround" the infeasible action (i.e., find a k-step path from s to a point on the mentor's nominal trajectory). If so, the learner knows that value will "flow" around the infeasible transition and thereby maintain the existing exploration bias. In this case, the learner concludes that the state is already "repaired" and augmented backups are suppressed. Otherwise, a random walk with expected radius of k-steps is undertaken to explore the area. This allows the learner to improve its model and discover potential repair paths. This walk is repeated at the next n visits of s or until a repair path is found. If no repair is found after

n attempts, the agent concludes that the infeasible transition is irreparable and augmented backups are suppressed permanently. Thus the mentor's influence persists in guiding the learner toward s until it is deemed to be unnecessary or misleading. The parameters k, and n must be tuned empirically, but can be estimated given knowledge of the connectivity of the domain and prior beliefs about how similar (in terms of length of average repair) the trajectories of the mentor and observer will be.

4   Empirical Demonstrations

Experimental evaluation of the original implicit imitation mechanism can be found in [3]. Our first experiment in this paper illustrates the necessity of feasibility testing. Agents must navigate an obstacle-free, 10-by-10 grid-world from upper-left corner to lower-right. We give a mentor with the "NEWS" action set (North, South, East and West movement actions) an optimal stationary policy. We study three learners, with the "Skew" action set (N, S, NE, SW) which are unable to duplicate the mentor exactly. The first learner imitates *with* feasibility testing, the second *without* feasibility testing, and the third control agent uses no imitation (i.e., is a standard RL-agent). Actions are perturbed 5% of the time. As in [3] the agents use model-based reinforcement learning with prioritized sweeping [14]. We used $k = 3$ and $n = 20$.

In Figure 1 the horizontal axis represents time and the vertical axis represents the average reward per 1000 time steps (averaged over 10 runs). The imitation agent with feasibility testing converges quickly to the optimal rate. The agent without feasibility testing achieves sporadic success early on, but due to frequent attempts to duplicate infeasible actions it never converges to the optimal rate (stochastic actions permit it to achieve goals eventually). The control agent without guidance due to imitation demonstrates a delay in convergence relative to the imitation agents, but converges to optimal rate in the long run. The gradual slope of the control agent is due to the higher variance in the control

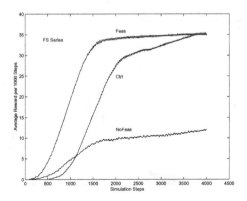

Fig. 1. Utility of Feasibility Testing

agent's discovery time for the optimal path. Thus, we see that imitation improves convergence, but feasibility testing is necessary when heterogeneous actions are present.

We developed feasibility testing and k-step repair to deal with heterogeneous actions, but the same techniques can be applied to agents operating in state space with different connectivity (these are equivalent notions ultimately). We constructed a domain where all agents have the *same* NEWS action set; but we introduce obstacles as shown in Figure 2, into the environment of the learners. The obstacles cause the imitator's actions to have different effects than the mentor's.

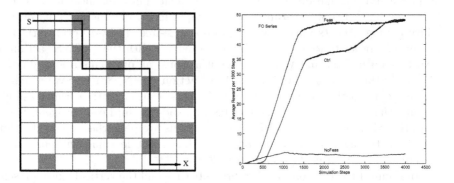

Fig. 2. Obstacle Map, Mentor's Path and Experiment Results

In Figure 2 we see that the imitator with feasibility testing performs best, the control agent converges eventually, and the agent without feasibility testing stalls. The optimal goal rate is higher in this scenario because the agents use the same "efficient" NEWS actions. We see local differences in connectivity are well handled by feasibility testing.

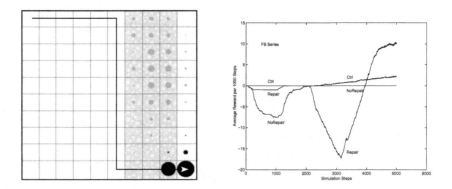

Fig. 3. River Scenario, Mentor's Path and Experiment Results

In simple problems it is likely that a learner's exploration may form possible repair paths before feasibility testing cuts off the guidance obtained from mentor observations. In more difficult problems (e.g., where the learner spends a lot of time exploring), it may conclude that a mentor's action is infeasible long before it has constructed its own repair path. The imitator's performance would then drop down to that of an unaugmented reinforcement learner.

To illustrate the effectiveness of k-step repair, we devised a domain where agents must cross a three-step wide "river" which runs vertically and exacts a penalty of -0.2 per step (see Figure 3). The goal state is worth +1.0. Without a long exploration phase, agents generally discover the negative states of the river and curtail exploration in this direction before actually making it across. If we examine the value function estimate (after 1000 steps) of an imitator with feasibility testing but no repair capabilities, we see that, due to suppression by feasibility testing, the high-value states (represented by large dark circles in Figure 3), backed up from the goal terminate abruptly at an infeasible transition before making it across the river. In fact, they are dominated by the lighter grey circles showing negative values. Once this barrier forms, only an agent with a very optimistic exploration policy will get to the goal, and then only after considerable exploration. In this experiment, we apply a k-step repair agent to the problem with $k = 3$.

Examining the graph in Figure 3, we see that both imitation agents experience an early negative dip as they are guided deep into the river by the mentor's influence. The agent without repair eventually decides the mentor's action is infeasible, and thereafter avoids the river (and the possibility of finding the goal). The imitator with repair also discovers the mentor's action to be infeasible, but does not immediately dispense with the mentor's guidance. It keeps exploring in the area of the mentor's trajectory using random walk, all the while accumulating a negative reward until it suddenly finds a repair path and rapidly converges on the optimal solution.[5] The control agent discovers the goal only once in the ten runs.

5   Conclusion

Implicit imitation makes use of the observer's own reward function and a model augmented by observations of a mentor to compute the actions an imitator should take without requiring that the observer duplicate the mentor's actions exactly. We have seen that feasibility testing extends implicit imitation in a principled manner to deal with the situations where the homogeneous actions assumption is invalid. Adding k-step repair preserves and extends the mentor's guidance in the presence of infeasible actions, whether due to differences in action capabilities or local differences in state spaces. Our approach also relates to the idea of "following" in the sense that the imitator uses local search in its model to repair discontinuities in its augmented value function before acting in the world.

---

[5] While repair steps take place in an area of negative reward in this scenario, this need not be the case. Repair doesn't *imply* short-term negative return.

We are currently extending our model to deal with partially-observable environments and to make explicit use of abstraction and generalization techniques in order to tackle a wider range of problems.

References

1. Wei Zhang and Thomas G. Dietterich. A reinforcement learning approach to job-shop scheduling. In *IJCAI-95*, pages 1114–1120, Montreal, 1995.
2. Justin A. Boyan and Andrew W. Moore. Learning evaluation functions for global optimization and boolean satisfiability. In *AAAI-98*, pages 3–10, July 26-30, 1998, Madison, Wisconsin, 1998.
3. Bob Price and Craig Boutilier. Implicit imitation in multiagent reinforcement learning. In *ICML-99*, pages 325–334, Bled, SI, 1999.
4. Paul Bakker and Yasuo Kuniyoshi. Robot see, robot do : An overview of robot imitation. In *AISB96 Workshop on Learning in Robots and Animals*, pages 3–11, Brighton,UK, 1996.
5. C. G. Atkeson and S. Schaal. Robot learning from demonstration. In *ICML-97*, pages 12–20, Nashville, TN, 1997.
6. Aude Billard and Gillian Hayes. Learning to communicate through imitation in autonomous robots. In *ICANN-97*, pages 763–68, Lausanne, Switzerland, 1997.
7. G. M. Hayes and J. Demiris. A robot controller using learning by imitation. Technical Report DAI No. 676, University of Edinburgh. Dept. of Artificial Intelligence, 1994.
8. Yasuo Kuniyoshi, Masayuki Inaba, and Hirochika Inoue. Learning by watching: Extracting reusable task knowledge from visual observation of human performance. *IEEE Transactions on Robotics and Automation*, 10(6):799–822, 1994.
9. T. M. Mitchell, S. Mahadevan, and L. Steinberg. LEAP: A learning apprentice for VLSI design. In *IJCAI-85*, pages 573–580, Los Altos, California, 1985. Morgan Kaufmann Publishers, Inc.
10. Paul E. Utgoff and Jeffrey A. Clouse. Two kinds of training information for evaluation function learning. In *AAAI-91*, pages 596–600, Anaheim, CA, 1991. AAAI Press.
11. Chrystopher Nehaniv and Kerstin Dautenhahn. Mapping between dissimilar bodies: Affordances and the algebraic foundations of imitation. In *EWLR-98*, pages 64–72, Edinburgh, 1998.
12. Dorian Šuc and Ivan Bratko. Skill reconstruction as induction of LQ controllers with subgoals. In *IJCAI-97*, pages 914–919, Nagoya, 1997.
13. Maja J. Mataric, Matthew Williamson, John Demiris, and Aswath Mohan. Behaviour-based primitives for articulated control. In *SAB-98*, pages 165–170, Zurich, 1998.
14. Andrew W. Moore and Christopher G. Atkeson. Prioritized sweeping: Reinforcement learning with less data and less real time. *Machine Learning*, 13(1):103–30, 1993.
15. Leslie Pack Kaelbling. *Learning in Embedded Systems*. MIT Press, Cambridge,MA, 1993.
16. George A. F. Seber. *Multivariate Observations*. Wiley, New York, 1984.
17. J. Mi and Allan R. Sampson. A comparison of the Bonferroni and Scheffé bounds. *Journal of Statistical Planning and Inference*, 36:101–105, 1993.

Knowledge and Planning in an Action-Based Multi-agent Framework: A Case Study

Bradley Bart[1], James P. Delgrande[1], and Oliver Schulte[2]

[1] School of Computing Science, Simon Fraser University,
Burnaby, B.C., Canada V5A 1S6, {bbart,jim}@cs.sfu.ca
[2] Department of Computing Science, University of Alberta, Edmonton, Alberta
Canada T6G 2E1, oschulte@cs.ualberta.ca

Abstract. The situation calculus is a logical formalism that has been extensively developed for planning. We apply the formalism in a complex multi-agent domain, modelled on the game of Clue. We find that the situation calculus, with suitable extensions, supplies a unified representation of (1) the interaction protocol, or structure of the game, (2) the dynamics of the knowledge and common knowledge of the agents, and (3) principles of strategic planning.

1 Introduction

The situation calculus is a logical formalism originally developed for planning by a single agent but more recently extended to deal with multiple agents and knowledge. In this paper we use a variant of the game of Clue as a testbed for gauging the power of the situation calculus in an epistemic, multi-agent setting. This has the potential to contribute to several areas of AI, such as the design of intelligent agents, game playing, and the formalism of the situation calculus itself. The situation calculus provides a general language for specifying interactions of a software agent; it can also be used to represent an agent's reasoning. Thus the situation calculus provides an integrated description of the action capabilities of agents and their reasoning and decision-making mechanisms. Similarly, in game playing the situation formalism can represent the rules of the game as well as knowledge about agents' strategies. Conversely, the connection with games opens up the possibility of applying efficient algorithms from games research for finding optimal strategies in multi-agent planning problems.

This paper focuses on issues concerning multi-agent interactions in the situation calculus. A novel aspect of this work is that we deal with knowledge that is *common* to a group of agents. We address these issues in a variant of the game of Clue, described below. Clue is a game in which the agents—players—have to discover the state of the world, rather than change it. We use the situation calculus to represent three aspects of the game:

1. The rules—what players can do when.
2. Information—what the players know at various stages of the game, including (objective) knowledge of the domain together with knowledge opf other agent's knowledge.

E. Stroulia and S. Matwin (Eds.): AI 2001, LNAI 2056, pp. 121–130, 2001.

3. Planning—how they can exploit that knowledge to find strategic plans for playing the game.

Most of the paper deals with the first two aspects. We found that the situation calculus is a remarkably natural formalism for describing a game structure. For representing the knowledge of the players during the game we employ an epistemic extension of the situation calculus that axiomatizes a knowledge fluent [8]. We require several extensions beyond the single-agent epistemic version of the situation calculus. First, we need an agent parameter for knowledge, to distinguish whose knowledge is referred to. Secondly, strategic reasoning involves an agent's reasoning about another agent's knowledge, as well as *common knowledge*.

We concentrate on a variant of Clue here, called MYST. The next section introduces Clue and MYST, and the situation calculus. The third section develops our axiomatisation of the game, while the fourth section addresses reasoning issues. We conclude with a short discussion. Further details are found in [1].

2   Background

Clue and MYST: We ignore those aspects of Clue that are irrelevant to the general problems of knowledge representation and planning. The premise of Clue is that there has been a murder; it is each player's goal to determine the murderer, weapon, and location of the murder. Each suspect, and possible weapon and location, are represented by a card. Initially the cards are divided into their three sorts (suspect, weapon, location), and from each sort one card is randomly selected and hidden. These three cards determine the details of the crime. The remaining cards are dealt to the players. At the outset a player sees only her own hand, and thus knows what cards she has been dealt, but not what the other players have received. Each player in turn asks one of the other players about a suspect, a weapon and a room. If the (queried) player has one of the queried cards, she shows it to the asker. The asker then knows that the player has that card; the other players know only that the (showing) player has *one* of the three cards. A player may guess the identity of the hidden cards at the end of their turn and, if correct, they win the game. The three hidden cards represent the state of the world. The joint knowledge of the players is sufficient to determine this information. However each player's goal is to learn the state of the world before the others do. Thus the game is of the same flavour as the "muddy children problem" [2], although more subtle and (we feel) interesting.

We reformulate the game of Clue as a simpler game that we call "MYST" (for "mystery"). In MYST there is a finite set of cards, but without the three sorts in Clue. There are m cards hidden in a "mystery pile" and n are given to each of p players. Hence there is a total of $k = m + (n \times p)$ cards. On their turn, a player asks a question about q cards of the form, "Do you have one of cards: $c_1, \ldots, c_q$?" This player is called the "poser". If the next player has one of these cards, they (privately) show the poser the card and the poser's turn is over. If the answer is "no", then the next player in turn is presented with the same query. After asking his question, a player may guess the contents of the mystery pile. If correct, he wins the game; otherwise, the player is relegated to answering posed queries only. The game ends if a player determines the contents of the mystery pile or if all players have been eliminated by unsuccessful guesses.

The Situation Calculus: The intuition behind the situation calculus is that the world persists in one state until an *action* is performed that changes it to a new state. Time is discrete, one action occurs at a time, time durations do not matter, and actions are irreducible entities. *Actions* are conceptualised as objects in the universe of discourse, as are *states* of the world. Hence, states and actions are *reified*. That is, the action of, for example, moving block a from block b to block c is an object.

The constant s_0 refers to the initial state, and $do(A, s)$ is the state resulting from doing action A in state s. Thus $do(stack(a, b), s_0)$ is the state resulting from a *stack* action performed on a and b in situation s_0. The fact that, after performing the stack action, "a is on b" could be represented by $on(a, b, do(stack(a, b), s_0))$. Time-varying predicates, such as *on*, are referred to as *fluents*. Actions have *preconditions* specifying the conditions under which an action can be performed, and *successor state axioms* giving the effects of an action. The predicate $Poss(A, s)$ is used by convention to "collect" the preconditions for action A in situation s. So for *stack* we can express that the preconditions are (1) the hand is holding the block to be stacked and the block to be stacked onto has a clear top:

$$Poss(stack(X, Y), s) \leftrightarrow inhand(X, s) \wedge clear(Y, s).$$

The fluent $on(X, Y, s)$ is true in a state resulting from X being stacked on Y so long as the stack action was possible:

$$Poss(stack(X, Y), s) \rightarrow on(X, Y, do(stack(X, Y), s)).$$

The only other time that an *on* is true in a non-initial state is when it was true in the previous state, and was not undone by an action:

$$Poss(A, s) \wedge A \neq unstack(X, Y) \wedge on(X, Y, s). \rightarrow on(X, Y, do(A, s)).$$

This last axiom is called a *frame axiom*, and specifies what remains unchanged during an action.

Hayes and McCarthy [6] originally proposed the situation calculus; we use the version from [5], making use of the formalisation of knowledge in [8], with variants that we describe later. A multiple-agent version of the situation calculus is described in [4]. There, information exchanges are modelled via "send" and "receive" commands. Here in contrast we axiomatise operations that result in a change of knowledge for an agent. Thus for example, if an agent *shows* another a card, then the second *knows* the value of the card.

3   Representing MYST in the Situation Calculus

In this section, we formalize the game of MYST by specifying a set of axioms in the language of the situation calculus. Of particular interest is the knowledge fluent that describes what players know at various stages of the game.

3.1   Situation Calculus Terms Used in the Formalisation of MYST

Constants: We assume enough arithmetic to define a sort *natural_num* with constants $0, 1, .., n, ...$ to have their intended denotation. We extend the situation calculus with two more sorts: the sort *player* and the sort *card*. We introduce the constants described in the following table.

Constant Symbol(s)	Sort	Meaning
p	*natural_num*	total number of players
k	*natural_num*	total number of cards
n	*natural_num*	number of cards in each player's hand
m	*natural_num*	number of cards in mystery pile
q	*natural_num*	number of cards in a query
$p_1, .., p_p$	*player*	p_i denotes player i.
$c_1, ..., c_k$	*card*	c_i denotes card i

To encode the fact that we deal with a finite set of distinct players and cards, we adopt a unique names assumption (UNA) and domain closure assumption (DCA) with respect to these sorts. That is, for the set of players we add axioms

$$\text{UNA}_P : (p_i \neq p_j) \text{ for all } 1 \leq i \neq j \leq p.$$
$$\text{DCA}_P : \forall x.\ player(x) \equiv (x = p_1 \vee \cdots \vee x = p_p).$$

Analogous axioms (UNA_C, DCA_C) are adopted for the set of cards. We have a further constant s_0 to denote the initial situation in MYST, which obtains immediately after the cards have been dealt.

Since the above predicates conceptually define a finite set of players (and cards), we adopt a set theoretic notation for players (and cards). Adopting a set notation—which we could embed in first-order logic—will make the axiomatisation neater and the language more mathematically familiar. Henceforth we will use the following notation

$$C := \{c_1, ..., c_k\} \text{ the set of all cards}$$
$$P := \{1, ..., p\} \quad \text{the set of all players (denoted by integers).}$$

Variables: We introduce variables ranging over components of MYST. We need two more sorts: *set_cards* for a set of cards, and *set_players* for a set of players. We will use variables as follows.

Symbol	Meaning
i, j	players ($i, j \in P$); typically i is the poser and j the responder
c_x	single card ($c_x \in C$)
G	subset of players ($G \subseteq P$)
Q	set of cards in a question ($Q \subseteq C$)
M	set of cards in a guess about the mystery pile ($M \subseteq C$)
C_j	set of cards held by player j ($C_j \subseteq C$)
C_0	set of cards in mystery pile ($C_0 \subseteq C$)
Σ	generic set of cards ($\Sigma \subseteq C$)
a	an action
s	a situation

We will not explicitly list "type-checking" predicates to ensure that c_x is a card (for instance).

Actions: The following is the list of action functions and their informal descriptions. The sequence in which actions may occur is defined by the predicate $Poss(a, s)$ below. Note that the first argument always represents the player performing the action.

Action function symbol	Meaning
$asks(i, Q)$	Player i asks question Q
$no(j)$	Player j says *no* to question Q
$yes(j)$	Player j says *yes* to question Q
$shows(j, i, c_x)$	Player j shows card $c_x \in Q \cap C_j$ to player i
$guess(i, M)$	Player i guesses that $C_0 = M$
$noguess(i)$	Player i makes no guess
$endturn(i)$	Player i ends his turn

Fluents: The following is a list of fluents and their informal descriptions. The evaluation of the fluents will depend on the situation s. Their truth values may change, according to successor state axioms.

Fluents Describing the Location of Cards:

$H(i, c_x, s)$: Player i holds card c_x.

$H(0, c_x, s)$: The mystery pile holds card c_x.

Fluents Describing Knowledge:

$Know(i, \phi, s)$: Player i knows ϕ.

$C(G, \phi, s)$: ϕ is common knowledge for all players in $G \subseteq P$.

$C(G, \phi, s)$ has the interpretation that, not only do all the players in G know that ϕ, but every player in G knows that the others know this, that they know that each knows this, and so on. There are well-known difficulties with axiomatizing a common knowledge operator, and well-known solutions as well (cf.[2]). We don't address these issues, but simply assume a language with a common knowledge modal operator.

Fluents Describing the State of the Game:

$In(i, s)$:   Player i has not yet been defeated due to a wrong guess.

$Question(Q, s)$: Question Q was the most recently asked question.

$Gameover(s)$:   The game is over.

Without going into the details, we may assume the presence of axioms that ensure that at most one query is asked per situation, that is, that $Question(Q, s)$ holds for at most one query Q.

Fluents Describing the Turn Order and Phases:

$Turn(i, s)$:   It is player i's turn.

$AnsTurn(j, s)$: It is player j's turn to answer the question.

As with queries, we assume the presence of axioms that ensure that it is exactly one player's turn and exactly one player's "answer turn".

Fluents Describing the Phases:

$AskPhase(s)$: It is the ask phase.

Similarly we have fluents for the answer phase ($AnsPhase(s)$), show phase ($ShowPhase(s)$), guess phase ($GuessPhase(s)$), and end phase ($EndPhase(s)$). Any situation s is in exactly one of these phases; we assume axioms that enforce this specification.

3.2   Axioms

The Initial Situation s_0: Different initial situations are possible depending on the initial random distribution of the cards. [8,5] modify the situation calculus to allow different initial situations by defining a predicate $K_0(s)$ that applies to situations that might be initial ones for all the agent knows. Our approach is different but equivalent: We use the single constant s_0 to refer to whatever initial situation results from dealing the cards, and represent the players' uncertainty by describing what fluents they do and do not know to hold in the initial situation. The following table of *initialization axioms* describes those fluent values common at s_0 in all games.

Initialization Axiom	Meaning
$\forall i.In(i, s_0)$	No player has been eliminated
$\forall Q.\neg Question(Q, s_0)$	No one has asked a question
$AskPhase(s_0),\ Turn(1, s_0)$	Player 1 is in the AskPhase of her turn
$\neg Gameover(s_0)$	The game is not over

The cards C are partitioned among the players and the mystery pile. The following axioms are the *partition axioms* for C. Here and elsewhere, free variables are understood to be universally quantified.

Exclusiveness $H(i, c_x, s_0) \rightarrow \forall j \neq i.\neg H(j, c_x, s_0)$.

    If player i holds card c_x, then no other player j (or the mystery pile) holds c_x. If the mystery pile holds card c_x, then c_x is not held by any player.

Exhaustiveness $\bigvee_{i=0}^{p} H(i, c_x, s_0)$.

    Every card is held by at least one player (or the mystery pile).

Set Size for Players(SSA)

    $\forall i \in \{1..p\}.\exists \Sigma.|\Sigma| = n \land (\forall x.H(i, c_x, s_0) \Leftrightarrow c_x \in \Sigma)$.

    For player i, there is a set of n cards containing just the cards held by i.

Set Size for the Mystery Pile

    $\exists \Sigma.|\Sigma| = m \land (\forall c_x.H(0, c_x, s_0) \Longleftrightarrow c_x \in \Sigma)$.

    There is a set of m cards containing just the cards in the mystery pile.

Preconditions: It is straightforward to define the preconditions of actions in terms of the fluents. We do not have space to give all the definitions in detail; instead, we specify the preconditions for the *asks* action as an example—the other preconditions are analogous. Player i can ask a question iff

1. it is her turn and
2. the game is in the AskPhase.

    Thus we have

$$Poss(asks(i, Q), s) \equiv Turn(i, s) \land AskPhase(s).$$

Successor State Axioms: We next describe the successor state axioms for the fluents. We begin with the *card holding fluent.*

The cards held by the players do not change over the course of the game.

$$H(i, c_x, do(a, s)) \equiv H(i, c_x, s) \qquad \text{for} \quad i \in \{0..p\}.$$

The fluent H is independent of the situation argument, and so we abbreviate $H(i, c_x, s)$ by $H(i, c_x)$. The fact that the card holdings are the same from situation to situation formally captures the fact that the world remains "static" as the game continues, so that players are not reasoning about changes in the world, but only about increasing information about a fixed but unknown constellation.

Next, we represent *turn taking.* Let $before(i) = i - 1$ if $i > 1$, and $before(1) = p$. Then we have the following axiom. A player's turn does not change until the previous player has taken the *endturn* action; the previous player is given by the *before* function.

$$Turn(i, do(a, s)) \equiv Turn(before(i), s) \wedge a = endturn((before(i))) \vee$$
$$Turn(i, s) \wedge \neg(a = endturn(i))$$

Other axioms describe the other fluents; we omit the details.

Axioms for Knowledge in MYST: We conceive of the players as perfect reasoners. Every player knows all tautologies and is able to derive all consequences of a set of formulas. As well, every player knows all the rules and axioms; see [2] for a full characterization. Although these assumptions do not do justice to the limitations of human and computational players, it makes the analysis of strategies mathematically easier.

Game theorists distinguish broad classes of games according to their epistemic structure. We locate our discussion of knowledge in MYST in these general game-theoretic terms; this will give an indication of the size of the class of multi-agent interactions that falls within our analysis. We shall give informal descriptions of the game-theoretic concepts, with a fairly precise rendering of the concept in terms of knowledge fluents for MYST. Game theory texts give precise definitions in game-theoretic terms; see for example [7].

A game has *complete information* if the rules of the game are common knowledge among the players. This is indeed the case for MYST; in the situation calculus, we can capture the complete information by stipulating that all the axioms describing the game structure is common knowledge in every situation. To illustrate, we have that $C(P, In(i, s_0), s_0)$ holds for $p \in \{1..p\}$ —it is common knowledge that at the beginning every player is in the game. A game has *perfect information* just in case every player knows the entire history of the game when it is his turn to move. Chess is a game of perfect information; MYST is *not.* For example, players don't know the entire initial distribution of cards, which is part of the history of the game. A game features *perfect recall* if no player forgets what she once knew or did. We express perfect recall by stipulating that once a player knows a fact in a situation, she continues to know it. Thus the general class of games for which something like our axiomatization should be adequate includes the class of games of complete, imperfect information with perfect recall.

The fluent $Know(i, \phi, s)$ expresses that player i knows that ϕ in situation s.[1] First, the players know which cards they hold in the initial situation s_0.

Axiom 1 (Knowledge Initialization) $Know(i, H(i, c_x, s_0), s_0)$.

Now for the knowledge successor state axioms. Since we assume that the players have perfect recall, we stipulate that knowledge once gained is not lost. Formally, let ϕ be a nonepistemic fluent that does not contain a $Know$ fluent. The case of special interest to the players is the fluent $H(i, c_x)$ (player i holds card x). The next axiom says that knowledge about ϕ is *permanent* in the sense that once gained, it is never lost later.

$$\forall i, s, s'.(s' \sqsubseteq s \land Know(i, \phi, s')) \rightarrow Know(i, \phi, s)$$
$$\forall i, s, s'.(s' \sqsubseteq s \land Know(i, \neg\phi, s')) \rightarrow Know(i, \neg\phi, s) \tag{1}$$

Inductively, it can be seen that knowing any of the knowledge of the form (1) is also permanent, and so on. Therefore Axiom (1) holds for the common knowledge fluent C as well as $Know$. Most of the reasoning about strategy rests on common knowledge between agents, that is, on the C fluent, rather than the separate knowledge of the agents expressed by the $Know$ fluent.

Players obtain new knowledge only when one player shows a card to another.

Axiom 2 $do(shows(j, i, c_x), s) \rightarrow C(\{i, j\}, do(shows(j, i, c_x), s), s)$.

Thus when player j shows a card to player i, it is common knowledge between them that this action took place. Note that it is then also common knowledge between i and j that player j holds card c_x. For one of the preconditions of $shows(j, i, c_x)$ is that j holds card c_x, and since the preconditions are common knowledge between the players, it is common knowledge that $(do(shows(j, i, c_x), s) \rightarrow holds(j, c_x, s)$.

When player j shows player i a card, it becomes common knowledge among the other players that j has at least one of the cards mentioned in i's query, although the other players won't necessarily know which card. Our axiomatization is powerful enough to represent the differential effect of showing cards on the various players, but for lack of space we do not go into the details here.

4   Deriving Knowledge in MYST

We state a result that follows from the definition of Clue within the axiomatized framework. This result describes what a player must know to prove the existence of a card in the mystery pile, and thus guides the derivation of winning strategies.

---

[1] See [8,5] for details. Suffice it to note that $Know$ is defined in first-order logic by explicitly axiomatising an (equivalent of an) accessibility relation [3].

Theorem 3. *Player i knows that a card c_x is in the mystery pile just in case i knows that none of the other players hold c_x. In symbols,*

$$Know(i, H(0, c_x), s) \equiv \forall j.Know(i, \neg H(j, c_x), s).$$

Furthermore, player i knows which cards are in the mystery pile just in case he knows which cards are not in the mystery pile. In symbols,

$$\forall c_x \in C_0.Know(i, H(0, c_x), s) \equiv \forall c_y \notin C_0.Know(i, \neg H(0, c_y), s).$$

The result follows more or less immediately from the partition axioms. The result establishes two subgoals for the main goal of determining that a card c_x is in the mystery pile: The first, sanctioned by the first part of the theorem, is to determine portions of the pile directly from "no" responses. The second, following the second part of the theorem, is to determine the locations of the $k - m$ cards outside the mystery pile from "yes" responses and then, by the set size axiom (SSA), deduce the m cards in the mystery pile. In either case, the set size axiom is crucial for drawing conclusions about the location of cards.

These observations are fairly obvious to a human analyzing the game. The point is that through our formalization of the game structure, a computational agent with theorem-proving capabilities can recognize these points and make use of them in planning queries.

In a multi-agent setting, optimal plans have an interactive and recursive structure, because an optimal plan for agent i must typically assume that agent j is following an optimal plan, which assumes that agent i is following an optimal plan ... Game-theoretic concepts that incorporate this recursive structure are the notion of Nash equilibrium and backward induction analysis (alpha-beta pruning) [7]. For restricted versions of MYST (for example, with two players only), we have determined the optimal backward induction strategies. Determining the Nash equilibria of MYST is an open question for future research.

We have also analysed aspects of the complexity of reasoning in MYST. Our analysis so far indicates that the computational complexity of this reasoning becomes intractable as the size of the game increases, but is quite manageable in relatively small spaces such as that of the original Clue game.

5   Conclusion

Clue and its variant MYST offer a number of challenges to a planning formalism for multi-agent interactions. We must represent the rules governing the interaction, uncertainty about the initial distribution of cards, the effects on knowledge and common knowledge of *show* actions, and assumptions about the reasoning of the agents, such as perfect recall. We showed that the epistemic version of the situation calculus, extended with a common knowledge operator, can represent all these aspects of the agents' interaction in a unified, natural and perspicuous manner. The formal representation permits agents to reason about each other's knowledge and their own, and to derive strategies for increasing their knowledge to win the game. Our results confirm the expectation that the situation calculus will be as useful for planning in multi-agent interactions in a game-theoretic setting as it has been for single-agent planning.

References

[1] B. Bart. Representations of and strategies for static information, noncooperative games with imperfect information. Master's thesis, Department of Computing Science, Simon Fraser University, 2000.

[2] R. Fagin, J. Y. Halpern, Y. Moses, and M. Vardi. *Reasoning about Knowledge*. The MIT Press, Cambridge, Massachusetts, 1995.

[3] G.E. Hughes and M.J. Cresswell. *A New Introduction to Modal Logic*. Routledge., London and New York, 1996.

[4] Y. Lespérance, H. Levesque, and R. Reiter. A situation calculus approach to modeling and programming agents. In M. Wooldridge and A. Rao, editors, *Foundations for Rational Agency*, pages 275–299. Kluwer, 1999.

[5] H.J. Levesque, F. Pirri, and R. Reiter. Foundations for the situation calculus. *Linköping Electronic Articles in Computer and Information Science*, 3(18), 1998.

[6] J. McCarthy and P.J. Hayes. Some philosophical problems from the standpoint of artificial intelligence. In D. Michie and B. Meltzer, editors, *Machine Intelligence 4*, pages 463–502. Edinburgh University Press, 1969.

[7] M. Osborne and A. Rubinstein. *A Course in Game Theory*. MIT Press, Cambridge, Mass., 1994.

[8] R. Scherl and H. Levesque. The frame problem and knowledge-producing actions. In *Proceedings of the Eleventh National Conference on Artificial Intelligence*, pages 698–695, Menlo Park, California, 1993. AAAI Press.

Learning about Constraints by Reflection

J. William Murdock and Ashok K. Goel

Georgia Institute of Technology
College of Computing
Atlanta, GA 30332-0280
`murdock,goel@cc.gatech.edu`

Abstract. A system's constraints characterizes what that system can do. However, a dynamic environment may require that a system alter its constraints. If feedback about a specific situation is available, a system may be able to adapt by reflecting on its own reasoning processes. Such reflection may be guided not only by explicit representation of the system's constraints but also by explicit representation of the functional role that those constraints play in the reasoning process. We present an operational computer program, SIRRINE2 which uses functional models of a system to reason about traits such as system constraints. We further describe an experiment with SIRRINE2 in the domain of meeting scheduling.

1 Introduction

All systems have constraints: restrictions on what things that system does. However, a dynamic environment may place demands on a system for which its constraints are not adequate. One potential use of machine learning is the modification of the constraints of a computer-based system to meet new requirements. It is often necessary (or at least useful) for a machine learning system to possess explicit representations of the concepts which it is learning about. Thus the goal of learning new constraints raises the question: how can a system represent and reason about its own constraints?

Consider, for example, the task of scheduling a weekly meeting among a group of users with fixed schedules. A system which performs this task is likely to have a wide variety of constraints, e.g., the set of times during which a meeting might be scheduled. If, however, a meeting scheduler has restrictions on the times that it can schedule meetings and those restrictions turn out to be invalid, it will have to modify those constraints.

One way that a system can determine that its constraints are inadequate is through feedback which is specific to a particular situation. A human user might not want to abstractly specify general constraints for all situations. Indeed such a user might not be able to completely define the constraints for a complex system. However, if a user can provide acceptable results for specific problems in which the meeting scheduler fails, it should be possible for that meeting scheduler to apply machine learning techniques to adapt to the desired functionality.

E. Stroulia and S. Matwin (Eds.): AI 2001, LNAI 2056, pp. 131–140, 2001.
© Springer-Verlag Berlin Heidelberg 2001

If an agent has a model of its own reasoning process, it may be possible to include constraints within that model, and thus represent not only what the constraint values are but also *what functional role they play* in the agent's reasoning. Under these circumstances, model-based diagnosis may be used to identify which constraints are having what effect on a specific output; the combination of this information with situation-specific feedback can thus enable adjustment of the constraints.

The SIRRINE2 system is an agent architecture for implementing agents with self-knowledge. The language for specifying agents in SIRRINE2 is the Task-Method-Knowledge (TMK) language which provides functional descriptions of reasoning processes. One aspect of these descriptions can be the explicit representation of agent's constraints and the functional role they play in the agent's behavior.

2   TMK Models

Agents in SIRRINE2 are modeled using the Task-Method-Knowledge (TMK) language. Variants and predecessors of this language have been used in a number of existing research projects such as AUTOGNOSTIC [5], ToRQUE [3], etc. A TMK model in SIRRINE2 is directly accessible to the evolutionary reasoning mechanism as declarative knowledge about the agent's processing. The work presented here extends the range of applications of TMK by focusing on its usefulness for the addition of new capabilities, rather than, for example, correcting failures in the original design, as is done in AUTOGNOSTIC.

In order to use a TMK model, the user also provides an initial *knowledge state* which the agent is to operate under (for example, a meeting scheduler might be provided with a list of schedules for the people in the meeting). During the execution of an agent, a *trace* of that execution is recorded. The trace and the model are both used by the portions of SIRRINE2 which perform evolution. These evolutionary reasoning mechanisms generate additional, intermediate knowledge. A particularly significant variety of intermediate knowledge is a *localization*, i.e., an identification of a potential candidate for modification by the system.

Processes in TMK are divided into *tasks* and *methods*. A task is a unit of computation which produces a specified result. A description of a task answers the question: *what* does this piece of computation do? A method is a unit of computation which produces a result in a specified manner. A description of a method answers the question: *how* does this piece of computation work? Task descriptions encode functional knowledge; the production of the specified result is the function of a computation. The representation of tasks in TMK includes all of the following information: :input and :output slots, which are lists of concepts which go in and out of the task; :given and :makes slots, which are logical expressions which must be true before and after the task executes; and some additional slots which refer to how that task is accomplished. The reference to how the task is accomplished may involve a simple table or piece of executable source code (in which case the task is said to be a *primitive task*) or it may involve a list of methods which accomplish the task.

Method descriptions encode the mechanism whereby a result is obtained. This mechanism is encoded as a collection of states and transitions, and the states refer to lower-level tasks which contribute to the effect of the method. Each non-primitive task is associated with a set of methods, any of which can potentially accomplish it under certain circumstances. Each method has a set of subtasks which combine to form the operation of the method as a whole. These subtasks, in turn, may have methods which accomplish them, and those methods may have further subtasks, etc. At the bottom level are the primitive tasks, which are not decomposed any further.

Descriptions of knowledge in TMK is done through the specification of *domain concepts*, i.e., kinds of knowledge and *task concepts*, i.e., elements of knowledge. For example, a domain concept in the domain of meeting schedulers would be a time slot. Two task concepts for this domain concept might be the time slot being considered for a meeting and a time slot in which some person is busy. TMK represents abstract knowledge about the kinds of constraints that exist in a domain as domain concepts. The connection of a particular set of constraints to a particular agent is then represented by a task concept.

In addition to the task concepts and domain concepts, modeling of knowledge in TMK includes information about relationships between knowledge elements. *Domain relations* are defined over domain concepts and abstractly describe the kinds of relationships that may exist over concepts in the domain. An example of a domain relation would be one that indicates that two time slots overlap. *Task relations* are defined over tasks concepts and involve a specific instantiation of a domain relation over some specific task concepts.

3   Evolution Algorithm

Below is a high-level overview of the algorithm which SIRRINE2 uses in the execution of an evolving agent.

```
function execute-agent(TMK-Model start-tmk, Knowledge-State start-ks)
      Trace tr
      Knowledge-State end-ks
      Knowledge-State desired-ks
      List of Localizations list-loc
      TMK-Model new-tmk
      (end-ks, tr) = execute-task(start-tmk, start-ks)
      If trace-outcome(tr) == success
        Return (end-ks, tr)
      desired-ks = acquire-feedback()
      list-loc = assign-credit(tr, start-tmk, end-ks, desired-ks)
      While list-loc != ()
        new-tmk = modify(start-tmk, first(list-loc))
        If new-tmk != start-tmk
          (end-ks, tr) = execute-agent(new-tmk, start-ks)
          Return (end-ks, tr)
        Else
          list-loc = rest(list-loc)
      Return (failure, tr)
```

The process begins with an initial TMK model and a starting knowledge state. For example, the execution of a meeting scheduling agent might begin with a description of that agent and a knowledge state which indicates a list of schedules to be considered. The primary task of the TMK model is then executed (this involves recursively selecting and invoking a method for that task, decomposing that method into subtasks, and then executing those subtasks). The task execution process returns both a trace and a resulting knowledge state (for example, a successful execution of a meeting scheduling agent might result in knowledge of a time slot for a meeting to be held). If the resulting trace indicates that the task has been successfully completed, the agent execution is successful. However, if the task was unsuccessful, some evolution of the agent is needed. At this point, the credit assignment process is used to identify possible causes for the agent's failure. The system then steps through the identified localizations one at a time until one of them allows the modification process to make a change to the TMK model. The modified TMK model thus describes a new, evolved agent. The original problem is then attempted again using this modified agent.

4   The Meeting Scheduler

One of the agents which have been modeled in SIRRINE2 is a relatively simple meeting scheduling system. The problem addressed by this meeting scheduler is finding a time slot for a weekly meeting of a given length for a group of people each with a given weekly schedule. For example, if three people want to meet, and one of them is always busy in the morning, and one is busy all day on Mondays, Wednesdays, and Fridays, and another is busy all day on Tuesday, the meeting scheduling agent will decide that the meetings should be held on Thursday afternoons.

Figure 1 presents the tasks and methods for the model of the meeting scheduling agent. The top level task of the agent is the task of scheduling a meeting. It has one method which it uses, that of enumerating a set of slots and checking those slots against the schedules. The slot-enumeration method sets up three subtasks: finding a first slot to try, checking that slot against the list of schedules, and finding a next slot to try. It also defines a set of transitions which order these subtasks; in particular, it starts with the find-first-slot subtask and then loops between the check-slot-schedules and find-next-slot until either the the check-slot-schedules task succeeds, (i.e., a slot has been found which satisfies all of the schedules) and thus the method has been successful or the find-next-slot task fails (i.e., there are no more slots to consider) and thus the method has been unsuccessful. Both the find-first-slot and find-next-slot tasks are primitive, i.e., they are directly implemented by simple procedures. The check-slot-schedules task, however, is implemented by the schedule-enumeration method. This method steps through each individual schedule in the list of schedules and checks the proposed slot against each of them until a conflict is determined or all of the schedules have been checked.

In addition to the tasks and methods illustrated in Figure 1, the TMK model of the meeting scheduler also contains explicit representations of the knowledge

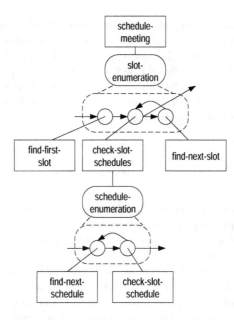

Fig. 1. The tasks and methods of a simple meeting scheduling agent. Rectangular boxes represent tasks; round boxes represent methods. The circle-and-arrow diagrams within the round dotted boxes represent the control portion of the methods, i.e., the transitions and their references to the subtasks.

contained by the meeting scheduler. The meeting scheduling agent contains eight domain concepts:

- length: A length of time, represented as a number of minutes
- day: A day of the week, e.g. Thursday
- time-of-Day: A time of the day, e.g. 2:00 PM
- time: A moment in time, represented by a combination of the day and time-of-day domain concepts, e.g., Thursday at 2:00 PM
- time-slot: An interval in time, containing two times: a start time and an end time, e.g. Thursday at 2:00 PM until Thursday at 3:00 PM
- schedule: A list of time-slots indicating when an individual is busy
- schedule-list: A list of schedules
- time-constraints: A list of time-slots indicating when meetings can be held, typically Monday through Friday from 9:00 AM to 5:00 PM

A description of a task in TMK explicitly refers to task concepts which describe the task's inputs and outputs. These task concepts explicitly refer to the domain concept of which the designated input or output should be an instance. For example, the schedule-meeting task has as its output a time slot for which a meeting should be held; this meeting time slot is a task concept which refers to the general time-slot domain concept.

The time-constraints domain concept is an example of an explicit representation of an agent's constraints. The meeting scheduler has one task concept for the time-constraints domain concept. This task concept, slot-generation-constraints, acts as an input to both the find-first-slot and find-next-slot tasks, constraining what kind of time slots these tasks can generate. The slot-generation-constraints task concept illustrates the crucial role that task concepts play in the integration of TMK models; it serves as the link between the find-first-slot and find-next-slot tasks which are influenced by the constraints, and the time-constraints domain concept which models the constraints.

5   Experiment

We describe here a brief experiment which illustrates the behavior of SIRRINE2 in a constraint evolution problem. Some time ago, our research group was faced with the problem of scheduling a weekly meeting to discuss technical issues. Our goal was to hold a 90 minute meeting. One member of the group sent out email asking what times people would be available for such a meeting. The members of the group sent back a list of times during which they were busy.

In order to conduct an experiment with our meeting scheduling agent, we decided to run the system on this data. The schedules were typed into the meeting scheduler. The scheduler considered a long sequence of 90 minute time slots, checking each one against the schedules of the people in the group. Every slot that it considered conflicted with at least one schedule; consequently, the meeting scheduler failed to generate a time for the meeting. Ultimately, it was decided (by the head of the group) that the meeting would be held on Tuesdays from 4:30 to 6:00 PM, i.e., the assumption that meetings must be held during standard business hours was violated. At this time, we provided SIRRINE2 feedback informing it of the time that was selected. At this point, the system was able to do some self-adaptation so that it would have generated this answer in the first place.

There are many possible changes that can be made which would have lead to this result. The meeting scheduler could be changed to always schedule meetings on Tuesdays 4:30 to 6:00 PM. Alternatively, it could be made to schedule meetings on Tuesdays 4:30 to 6:00 PM only when it receives exactly the same set of schedules as it did in the experiment and to simply use its existing mechanisms in all other cases. A reasonable compromise would be to allow meetings to generally be scheduled until 6:00 PM. However, the current model of the meeting scheduling domain does not provide sufficient information to identify a reasonable compromise. Consequently, a simpler change was made in which the Tuesdays 4:30 to 6:00 slot is suggested whenever a 90 minute time slot is requested and no other time is available.

During this experiment, the meeting scheduler went through the following stages:

Execution: The meeting scheduler runs and attempts to solve the problem as specified. During execution, a trace of reasoning is generated. For this problem, the agent fails, because it is unable to find a slot which fits into all of the schedules indicated.

Feedback Acquisition: Information is provided by the user which indicates that the slot which should have been selected is Tuesdays from 4:30 to 6:00. This fact is provided in the form of a desired output knowledge state.

Credit Assignment: If the meeting scheduler fails, as it does in the example, SIRRINE2 attempts to identify a particular procedural element (task or method) which may be responsible for the failure. This process returns a list of possible localizations of failure since there may be many possible causes for the observed result. The element of particular interest in this example is the find-next-slot task. This task should have produced a time slot but, in the final iteration of the system, didn't; because SIRRINE2 was given a time slot as feedback, it posits that the failure of the system may be a result of this task not producing that time slot. Note that this step is the one which critically depends on the presence of explicit constraint knowledge; the assignment of credit for the find-next-slot uses the :input slot of that task to determine that the slot-generation-constraints task concept influences its results.

Modification: Given a particular failure localization, the modification mechanism is intended to make a change to the system which corrects the identified fault. Figure 2 illustrates the revised meeting scheduler. The primitive find-next-slot task is modified to be a non-primitive task with two methods: find-next-slot-base-method simply invokes the existing primitive for finding slots, and find-next-slot-alternate-method always produces the produces the Tuesdays from 4:30 to 6:00 slot. The :given slot for the alternate method indicates that it is to be run if and only if a 90 minute time slot is requested under knowledge conditions similar to the ones found here. Similarity, in this situation, is defined by the :input slot of the task, i.e., the alternate method is chosen whenever the values of the task concepts specified in the :input slot exactly match their values in the earlier execution. The redesign strategy presented here is one example of a way to expand upon a set of constraints: by providing an alternative functional element with different constraints and establishing appropriate conditions for selecting that elements, the overall constraints of the model are expanded.

Execution: Finally, the meeting scheduler is run again with the same set of schedules. During this execution, the original find-next-slot primitive is run repeatedly until no other time is available and then the new primitive is run. Thus the scheduler correctly finds the Tuesdays from 4:30 to 6:00 slot, confirms that it does fit the schedules presented, and then terminates successfully.

Note that a specific result of this experiment is that learning is enabled by the explicit representation of the constraints, *combined* with the connection between this representation and the functional descriptions of the computational units; the task concepts in the TMK models provide the integration of constraint representation and that representation's functional role. The learning of new constraints here takes place with only a single trial; one problem is presented and one piece of feedback is received. Furthermore, it is done without any direct mapping from constraint knowledge to final results; the model simply indicates that the constraints data structure affects the find-first-slot and find-next-slot tasks. Credit assignment over the model and an execution trace is needed to

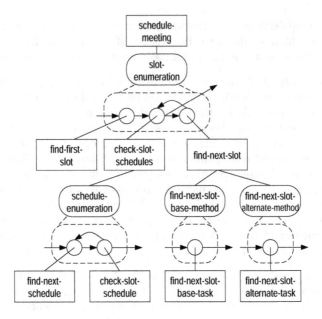

Fig. 2. The revised meeting scheduling agent in which the find-next-slot task has been altered.

determine how the constraints affected the results during the execution. The modification made is guided by this credit assignment and leads to an enhanced system whose constraints are consistent with the feedback provided by the user.

6   Discussion

Meeting scheduling is one member of the broad class of scheduling problems. The issue of learning new constraints seems particularly applicable to scheduling problems because the nature of many of the constraints is reasonably well defined and understood: the goal is to produce a schedule for one or more actions, and the constraints are those things that define what actions can potentially be taken and when. The CAP system [1] explores one approach to the incremental enhancement of a meeting scheduling agent: the system's autonomous actions (in this case, suggesting default values for meeting parameters such as time and location) are treated as classification problems. A set of inductive machine-learning mechanisms are available in this system to classify situations in terms of the desired action to take (i.e, the desired default value to suggest). The machine-learning algorithms used in CAP are very effective at forming useful generalizations over large data sets and require very little explicit domain knowledge. Unlike the SIRRINE2 approach, there is no need to provide a high-level description of the overall behavior of the system; each individual decision point acts as an independent classification problem and receives its own direct feedback. It is not clear, however, how well this approach generalizes to situations in which the feedback available has less quantity or less direct connection to the actual decision made.

In [4] decisions are also treated as separate classification problems. This system involves different kinds of decisions (learning over interface actions rather than over parameter values) and has a different set of learning algorithms (including reinforcement learning). However, this system, like CAP, does not possess an explicit description of the relationships between the elements of the system and thus is not able to reason across these elements except in regards to tendencies over very many examples. As in CAP, feedback comes in the form of relatively non-intrusive observations of actual user actions, which makes it feasible to collect large volumes of data. However, this approach may not be appropriate for problems such as the one found in our experiment in which the agent performs comparatively elaborate autonomous reasoning, and only very little information is provided by the user during the agent's execution.

Model-based reflection, embodied in SIRRINE2 and related systems, is a mechanism for developing flexible intelligent agents. One significant alternative to this approach involves automatically combining agent operations using one of the many available planning systems [2,6]. The planning approach is a very appealing one because it does not require a designer at all; a user simply describes the primitive operations available in a domain (similar to primitive tasks in TMK) and some goal (similar to a top level task in TMK), and the planning system combines these operations into a plan for achieving that goal. Also, the planning system does not require as inputs all of the intermediate levels of methods and tasks between the overall task and the primitive operations. Furthermore, a planning system is almost infinitely flexible for a given set of operations; the system has *no* preconceived notions of how operations could be combined and thus can provide a completely new sequence of actions for any new input.

There is, however, a key difference between primitive tasks in TMK and operators in a typical planning system. The :given and :makes slots which describe the known properties of the inputs and outputs of the primitive can be significantly underspecified. This makes it possible for some TMK primitives to be much more complex, coarser grained entities than a planning operator can be. Furthermore, the planning system which combines fine-grained planning operators may be prohibitively slow since it has so much information to reason about. The fact that TMK agents must be designed in advance is a limitation of the method in that it is a strong knowledge requirement, but it is also a benefit in that interpreting a predesigned combination of actions is generally much more efficient that constructing a combination of actions during execution.

Domains which are much more complex then they are dynamic are likely to be well served by hard-coded software agents which avoid the need for an explicit model of the domain altogether. Domains which are much more dynamic than they are complex may be relatively easy to encode in a planning system which can provide virtually unlimited flexibility. Model-based reflection seems best suited to domains which present a balance of complexity and dynamics. SIR-RINE2 has been tested on a variety of domains in addition to meeting scheduling. These domains include web browsing, bookkeeping, and conceptual design. All of these domains frequently require consistent, repetitive behavior but occasionally make unpredictable demands which require variations on that behavior. By using models of processes and adapting them as needed, SIRRINE2 is able to efficiently handle routine situations *and* effectively react to new challenges.

Acknowledgments. Effort sponsored by the Defense Advanced Research Projects Agency, and the United States Air Force Research Laboratory, Air Force Materiel Command, USAF, under agreement number F30602-96-2-0229. The U.S. Government is authorized to reproduce and distribute reprints for governmental purposes notwithstanding any copyright annotation thereon. The views and conclusions contained herein are those of the authors and should not be interpreted as necessarily representing the official policies or endorsements, either expressed or implied, of the Defense Advanced Research Projects Agency, Air Force Research Laboratory, or the U.S. Government.

References

[1] Lisa Dent, Jesus Boticario, Tom Mitchell, David Sabowski, and John McDermott. A personal learning apprentice. In William Swartout, editor, *Proceedings of the 10th National Conference on Artificial Intelligence - AAAI-92*, pages 96–103, San Jose, CA, July 1992. MIT Press.

[2] R. E. Fikes and N. J. Nilsson. STRIPS: a new approach to the application of theorem proving to problem solving. *Artificial Intelligence*, 2(3–4):189–208, 1971.

[3] Todd Griffith and J. William Murdock. The role of reflection in scientific exploration. In *Proceedings of the Twentieth Annual Conference of the Cognitive Science Society*, 1998.

[4] Pattie Maes and Robyn Kozierok. Learning interface agents. In *Proceedings of the 11th National Conference on Artificial Intelligence - AAAI-93*, pages 459–464, Menlo Park, CA, USA, July 1993. AAAI Press.

[5] Eleni Stroulia and Ashok K. Goel. A model-based approach to blame assignment: Revising the reasoning steps of problem solvers. In *Proceedings of the National Conference on Artificial Intelligence - AAAI-96*, Portland, Oregon, August 1996.

[6] D. E. Wilkins. Can AI planners solve practical problems? *Computational Intelligence*, 6(4):232–246, 1990.

Learning Bayesian Belief Network Classifiers: Algorithms and System

Jie Cheng[1] and Russell Greiner[2]

[1]Global Analytics, Canadian Imperial Bank of Commerce,
Toronto, Ontario, Canada M5J 2S8
Jie.Cheng@CIBC.ca
[2]Department of Computing Science, University of Alberta
Edmonton, Alberta, Canada T6G 2H1
Greiner@cs.UAlberta.ca

Abstract. This paper investigates the methods for learning predictive classifiers based on Bayesian belief networks (BN) – primarily unrestricted Bayesian networks and Bayesian multi-nets. We present our algorithms for learning these classifiers, and discuss how these methods address the overfitting problem and provide a natural method for feature subset selection. Using a set of standard classification problems, we empirically evaluate the performance of various BN-based classifiers. The results show that the proposed BN and Bayes multi-net classifiers are competitive with (or superior to) the best known classifiers, based on both BN and other formalisms; and that the computational time for learning and using these classifiers is relatively small. These results argue that BN-based classifiers deserve more attention in the data mining community.

1 Introduction

Classification is the task of identifying the class labels for instances based on a set of features (attributes). Learning accurate classifiers from pre-classified data is a very active research topic in machine learning and data mining. In the past two decades, many algorithms have been developed for learning decision-tree and neural-network classifiers. While Bayesian networks (BNs) [22] are powerful tools for knowledge representation and inference under conditions of uncertainty, they were not considered as classifiers until the discovery that Naïve-Bayes, a very simple kind of BNs that assumes the attributes are independent given the class node, are surprisingly effective [17].

This paper further explores this role of BNs. Section 2 provides the framework of our research, introducing Bayesian networks and Bayesian network learning and then briefly describing five classes of BNs. Section 3 describes our methods for learning unrestricted BNs. It also describes our approaches to avoiding overfitting and to selecting feature subsets. Section 4 presents and analyzes our experimental results over a standard set of learning problems obtained from the UCI machine learning repository.

---

[1] Previous work done at the University of Alberta.

E. Stroulia and S. Matwin (Eds.): AI 2001, LNAI 2056, pp. 141-151, 2001.

2 Framework

2.1 Bayesian Networks

A Bayesian network $B = \langle N, A, \Theta \rangle$ is a directed acyclic graph (DAG) $\langle N, A \rangle$ where each node $n \in N$ represents a domain variable (eg, a dataset attribute), and each arc $a \in A$ between nodes represents a probabilistic dependency, quantified using a conditional probability distribution (CP table) $\theta_i \in \Theta$ for each node n_i (see [22]). A BN can be used to compute the conditional probability of one node, given values assigned to the other nodes; hence, a BN can be used as a classifier that gives the *posterior probability distribution* of the class node given the values of other attributes. A major advantage of BNs over many other types of predictive models, such as neural networks, is that the Bayesian network structure explicitly represents the inter-relationships among the dataset attributes (Fig. 7). Human experts can easily understand the network structures and if necessary modify them to obtain better predictive models. By adding decision nodes and utility nodes, BN models can also be extended to *decision networks* for decision analysis [20].

Applying Bayesian network techniques to classification involves two sub-tasks: BN learning (training) to get a model and BN inference to classify instances. In Section 4, we will demonstrate that learning BN models can be very efficient. As for Bayesian network inference, although it is NP-hard in general [7], it reduces to simple multiplication in our classification context, when all the values of the dataset attributes are known.

2.2 Learning Bayesian Networks

The two major tasks in learning a BN are: learning the graphical structure, and then learning the parameters (CP table entries) for that structure. As it is trivial to learn the parameters for a given structure that are optimal for a given corpus of complete data – simply use the empirical conditional frequencies from the data [8] – we will focus on learning the BN structure.

There are two ways to view a BN, each suggesting a particular approach to learning. First, a BN is a structure that encodes the joint distribution of the attributes. This suggests that the best BN is the one that best fits the data, and leads to the *scoring-based* learning algorithms, which seek a structure that maximizes the Bayesian, MDL or Kullback-Leibler (KL) entropy scoring function [13][8].

Second, the BN structure encodes a group of conditional independence relationships among the nodes, according to the concept of *d-separation* [22]. This suggests learning the BN structure by identifying the conditional independence relationships among the nodes. These algorithms are referred as *CI-based* algorithms or constraint-based algorithms [23][1].

Friedman *et al.* [10] show theoretically that the general scoring-based methods may result in poor *classifiers* since a good classifier maximizes a different function – *viz.*, classification accuracy. Greiner *et al.* [12] reach the same conclusion, albeit via a different analysis. Moreover, the scoring-based methods are often less efficient in practice. This paper demonstrates that the CI-based learning algorithms can effectively learn BN *classifiers*.

2.3 Bayesian Network Classifiers

We will consider the following five classes of BN classifiers: Naïve-Bayes, Tree augmented Naïve-Bayes (TANs), Bayesian network augmented Naïve-Bayes (BANs), Bayesian multi-nets and general Bayesian networks (GBNs).

Naïve-Bayes. A Naïve-Bayes BN, as discussed in [9], is a simple structure that has the class node as the parent node of all other nodes (see Fig. 1.a). No other connections are allowed in a Naïve-Bayes structure.

Naïve-Bayes has been used as an effective classifier for many years. As Naïve-Bayes assumes that all the features are independent of each other, these BN-based classifiers are easy to construct, as no *structure* learning procedure is required. Although this independence assumption is obviously problematic, Naïve-Bayes has surprisingly outperformed many sophisticated classifiers over a large number of datasets, especially where the features are not strongly correlated [17].

In recent years, a lot of effort has focused on improving Naïve-Bayesian classifiers, following two general approaches: selecting feature subset [18][14][21] and relaxing independence assumptions [16][10]. Below we introduce BN models that extend Naïve-Bayes in the second fashion, by allowing dependencies among the features.

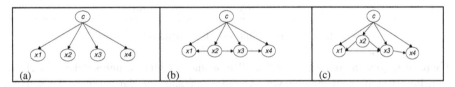

Fig. 1. (a) Naïve-Bayes. (b) Tree Augmented Naïve-Bayes. (c) BN Augmented Naïve-Bayes.

Tree Augmented Naïve-Bayes (TAN). TAN classifiers extend Naïve-Bayes by allowing the attributes to form a tree – cf, Fig. 1.b: here c is the class node, and the features x_1, x_2, x_3, x_4, without their respective arcs from c, form a tree. Learning such structures can be easily achieved by using a variation of the Chow-Liu [6] algorithm. The performance of TAN classifiers is studied in [10][5].

BN Augmented Naïve-Bayes (BAN). BAN classifiers extend TAN classifiers by allowing the attributes to form an arbitrary graph, rather than just a tree [10] – see Fig. 1.c. Learning such structures is less efficient. Friedman *et al.* [10] presents a minimum description length scoring method for learning BAN. Cheng and Greiner [5] study a different algorithm based on conditional independence (CI) tests. Both papers also investigate the performance of BAN classifiers.

Bayesian Multi-net. Bayesian Multi-nets were first introduced in [11] and then studied in [10] as a type of classifiers. A Bayesian multi-net is composed of the prior probability distribution of the class node and a *set* of local networks, each corresponding to a value that the class node can take (see Fig. 2.a). Bayesian multi-nets can be viewed as a generalization of BANs. A BAN forces the relations among the features to be the same for all the values that the class node takes; by contrast a Bayesian multi-net allows the relations among the features to be different – i.e., for different values the class node takes, the features can form different local networks with different structures. In a sense, the class node can be also viewed as a parent of all the feature nodes since each local network is associated with a value of the class node. Note that these multi-net structures are strictly more expressive than Naïve-Bayes, TAN or BAN structures. To motivate this, consider the tasks in pattern recognition – different patterns may have different relationships among features.

As the multi-net structure imposes no restrictions on the relationships among the attributes, they are a kind of *unrestricted* BN classifier. However, while multi-net is more general than BAN, it is often less complex than BAN since some of the local networks can be simpler than others, while BAN needs to have a complex structure in order to express all the relationships among the features.

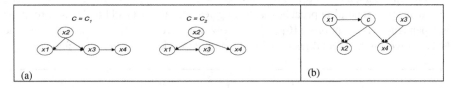

(a)   (b)

Fig. 2. (a) Bayesian Multi-net. (b) General Bayesian net.

General Bayesian Network (GBN). GBN is another kind of unrestricted BN classifier, however, of a different flavor. A common feature of Naïve Bayes, TAN, BAN and multi-net is that the class node is treated as a special node – the parent of all the features. However, GBN treats the class nodes as an ordinary node (see Fig. 2.b), it is not necessary a parent of all the feature nodes. The learning methods and the performance of GBN for classification are studied in [10][5].

Comparison: To compare GBNs and Bayesian multi-nets, observe that GBNs assume that there is a single probabilistic dependency structure for the entire dataset; by contrast, multi-nets allow different probabilistic dependencies for different values of the class node. This suggests that GBN classifiers should work better when there is a single underlying model of the dataset and multi-net classifier should work better when the underlying relationships among the features are very different for different classes.

2.4 Motivations

In our earlier work [5], we studied the CI-based methods for learning GBN and BAN and showed that our CI-based methods appear not to suffer from the drawbacks of scoring-based methods (see Section 2.2). With a wrapper algorithm (see Section 3.2), these more general types of BN classifiers do work well. This paper continues our research in BN classifiers in the following aspects.

1. Our earlier work suggested that the more general forms of BN classifiers can capture the relationships among the features better and therefore make more accurate predictive models. However, it did not consider an important class of BN classifiers – Bayesian multi-net. Here we evaluate its learning efficiency and performance for classification.
2. A node ordering specifies an order of the nodes, with the understanding no node can be an ancestor of a node that appears earlier in the order. Our earlier work assumed this node ordering was given. Here we investigate the effect of such orderings by learning the BN classifiers with and without node orderings.
3. The learned GBN structure immediately identifies the relevant feature subset – the *Markov blanket* (Section 3.3) around the class node. Here we study the effectiveness of such feature subsets by using it to simplify Bayesian multi-net classifiers.

3 Learning Unrestricted BN Classifiers

This section presents algorithms for learning general Bayesian networks and Bayesian multi-nets. It also presents the wrapper algorithm that can wrap around these two learners to help find good settings for the "independence test threshold", and an algorithm for learning multi-nets using feature subsets.

3.1 The Learning Algorithms for Multi-nets and GBNs

Fig. 3 and Fig. 4 sketches the algorithms for learning multi-nets and GBNs. They each use the CBL_1 algorithms, which are general purpose BN-learning algorithms: one for the case when node ordering is given (the CBL_1 algorithm [1]); the other for the case when node ordering is not given (the CBL_2 algorithm [2]).

Both CBL_1 and CBL_2 are CI-based algorithms that use information theory for dependency analysis. CBL_1 requires $O(N^2)$ mutual information tests to learn a general BN over N attributes, and CBL_2 requires $O(N^5)$ mutual information tests. The efficiency of these algorithms is achieved by a three-phase BN learning algorithm: *drafting*, which is essentially the Chow-Liu [6] tree construction algorithm; *thickening*, which adds edges to the draft; and *thinning*, which removes unnecessary edges. As these learners use a finite set of samples, they need to use some threshold $\tau \in \Re^+$ when determining whether some statistical condition is met (see below). Modulo this issue, these algorithms are guaranteed to learn the optimal structure, when the underlying model of the data satisfies certain benign assumptions. For the correctness proof, complexity analysis and other detailed information, please refer to [1][2].

```
MNᵢ(S: training set;   F: feature set; [O: Node Ordering]):
        returns Bayesian Multi-net
1. Partition the training set into subsets Sᵢ, by the values of the
   class node.
2. For each training subset Sᵢ,
   Call BN-structure learning algorithm CBLᵢ on  S, F  (and O if
   i=1)
   Compute the parameters (using observed frequencies) of each local
   network.
3. Estimate the prior probability distribution of the class node.
```

Fig. 3. The MNᵢ Algorithm.

```
GBNᵢ(S: training set;  F: feature set; [O: Node Ordering]):
        returns general BN
1. Call BN-structure learning algorithm CBLᵢ on  S, F  (and O if
   i=1)
2. Find the Markov blanket  B ⊆ F  of the class node.
3. Delete all the nodes that are outside the Markov blanket.
4. Compute the parameters (using observed frequencies)
```

Fig. 4. The GBNᵢ Algorithm.

3.2   The Wrapper Algorithm

Unlike Naïve-Bayes and TAN learners, there is no restriction on the structures that the GBN learner and multi-net learner can learn. Therefore, it is possible that a BN model will *overfit* – ie, fit the training set too closely instead of generalizing, and so will not perform well on data outside the training samples. In [5], we proposed a wrapper algorithm to determine the best setting for the threshold τ; we observed that this increased the prediction accuracy up to 20% in our experiments. Suppose X-learner is a learning algorithm for classifier X, the wrapper algorithm can wrap around X-learner in the following way.

```
Wrapper (X-learner: LearningAlgorithm, D: Data): returns Classifier
1. Partition the input training set D = T ∪ H  into internal train-
   ing set T and internal holdout set H.
2. Call X-learner on the internal training set T   m times, each
   time using a different threshold setting τᵢ; this produces a set
   of m classifiers { BNᵢ }
3. Select a classifier BN* = ⟨N, A*, θ*⟩ ∈ {BNᵢ} that performs best on
   the holdout set H.
4. Keep this classifier's structure ⟨N, A*⟩ and re-learn the parame-
   ters (conditional probability tables) Θ′ using the whole train-
   ing set D.
5. Output this new classifier.
```

Fig. 5. The wrapper algorithm.

When the training set is not large enough, k-fold cross validation should be used to evaluate the performance of each classifier. This wrapper algorithm is fairly efficient since it can reuse all the mutual information tests. Note that mutual information tests often take more than 95% of the running time of the BN learning process [2].

3.3 Feature Subset Selection

Overfitting often happens when there are too many "parameters", for a given quantity of data. Here, this can happen if there are too many nodes, and hence too many CPtable entries. One way to reduce the chance of this happening is by considering only a subset of the features; this is called "feature selection", and is an active research topic in data mining. For example, Langley and Sage [18] use forward selection to find a good subset of attributes; Kohavi and John [15] use best-first search, based on accuracy estimates, to find a subset of attributes.

A byproduct of GBN learning is that we can get a set of features that form the Markov blanket of the class node. The *Markov blanket* of a node n is the union of n's parents, n's children, and the parents of n's children. This subset of nodes "shields" n from being affected by any node outside the blanket. When using a BN classifier on complete data, the Markov blanket of the class node forms a natural feature selection, as all features outside the Markov blanket can be safely deleted from the BN. This can often produce a much smaller BN without compromising the classification accuracy.

To examine the effectiveness of such feature subset, we use it to simplify the multi-net learner. The algorithm is described below.

```
MN-FSᵢ(S: training set;  F: feature set; [O: Node Ordering]):
       returns Bayesian Multi-net
1. Call Wrapper( GBNᵢ ) with the training set S and all features
   F.
2. Get the Markov blanket B ⊆ N of the class node.
3. Call Wrapper (MNᵢ) with the training set S  and the feature
   subset B.
4. Output the multi-net classifier.
```

Fig. 6. The MN-FS₍ᵢ₎ algorithm.

4   Empirical Study

4.1 Methodology

Our experiments involved five datasets downloaded from the UCI machine learning repository [19] – see Table 1. When choosing the datasets, we selected datasets with large numbers of cases, to allow us to measure the learning and classification efficiency. We also preferred datasets that have few or no continuous features, to avoid information loss in discretization and to be able to compare the learning accuracy with other algorithms fairly. When we needed to discretize the continuous features, we used the discretization utility of MLC++ [14] on the default setting.

Table 1. Datasets used in the experiments.

Dataset	Attributes.	Classes	Instances	
			Train	Test
Adult	13	2	32561	16281
Nursery	8	5	8640	4320
Mushroom	22	2	5416	2708
Chess	36	2	2130	1066
DNA	60	3	2000	1186

The experiments were carried out using our Bayesian Network PowerPredictor 1.0 [4]. For each data set, we learned six BN classifiers: Wrapper(GBN) = W-GBN, Wrapper(GBN with ordering) = W-GBN-O, Wrapper(multi-net) = W-MN, Wrapper(multi-net with ordering) = W-MN-O, Wrapper(multi-net with feature selection) = W-MN-FS and Wrapper(multi-net with feature selection with ordering) = W-MN-FS-O. The ordering for the Chess data set is the reversed order of the features that appear in the data set since it is more reasonable, the ordering we use for other data sets are simply the order of the features that appear in the data set. For the GBN learner, we also assume that the class node it is a root node in the network.

The classification process is also performed using BN PowerPredictor. The classification of each case in the test set is done by choosing, as class label, the value of class variable that has the highest posterior probability, given the instantiations of the feature nodes. The classification accuracy is defined as the percentage of correct predictions on the test sets (i.e., using a 0-1 loss function).

The experiments were performed using a Pentium II 300 MHz PC with 128MB of RAM, running MS-Windows NT 4.0.

4.2 Results

Table 2 provides the prediction accuracy and standard deviation of each classifier. We ordered the datasets by their training sets from large to small. The best results of each dataset are emphasized using a boldfaced font. Table 2 also gives the best results reported in the literature on these data sets (as far as we know). To get an idea of the structure of a learned BN classifier, please see Figure 7.

From Table 2 we can see that all six unrestricted BN classifiers work quite well. Bayesian multi-net works better on Nursery and Mushroom; while GBN works better on DNA. The two types of classifiers have similar performance on Adult and Chess. This suggest that some data sets are more suitable for multi-net classifiers while others are more suitable for GBN, depending on whether the underlying relationships among the features are different for different class node values.

We can also see that the feature ordering does not make much difference to the performance of the classifiers. We also tried to provide the BN learners with obviously wrong ordering. Its effect to the classifier's performance is very small. However, with wrong ordering, the classifiers tend to be more complex.

By comparing the performance of the multi-nets *without* feature selection to the multi-nets *with* feature selection, we can see that the difference is quite small. However, the multi-nets with feature selection are much simpler. By comparing the running time of learning these classifiers (see Table 3), we can see that multi-nets with feature selection can be learned faster.

Table 3 gives the total learning time of each BN classifier using the wrapper algorithm. Because the feature ordering makes little difference on the efficiency, we only give the running time of the learning procedure without the ordering. (In practice, CBL1 and CBL2 are both linear in the number of instances and appear $O(N^2)$ in the number of features N.) The table shows that all BN classifiers can be learned efficiently as the longest learning time is less than 25 minutes. Note that the running time for learning the multi-nets with feature selection includes the running time for learning GBN in the first step of the feature subset selection algorithm (see Section 3.3). In general, the wrapper algorithm is about 3 to 5 times slower than only using the learner alone, even though the wrapper algorithm usually tries 7 to 15 different models before it output the best performer.

Table 2. The results of unrestricted BN classifiers(The numbers in the parentheses are the number of selected features / total number of features).

	W-GBN	W-GBN-O	W-MN	W-MN-O	W-MN-FS	MN-FS-O	Bestre-ported
Adult	**86.33±0.53** (7/13)	85.88±0.53 (8/13)	84.83±0.55	85.54± 0.54	85.79±0.54 (7/13)	85.46 ±0.54 (8/13)	85.95
Nurs-ery	91.92±0.81 (8/8)	91.60±0.83 (8/8)	97.13±0.50	**97.31± 0.48**	Same as W-MN	Same as W-MN-O	N/A
Mush room	98.67±0.43 (7/22)	98.74±0.42 (5/22)	99.96±0.07	**100**	98.67±0.43 (7/22)	99.11 ±0.35 (5/22)	100
Chess	93.53±1.48 (11/36)	93.62±1.47 (11/36)	**96.44±1.11**	94.56 ±1.36	93.25±1.51 (11/36)	93.4 3±1.49 (11/36)	99.53 ±0.21
DNA	95.70±1.15 (14/60)	**96.63±1.03** (15/60)	94.10±1.34	93.51 ±1.40	95.36±1.20 (14/60)	95.70 ±1.15 (15/60)	96.12 ±0.6

Table 3. Running time (CPU seconds) of the classifier learning procedures.

	W-GBN	W-MN	W-MN-FS
Adult	1046	1466	1200
Nursery	54	79	N.A.
Mushroom	322	533	345
Chess	84	163	109
DNA	210	1000	266

In our experiments, we found that the classification process is also very efficient. PowerPredictor can perform 200 to over 1000 classifications per second depending on the complexity of the classifier.

5 Conclusion

In this paper, we studied two types of unrestricted BN classifiers – general BNs and Bayesian multi-nets. The results show that our CI-based BN-learning algorithms are very efficient, and the learned BN classifiers can give very good prediction accuracy.

This paper also presents an effective way for feature subset selection. As we illustrate in Figure 7, the BN classifiers are also very easy to understand for human being. By checking and modifying the learned BN predictive models, domain experts can study the relationships among the attributes and construct better BN predictive models.

Based on these results we believe that the improved types of BN classifiers, such as the ones shown here, should be used more often in real-world data mining applications.

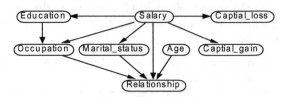

Fig. 7. The learned W-GBN classifier for "Adult" data set.

References

1. Cheng, J., Bell, D.A. and Liu, W. (1997a). An algorithm for Bayesian belief network construction from data. In *Proceedings of AI & STAT'97* (pp.83-90), Florida.
2. Cheng, J., Bell, D.A. and Liu, W. (1997b). Learning belief networks from data: An information theory based approach. In *Proceedings of ACM CIKM'97*.
3. Cheng, J. (1998). *PowerConstructor* System. http://www.cs.ualberta.ca/~jcheng/bnpc.htm.
4. Cheng, J. (2000). *PowerPredictor* System. http://www.cs.ualberta.ca/~jcheng/bnpp.htm.
5. Cheng, J., Greiner, R. (1999). Comparing Bayesian network classifiers. In *UAI-99*.
6. Chow, C.K. and Liu, C.N. (1968). Approximating discrete probability distributions with dependence trees. *IEEE Trans. on Information Theory*, 14 (pp. 462-467).
7. Cooper, G.F. (1990) Computational complexity of probabilistic inference using Bayesian belief networks, In *Artificial Intelligence*, 42 (pp. 393-405).
8. Cooper, G.F. and Herskovits, E. (1992). A Bayesian Method for the induction of probabilistic networks from data. *Machine Learning*, 9 (pp. 309-347).
9. Duda, R. and Hart, P. (1973). *Pattern classification and scene analysis*. John Wiley & Sons.
10. Friedman, N., Geiger, D. and Goldszmidt, M. (1997). Bayesian Network Classifiers. *Machine Learning*, 29, (pp. 131-161).
11. Geiger, D. and Heckerman, D. (1996). Knowledge representation and inference in similarity networks and Bayesian multinets. In *Artificial Intelligence* 82 (pp. 45-74).
12. Greiner, R. Grove, A. and Schuurmans, D. (1997). Learning Bayesian nets that perform well. In *UAI-97*.
13. Heckerman, D. (1995). A tutorial on learning Bayesian networks. *Technical Report MSR-TR-95-06*. Microsoft Research.
14. Kohavi, R., John, G., Long, R. Manley, D. and Pfleger, K. (1994). MLC++: A machine learning library in C++. In *Proceedings of Sixth International Conference on Tools with Artificial Intelligence*. IEEE Computer Society.
15. Kohavi, R., John G. (1997) Wrappers for Feature Subset Selection. In *Artificial Intelligence journal*, special issue on relevance, Vol. 97, No. 1-2 (pp. 273-324).
16. Kononenko, I. (1991). Semi-naïve Bayesian classifier. In Y. Kodratoff (Ed.), *Proceedings of sixth European working session on learning (pp.206-219)*. Springer-Verlag.
17. Langley, P., Iba, W. and Thompson, K. (1992). An analysis of Bayesian classifiers. In *Proceedings of AAAI-92* (pp. 223-228).
18. Langley, P. and Sage, S. (1994). Induction of Selective Bayesian Classifiers. In *UAI-94*.

19. Murphy, P.M. and Aha, D.W. (1995). UCI repository of machine learning databases. http://www.ics.uci.edu/~mlearn/MLRepository.html.

20. Neapolitan, R.E. (1990), *Probabilistic reasoning in expert systems: theory and algorithms*, John Wiley & Sons.

21. Pazzani, M.J. (1995). Searching for dependencies in Bayesian classifiers. In *AI & STAT'95*.

22. Pearl, J. (1988). *Probabilistic Reasoning in Intelligent Systems: networks of plausible inference*, Morgan Kaufmann.

23. Spirtes, P., Glymour, C. and Scheines, R. (1993). *Causation, Prediction, and Search*. http://hss.cmu.edu/html/departments/philosophy/TETRAD.BOOK/book.html.

Local Score Computation in Learning Belief Networks

Y. Xiang and J. Lee

Dept. of Computing and Information Science
University of Guelph, Guelph, Ontario, Canada N1G 2W1
{yxiang, lee}@snowhite.cis.uoguelph.ca
http://snowhite.cis.uoguelph.ca/faculty_info/yxiang/

Abstract. We propose an improved scoring metrics for learning belief networks driven by issues arising from learning in pseudo-independent domains. We identify a small subset of variables called a *crux*, which is sufficient to compute the incremental improvement of alternative belief network structures. We prove formally that such local computation, while improving efficiency, does not introduce any error to the evaluation of alternative structures.

Keywords: Knowledge discovery, data mining, machine learning, belief networks, uncertain reasoning.)

1 Introduction

Learning belief networks from data has been an active research area in recent years [2,7,4,15,3]. Successive graphical structures are evaluated with a scoring metrics until a stopping condition is met. As the task is NP-hard [1], a common method in selection the structure is the single-link lookahead, where successive structures adopted differ by a single link. It has been shown that a class of probabilistic models called *pseudo-independent* (PI) models cannot be learned by single-link search [14]. A more sophisticated method (multi-link lookahead) is proposed in [15] and is improved in [5] for learning decomposable Markov networks (DMNs) from data.

DMNs are less expressive than Bayesian networks (BNs). However, DMNs are the runtime representation of several algorithms for inference with BNs [8,6, 10], and can be the intermediate results for learning BNs. For example, learning PI models needs multi-link lookahead and the search space for DAGs is much larger than that of chordal graphs. Learning DMNs first can then restrict the search for DAGs to a much smaller space, improving the efficiency.

In this work, we focus on learning DMNs using the entropy score which is closely related to other scoring metrics [15] such as Bayesian [2], minimum description length (MDL) [7], and conditional independence [9,11]. The score of a DMN is defined as the entropy of the DMN computed from its joint probability distribution (jpd). Previous work [15,5,13] used entropy score as the sole control of both goodness-of-fit and complexity of the output structure. An increment

E. Stroulia and S. Matwin (Eds.): AI 2001, LNAI 2056, pp. 152–161, 2001.

threshold Δh of the entropy score is set by the user. Learning stops when no structure (allowed by the given lookahead search) can improve the score beyond Δh. The smaller the value of Δh, the better the goodness-of-fit of the output structure, and the more complex the structure is.

Such stopping control works fine with the single-link lookahead. However, an issue arises when multi-link lookahead is performed: It is possible at some point of learning that a best single link may produce a score improvement 0.0099 and get rejected since $\Delta h = 0.01$. On the other hand, a best double-link that produces a score improvement of 0.01 will be adopted. It can be argued that the double-link increases the complexity of the structure much more than it contributes to the goodness-of-fit. Hence if any link is to be added at all, a single link is a better choice than a double-link. However, using the entropy improvement as the sole stopping control, this issue cannot be resolved.

In this work, we address this issue by explicitly describing the model complexity in the score (a common approach in learning). We define a new score as

$$\Gamma(M) = \Gamma_1(M) + \alpha \, \Gamma_2(M) \, ,$$

where M is a DMN, $\Gamma_1(M)$ measures the goodness-of-fit of M, and $\Gamma_2(M)$ measures the complexity of M. The constant α is set by the user to trade goodness-of-fit with the complexity of the output DMN. Learning stops when no DMN M' can improve $\Gamma(M)$ for the current DMN M. Hence, threshold is no longer needed. The above issue will be resolved since the single link will improve $\Gamma(M)$ more than the double link.

In the rest of the paper, we propose how to compute the incremental change in $\Gamma(M)$ due to link addition by local computation using a small subset of variables called *crux*. We prove the correctness of the algorithms formally.

2   Background

Let $G = (V, E)$ be a graph, where V is a set of nodes and E a set of links. A graph is a *forest* if there are no more than one path between each pair of nodes. A forest is a *tree* if it is connected. A set X of nodes is *complete* if elements of X are pairwise adjacent. A maximal set of nodes that is complete is a *clique*. A path or cycle ρ has a *chord* if there is a link between two non-adjacent nodes in ρ. G is *chordal* if every cycle of length ≤ 4 has a chord.

A *cluster graph* is a triplet (V, Ω, S), where V is called a *generating* set, Ω is a set of nodes each of which is labeled by a nonempty subset of V and is called a *cluster*, S is a set of links each of which is labeled by the intersection of the two clusters connected and is called a *separator*. A cluster forest is a *junction forest* (JF) if the intersection of every pair of connected clusters is contained in every cluster on the path between them. Let $G = (V, E)$ be a chordal graph, Ω be the set of cliques of G, and F be a JF (V, Ω, S). We will call F a *corresponding* JF of G. Such a JF exists if and only if G is chordal.

A DMN is a triplet $M = (V, G, \mathcal{P})$, where V is a set of discrete variables in a problem domain, and $G = (V, E)$ is a chordal graph. $\mathcal{P}$ is a set of probability distributions one for each cluster defined as follows: Let F be a corresponding JF of G. Direct links of F such that each cluster has no more than one parent cluster. For each cluster C with a parent Q, associate C with $P(C|Q)$. The jpd of M is defined as $P(V) = \prod_C P(C|Q)$. Probabilistic conditional independence among variables in V is conveyed by node separation in G, and by separator separation in F. It has been shown [12] that G and F encode exactly the same dependence relations within V. Hence, we will switch between the two graphical views from time to time.

3   Local Computation for Measure of Goodness-of-Fit

The goodness-of-fit of a DMN M to an underlying (unknown) domain model can be measured by the K-L cross entropy between them. It has been shown [15] that to minimize the K-L cross entropy, it suffices to minimize the entropy of M which can be computed as

$$H_M(V) = \sum_C H(C) - \sum_S H(S) , \tag{1}$$

where C is a cluster in the corresponding JF and S is a separator. Hence we shall use the entropy of a DMN M as the measure of goodness-of-fit, denoted as $\Gamma_1(M) = H_M(V)$.

During learning, a large number of alternative DMN structures need to be evaluated using the score. Since most of the clusters and separators do not change between successive structures, it is inefficient to compute the entropy of all of them for each structure. It is much more efficient to identify a small set of clusters and separators that contribute to the incremental change of the score after a set of links has been added to the current structure. In the following, we study how these clusters and separators can be identified effectively.

First, we define the context in which the learning takes place: At each step of learning, a set of links L is added to the current structure G to obtain a supergraph G' of G. The cardinality $|L|$ depends on whether it is single-link lookahead ($|L| = 1$) or multi-link lookahead ($|L| > 1$). The initial G at the start of learning is an empty (chordal) graph. We require that at each step, G' is also a chordal graph and the endpoints ED of L are contained in a clique of G'. We shall call G' the *chordal supergraph* of G induced by L. We denote the corresponding JF of G' by F'.

4   The Notion of Crux

In this section, we identify a small subset of V called *crux* that are defined by the structural change due to adding links L to a chordal graph. We establish some properties of crux. In the next section, we show that the crux is a sufficient subset of variables necessary to compute the incremental change of of entropy.

Lemma 1 *Let G be a chordal graph and G' be a chordal supergraph of G induced by a set L of links. Then the clique that contains ED, the set of endpoints of L, is unique.*

Proof:

Suppose that two distinct cliques C and Q exist in G' that contain ED. Then there exist $c \in C$ and $q \in Q$ such that $c \notin Q$ and $q \notin C$. That is, $\{c, q\}$ is not a link in G' and hence not in G as well.

Let $\{x, y\}$ be any link in L. Since x, y and c are all in C, they must be complete in G'. Since $\{x, c\}$ and $\{y, c\}$ are not in L, they must be links in G. Similarly, $\{x, q\}$ and $\{y, q\}$ must be links in G. We have therefore found a cycle (x, c, y, q, x) in G and neither $\{x, y\}$ nor $\{c, q\}$ is a link in G: a chordless cycle. This contradicts that G is chordal.   □

Definition 2 *Let G be a chordal graph and G' be a chordal supergraph of G induced by a set L of links. Let C be the unique clique in G' that contains the endpoints of L. Let Q be any clique of G' such that $Q \cap C \neq \emptyset$ and Q is not a clique in G. Denote the set of all such cliques by Φ. Then the union of elements in Φ, namely, $\bigcup_{Q \in \Phi} Q$ is called the* **crux** *induced by G and L, and the set Φ is called the* **generating set** *of the crux.*

Note that the crux contains C. Note also that since each pair of cliques in a chordal graph is incomparable, given the crux R, its generating set Φ can be uniquely identified.

Figure 1 illustrates the concept of crux in different cases. In each box, the upper graphs are chordal graphs G and G' where dashed link(s) indicate the set L of links added. The lower graphs in each box depict the corresponding JFs where the dashed cluster(s) form the generating set Φ. For example, in (a) and (b), the generating set Φ contains only a single cluster which is the crux itself. In (c), however, Φ consists of $\{b, c, f\}$ and $\{c, e, f\}$ while the crux is $\{b, c, e, f\}$.

The following proposition says that each clique in Φ contains the endpoints of at least one link in L, and Φ is made of all such cliques.

Proposition 3 *Let G be a chordal graph and G' be a chordal supergraph of G induced by a set L of links. Let R be the crux induced by G and L and Φ be its generating set.*

1. *For each $Q \in \Phi$, there exists a link $\{x, y\} \in L$ such that $\{x, y\} \subset Q$.*
2. *For each clique Q in G', if there exists a link $\{x, y\} \in L$ such that $\{x, y\} \subset Q$, then $Q \in \Phi$.*

Proof:

(1) Suppose for $Q \in \Phi$, no such $\{x, y\}$ is contained in Q. Then Q is not a clique newly created or enlarged by the addition of L to G. That is, G is a clique in G: contradiction to $Q \in \Phi$.

(2) Let Q be a clique in G' such that the stated condition holds. The $Q \cap C \neq \emptyset$ and Q is not a clique in G. □

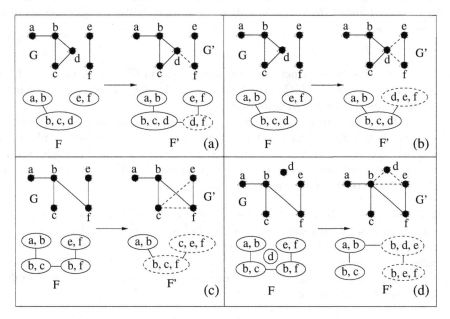

Fig. 1. Illustration of crux

The following proposition shows that the crux is in fact the union of all cliques newly formulated due to the addition of L. In the proposition, "\" is the set difference operator.

Proposition 4 *Let G be a chordal graph and G' be a chordal supergraph of G induced by a set L of links. Let Ω be the set of cliques in G, Ω' be the set of cliques in G', R be the crux induced by G and L, and Φ be the generating set of R. Then $\Phi = \Omega' \setminus \Omega$.*

Proof:

Each clique contained in R is in $\Omega' \setminus \Omega$ by the definition of crux. We only need to show that each $Q \in \Omega' \setminus \Omega$ is also contained in R, that is $Q \cap C \neq \emptyset$, where C is the unique clique in G' that contains endpoints ED of L. Each clique Q in G' that is created or is modified from cliques of G due to adding L must contain elements of ED, and hence $Q \cap C \neq \emptyset$.   □

Although Proposition 4 gives a much simplier definition of crux, Definition 2 allows more efficient computation of the crux. Based on Proposition 4, the crux can be obtained by computing $\Omega' \setminus \Omega$. The complexity is $O(|\Omega|^2)$ since $|\Omega'| \approx |\Omega|$. On the other hand, based on Definition 2, one pass through Ω' is needed to find C, another pass is needed to find cliques intersecting with C (assuming k such cliques are found), and additional k passes through Ω are needed to identify the newly created or enlarged cliques. The complexity is $O((k + 2) |\Omega|)$. The value of k is usually a very small integer. Hence for large problem domains, $k + 2$ is much smaller than $|\Omega|$. Since the crux needs be obtained for every structure to be evaluated, significant computational savings can be obtained if Definition 2 is followed.

The following proposition says that the generating set of the crux forms a subtree in F'.

Proposition 5 *Let G be a chordal graph and G' be a chordal supergraph of G induced by a set L of links. Let R be the crux induced by G and L and F' be the corresponding JF of G'. The generating set Φ of R forms a connected subtree in F'.*

Proof:

We prove by contradiction. Let C be the unique clique of G that contains endpoints ED of L. Suppose that members of Φ do not form a connected subtree in F'. Then there exists a cluster $Q \in \Phi$ and a cluster $Z \notin \Phi$ such that Z is on the path between C and Q in F'. This implies $Z \supset C \cap Q$. By Proposition 3, there exists $\{x, y\} \in L$ such that $\{x, y\} \subset Q$. By Lemma 1, we also have $\{x, y\} \subset C$. Therefore, we have $\{x, y\} \in Z$. By Proposition 3, this implies that $Z \in \Phi$: a contradiction. $\square$

5   Sufficient Subdomain for Entropy Score Computation

The following proposition shows that if the two corresponding junction forests F and F' share some clusters, then there exists one such cluster that is terminal in F'.

Proposition 6 *Let G be a chordal graph and G' be a chordal supergraph of G induced by a set L of links. Let F and F' be the corresponding JF of G and G', respectively. If F' shares clusters with F, then at least one of them is terminal in F'.*

Proof:

Suppose the conclusion does not hold. Let R be the crux induced by G and L. Then the generating set of R will not form a connected subtree in F': a contradiction with Proposition 5. $\square$

The following proposition says that if a cluster shared by F and F' is terminal in F', then its boundary is complete and identical in both chordal graphs, G and G'.

Proposition 7 *Let G be a chordal graph and G' be a chordal supergraph of G induced by a set L of links. Let F and F' be the corresponding JF of G and G', respectively. Let Q be a cluster shared by F and F', and is terminal in F'. Then the boundary between Q and $V \setminus Q$ in both G and G' is complete and identical.*

Proof:

Since Q is terminal in F', its boundary with $V \setminus Q$ in G' is complete. Since Q is shared by F and F', it does not contain any $\{x, y\} \in L$ by Propositions 3 and 4. Hence, its boundary with $V \setminus Q$ in G was not altered by adding L to G. This implies that its boundary with $V \setminus Q$ in G is identical to that in G'. □

The following proposition shows that the increment of entropy score can be correctly computed without variables in a shared terminal cluster. Let G be the structure of a DMN M over V. Let Q be a clique in G with a complete boundary S. If we remove variables $Q \setminus S$ from V and remove the corresponding nodes from G, the resultant graph is still chordal and is a valid structure of a DMN. We call the resultant DMN a *reduced* DMN.

Proposition 8 *Let G be the structure of a DMN M over V and G' be the structure of another DMN M' that is a chordal supergraph of G induced by a set L of links. Let $H(V)$ and $H'(V)$ be the entropy of M and M', respectively. Let Q be a cluster shared by F and F', and is terminal in F'. Let S be the separator of Q in F'. Then $\delta h = H(V) - H'(V)$ can be computed using reduced DMNs where variables in $V \setminus (Q \setminus S)$ are removed.*

Proof:

Denote $V^* = V \setminus (Q \setminus S)$. Since S is the boundary of Q in G', we have

$$H'(V) = H'(V^*) + H(Q) - H(S) ,$$

where $H'(V^*)$ is the entropy of the DMN obtained by removing variables $Q \setminus S$ from M'. By Proposition 7, S is also the boundary of Q in G. We have

$$H(V) = H(V^*) + H(Q) - H(S) ,$$

where $H(V^*)$ is the entropy of the DMN obtained by removing variables $Q \setminus S$ from M. Hence $\delta h = H(V) - H'(V) = H(V^*) - H'(V^*)$. □

By recursively applying Proposition 8, the following theorem establish the correctness of local computation for the incremental entropy score.

Theorem 9 *Let G be the structure of a DMN M over V and G' be the structure of another DMN M' that is a chordal supergraph of G induced by a set L of links. Let $H(V)$ and $H'(V)$ be the entropy of M and M', respectively. Then the crux R induced by G and L is a sufficient subset of V needed to compute $\delta h = H(V) - H'(V)$.*

Proof:

Let F be the corresponding JF of G, and F' be that of G'. If F and F' have shared clusters, by Proposition 6 a terminal cluster Q shared by F and F' can be found. Denote the separator of Q in F' by S and $V^* = V \setminus (Q \setminus S)$. By Proposition 8, δh can be computed as $H(V^*) - H'(V^*)$. By recursively applying

Propositions 6 and 8, eventually we can remove all clusters shared by F and F'. The remaining clusters is the generating set Φ of R, and hence δh can be computed as $\delta h = H(R) - H'(R)$. $\square$

Theorem 9 suggests the following method to compute δh by local computation: First compute the crux R based on Definition 2. Then compute the subgraphs of G and G' spanned by R. Convert the subgraphs into junction forest representations and compute δh using equation 1.

6 Complexity of a Decomposable Markov Network

We now shift to the computation of the complexity of a DMN, which we define as the total number of unconstrained parameters needed to specify $\mathcal{P}$. We denote the space of a set X of variables by D_X. The following Lemma derives the complexity of two adjacent cluster representations in a DMN. Due to space limit, the proofs for all formal results on the complexity will be included in a longer version of this paper.

Lemma 10 *Let C be a cluster in the junction forest representation of a DMN, Q be its terminal parent, and S be their separator. Then the total number of unconstrained parameters required to specify $P(C \cup Q)$ is $|D_C| + |D_Q| - |D_S| - 1$.*

The following theorem derives the complexity of a DMN whose structure is a JT.

Theorem 11 *Let Ω be the set of clusters in the junction tree representation of a DMN over variables V and Ψ be the set of separators. Then the total number of unconstrained parameters needed to specify $P(V)$ is*

$$ N = \sum_{C_i \in \Omega} |D_{C_i}| - \sum_{S_j \in \Psi} |D_{S_j}| - 1 . $$

The following corollary extends Theorem 11 on the complexity of a JT representation to a junction forest representation.

Corollary 12 *Let Ω be the set of clusters in a junction forest representation of a DMN over V and Ψ be the set of separators. Let the junction forest consist of k junction trees. Then the total number of unconstrained parameters needed to specify $P(V)$ is*

$$ N = \sum_{C_i \in \Omega} |D_{C_i}| - \sum_{S_j \in \Psi} |D_{S_j}| - k . $$

Based on Corollary 12, we have the measure of complexity of a DMN M as

$$ \Gamma_2(M) = \sum_{C_i \in \Omega} |D_{C_i}| - \sum_{S_j \in \Psi} |D_{S_j}| - k . $$

7   Local Computation of DMN Complexity

Following the same idea of local computation of δh, we want to find a small subset of variables sufficient to compute the incremental change of complexity due to the addition of links L to the current DMN. We show below that the crux is just such a subset.

The following proposition says that a terminal cluster unchanged by the addition of L is irrelevant to the computation of the incremental complexity.

Proposition 13 *Let G be the structure of a DMN M over V and G' be the structure of another DMN M' that is a chordal supergraph of G induced by a set L of links. Let N and N' be the total number of unconstrained parameters needed to specify $P(V)$ for M and $P'(V)$ for M', respectively. Let Q be a cluster shared by F and F', and is terminal in F'. Let S be the separator of Q in F'. Then $\delta n = N' - N$ can be computed using reduced DMNs where variables in $V \setminus (Q \setminus S)$ are removed.*

The following theorem shows that the crux is sufficient for computing the incremental complexity.

Theorem 14 *Let G be the structure of a DMN M over V and G' be the structure of another DMN M' that is a chordal supergraph of G induced by a set L of links. Let N and N' be the total number of unconstrained parameters needed to specify $P(V)$ for M and $P'(V)$ for M', respectively. Then the crux R induced by G and L is a sufficient subset of V needed to compute $\delta n = N' - N$.*

Theorem 14 suggests the following method to obtain the incremental change to the DMN complexity by local computation: First compute the crux R based on Definition 2. Then compute the subgraphs of G and G' spanned by R. Convert the subgraphs into junction forest representations and compute δn using Corollary 12.

8   Conclusion

We have shown that crux forms a subset of variables sufficient to compute the incremental change of both goodness-of-fit and complexity of a DMN during search of alternative dependence structures. The overall incremental improvement due to adding links L is $\delta \Gamma = \delta h - \alpha\, \delta n$, computed using the crux. Search can terminate when no alternative structures provide positive $\delta \Gamma$. The computation is much more efficient than direct evaluation as the crux is small and computation is local. There is no loss of accuracy due to the local computation. The method is currently being implemented in WEBWEAVR-III toolkit.

Acknowledgements. This work is supported by Research Grant OGP0155425 from NSERC of Canada and a grant from IRIS in the Networks of Centres of Excellence Program of Canada.

References

1. D. Chickering, D. Geiger, and D. Heckerman. Learning Bayesian networks: serach methods and experimental results. In *Proc. of 5th Conf. on Artificial Intelligence and Statistics*, pages 112–128, Ft. Lauderdale, 1995. Society for AI and Statistics.

2. G.F. Cooper and E. Herskovits. A Bayesian method for the induction of probabilistic networks from data. *Machine Learning*, (9):309–347, 1992.

3. N. Friedman, K. Murphy, and S. Russell. Learning the structure of dynamic probabilistic networks. In G.F. Cooper and S. Moral, editors, *Proc. 14th Conf. on Uncertainty in Artificial Intelligence*, pages 139–147, Madison, Wisconsin, 1998. Morgan Kaufmann.

4. D. Heckerman, D. Geiger, and D.M. Chickering. Learning Bayesian networks: the combination of knowledge and statistical data. *Machine Learning*, 20:197–243, 1995.

5. J. Hu and Y. Xiang. Learning belief networks in domains with recursively embedded pseudo independent submodels. In *Proc. 13th Conf. on Uncertainty in Artificial Intelligence*, pages 258–265, Providence, 1997.

6. F.V. Jensen, S.L. Lauritzen, and K.G. Olesen. Bayesian updating in causal probabilistic networks by local computations. *Computational Statistics Quarterly*, (4):269–282, 1990.

7. W. Lam and F. Bacchus. Learning Bayesian networks: an approach based on the MDL principle. *Computational Intelligence*, 10(3):269–293, 1994.

8. S.L. Lauritzen and D.J. Spiegelhalter. Local computation with probabilities on graphical structures and their application to expert systems. *J. Royal Statistical Society, Series B*, (50):157–244, 1988.

9. J. Pearl. *Probabilistic Reasoning in Intelligent Systems: Networks of Plausible Inference*. Morgan Kaufmann, 1988.

10. G. Shafer. *Probabilistic Expert Systems*. Society for Industrial and Applied Mathematics, Philadelphia, 1996.

11. P. Spirtes and C. Glymour. An algorithm for fast recovery of sparse causal graphs. *Social Science Computer Review*, 9(1):62–73, 1991.

12. Y. Xiang. A characterization of single-link search in learning belief networks. In P. Compton H. Motoda, R. Mizoguchi and H. Liu, editors, *Proc. Pacific Rim Knowledge Acquisition Workshop*, pages 218–233, Singapore, 1998.

13. Y. Xiang, J. Hu, N. Cercone, and H. Hamilton. Learning pseudo-independent models: analytical and experimental results. In H. Hamilton, editor, *Advances in Artificial Intelligence*, pages 227–239. Springer, 2000.

14. Y. Xiang, S.K.M. Wong, and N. Cercone. Critical remarks on single link search in learning belief networks. In *Proc. 12th Conf. on Uncertainty in Artificial Intelligence*, pages 564–571, Portland, 1996.

15. Y. Xiang, S.K.M. Wong, and N. Cercone. A 'microscopic' study of minimum entropy search in learning decomposable Markov networks. *Machine Learning*, 26(1):65–92, 1997.

Personalized Contexts in Help Systems

Vive S. Kumar, Gordon I. McCalla, and Jim E. Greer

ARIES Laboratory, Department of Computer Science,
University of Saskatchewan, Canada
vive.kumar@usask.ca

Abstract. Help systems offer a variety of services ranging from providing references to online documents to providing task-specific on-the-job training. One of the pervasive characteristics of any help system is the conception of a help-context. Depending on the type of service being offered, help systems may require different help-contexts. The context captures knowledge about the person who provides help, the person who consumes help, the help material, and the tool that delivers the material. The knowledge about the helper and the helpee can be stored in user models. In this paper we discuss how help-contexts are created in the Helper's Assistant and how user models enhance the quality of help-contexts and the quality of help being delivered.

1. Contexts in Help Systems

Computer-based tools often necessitate different degrees of adaptation to users with varying amounts of computer expertise in task-domains of different complexities, resulting in a variety of user impasses. This requires software tools to place increasing emphasis on help systems to handle such impasses. Help systems range from sophisticated graphical interfaces that guide the users, to proactive systems that can intervene in the user-software dialogue. They can be passive or active, provided with canned solutions or knowledge-based inferences, generic or task specific, collaborative, or autonomous. They can be centric or distributed in terms of help components.

Help systems have been extensively investigated since the early 80s [4]. Most contemporary software tools have generic help facilities including metaphoric help (user-friendly interfaces) and online help (www manuals). OFFICE [9] is a help system that represents the authority and responsibility structure of the office workers and the profiles of the workers in specific roles within the organization. EUROHELP [10] has an extensive model that represents users' learning and forgetting. The model is used to estimate knowledge strength of the user on a topic, to verify didactic goals related to the topic being learned, and to identify prerequisite knowledge of the user.

There is a compelling trend to try to improve the quality of help by increasing the bandwidth of information available to the help system. There are different dimensions to increasing the bandwidth of help information. The bandwidth can be increased with additional help material to augment the information about the subject/topic/domain of the help request. The bandwidth can be enhanced with help components/tools that can deliver help in a diverse manner or with knowledge of the helper (who provides help) and helpee (who consumes help) to personalize the delivery of help. The bandwidth

E. Stroulia and S. Matwin (Eds.): AI 2001, LNAI 2056, pp. 162–171, 2001.
© Springer-Verlag Berlin Heidelberg 2001

can be supplemented with pedagogical principles that can guide the process of help delivery. The system can bring in appropriate/additional helpers to establish a realistic collaborative help scenario to expand bandwidth even further.

A help system can have a combination of these dimensions that extend the help bandwidth. We call this a help-context. A help context is a frame of reference for help – a collection of knowledge that surrounds the help situation in order to support the help interaction. Every help system operate based on some help context. Establishing a suitable context is a primary problem in any help system. Success of peer help among friends and colleagues is due to the establishment of personal, shared contexts. In most cases, such contexts are established in an opportunistic fashion and the quality of help depends on the capability of the individual delivering help.

Some of the notable systems that explicitly establish a range of help-contexts include Microsoft's Intellisense™ technology [8] and I-Help [3]. Both systems allow the depth of the help-contexts to be tuned to different levels depending on different requirements. Microsoft's Office Assistant does not possess an explicit model of the user. However, it helps users to discover the full functionality of Office Products by tracking users' recent actions, anticipating users' needs, and providing suggestions about how to complete tasks more easily and efficiently. The inadequacy of the Intellisense™ technology derives primarily from the lack of user-specific contextual information, where the captured information about the user is neither used extensively nor kept over time. I-Help is an agent-oriented matchmaker tool that identifies suitable human helpers. I-Help establishes coherent user-groups based on user preferences. What the I-Help system lacks is personalized context-specific support for the helper.

Personalization is one of the essential dimensions of a help-context. Human help is inherently personalized and is superior to machine help since relevant context is established between the helper and the helpee. This is true because human helpers can understand subtle contextual cues better than any help system. In mimicking such humane behaviour, help systems attempt to customize the contextual assistance in tune with the personal requirements. A help-context can be customized around the help being requested. In a programming environment, a preliminary personalized help-context can be built based on recent interactions of the helpee with the Integrated Development Environment (or the recent command line executions of the helpee). Shared collaborative applications (whiteboards) and shared input/output devices can provide personal but non-portable contexts. We claim that instead of embedding the context in the interface itself, it is possible to capture the context as a software entity. Such a portable context can be used to personalize the interface at runtime. For example, if the help-context is known to the helper, he or she can create a better explanation, using tools and material relevant to the help context.

Personalization can focus on the helper, or the helpee, or a partnership between the two. In this paper, we will restrict our focus to developing a personalized context for the helper. There are many aspects to personalization in help systems. The interface presenting the help-context to the helper can be personalized; the suite of help tools that are preferred by the helper can be chosen; favourite tutorial strategies of the helper can be preferred. In addition, the helper can choose the helpees who he/she would like to help, when he/she would like to deliver help, and how he/she would like to portray himself/herself over the network. Personalized help-contexts can choose between proactive *versus* reactive help. It is quite possible that in most cases reactive help is sufficient to satisfy help requests. That is, help is offered only when requested. On those occasions, the impact and utility of the help-context can be minimal. Input for reactive help comes primarily from the recent interaction of the helpee with the system. However, there are situations when proactive help can be found very useful. The proactive mode of help can also allow a helpee to join in a help interaction going on between a helper and another helpee. Such a situation is possible when the helpee notices that his/her help request is addressed in a help interaction and would like to join in, contribute, and expand the scope of the interaction. Input for proactive help comes from observations of past and recent interaction of the helpee with the system.

User modelling is the key to personalization in help systems. A model is an observable representation of attributes of the entity being modelled. A user model acquires knowledge about users, relative to the learning goals. Normally, acquisition is carried out dynamically as the user engages in interactions with the system. User models can be used in help systems in a variety of contexts, including adaptation of user interfaces, selection of instructional exercises, support for collaboration, customization of information content, and prediction of users' future behaviour. However, it is not a trivial task to obtain user model information from observed user actions. Further, making help inferences from the information contained in a user model is a complex task. Beyond that, it is even more complicated to identify and deliver appropriate help-actions based on the inferred information. Nevertheless, a pragmatic, generic, and sophisticated user model has been designed, developed, and deployed in a help system called "Helper's Assistant", which generates a comprehensive help-context to personalize help delivery.

2. Personalized Contexts in Helper's Assistant

Helper's Assistant [6] is a framework as well as a tool that assists a helper to better understand the help request, the background knowledge about the helpee, potentially successful tutorial strategies, preferred help tools, and other help delivery constraints. It presents the help request in its raw form; provides references to similar requests made by other helpees; provides help material and help tools that match the help request; advises the helper about appropriate tutorial strategies; presents a glimpse of the subject knowledge, help history, and preferences of the helpee. Helper's Assistant also attempts to incorporate input from the helpee to supplement the help-context.

The current prototype implementation of Helper's Assistant is a support system for helpers who are engaged in providing Java programming help to novice learners over a computer network. A help-request originating from a helpee initiates a help session between a helper and a helpee. At this point, the helper can choose to invoke and use Helper's Assistant. The helper can interact with Helper's Assistant before or during the help session. Using the models of the helper and the helpee, Helper's Assistant creates a help-context that provides task-oriented, personalized support for the helper.

Fig. 1 outlines the flow of information from various sources to the help-context. The resources are completely independent of each other and they interact with the help-context object using a CORBA-based client-server platform. For example, the helpee can initiate a help request from any application as long as that application or the helper (using any application) sends in a message to the "Help Request Server" to invoke Helper's Assistant.

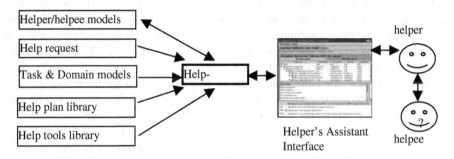

Fig. 1. An outline of flow of help-context information

The help-context acts as a channel between the system and the resources. Internally, it is represented as an object. It contains simple data, inferred data, and methods to retrieve and update values. It uses three types of knowledge-based inferences: rule-based, Bayesian, and constraint-based resolution. Section 3 details from where the help-context data is obtained, how it is inferred, and in what form it is presented to the helper. An abridged list of the help-context slots is presented in Table 1.

Table 1. Slots of help-context

Help context categories
1   Help request material, related material, help request statistics, similar sessions
2   Help concept, related concepts, concept statistics, instantiated concept hierarchy
3   Helpee keywords, related keywords
4   Associated task, task models, task statistics for class, task statistics for helpee
5   Helpee preferences: when, how long, type, mode, form, interface, pedagogy…
6   System preferences: when, how long, type, mode, form, interface, pedagogy…
7   Helper preferences: when, how long, type, mode, form, interface, pedagogy…
8   Help plan library, help principle, instantiated help plan
9   Tool library, models of tools

The first three slots contain a number of key-value pairs, where each slot requires some input from the helpee that is enhanced by the system and/or the helper. For the first slot, the helpee provides the help request question/material (example, Java code) and the system attempts to extract similar question/material, related statistics, and the helpee's help request statistics.

The second slot requires the helpee to select one or more related concepts from a hierarchy. The system enhances the selection with a set of concepts attributed to parent, child, adjacent, related, and prerequisite relations. The system then instantiates the values for the resultant set of concepts (reflecting the subject knowledge of the helpee). The third slot accepts a set of keywords and the system enhances with a set of related keywords.

The next four slots are filled by the system in cooperation with the helper. The fourth slot corresponds to the curriculum-related information. Associated tasks are tasks that the helpee is expected to perform within the scope of the curriculum. Task models are predetermined references to procedural knowledge associated with a task. For example, different algorithms form the task models for a programming problem. Performance statistics of the helpee and the related group (example, a class of students) can also be extracted for each task as part of the help-context. The fifth, sixth, and seventh slots of the help-context capture preferential data for the helper, the helpee, and the system. Preferential data includes the type of help responses (*short answer, analogy,..*), the mode of help-delivery (*offline, online, just-in-time, every 10 minutes, session transferable, interruptible, joinable,..*), the form of help communication (*manual, automated, collaborative, anonymous,..*), interface preferences (*tab-options, look-and-feel,..*), tool preferences (*web forum, chat,..*), pedagogical preferences (*min-to-max material, analogy, articulation,..*), interaction partner preferences (*gender, ethnicity, group,..*), when (*just-in-time, within 15 minutes,..*), how long (*5 minutes, until-done,..*), willingness (*helpee-category, curriculum-category,..*), conflicts (*resolution priority, resolution rules, ...*), etc.

The eighth slot corresponds to the chosen help plan derived by the system. The process of instantiation of a help plan based on the personal preferences of the helper is described elsewhere [5,7]. The final slot contains information related to the external application tools that Helper's Assistant can invoke. Presently, the models of these tools only contain usage history with respect to individual users. However, it is possible to conceive a detailed application model for each tool, which will give a comprehensive usage history for the users of these tools.

Fig. 1 shows a screen shot of the interface of Helper's Assistant. The interface is determined based on the helper's preferences stored in the helper's user model, symbolized in terms of the tabs that are shown at the top of the figure. The first tab brings in the help request, references to other help sessions on similar topic(s), and statistics related to similar help requests. The second tab presents a customized list of WWW links and a search engine. The third tab summarizes the helpee's curriculum related efforts and relevant user model information. The fourth tab allows the helper to locally compile a Java program, inspect the compiled output, and look at the bug statistics of the helpee from time to time. The fifth tab presents the help plan.

Each tab presents a piece of the help-context information. As mentioned earlier, a help-context is an extended representation of a help request. It is a container for all the relevant references associated with the help request. It acts as the object of reference during help sessions. The help-context has many slots of key-values structure. The values for help-context are obtained from a variety of resources.

Once created, the help-context generates the interface for Helper's Assistant. As depicted in Fig. 2, the interface contains seven components: "help request", "WWW search", "Concepts UM info", "Tasks", "Compile", "Help plan", and "Help tools".

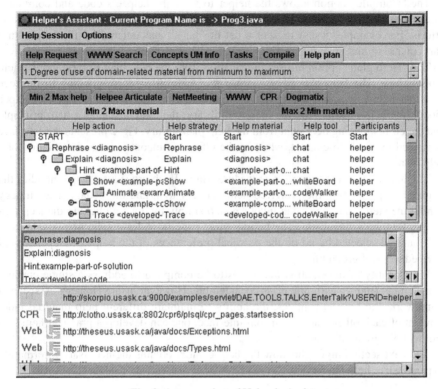

Fig. 2. A screen shot of Helper's Assistant

The "help request" option retrieves the question posed by the helpee, and creates references to similar questions posed earlier, related help material, and other ongoing help sessions that might be of interest. The question is retrieved from the application the helpee was using when he or she requested help. Similar questions, related help material, and similar ongoing sessions are obtained using a keyword-based search.

The "WWW search" option presents a domain-specific, predetermined WWW search space, which is deployed using JavaHelp™ (as Java programming is our domain). The "Concepts UM info" option presents conceptual knowledge of the helpee in terms of "Abstract Syntax Tree" elements of the Java programming language. The conceptual knowledge is represented in the interval of [0 – 1] and the values of these concepts are retrieved from the helpee's user model. In addition, the preferences of the helpee, the helper, and resolved preferences in case of conflicts are also presented to the helpee.

The "Tasks" option presents the helpee's progress in a course, including the start date of the curriculum element (e.g., start date of assignment 1), the end date, the associated concepts, whether completed, and the score. This information is obtained from domain models. In addition, the helper is given references to specific, preconceived solutions for individual curriculum elements (e.g., solutions for an assignment using different algorithms), which is obtained from the task models.

The "Compile" option allows the helper to view the helpee's code and compile it locally. It also presents statistical information about the helpee's earlier compilation efforts. For example, it can present a list of "bugs" encountered by the helpee in a particular assignment, and their frequency, retrieved from the helpee's user model.

The "Help plan" option utilises information from the help plan library and the help tools library. The help plan library consists of help plans corresponding to fourteen common help principles. Using the information from the helper model, the helpee model, the help request, and the help tool library, the system selects a help principle and the corresponding help plan from the help plan library. Fig. 2 presents the interface generated by the help-context, which is the ultimate outcome of the instantiation of a help plan.

The help plan is a sequence of procedural steps. Each procedural step embodies the required help material, the preferred help delivery tool, and the pedagogical strategy behind the step. The helper can invoke a step simply by double-clicking the step (example, Rephrase:diagnosis). The bottom-most pane provides a suite of relevant tools and material selected based on the personal preferences of the helper, independent of any pedagogical grounding.

The quantity of information that needs to be compiled to address a single curriculum element (like an assignment) is considerable. However, using Helper's Assistant's framework, the built-in routines, the ability to maintain different help material independent of each other, and the custom interface, one can develop a practical help system without great difficulty.

The next section highlights how the help-context obtains the necessary information to personalize help interaction.

3. Creation of Help-Context in Helper's Assistant

The majority of help-context information is about the personal aspects of the helper and the helpee, which are stored in the respective user models. Some of the slots in the help-context contain simple data ("user-id", "willing-to-help (yes/no), etc). Interestingly, some of the slots contain complex information that is used in knowledge-based inferences. Considering this requirement, the help-context has been implemented as an object that possesses several inference methods.

One of the knowledge-based techniques used in Helper's Assistant is its ability to use human help as part of the machine help, what we call the human-in-the-loop approach. In order to make this integration successful it is imperative that the system can present personalized information to the helper. One simple type of personalization is the system's ability to consider the gender preferences of the helper. For example, the helper and the helpee can store their gender (or many other) preferences as production rules, in their respective user models. Helper's Assistant keeps track of the success rate of same-gender and cross-gender interactions of the helper and the helpee. Based on these values, Helper's Assistant executes the production rules to obtain a measure of relevance for the helper-helpee pair. Java Expert System Shell is used for rule-based reasoning [2]. An example rule is given below:

```
if helper-same-gender-interaction is worse or bad  AND
   helper-cross-gender-interaction is okay or good AND
   helper-gender-preference is female AND
   helpee-gender is female AND
   helpee-cross-gender-interaction is okay or good
then helper-helpee-gender-pairing is acceptable
```

At this point in time the helper has already been chosen. However, the system evaluates the compatibility between the helper and the helpee using these rules and updates the gender-related statistics with the outcome of the help interaction (success or failure). This statistic can be used by the matchmaker application (or server).

Helper's Assistant uses Bayesian reasoning to update conceptual knowledge of the users. For example, the conceptual knowledge of the Java programming language is stored in an abstract syntax tree, where each node refers to a syntactical component of the language. The structure of the abstract syntax tree is replicated in the Bayes network as a causal structure. Each concept node in the network is initialized with a default value. The competence of a user corresponding to a concept node is represented in the range of [0 – 1]. The evidence observed from the external applications, related to the appreciation or the deprecation of the user's knowledge of the concept nodes are fed into the network. The evidential values are updated within each node and then propagated upwards towards the root of the syntax tree using the Bayesian inference methods ingrained in JavaBayes [1].

Helper's Assistant uses constraint-based reasoning to traverse a network of help-actions, which results in an instantiated help plan [5,7]. Each help-action node in the network represents a unique, byte-sized, help procedure. There is a start node and an end node in the network. There can be many paths starting from the start node to the end node through a number of help-action nodes. Each arc connecting two help-action nodes is associated with a number of *"pedagogical constraints"*. Pedagogical constraint ensure prerequisite relations between two consecutive nodes; limit the number of execution of cyclic nodes; ensure helper/helpee preferences are considered; guarantee the availability of help resources; and enforce time limits. The particular traversal of the help-plan-network results in a specific help-plan. The traversal however is dependent on the pedagogical constraints. That is, the traversal is stopped when all the constraints associated with a particular node (called "failed node") are not satisfied. The path traversed up to the failed node yields the help plan.

The help plan network contains many paths from the start node to the end node. The system explores all possible paths (depth-first search) to identify a set of candidate paths. Many candidate help-plans are arrived at for a single help-context corresponding to the set of candidate paths. The candidate help-plans are presented to the helper who can select an appropriate one for execution. For example, in Fig. 2, the system presents a candidate set of eight help plans (min-to-max help, helpee articulate, Netmeeting, WWW, CPR, Dogmatix, min-to-max material, and max-to-min material). The helper can select any help plan from this list as a contextual reference for the help session. By double-clicking on any of the help plans, the helper can expand the corresponding help-actions.

In many ways the user model of helper and helpee informs the help-context in Helper's Assistant. Both user models and help-context are objects. They have similar input resources, similar inference procedures, and share a number of common variables. However, there are some differences in terms of their scope and functionality. The help-context is relevant only for the duration of the current help request, while the user models deal with the accumulation of user-related information over a much longer period of time. User model gets input from a variety of external applications, while help-context gets input primarily from the task models, the domain models, the helpee, and the user models. For a single variable, the user model provides a range of update methods that the user can choose from. The help-context provides only one update method that sends the value of a variable to the user model. The key aspect is that both the help-context and the user model feed on each other.

4. Conclusion

We conducted a usability study to informally evaluate how Helper's Assistant will be received among student helpers, both novice peers and experts, in a university environment. The design of the study and the results are described elsewhere [5,6]. In this paper, we report the results pertaining to differences in novice-peer and expert perception and usage of Helper's Assistant, particularly as it pertains to the utility and accuracy of the help-context. The data is obtained primarily from a questionnaire that helpers filled in after they completed their help sessions with and without using Helper's Assistant. Usage statistics of the system were obtained automatically.

Experts found Helper's Assistant to be useful 56% (18 out of 32) of the times while novice peers found Helper's Assistant to be useful 72% (23 out of 32) of the times. We concluded that novice peer-helpers found the system to be more often useful than experts did.

Experts were successful in answering a question with Helper's Assistant 88% (22 out of 25) of the times and they were successful in answering a question without Helper's Assistant 85% (17 out of 20) of the times. On the other hand, 87% (20 out of 23) of the times novice peers were successful in answering a question with Helper's Assistant and 50% (12 out of 24) of the times novice peers were successful in answering a question without Helper's Assistant. Novice peers found Helper's Assistant to be more useful in successfully answering a question than experts did.

By observing the number of mouse-clicks it is determined that novice peers used Helper's Assistant (277 total clicks) much more than experts did (78 total clicks). Obviously, novice peers sought more support from the system than the experts did.

Based on a question concerning the cost/benefit analysis we find that 31% of the times experts felt that the cost (extra overhead) of using Helper's Assistant is more than the benefits of using Helper's Assistant. On the other hand, 50% of the times peer helpers found Helper's Assistant not worth the extra effort it caused them. That is, half the novice peer-helpers felt that Helper's Assistant is not worth the trouble of learning about the system. This result indicates that there is an opportunity to improve the system to make it more comfortable for the novice peer helpers.

In general, these results suggest that the novice peer helpers found personalized Helper's Assistant to be more useful than the expert helpers. Obviously, novice peer helpers need more personalized support to make the help sessions more conducive to their individual ability, style, and time frame.

One of the goals of the help system community is to find and deploy techniques to tutor, train, support, and help users in various domains in a personalized manner. Helper's Assistant presents one such framework that can provide personalized, customized, and possibly just-in-time help to the helper. The framework is quite generic and can be used in a variety of situations. User models and help-contexts are the core personalization resources of Helper's Assistant. Information derived from the user models is used to personalize the help-context and hence personalize the help interaction. It is our conviction that personalized help-context is central to any successful help system.

Acknowledgements. We would like to thank the Natural Sciences and Engineering Research Council of Canada, the University of Saskatchewan graduate scholarship program and the Canadian TeleLearning Network of Centres of Excellence for financial support of this project.

References

1. Cozman F.G. (2000). Java Bayes: Bayesian networks in Java. http://www.cs.cmu.edu/~javabayes/Home/index.html.
2. Friedman-Hill E. (2000). http://herzberg.ca.sandia.gov/jess/.
3. Greer J.E., McCalla G.I., Cooke J.E., Collins J.A., Kumar V.S., Bishop A.S., & Vassileva J.I. (2000). Integrating Cognitive Tools for Peer Help: The Intelligent IntraNet Peer Help-Desk Project. In Lajoie S. (Ed.), *Computers as Cognitive Tools: The Next Generation* (pp. 69-96). Lawrence Erlbaum.
4. Houghton R.C. (1984). Online help systems: A conspectus. *CACM, 27*(2), 126-133.
5. Kumar V., McCalla G., & Greer J. (1999). Helping the peer helper. International conference on AI in Education. Le Mans, France. 325-332.
6. Kumar V. (1999). Helping the peer helper in knowledge-based, collaborative, distributed peer help networks [thesis proposal]. U. Saskatchewan.
7. Kumar V., Greer J., & McCalla G. (2000). Pedagogy in peer-supported helpdesks. International Conference on Knowledge-based Computer Systems. Mumbai, India.
8. Microsoft (TM). (1998). Microsoft Office IntelliSense White Paper. http://www.microsoft.com/macoffice/prodinfo/office/intel.htm.
9. Nirenburg S., & Lesser V. (1988). Providing intelligent assistance in distributed office environments. In Bond A.H. & Gasser L. (Eds.), *Readings in Distributed Artificial Intelligence* (pp. 590-598). Morgan Kaufmann.
10. Winkels R. (1998). EUROHELP. http://www.lri.jur.uva.nl/~winkels/eurohelp.html.

QA-LaSIE: A Natural Language Question Answering System

Sam Scott[1] and Robert Gaizauskas[2]

[1] Institute for Interdisciplinary Studies
Carleton University, Ottawa, K1S 5B6, Canada
sscott@ccs.carleton.ca
[2] Department of Computer Science
University of Sheffield, Sheffield, S1 4DP, UK
r.gaizauskas@dcs.shef.ac.uk

Abstract. QA-LaSIE was the heart of the University of Sheffield entry to the Question Answering track of TREC-9. By relaxing some of the strongest linguistic constraints, we achieved a very significant performance improvement over our TREC-8 system on both the TREC-8 and TREC-9 tasks. Whereas most systems returned answers that were always close to the maximum allowable length, our system was one of the only entries that tried to return an "exact answer" to a question.

1 Introduction

This paper describes a system to discover answers to questions posed in natural language against large text collections. The system was designed to participate in the Question Answering (QA) Track of the Text Retrieval Conferences (see http://trec.nist.gov) and therefore the definitions of "question" and "answer" that we adopt for this paper are those used in the TREC QA track (see section 2 below). While the system is a research prototype, it is clear that systems of this sort hold great potential as tools to enhance access to information in large text collections (e.g. the Web). Unlike a search engine, which returns a list of documents ranked by presumed relevance to a user query, leaving the user to read the associated documents to fulfil his information need, a question answering system aims to return the precise answer to a question leaving the user no further searching (though of course a link to the source document enables the user to confirm the answer).

The task of question answering should be of interest to the AI community for the simple reason that some form of Natural Language Processing must be used. There was not a single system entered in the TREC-9 QA Track that did not use some form of linguistic knowledge – no group took a purely statistical word counting approach.[1] Thus, unlike other tasks in Information Retrieval, question answering is one in which some form of NLP seems unavoidable. Nevertheless,

---

[1] The least NLP to be found was in one of the IBM groups' submissions. But even this system used the WordNet hypernym hierarchy to gain an edge over a simple bag-of-words representation. Most systems used considerably more NLP.

E. Stroulia and S. Matwin (Eds.): AI 2001, LNAI 2056, pp. 172–182, 2001.

our own experience over two years of participation shows that an overly strict or formalistic approach may not succeed as well as one based on a mixture of formal NLP and ad-hoc heuristics. This year we achieved much better performance by relaxing some of the strict constraints we had employed for TREC-8.

The essence of our approach is to pass the question to an information retrieval (IR) system which uses it as a query to do passage retrieval against the text collection. The top ranked passages from the IR system are then passed to a modified information extraction (IE) system. Partial syntactic and semantic analysis of these passages, along with the question, is carried out to identify the "sought entity" from the question and to score potential matches for this sought entity in each of the retrieved passages. The five highest scoring matches become the system's response. It is our hypothesis that NLP techniques can contribute positively to QA capability.

2   The TREC Question Answering Track

The TREC-9 QA Track task was to return a ranked list of up to 5 answers to each of 693 previously unseen questions. The answers had to be passages from texts found in a (provided) 4GB newswire text collection. In TREC-9 there were two subtasks: 50-byte and 250-byte answers (maximum). The score assigned to each question was the reciprocal of the rank at which the first correct answer was found, or 0 if no answer was correct. So a system got 1 point for a correct answer at rank 1, 1/2 for rank 2, etc. The final score assigned to the system was the Mean Reciprocal Rank over the entire question set. For more details see the QA track guidelines document [5].

3   System Description

3.1   Overview

The key features of our system setup, as it processes a single question, are shown in Figure 1. First, the (indexed) TREC document collection is passed to an IR system which treats the question as a query and returns top ranked passages from the collection. As the IR system we use the Okapi system [6][2] to retrieve passages between 1 and 3 paragraphs in length – a configuration arrived at experimentally (details in [7]). Following the passage retrieval step, the top 20 ranked passages are run through a filter to remove certain formatting features which cause problems for downstream components. Finally, the question itself and the filtered top ranked passages are processed by a modified version of the LaSIE information extraction system [3], which we refer to below as QA-LaSIE. This yields a set of top ranked answers which are the system's overall output.

The reasoning behind this choice of architecture is straightforward. The IE system can perform detailed linguistic analysis, but is quite slow and cannot process the entire TREC collection for each query, or even realistically pre-process it in advance to allow for reasonable question answering performance

---

[2] Software available at: http://dotty.is.city.ac.uk/okapi-pack/ .

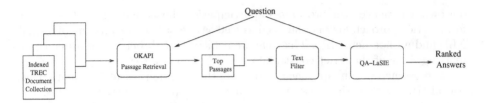

Fig. 1. System Setup for the Q & A Task

during the test run. IR systems on the other hand are designed to process huge amounts of data. By using an IR system as a filter to an IE system we hope to benefit from the respective strengths of each.

3.2   LaSIE

The system used to perform detailed question and passage analysis is largely unchanged in architecture from the LaSIE system entered in the last Message Understanding Conference (MUC-7) [3]. The system is essentially a pipeline consisting of the following modules, each of which processes the entire text[3] before the next is invoked.

Tokenizer. Identifies token boundaries and text section boundaries (text header, text body and any sections to be excluded from processing).

Gazetteer Lookup. Identifies single and multi-word matches against multiple domain specific full name (locations, organisations, etc.) and keyword (company designators, person first names, etc.) lists, and tags matching phrases with appropriate name categories.

Sentence Splitter. Identifies sentence boundaries in the text body.

Brill Tagger. Assigns one of the 48 Penn TreeBank part-of-speech tags to each token in the text [1].

Tagged Morph. Simple morphological analysis to identify the root form and inflectional suffix for tokens which have been tagged as noun or verb.

Parser. Performs two pass bottom-up chart parsing, pass one with a special named entity grammar, and pass two with a general phrasal grammar. A "best parse" is then selected (which may be only a partial parse) and a predicate-argument representation, or quasi-logical form (QLF), of each sentence is constructed compositionally.

Name Matcher. Matches variants of named entities across the text.

Discourse Interpreter. Adds the QLF representation to a semantic net, which encodes background world and domain knowledge as a hierarchy of concepts. Additional information inferred from the input using this background knowledge is added to the model, and coreference resolution is attempted between instances mentioned in the text, producing an updated discourse model.

---

[3] In the current implementation a "text" is either a single question or a candidate answer passage.

3.3   QA-LaSIE

The QA-LaSIE system takes a question and a set of passages delivered by the IR system and returns a ranked list of proposed answers for the question. The system is composed of the eight modules described in the preceding section plus one new module. Four key adaptations were made to move from the base IE system to a system capable of carrying out the QA task:

1. a specialised grammar was added to the parser to analyse questions;
2. the discourse interpreter was modified to allow the QLF representation of each question to be matched against the discourse model of a candidate answer passage;
3. the discourse interpreter was modifed to include an answer identification procedure which scores all discourse entities in each candidate passage as potential answers;
4. a TREC Question Answer module was added to examine the discourse entity scores across all passages, determine the top 5, and then output the appropriate answer text.

Parsing: Syntactic and Semantic Interpretation. In the LaSIE approach, both candidate answer passages and questions are parsed using a unification-based feature structure grammar. The parser processes one sentence at a time and along with the original words of the sentence also receives as input a part-of-speech tag for each word, morphological information for each noun and verb (word root plus affix), and zero or more phrases tagged as named entities. As output the parser produces a representation of the sentence in a "quasi-logical form" – a predicate-argument representation that stands somewhere between the surface form of the sentence and a fully interpreted semantic representation in a standard logical language. In particular the QLF representation defers issues of quantifier scoping and of word sense disambiguation.

To take a simple example, the sentence fragment *Morris testified that he released the worm* ... is parsed and transduced to the representation

```
person(e1),name(e1,'Morris'),gender(e1,masc),testify(e2),
time(e2,past),aspect(e2,simple),voice(e2,active),lsubj(e2,e1),
release(e3),time(e3,past),aspect(e3,simple),voice(e3,active),
pronoun(e4,he),lsubj(e3,e4),worm(e5),number(e5,sing),
det(e5,the),lobj(e3,e5),proposition(e6),main_event(e6,e3),
lobj(e2,e6)
```

The name information is derived from the Gazetteer lookup stage (where *Morris* is recorded as a male first name), the tense information from the morphological analysis stage, and the grammatical role information from annotations on context-free rules in the grammar. In this case these rules encode that in English sentences which consist of a noun phrase followed by a verb phrase, which in turn consists of a verb in the active voice and a sentential complement, the noun phrase prior to the verb is the subject and the sentence following it is the object. For common nouns and verbs, the lexical root of the word becomes a predicate in the QLF language.

Both noun phrase heads and verb group heads are given unique discourse entity references of the form e_n. This allows modification relations (e.g. of prepositional phrases) or grammatical role information (e.g. subject and object relations) to be captured via binary predicates holding of these entities. In cases where parsing fails to capture all this information (e.g. when only simple noun phrase, verb group, prepositional phrase or relative clause chunks are found and not a spanning parse for the sentence) then partial QLF information can be returned, making the system robust in the face of grammatical incompleteness.

Each sentence in a candidate answer passage is analysed in this fashion. So is the question, using a special question grammar. This grammar produces a QLF for the question in much the same style as above. For example, a question such as *Who released the internet worm?* would be analysed as:

```
qvar(e1),qattr(e1,name),person(e1),release(e2),time(e2,past),
aspect(e2,simple),voice(e2,active),lsubj(e2,e1),
worm(e3), number(e3,sing),det(e3,the),lobj(e2,e3),
name(e4,'Internet'),qual(e3,e4)
```

Note the use of the special predicate, qvar (question variable), to indicate the "sought entity" requested by the question. In this case the qvar can also be typed because *who* tells us the entity of concern is a person, and we presume (by encoding this in the transduction rules) that the attribute we are seeking here is a name (and not, e.g., a definite description such as *a guy at MIT*). The fact that the system should return a name is encoded in the qattr predicate. In other cases where the interrogative pronoun is more generic (e.g. *what*) the type of the qvar and the attribute sought of it may not be so readily determinable.

Discourse Interpretation of Candidate Answer Passages. Once a passage has been parsed and each sentence has been assigned a QLF representation, the discourse interpreter integrates the passages into a discourse model - a specialisation of a semantic net which supplies the system's background domain knowledge. For IE applications, this domain-specific background knowledge assists in extraction tasks by allowing template slot values to be inferred from it together with information supplied in the text being analyzed. However, for the TREC QA task there is no specific domain, and so this role of the semantic net is not relevant (though a very basic "generic" world model is employed).

The real function of the semantic net in the QA task is to provide a framework for integrating information from multiple sentences in the input. As the QLF representation of each sentence is received by the discourse interpreter, each entity is added as an instance node in the semantic net associated with its type node (the single unary predicate in which it occurs) – e.g. given worm(e5), e5 is linked to the worm node in the net, if it already exists, and to a new, dynamically-created node labelled worm if not. Added to each such entity node is an attribute-value structure, or property list, containing all the attribute and relational information for this entity (all binary predicates in which it occurs).

In addition to adding a sentence's QLF to the semantic net in this fashion, one further node is added representing the sentence itself. This sentence entity has a sequence number indicating the sentence's position in the passage, and also has an attribute recording the entity numbers of every entity occurring in the passage. Thus, the discourse model aims to model not only the content of the discourse, but simple aspects of the discourse structure itself.

After each sentence has been added to the discourse model, the discourse interpreter begins its main task – to determine coreference relations between entities in the current sentence and entities already added to the model from previous sentences in the input. There is not space to detail this algorithm here (see [2]), but in essence it relies upon factors including the semantic type compatibility, attribute compatibility, and textual proximity of potential coreferents. Once a coreference has been established between two entities, the two are merged by replacing all references to the two entity numbers by references to just one of them. However, the surface realisations which initially served as triggers for the creation of each distinct entity node are retained as attributes of the merged entity, and can be used later, e.g. to generate a text string as an answer.

Answer Identification. After the discourse model has been constructed for a candidate answer passage, the QLF of the question is added to this model and treated as sentence 0. The coreference procedure is run and as many coreferences as possible are established between entities in the question and those in the passage[4].

In the TREC-8 version of QA-LaSIE [4] this procedure was the primary question answering mechanism: if the qvar was resolved with an entity in the candidate answer passage then this entity became the answer; if not, then no answer was proposed. This approach had several major drawbacks. First, it permitted only one answer per question, whereas the QA track allows up to five answers to be proposed. Second, it was very fragile, as coreference tends to be difficult to establish.

Given these weaknesses, the TREC-9 system follows a significantly different approach. Instead of attempting to directly corefer the qvar with an entity in the candidate answer passage, entities in the passage are scored in a way which attempts to value their likelihood as answers. The best scores are then used to select the answers to be returned from the passage.

The discourse model is transversed twice, sentence by sentence.

1. *Sentence Scoring* On the first pass, the sentences are given an integer score. The entities in the question are interpreted as "constraints" and each sentence in the answer passage gets one point for each constraint it contains. This rewards sentences for containing entities that have been detected as coreferring with entities in the question. Typically these will be sentences

---

[4] The standard coreference procedure uses a distance metric to prefer closer to more distant potential coreferences. Clearly this is irrelevant for questions which are not part of the original candidate answer passage. Hence we switch off the distance-preference heuristic for coreference in this case.

which contain named entities mentioned in the question, or sentences which contain definite noun phrases or pronouns which have already been resolved (as part of discourse interpretation of the passage). Sentences also get an extra point if they contain an event entity of the same type as the event derived from the matrix verb of the question (unless that verb is *to be*).

2. *Entity Scoring* On the second pass, the system looks in each sentence for the best possible answer entity. To be considered, an entity must be an object (not an event), and must not be one of the constraints from the previous step. If the `qvar` has a `qattr`, then the entity must also have the specified attribute to be considered a possible answer. The entities in a given sentence are compared to the `qvar` and scored for semantic similarity, property similarity, and for object and event relations.

Semantic and property similarity scores are determined as for generic coreferencing. The semantic similarity score indicates how closely semantically related two things are (on a scale of 0 to 1). The semantic similarity is related to the inverse of the length of the path that links the two semantic types in the ontology. If the `qvar` and an entity have the same type (e.g. `person`), then that entity will receive a semantic similarity of 1. If the two semantic types are on different branches of the hierarchy, the score is 0.

The property similarity score is also between 0 and 1 and is a measure of how many properties the two instances share in common and how similar the properties are.

The object relation and event relation scores were motivated by failure analysis on the original system and were tuned through test runs. The object relation score adds 0.25 to an entity's score if it is related to a constraint within the sentence by apposition, a qualifying relationship, or with the prepositions *of* or *in*. So if the question was *Who was the leader of the teamsters?*, and a sentence contained the sequence ... *Jimmy Hoffa, Leader of the Teamsters, ...* then the entity corresponding to *Jimmy Hoffa* would get the object relation credit for being apposed to *Leader of the Teamsters*.

The event relations score adds 0.5 to an entity's score if:

a) there is an event entity in the QLF of the question which is related to the `qvar` by a `lsubj` or `lobj` relation and is not a `be` event (i.e. derived from a copula construction), and

b) the entity being scored stands in the same relation (`lobj` or `lsubj`) to an event entity of the same type as the `qvar` does. So if the question was, *What was smoked by Sherlock Holmes?* and the answer sentence was *Sherlock Holmes smoked a pipe*, then the entity *a pipe* would get the event relations credit for being in the `lobj` relation to the verb *to smoke*.

This represents a significant weakening of the requirement in our TREC-8 system that the `qvar` had to match with an entity in the answer passage which stood in the same relation to its main verb as the `qvar` did with the main verb in the question, as well the main verbs and other complements being compatible. Here a bonus is awarded if this the case; there it was mandatory.

Finally, the entity score is normalized to bring it into the range [0,1]. This is motivated by the idea that if two sentences have equal scores from step

1 above, the entity score should break the tie between the two, but should not increase their scores to be higher than a sentence that had a better score from step 1. Normalizing the score improved performance slightly in tests on the TREC-8 questions.

3. *The Total Score* For every sentence, the "best" answer entity is chosen according to the Entity Scoring described above. The sentence and entity scores are then added together and normalized by dividing by the number of entities in the question plus 1. The sentence instance is annotated to include the total score, the best entity (if one was found), and the "exact answer". The exact answer will be the name of the best entity if one was identified during parsing. Otherwise this property is not asserted.

Answer Output. The answer output procedure gathers the total scores, as described in the preceding section, from each sentence in each of the passages analyzed by QA-LaSIE, sorts them into a single ranking, and outputs answers from the overall five highest scoring sentences.

We submitted four runs to the TREC-9 evaluation – two in the 50-byte category and two in the 250 category. These four runs are explained below:

shef50ea. This is the exact answer run. If a high scoring sentence was annotated with a trec9_exact_answer attribute then this is assumed to be the answer. If there is no exact answer, then the code looks for a trec9_answer_entity and outputs the longest realization of that entity as the answer. If there is no answer entity, which can happen occasionally, then a default string is output. In all cases, the string is trimmed to 50 bytes if necessary, by trimming characters from the left hand side.

shef50. For this run, the system looks for the first occurrence of the trec9_-answer_entity in the sentence and then outputs 50 bytes of the sentence centered around that entity. The 50-bytes will never go outside of the answer sentence (if the first occurrence is the first word, then the 50 bytes will be the first 50 bytes of the sentence, and so on). If the sentence is shorter than 50 bytes, then the full sentence is output as the answer. If there is no answer entity, the middle 50 bytes are output.

shef250. Same as shef50, but up to 250-bytes or the full sentence is output (whichever is shorter).

shef250p. For this run, the answer for shef250 is computed, then the answer is padded to 250 bytes if necessary by adding characters from the file to both ends, going outside the confines of the sentence if necessary.

4   Results

4.1   Development Results (TREC-8)

Development results for the four run types described in the preceding section are shown in Table 1. shef-trec8 refers to the official results obtained by our TREC-8 system in TREC-8. okapi-baseline refers to a naive approach that simply used Okapi passage retrieval with a maximum passage length of one

Table 1. Results on TREC-8 Questions. Rank hypothetical where marked.

System	Run	Mean Reciprocal Rank	Correct Answers	Rank in Class
shef-trec8	50	.081	N/A	15/17
okapi-baseline	50	.157	N/A	14/17 (hyp)
shef50ea	50	.329	89/164	4/17 (hyp)
shef50	50	.368	98/164	3/17 (hyp)
shef-trec8	250	.111	N/A	22/24
okapi-baseline	250	.395	N/A	11/24 (hyp)
shef250	250	.490	127/164	4/24 (hyp)
shef250p	250	.506	130/164	4/24 (hyp)

paragraph and then trimmed this paragraph to 50 or 250 bytes. This method led to Mean Reciprocal Rank scores of 0.157 for the 50 byte responses and .395 for the 250 byte responses. This totally naive approach would have placed 14th of 17 entrants in the TREC-8 50-byte system ranking and joint 11th of 24 in the 250-byte system ranking. In both cases these results were considerably higher than our own entries in TREC-8. Thus, we started with a sobering baseline to contend with. However, following development of the new approach described above in section 3.3 and numerous experiments with various parameter settings we arrived at the best development results presented in Table 1.

4.2 Final Evaluation Results (TREC-9)

Mean reciprocal rank scores for the four Sheffield TREC-9 runs are shown in Table 2, for both lenient and strict scorings.[5] We have also included our system's ranking over all the systems entered and the mean score for all systems entered. In all cases the performance of the Sheffield system is very close to the mean. We have also used the Perl patterns supplied by NIST for the TREC-9 results to score the submitted runs and an `okapi-baseline` system ourselves. These results are reported in the Auto column.

5 Discussion

The TREC-9 results also reported on the mean byte length of answers for each submitted run. Most participants gave as much text as was allowed, resulting in mean byte lengths of more than 45 bytes in the 50 byte category for all but a handful of systems. Our shef50ea run (the exact answer run) was one of the few that had a lower mean answer length – less than 10 bytes in fact. While we do not know yet what the mean byte length would have been for correct answers, we can report that our system had the highest score of the four systems that returned answers with an average length under 10 bytes.

---

[5] In strict scoring, an otherwise correct answer was marked as wrong if there was no support for it in the text from which it was extracted.

Table 2. TREC-9 Results.

System	Run	Mean Reciprocal Rank			% Correct Answers in Top 5			Rank in
		Strict	Lenient	Auto	Strict	Lenient	Auto	Class
shef50ea	50	.159	.172	.171	23.6	25.7	25.8	28/35
shef50	50	.206	.217	.233	31.1	32.1	35.2	21/35
mean (of 35)	50	.220	.227		31.0	32.2		
okapi-baseline	50			.111			21.9	
shef250	250	.330	.343	.348	48.5	49.4	51.5	28/43
shef250p	250	.345	.357	.365	50.9	51.3	53.7	23/43
mean (of 43)	250	.351	.363		49.0	50.5		
okapi-baseline	250			.328			55.6	

At this point we do not have the information to allow us to apportion faults between Okapi and QA-LaSIE. In training on the TREC-8 questions Okapi was returning answer-containing passages for about 83% of the questions. On this basis the best QA-LaSIE mean reciprocal rank scores obtained in development were around .37 for the 50-byte runs and just over .50 for 250-byte runs, as presented above in Table 1.

Thus the TREC-9 test results represent a significant drop with respect to training results. Nevertheless, with respect to our best TREC-8 Mean Reciprocal Rank results (.081 for the 50-byte run, .111 for the 250-byte run), these figures represent a very significant improvement, especially given that the question set is significantly larger and the questions are "real", as opposed to what were artificially created back-formulations in many cases in TREC-8. And, they validate the central hypothesis of our TREC-9 work that we should abandon our previous rigid approach in which candidate answer entities either met constraints imposed by the question or did not, in favour of a looser approach which scored them in terms of various factors which suggested that they might be an answer. Finally, note that in both training and testing, for 250 as well as 50 byte answers, QA-LaSIE performed better than the Okapi baseline system, indicating that the NLP analysis is yielding increased value over a naive IR-only approach.

References

1. E. Brill. A simple rule-based part-of-speech tagger. In *Proc. of the Third Conference on Applied Natural Language Processing*, pages 152–155, Trento, Italy, 1992.
2. R. Gaizauskas and K. Humphreys. Quantitative Evaluation of Coreference Algorithms in an Information Extraction System. In S. Botley and T. McEnery, editors, *Discourse Anaphora and Anaphor Resolution*. John Benjamins, London, 2000.
3. K. Humphreys, R. Gaizauskas, S. Azzam, C Huyck, B. Mitchell, H. Cunningham, and Y. Wilks. Description of the LaSIE-II system as used for MUC-7. In *Proceedings of the Seventh Message Understanding Conference (MUC-7)*, 1998.
4. K. Humphreys, R. Gaizauskas, M. Hepple, and M. Sanderson. University of Sheffield TREC-8 Q & A System. In *NIST Special Publication 500-246: The Eighth Text REtrieval Conference (TREC 8)*, 1999.

5. TREC-9 Question Answering Track Guidelines.
   http://trec.nist.gov/act_part/guidelines/QA_guidelines.html, 2000.
6. S. Robertson and S. Walker. Okapi/Keenbow at TREC-8. In *NIST Special Publication 500-246: The Eighth Text REtrieval Conference (TREC 8)*, 1999.
7. S. Scott and R. Gaizauskas. University of Sheffield TREC-9 Q & A System. In *Proceedings of The Ninth Text REtrieval Conference (TREC 9)*, 2000. To appear.

Search Techniques for Non-linear Constraint Satisfaction Problems with Inequalities

Marius-Călin Silaghi, Djamila Sam-Haroud, and Boi Faltings

Artificial Intelligence Laboratory
Swiss Federal Institute of Technology 1015 Lausanne, Switzerland
{silaghi,haroud,faltings}@lia.di.epfl.ch

Abstract. In recent years, interval constraint-based solvers have shown their ability to efficiently solve challenging non-linear real constraint problems. However, most of the working systems limit themselves to delivering point-wise solutions with an arbitrary accuracy. This works well for equalities, or for inequalities stated for specifying tolerances, but less well when the inequalities express a set of equally relevant choices, as for example the possible moving areas for a mobile robot. In that case it is desirable to cover the large number of point-wise alternatives expressed by the constraints using a reduced number of sets, as interval boxes. Several authors [2,1,7] have proposed set covering algorithms specific to inequality systems. In this paper we propose a lookahead backtracking algorithm for inequality and *mixed equality/inequality* constraints. The proposed technique combines a set covering strategy for inequalities with classical interval search techniques for equalities. This allows for a more compact representation of the solution set and improves efficiency.

1   Introduction

A wide range of industrial problems require solving constraint satisfaction problems (CSPs) with numerical constraints. A numerical CSP (NCSP), (V, C, D) is stated as a set of variables V taking their values in domains D over the reals and subject to constraints C. In practice, the constraints can be equalities or inequalities of arbitrary type and arity, usually expressed using arithmetic expressions. The goal is to assign values to the variables so that all the constraints are satisfied. Such an assignment is then called a solution. Interval constraint-based solvers (e.g. Numerica [8], Solver [4]) take as input a numerical CSP, where the domains of the variables are intervals over the reals, and generate a set of boxes which *conservatively* enclose each solution (no solution is lost). While they have proven particularly efficient in solving challenging instances of numerical CSPs with non-linear constraints, they are commonly designed to deliver *punctual* solutions. This fits well the needs inherent to equality systems but is less adequate for several problems with inequalities. Inequalities can be used to state tolerances, like for example *beam-dimension* $= k \pm \varepsilon$, and it is then admissible to solve them using punctual solvers. However, in their most general form, they rather express spectra of equally relevant alternatives which need to be identified as precisely and exhaustively as possible. Such inequalities will, for example,

E. Stroulia and S. Matwin (Eds.): AI 2001, LNAI 2056, pp. 183–193, 2001.
© Springer-Verlag Berlin Heidelberg 2001

define the possible moving areas of a mobile robot, the collision regions between objects in mechanical assembly, or different alternatives of shapes for the components of a kinematic chain. In all these cases, it is not acceptable to arbitrarily focus on a specific solution, especially when this choice is forced by idiosyncrasies of the used solver.

A natural alternative to the punctual approach is to try to cover the spectrum of solutions for inequalities using a reduced number of subsets from $\mathbb{R}^n$. Usually, these subsets are chosen with known and simple properties (interval boxes, polytopes, ellipsoid,..) [5]. In recent years, several authors have proposed set covering algorithms with intervals boxes [5,2,7,1]. These algorithms, except for [5], are designed for inequality systems[1], are based on domain splitting and have one of the two following limitations. Either the constraint system is handled as an indivisible whole[2], or the splits are performed statically which means that their results are not, or only partially, further propagated to the related variables. In the first case the tractability limits are rapidly reached while in the second, the information resulting from a split is sub-optimally used. This paper proposes an algorithm for *dynamically* constructing an interval-box covering, for a set of equality/inequality constraints, according to a "maintaining local consistency" search schema. In numerical domains, local consistency usually takes the form of either Box, Hull, kB or Bound consistency [8,6], generally referred to as bound consistency in the rest of the paper. Maintaining bound consistency (MBC) is a powerful lookahead search technique for numerical CSPs which allows the splits performed on a given variable domain to be propagated on domains of other variables, thus reducing the splitting effort. The proposed technique builds on the feasibility test proposed in [1]. This allows for robustly constructing sound boxes and devising efficient splitting heuristics for search. The output is a union of boxes which conservatively encloses the solution set. As shown by the preliminary experiments, the new algorithm improves efficiency as well as the compactness of the output representation. In order to reduce the space requirements, our algorithm can alternatively be used to compute a new form of consistency called $\varepsilon_1\varepsilon_2$-consistency. $\varepsilon_1\varepsilon_2$-consistency is a weakening of global consistency which only considers certain projections of the solution space. It can be used as a preprocessing technique for speeding up further queries.

2   Background

We start by recalling the necessary background and definitions. Parts of the material described in this section are presented in [1].

2.1   Interval Arithmetic

Intervals. The finite nature of computers precludes an exact representation of the reals. The set $\mathbb{R}$, extended with the two infinity symbols, and then denoted

---

[1] In [7,1] equalities are approximated by inequalities.

[2] All the variables are split uniformly [5], or the entire set of constraints must be algebraically reformulated [2].

by $\mathbb{R}^\infty = \mathbb{R} \bigcup \{-\infty, +\infty\}$, is in practice approximated by a finite subset $\mathbb{F}^\infty$ containing $-\infty$, $+\infty$ and 0. In interval-based constraint solvers, $\mathbb{F}^\infty$ usually corresponds to the floating point numbers used in the implementation. Let $<$ be the natural extension to $\mathbb{R}^\infty$ of the order relation $<$ over $\mathbb{R}$. For each l in $\mathbb{F}^\infty$, we denote by l^+ the smallest element in $\mathbb{F}^\infty$ greater than l, and by l^- the greatest element in $\mathbb{F}^\infty$ smaller than l.

A closed interval $[l, u]$ with $l, u \in \mathbb{F}$ is the set of real numbers $\{r \in \mathbb{R} \mid l \leq r \leq u\}$. Similarly, an open/closed interval (l, u) (respectively $(l, u]$) with $l, u \in \mathbb{F}$ is the set of real numbers $\{r \in \mathbb{R} \mid l \leq r < u\}$ (respectively $\{r \in \mathbb{R} \mid l < r \leq u\}$). The set of intervals, denoted by $\mathbb{I}$ is ordered by set inclusion. In the rest of the paper, intervals are written uppercase, reals or floats are sans-serif lowercase, vectors in boldface and sets in uppercase calligraphic letters. A *box*, $\mathbf{B} = I_1 \times \ldots I_n$ is a Cartesian product of n intervals. A *canonical interval* is a non-empty interval of the form $[l..l]$ or of the form $[l..l^+]$. A canonical box is a Cartesian product of canonical intervals.

Numerical Constraints. Let $\mathcal{V}_\mathbb{R} = \{x_1 \ldots x_n\}$ be a set of variables taking their values over $\mathbb{R}$. Given $\sum_\mathbb{R} = \{\mathbb{R}, \mathcal{F}_\mathbb{R}, \mathcal{R}_\mathbb{R}\}$ a structure where $\mathcal{F}_\mathbb{R}$ denotes a set of operators and $\mathcal{R}_\mathbb{R}$ a set of relations defined in $\mathbb{R}$, a *real constraint* is defined as a first order formula built from $\sum_\mathbb{R}$ and $\mathcal{V}_\mathbb{R}$. Interval arithmetic methods [3] are the basis of interval constraint solving. They approximate real numbers by intervals and compute conservative enclosures of the solution space of real constraint systems.

Relations and Approximations. Let $c(x_1, \ldots x_n)$ be a real constraint with arity n. The *relation* defined by c, denoted by ρ_c, is the set of tuples satisfying c. The relation defined by the negation, $\neg c$, of c is given by $\mathbb{R}^n \setminus \rho_c$ and is denoted by $\rho_{\bar{c}}$. The global *relation* defined by the conjunction of all the constraints of an NCSP, $\mathcal{C}$ is denoted $\rho_\mathcal{C}$. It can be approximated by a computer-representable superset or subset. In the first case the approximation is *complete* but may contain points that are not solutions. Conversely, in the second case, the approximation is *sound* but may lose certain solutions. A relation ρ can be approximated conservatively by the smallest (w.r.t set inclusion) union of boxes, $\mathbf{Union}\rho$, or more coarsely by the smallest box $\mathbf{Outer}\rho$, containing it. By using boxes included into ρ, sound (inner) approximations $\mathbf{Inner}\rho$ can also be defined. In [1], $\mathbf{Inner}\rho$ is defined as the set $\{r \in \mathbb{R}^n \mid \mathbf{Outer}\{r\} \subseteq \rho\}$. Figure 1 illustrates the different forms of approximations.

The computation of these approximations relies on the notion of *contracting operators*. Basically, a contracting operator narrows down the variable domains by discarding values that are locally inconsistent. This is often done using bound consistency. In this paper we use the notion of outer contracting operator, defined as follows:

Definition 1 (Outer contracting operator). *Let $\mathbb{I}$ be a set of intervals over $\mathbb{R}$ and ρ a real relation. The function $\mathbf{OC}_\rho : \mathbb{I}^n \to \mathbb{I}^n$ is a contracting operator for the relation ρ iff for any box $\mathbf{B}, \mathbf{B} \in \mathbb{I}^n$, the next properties are true:*

$$(1)\ \mathbf{OC}_\rho(\mathbf{B}) \subseteq \quad \mathbf{B} \quad \text{(Contractiveness)}$$
$$(2)\ \ \rho \cap \mathbf{B} \ \subseteq \mathbf{OC}_\rho(\mathbf{B})\ \text{(Completeness)}$$

Often, a monotonicity condition is also required [3].

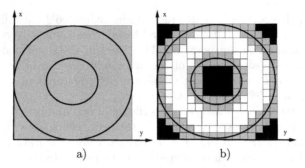

Fig. 1. a) is an **Outer** approximation; b) The set of white boxes give an **Inner** approximation, together with all the grey boxes they give a **Union** approximation.

2.2   Implementing Approximations of Type Union

In this paper we consider the problem of computing **Union** approximations. Several authors have recently addressed this issue. In [5], a recursive dichotomous split is performed on the variable domains. Each box obtained by splitting is tested for inclusion using interval arithmetic tools. The boxes obtained are hierarchically structured as 2^k-trees. The authors have demonstrated the practical usefulness of such techniques in robotics, etc. In [7], a similar algorithm is presented. However, only binary or ternary subsets of variables are considered when performing the splits. This means that for problems of dimension n, only quadtrees or octrees need to be constructed instead of the entire 2^n-tree. The approach is restricted to classes of problems with convexity properties. The technique proposed in [2] constructs the union algebraically, using Bernstein polynomials which give formal guarantees on the result of the inclusion test. The approach is restricted to polynomial constraints. Finally, [1] has addressed the related problem of computing **Inner** approximations, which are also unions of boxes but entirely contained in the solution space.

3   Conservative Union Approximation

Interval-based search techniques for CSPs with equalities and inequalities are essentially dichotomous. Variables are instantiated using intervals. When the search reaches an interval that contains no solutions it backtracks, otherwise the interval is recursively split in two halves up to an established resolution. The most successful techniques enhance this process by applying an outer-contracting operator to the overall constraint system, after each split. In all the known algorithms, equalities and inequalities are treated the same way. Splitting is performed until canonical intervals are reached and as long as the error inherent to the outer-contracting operator is smaller than the interval to split. This policy, referred to as DMBC (Dichotomous MBC) in the rest of the paper, works generally well for equality systems but leaves place for improvement when inequalities are involved. Let us consider a small NCSP with the following constraints:

$$P_1 = \{x_0 = x_1 + 1, x_2 + 1 = x_0 + x_1, x_2 \geq x_0 + 2, x_1 + 2x_3 \geq x_4, x_2 - x_3 \leq 3\}$$

where the domains are [-10,10]. For this example, the usual technique, efficiently implemented in ILOG Solver, a popular constraint-based solver, generates 8280 small boxes when all the solutions are explicitly asked for[3]. Using a set covering strategy for inequalities, the technique we propose delivers all the solutions, with the same precision, using only 199 boxes and with a speed up of three times.

The reason behind these results is that in the first case, the splitting is done blindly, without taking into account the topology of inequalities. Instead, the technique we propose includes a feasibility (soundness) test for boxes, which allows better splitting decisions. Given a constraint and a box, the feasibility test checks whether all the points in the box satisfy the constraint. Recently, an original idea was proposed in [1] for safely implementing such tests for general constraints. Given a constraint c and a box $\mathbf{B}$, it consists of proving that $\{r \in \mathbf{B} \mid r \in \rho_{\overline{c}}\} = \emptyset$. The proof is done by construction using DMBC on $\neg c$ and is valid due to the completeness of DMBC. We use a related approach for computing an outer approximation of type **Union**. We define a union conservative contracting operator as follows:

Definition 2 (Union Conservative Contracting Operator). *Let ρ be an n-ary real relation. A union conservative contracting operator for ρ, $\mathbf{UC}_c : \mathbb{I}^n \to \mathcal{P}(\mathbb{I})^n$ verifies:*

$$\forall \mathbf{B} : \mathbf{UC}_\rho(\mathbf{B}) \supseteq \mathbf{Union}(\mathbf{B} \bigcap \rho) \tag{1}$$

In this paper we use an outer contracting operator on inverted inequalities to avoid splitting completely feasible boxes. The goal is to generate a more compact output and to reduce the replication of search effort.

4   Algorithms

We now present an algorithm named UCA6 (Algorithm 1) that computes a **Union** approximation for numerical CSPs with equalities and inequalities. We note lists in the Prolog style $[Head|Tail]$. $\mathcal{B}$ denotes the list of children to be checked for a node, and $\mathcal{P}$ denotes the list of all $\mathcal{B}$. The algorithm presented is depth-first. Breadth-first and other heuristics can be obtained by treating the lists $\mathcal{B}$ and $\mathcal{P}$ as sets, $\mathcal{P}$ becoming respectively the union of all the sets of type $\mathcal{B}$. The algorithm UCA6 iteratively calls the function **getNext** which delivers a new **Outer** approximation for a subspace in the solution space. By construction, the new **Outer** approximation will not intersect with any previously computed box. The function **getNext** has two main components: a reduction operator, **reduc** (Algorithm 2), and a splitting operator, **split** (Algorithm 3). These operators are interleaved as in a classical maintaining bound consistency algorithm. Practically, it is preferable to stop the dichotomous split when the precision of the numeric search tool (splitting and contracting operators) can lead to unsafe solutions at a given precision ε. An unsafe solution is a box that may contain no real solution. **reduc**, checks this state using a function called *Indiscernible*(constraint, **Box, OC**, ε), which is not discussed here in detail[4].

---

[3] Typically, the algorithms are optimized for delivering the first solution.

[4] The simplest strategy consists of checking that all the intervals are smaller than ε, but more sophisticated techniques can be built by estimating computational errors.

Each search node is characterized by the next structures:

* The list $\mathcal{B}$ corresponds to a set of splits for the current search node. It defines the next branches of search. Each split correspond to a new node of the search.
* A box $\mathbf{B}$ defining the domains of the current NCSP.
* The current NCSP $\mathcal{C}$ containing only the constraints of the initial NCSP that can participate in pruning the search space. The constraints that are indiscernible or entirely feasible in $\mathbf{B}$ are eliminated.
* Each constraint q in a node is associated with a box, $\mathbf{B_q}$, such that all the space in $\mathbf{B} \setminus \mathbf{B_q}$ is feasible.

Each $\mathbf{B_q}$ is initially equal with the projection of the initial search space on the variables in the constraint q, after applying $\mathbf{OC}_{\rho_{\overline{q}}}$. One of the features of **reduc** is that it removes redundant completely feasible or indiscernible constraints. If the recent domain modifications of some inequality q have modified $\mathbf{B_q}$, q is checked for feasibility at line 4, and eventually removed from the current CSP (line 6). Equalities are similarly eliminated at line 9 when they become indiscernible.

4.1 Splitting Operator

The function **split** (Algorithm 3) allows for using three splitting strategies. The first one, **splitFeasible**, extracts sound subspaces for some inequality, as long as these subspaces fragment the search space in a ratio limited by a given *fragmentation threshold*, denoted by *frag* (line 3). The second and the third strategies (**splitIneq**, respectively **splitEq**), consist of choosing for dichotomous split, a variable involved in an inequality (respectively an equality) of the current NCSP $\mathcal{C}$. The heuristics used at lines 3, 3, 3, and 3 in Algorithm 3 can be based on the occurrence of variables in the constraints of $\mathcal{C}$, or according to a round robin technique. The domain of the chosen variable is then split in two halves. Techniques based on the occurrences of variables in constraints can also be used to devise heuristics on ordering the bounds at line 3 in **splitFeasible**. The criteria for choosing a constraint at line 3 can look for maximizing the size of the search space for which a given constraint is eliminated, minimize the number of children nodes, or maximize the number of constraints that can benefit[5] from the split.

Given two boxes $\mathbf{B}$ and $\mathbf{B_q}$, where $\mathbf{B}$ contains $\mathbf{B_q}$, and given a bound b in $\mathbf{B_q}$ for a variable x, we use the next notations:

* $\mathbf{B}_{\mathbf{f}(x,b)[\mathbf{B_q},\mathbf{B}]}$ is the (feasible) box not containing $\mathbf{B_q}$ obtained from $\mathbf{B}$ by splitting the variable x in b.
* $\mathbf{B}_{\mathbf{u}(x,b)[\mathbf{B_q},\mathbf{B}]}$ is the (indiscernible) box containing $\mathbf{B_q}$ obtained from $\mathbf{B}$ by splitting the variable x in b.
* $\mathbf{B}_{\frac{1}{2}\mathbf{r}(x)[\mathbf{B}]}$ is the (indiscernible) box obtained from $\mathbf{B}$ by splitting the variable x in half and retaining its upper half.
* $\mathbf{B}_{\frac{1}{2}\mathbf{l}(x)[\mathbf{B}]}$ is the (indiscernible) box obtained from $\mathbf{B}$ by splitting the variable x in half and retaining its lower half.

These concepts are illustrated in the Figure 2.

---

[5] The constraints for which the domains are split may propagate more when $\mathbf{OC}$ is applied.

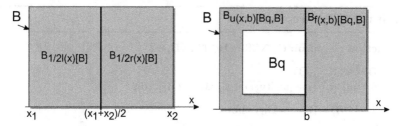

Fig. 2. Splitting operators.

Algorithm 1: *Search*

---

procedure UCA6 *(C = (V, C, D): NCSP)*
  $\mathcal{P} = [[\{\mathbf{OC}_{\rho_C}(D), C, \{\mathbf{B_q}(\mathbf{OC}_{\rho_C}(D))\}\}]]$
  while *(getNext(P, C, solution))* **do**
    $\mathcal{U} \leftarrow \{\text{solution}\} \cup \mathcal{U}$
  end
  return $\mathcal{U}$
end.
function getNext *(inout:* $\mathcal{P} = [\mathcal{B} = [\{\mathbf{B} \in \mathbb{I}^n, \mathcal{C}: \text{NCSP}, \{\mathbf{B_q} \in \mathbb{I}^n\}\} \mid T_{\mathcal{B}}] \mid T_{\mathcal{P}}]$;
in: $\mathcal{C_G} \in$ NCSP; **out:** *solution*$\in \mathbb{I}^n$ *)* $\rightarrow$ *bool*
  forever do

    if *(B = [ ])* **then**

      if *(T_{\mathcal{P}} = [ ])* **then**

        return (false)
      else

        $\mathcal{P} \leftarrow T_{\mathcal{P}}$
      end
      continue
    end
    $(\mathcal{C}', \mathbf{B}', \{\mathbf{B_q}'\}) \leftarrow \mathbf{reduc}(\mathcal{C}, \mathbf{B}, \{\mathbf{B_q}\})$
    $\mathcal{B} \leftarrow T_{\mathcal{B}}$
    if *(B' <> ∅)* **then**

      if *(C' = ∅)* **then**

        solution $\leftarrow \mathbf{B}'$
        return (true)
      end
      $\mathcal{B}' \leftarrow \text{split}(\mathbf{B}', \mathcal{C}', \{\mathbf{B_q}'\})$
      $\mathcal{P} \leftarrow [\mathcal{B}' \mid \mathcal{P}]$
    end
  end
end.

Algorithm 2: *Problem Reduction*

$\quad$ **function reduc** *(in: C : NCSP, $\mathbf{B} \in \mathbb{I}^n$, $\{\mathbf{B_i} \in \mathbb{I}^n\}$) $\rightarrow$ (NCSP, $\mathbb{I}^n$, $\{\mathbb{I}^n\}$)*

$\quad\quad$ $\mathbf{B}' \leftarrow \mathbf{OC}_{\rho_C}(\mathbf{B})$
$\quad\quad$ **for all** *(q={inequality}, $q \in C$, $\mathbf{B_q} \in \{\mathbf{B_i}\}$)* **do**

$\quad\quad\quad$ **if** *($\mathbf{B}' \cap \mathbf{B_q} <> \mathbf{B_q}$)* **then**

$\quad\quad\quad\quad$ $\mathbf{B_q} \leftarrow \mathbf{OC}_{\rho_{\neg q}}(\mathbf{B}' \cap \mathbf{B_q})$
$\quad\quad\quad\quad$ **if** *(($\mathbf{B_q} = \emptyset$)$\vee$Indiscernible(q,$\mathbf{B_q}$))* **then**

$\quad\quad\quad\quad\quad$ $C \leftarrow C \setminus \{q\}$, $\{\mathbf{B_i}\} \leftarrow \{\mathbf{B_i}\} \setminus \mathbf{B_q}$
$\quad\quad\quad\quad$ **end**
$\quad\quad\quad$ **end**
$\quad\quad$ **end**
$\quad\quad$ **for all** *(q=equality, $q \in C$)* **do**

$\quad\quad\quad$ **if** *(Indiscernible(q,$\mathbf{B}'$))* **then**

$\quad\quad\quad\quad$ $C \leftarrow C \setminus \{q\}$, $\{\mathbf{B_i}\} \leftarrow \{\mathbf{B_i}\} \setminus \mathbf{B_q}$
$\quad\quad\quad$ **end**
$\quad\quad$ **end**
$\quad\quad$ return $(C, \mathbf{B}', \{\mathbf{B_i}\})$
$\quad$ **end.**

Proposition 1. *Let $C = (V, C, D)$ be an NCSP. UCA6 computes a union conservative contractive operator for ρ_C.*

Sketch of proof. Both the splitting and the contracting operators are complete and conservative. As invariant, the union of $\mathcal{P}$ with the set of already returned solutions corresponds to the output of a union conservative contractive operator. Therefore, when $\mathcal{P}$ is empty, the output solutions satisfy the property.

5   Handling Space Limitations

When a representation of all the solutions of a NCSP has to be built, or even its projection to a quite limited number of variables, the precision is the most constraining factor. The space required depends exponentially on this precision. The analytic representation itself is very efficient in space, but is less easy to visualize and offers less topological information. The amount of aggregation on solutions is a second factor that controls the required space. The improvements that can be achieved depend on the problem at hand. In order to characterize the representations that can be obtained we introduce the notion of $\varepsilon_1\varepsilon_2$-consistency which allows for constructing the representation of the solution space only for a given subset of variables.

Definition 3 (ε-solution). *An ε-solution of a NCSP $\mathcal{N}$ is a box denoted by $\nu_{\mathcal{N},\varepsilon} = I_1 \times \ldots \times I_n$ (n is the number of variables in $\mathcal{N}$) such that the search tools with resolution ε (splitting and contracting operators) cannot reduce it or decide the absence of solutions inside it.*

Algorithm 3: *Splitting*

---

function split$(in: \mathbf{B} \in \mathbb{I}^n, \mathcal{C} : \text{NCSP}, \{\mathbf{B_i} \in \mathbb{I}^n\}) \to [\{\mathbb{I}^n, \text{NCSP}, \{\mathbb{I}^n\}\} \mid \_]$

  $fun \leftarrow choose\ appropriate(\text{splitFeasible, splitIneq, splitEq})$
  $\mathcal{B} \leftarrow [\,]$
  $fun(\mathbf{B}, \mathcal{C}, \{\mathbf{B_i}\}, \mathcal{B})$
  $return\ \mathcal{B}$
end.
procedure splitFeasible$(in:\mathbf{B},\mathcal{C},\{\mathbf{B_i}\};inout:\mathcal{B} \in [\{\mathbb{I}^n, \text{NCSP}, \{\mathbb{I}^n\}\} \mid \_])$

  $q \leftarrow choose\ \{inequality\} \in \mathcal{C},\ \mathbf{B_q} \in \{\mathbf{B_i}\}$
  foreach *(bound* b *of some variable* x *of* q *in* $\mathbf{B_q}$ *(e.q. in descending order*
  of the relative distance rd *to the corresponding bound in* **B**$)$ *)* **do**

      if (rd $<frag$) continue
      $\mathbf{B'} \leftarrow \mathbf{B}_{f(x,b)[\mathbf{B_q},\mathbf{B}]}$
      $\mathbf{B} \leftarrow \mathbf{B}_{u(x,b)[\mathbf{B_q},\mathbf{B}]}$
      $\mathcal{B} \leftarrow [\{\mathbf{B'},\mathcal{C} \setminus \{q\},\{\mathbf{B_i}\} \setminus \mathbf{B_q}\} \mid \mathcal{B}\,]$
  end
  $\mathcal{B} \leftarrow [\{\mathbf{B},\mathcal{C},\{\mathbf{B_i}\}\} \mid \mathcal{B}\,]$
end.
procedure splitIneq$(in:\mathbf{B},\mathcal{C},\{\mathbf{B_i}\};inout:\mathcal{B} \in [\{\mathbb{I}^n, \text{NCSP}, \{\mathbb{I}^n\}\} \mid \_])$

  $q \leftarrow choose\ \{inequality, \mathbf{B_q} \in \mathbb{I}^n\} \in \mathcal{C}$
  $x \leftarrow choose\ variable\ of\ q\ given\ \mathcal{C}$
  $\mathcal{B} \leftarrow [\{\mathbf{B}_{\frac{1}{2}r(x)[\mathbf{B}]},\mathcal{C},\{\mathbf{B_i}\}\} \mid \mathcal{B}\,]$
  $\mathcal{B} \leftarrow [\{\mathbf{B}_{\frac{1}{2}l(x)[\mathbf{B}]},\mathcal{C},\{\mathbf{B_i}\}\} \mid \mathcal{B}\,]$
end.
procedure splitEq$(in:\mathbf{B},\mathcal{C},\{\mathbf{B_i}\};inout:\mathcal{B} \in [\{\mathbb{I}^n, \text{NCSP}, \{\mathbb{I}^n\}\} \mid \_])$

  $q \leftarrow choose\ \{equality\} \in \mathcal{C}$
  $x \leftarrow choose\ variable\ of\ q\ given\ \mathcal{C}$
  $\mathcal{B} \leftarrow [\{\mathbf{B}_{\frac{1}{2}r(x)[\mathbf{B}]},\mathcal{C},\{\mathbf{B_i}\}\} \mid \mathcal{B}\,]$
  $\mathcal{B} \leftarrow [\{\mathbf{B}_{\frac{1}{2}l(x)[\mathbf{B}]},\mathcal{C},\{\mathbf{B_i}\}\} \mid \mathcal{B}\,]$
end.

Definition 4 $(\varepsilon_1\varepsilon_2\text{-}\mathbf{consistency})$. *A constraint* $c(x_1,...x_k)$ *of a NCSP* $\mathcal{N} = (V,C,D)$ *is* $\varepsilon_1\varepsilon_2$-*consistent related to the variables in* $X = \{x_1,...,x_k\}$, $X \subseteq V$, *iff:*

$$\rho_N \mid_X \subseteq \rho_c,\ \forall \overline{v} \in D_{x_1} \times ... \times D_{x_k},\ \overline{v} \in \rho_c \Rightarrow \exists \nu_{N,\varepsilon_2},\ \exists \overline{b} \in \nu_{\mathcal{N},\varepsilon_2} \mid_X,\ \mid \overline{v}-\overline{b} \mid < \varepsilon_1$$

The procedure **UCA6** can be modified for generating the boxes for representing an $\varepsilon_1\varepsilon_2$-consistent constraint on a set X of variables. This is done by filtering out of $\mathcal{P}$, the portions of search space, closer to the found solution (line 1) than a distance ε_1. The distance is computed in the space defined by the variables in X.

6   Experiments

Only a small amount of work exists on computing union approximations for numerical problems with mixed equality/inequality constraints. Often these problems are recast as optimization problems, with artificial optimization criteria, to fit the solvers. Hence, no significant set of benchmarks is presently available in this area. In this section we present a preliminary evaluation on the following small set of problems.

WP is a 2D simplification of the design model for a kinematic pair consisting of a wheel and a pawl. The constraints determine the regions where the pawl can touch the wheel without blocking its motion.

$$WP = \{20 < \sqrt{x^2 + y^2} < 50, 12y/\sqrt{(x-12)^2 + y^2} < 10, x : [-50, 50], y : [0, 50]\}$$

SB describes structural and safety restrictions for the components of a floor consisting of a concrete slab on steel beams.

$$SB = \{u + c_1 w^{1.5161} - p = 0, u - (c_6 h_s + c_7)s \le 0,$$
$$c_2 - c_3 s + c_4 s^2 - c_5 s^3 - h_s \le 0, c_8 (pw^2)^{0.3976} - h_b \le 0, c_9 (pw^3)^{0.2839} - h_b \le 0\}$$

Finally, SC is a collision problem requiring some minimal distance between a trajectory and an object [1].

$$SC = \{\forall t, \sqrt{(2.5 \sin t - x)^2 + (2.5 \cos t - y)^2} \ge 0.5, t : [-\pi..\pi], x, y : [-5..5]\}$$

On problems with exactly one inequality and no equalities, UCA6(**EqFeasibleIneq**) defined further is equivalent to ICAb5 presented in [1].

For the **splitFeasible** strategy our implementation chooses the inequality, q, whose split yields the child node with maximal search space where q is eliminated as completely feasible. For the other two splitting strategies, constraints and variables are chosen in a round robin fashion. We use *frag*=0.2. We have tested three combinations of these strategies: **EqIneq**:(splitEq,splitIneq), **IneqEq**:(splitIneq,splitEq), and **EqFeasibleIneq**:(splitEq,splitFeasible,splitIneq). The **OC** operator is 3B-consistency. DMBC is implemented with ILOG Solver. The obtained results are described in the following array:

Problem	DMBC (boxes / seconds)	EqIneq	IneqEq	EqFeasibleIneq
P_1 ($\varepsilon = .1$)	8280 / 3.38s	276 / 1.67s	410 / 1.47s	199 / 0.88s
SB ($\varepsilon = .02$)	67122 / 182.2s	122 / 0.47s	148 / 0.46s	92 / 0.35s
WP ($\varepsilon = .1$)	>100000 / >238s	5021 / 2.01s	5021 / 2.01s	5561 / 15.18s
SC ($\varepsilon = .1$)	16384 / 68.36s	3022 / 54.88s	3022 / 54.88s	2857 / 53s

7   Conclusion

Interval-constraint based solvers are usually designed to deliver punctual solutions. Their techniques work efficiently for problems with equalities, but might alter both efficiency and compactness of the output representation for many problems with inequalities. In this paper, we propose an algorithm for numerical CSPs with mixed equality/inequality constraints that remedies this state of affairs. The approach combines the classical interval search techniques for equalities with set covering strategies designed to reduce the number of boxes approximating inequalities.

References

1. F. Benhamou and F. Goualard. Universally quantified interval constraints. In *Procs. of CP'2000*, pages 67–82, 2000.
2. J. Garloff and B. Graf. Solving strict polynomial inequalities by Bernstein expansion. *Symbolic Methods in Control System Analysis and Design, London: IEE*, pages 339–352, 1999.
3. L. Granvilliers. *Consistances locales et transformations symboliques de contraintes d'intervalles*. PhD thesis, Université d'Orléans, déc 98.
4. ILOG. *Solver 4.4, Reference Manual*. ILOG, 1999.
5. L. Jaulin. *Solution globale et garantie de problèmes ensemblistes ; Application à l'estimation non linéaire et à la commande robuste*. PhD thesis, Université Paris-Sud, Orsay, Feb 94.
6. O. Lhomme and M. Rueher. Application des techniques CSP au raisonnement sur les intervalles. *Revue d'intelligence artificielle*, 11(3):283–311, 97. Dunod.
7. D. Sam-Haroud and B. Faltings. Consistency techniques for continuous constraints. *Constraints, An International Journal,1*, pages 85–118, 96.
8. P. Van Hentenryck. A gentle introduction to Numerica. *AI*, 103:209–235, 98.

Searching for Macro Operators with Automatically Generated Heuristics

István T. Hernádvölgyi*

University of Ottawa
School of Information Technology & Engineering
Ottawa, Ontario, K1N 6N5, Canada
istvan@site.uottawa.ca

Abstract. Macro search is used to derive solutions quickly for large search spaces at the expense of optimality. We present a novel way of building macro tables. Our contribution is twofold: (1) for the first time, we use automatically generated heuristics to find optimal macros, (2) due to the speed-up achieved by (1), we merge consecutive subgoals to reduce the solution lengths. We use the Rubik's Cube to demonstrate our techniques. For this puzzle, a 44% improvement of the average solution length was achieved over macro tables built with previous techniques.

1 Introduction

In state space search a solution is a sequence of operators. A solution is optimal if no shorter operator sequence exists that reaches the goal state from the start state. It is often the case that a suboptimal solution can be obtained much faster than an optimal one. Our aim is to find *near optimal* solutions *quickly*. Macro search reduces search effort by decomposing the original problem into a series of subproblems, which can be solved separately. The individual solution paths concatenated form the final solution. Restricting the solution path to go through subgoal states unfortunately results in suboptimal solutions. The less the number of subgoals, the shorter the solutions but also the larger the individual search spaces and the more the number of macros. In this paper, we reduce the number of subgoals by merging consecutive ones. To cope with larger search spaces, we employ automatically generated heuristics. Subgoals which require a large number of macros to calculate are solved by heuristic search for each problem instance instead of precomputing and storing the macros. We demonstrate these techniques on the Rubik's Cube and compare our results to various approaches. We conclude that our method is effective and results in significant reduction in solution length at reasonable extra computational effort.

---

* I like to thank Dr. Robert C. Holte and Dr. Jonathan Schaeffer for helpful comments. This research was partially founded by an NSERC grant.

E. Stroulia and S. Matwin (Eds.): AI 2001, LNAI 2056, pp. 194–203, 2001.

2 Subgoals and Macros

In macro search, a problem is decomposed into a series of subgoals. A state is represented by a vector of state variables and the subgoals correspond to establishing the goal values of these variables while leaving the values intact for those state variables which were fixed for previous subgoals. The state variables fixed for subgoal s_i are always a subset of the state variables for subgoal s_{i+1}. The last element of the subgoal sequence is the goal state itself. Korf [7] gives sufficient properties for spaces which make macro search applicable.

The macros are operator sequences composed of the original operators, which can be used to fix subgoals. The macros for subgoal s_i fix the values of those state variables which are specified for this subgoal and leave the values of the already fixed variables for subgoal s_{i-1} intact. The number of macros for subgoal s_i depends on how many ways the state variables to be fixed for this subgoal can occur such that the state variables fixed for subgoal s_{i-1} have their goal values. The *macro table* stores the macros needed to fix each subgoal.

The solution is the concatenation of macros solving the subgoals. At each subgoal, the macro which solves the current subgoal for the actual values of the state variables is retrieved and appended to the solution path.

A macro is *optimal* if no shorter operator sequence exists which fixes the subgoal variables without disturbing the ones already fixed. Traditionally macros were found by uninformed techniques. Short optimal macros can be found by breadth-first search or by iterative deepening. These methods are general and work well for short macros, but longer macros require more sophisticated techniques.

Partial-match, bi-directional search [9] is a breadth-first expansion from the start and the goal state simultaneously. If the two search frontiers meet, an optimal macro has been found. There are two drawbacks to using this method. First, all operators must be invertible. Second, the search frontiers must be kept in memory. While memory requirements are reduced to the square root of breadth-first search, for long macros and spaces with large branching factor, this method is infeasible.

Macro composition is a technique developed by Sims [12]. Suppose macros m_1 and m_2 have the same invariant state variables. The idea is to compose m_1 with m_2^{-1} to obtain a new macro $m_1 m_2^{-1}$ which has extra invariants. The technique is widely used in Computational Group Theory and is often referred to as the Schreier-Sims method. Korf used macro composition to find those macros which he could not find by bi-directional search due to lack of memory. The Schreier-Sims method [1] only uses macro compositions and is proved to be of polynomial order in the number of state variables. The drawback of this method is that macros obtained this way are not optimal.

The number of subgoals can be reduced by fixing more than one state variables for a single subgoal. This almost inevitably results in the explosion of the number of macros needed. The additional state variables to fix could potentially have a large combination of legal value assignments. When the number of macros is excessively large, heuristic search may be employed to fix the subgoal in question. In fact, this is the approach we take in our Rubik's Cube experiment.

The length of the optimal macros for merged subgoals may also increase but will certainly not exceed the sum of the optimal macros corresponding to the individual subgoals. This is where the solution length reduction comes from.

3   Automatic Generation of Admissible Heuristics

Each subgoal in the macro table represents a different search space. If we are to find macros with heuristic search, we need different heuristics for every space. Effective admissible heuristics are hard to hand craft and for macro search we need heuristics for every subgoal. The first automatically generated heuristic for the Rubik's Cube is due to Prieditis [11]. Korf [10] used the *pattern database* method of Culberson and Schaeffer [2] to find optimal solutions to random instances of the Rubik's Cube for the first time. A pattern database is a hash table of heuristic values indexed by pattern states. Each pattern state represents a number of states from the original space and is obtained by replacing some of the values of the state variables with "blanks". The space of pattern states is an abstraction of the original space where optimal distances between an abstract state and the abstract goal state provide admissible heuristic values for search algorithms in the original space. The size of the pattern database is the size of the abstract space. The pattern abstractions used by Culberson and Schaeffer for the 15-Puzzle and the abstractions used by Korf for the Rubik's Cube were hand-crafted. Our method of *domain abstraction* [4] generalizes the notion of pattern databases. Instead of just using "blanks" we proved [3] that any map of the original domain to a smaller cardinality domain generates a homomorphism which can be used to derive admissible heuristic values. These maps of the domain can be automatically generated. We verified a conjecture due to Korf [10] in a large scale experiment [5] that the larger the pattern database the fewer the number of states expanded in the original space and that this trade-off is close to linear. In our framework, the larger the cardinality of the image domain the larger the pattern database. We obtain the pattern database by first building the *transpose graph* of the abstract space. This is a graph with vertices of the pattern states but the direction of the operators is reversed. We then perform a breadth-first expansion of this graph from the abstract goal state. We use the transpose graph because we do not require the operators to be invertible.

4   The Rubik's Cube Experiment

The Rubik's Cube is a well known combinatorial puzzle often used as a benchmark problem for new algorithms. Optimal solutions (a dozen or so) were only recently obtained [10]. Finding short solutions quickly still remains a challenge. The cube has six colored faces with nine colored stickers each. The moves are the quarter turns of the faces. The goal of the game is to bring the same color stickers back on each face after the puzzle has been scrambled. Structurally the cube is made up of twenty six little blocks called cubies. There are eight corner cubies each with three different colored stickers, twelve edge cubies with two colored faces and six center cubies with one color sticker each (Figure 1). The center cubies do not move with respect to each other, hence they should not be part of an encoding of the space. The space has $4.3 \cdot 10^{19}$ states. The quarter turn

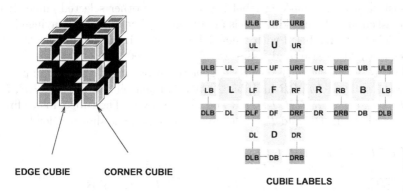

EDGE CUBIE   **CORNER CUBIE**

CUBIE LABELS

Fig. 1. The Rubik's Cube

operators U, L, R, F, B and D correspond to a clock-wise quarter turn of the *up, left, right, front, back* and *down* faces respectively. We count two consecutive quarter turns of the same face in the same direction as a single move ($B\ B = B^2$). The edge and corner cubies are labeled as shown on Figure 1.

For the experiment, we built 3 macro tables. Table $T_{18,1}$ is a macro table with 18 subgoals (the order of these subgoals is listed in Table 1 and correspond to our preference to solve the cube by hand). T_6 is a macro table with six subgoals. The subgoals of T_6 (Table 2) were obtained by merging consecutive subgoals from $T_{18,1}$. The first subgoal of T_6 is to fix all cubies on the "up" face at once. Rather than precomputing and storing in a table the 96 million macros required for this subgoal, we instead solve each instance of it, as needed, by a heuristic search with automatically generated heuristics. $T_{18,2}$ is also a macro table with 18 subgoals. It uses the same subgoal sequence as Korf did in his original work [6]. At the time, he could not calculate all the optimal macros (because of small memory computers) and obtained 7 by macro composition. We replaced these 7 by the optimal macros found by our method.

The pattern databases were automatically generated by domain abstraction. The original domain is composed of the cubie and orientation labels. The non invariant cubies are masked by a special label $*$ (they will be fixed for later subgoals).

Our domain map generator selects two corner cubies or two edge cubies. First, it randomly decides to either mask their orientation or their identity. Then it expands the abstract space. If in this expansion the state limit N is reached, the process is aborted and two more cubies are masked. This continues until a pattern database with less than N states is built. The orientation is 0 or 1 for edge cubies and 0, 1 or 2 for corner cubies. They can be masked with the label x indicating that the cubie's orientation is not taken into account. When the identities of the cubies are masked, instead of their orientation, the following cases may occur. If the two selected cubies haven't been masked yet, a new masking label is assigned to both so they are indistinguishable. If exactly one is masked, then its masking label is given to the other selected cubie. If both are masked and the masking labels are different, then all cubies having either of these labels are relabeled with a new label. Our limit on the number of pattern states in the database in all cases was $N = 2,000,000$.

Let us demonstrate the heuristic generation process with an example. Consider the subgoal RF, RB in Table 2. At this point, cubies URF, URB, ULB, ULF, UF, UL, UR, UB, LF, LB and DL are fixed. The subgoal is to find the macros which fix RF and RB. The goal state $g_{RF,RB}$ is shown below[1].

$$\left\{ \begin{array}{llllllll} URF_0 & URB_0 & ULB_0 & ULF_0 & * & * & * & * \\ URF & URB & ULB & ULF & DRF & DRB & DLB & DLF \\ \hline UF_0 & UL_0 & UR_0 & UB_0 & LF_0 & LB_0 & DL_0 & \mathbf{RF_0}\ \mathbf{RB_0}\ *\ \ *\ \ * \\ UF & UL & UR & UB & LF & LB & DL & RF\ \ RB\ DF\ DB\ DR \end{array} \right\}$$

After a few iterations, the domain abstraction generator could have relabeled the domain so that the above goal state became

$$\left\{ \begin{array}{llllllll} A_0 & A_0 & B_x & B_x & * & * & * & * \\ URF & URB & ULB & ULF & DRF & DRB & DLB & DLF \\ \hline C_x & C_x & C_x & C_x & D_x & D_x & D_x & \mathbf{RF_0}\ \mathbf{RB_0}\ *\ \ *\ \ * \\ UF & UL & UR & UB & LF & LB & DL & RF\ \ RB\ DF\ DB\ DR \end{array} \right\}$$

In this case, cubies URF and URB were relabeled to A but their orientations were kept unique. The other two invariant corner cubies were labeled B and they also had their orientations masked. Four of the edge cubies were labeled C and three were masked with label D. The orientations of the invariant edge cubies were all masked except for RF and RB. Their identity and orientation is kept unique in order to obtain accurate heuristics for the start states.

For the initial subgoals we used only one pattern database. Subsequent subgoals used some of the pattern databases from the preceding subgoal as well. The heuristic values were combined by the max function to guarantee admissible heuristic values.

We also performed post processing on the solution paths. First, operators followed by their inverses cancel. Second, consecutive occurrences of the same operator may be replaced by a power. In particular, opposing faces of the Rubik's Cube do not move common cubies. This allows us to rearrange the operators in the path such that the path shortening described above can be further applied.

---

[1] cubies are subscripted by their orientation and indexed by position, the line divides the corner and edge cubies in the vector

5   Results & Discussion

We generated 10,000 random instances of the Rubik's Cube by random walks of 500 moves each. These problem instances were then evaluated by the 18 subgoal and the 6 subgoal macro tables. The histograms are shown on Figure 2. It is clear

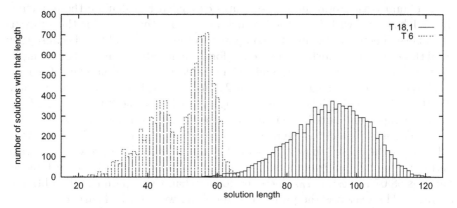

Fig. 2. Histograms of solution lengths obtained for 10,000 random cube states

from these histograms that the longest solutions with the 6 subgoal macro table are as good as the shortest solutions with the 18 subgoal macro table. It would be worthwhile to compare these results to the optimal solutions but today even with the latest methods this is impossible. It is conjectured [10] that the longest shortest path (diameter) between two states is no more than 20 moves and the vast majority of states are 18 moves away from the goal state. In light of these numbers, we estimate that our solutions with T_6 are on average 3 times and in the worst case 4 times of optimal. With $T_{18,1}$ the solutions are 5 times longer on average and in the worst case 7 times of the optimal length. The average solution length on these 10,000 random instances for T_6 is 50.3 and for $T_{18,1}$ it is 89.8. $T_{18,1}$ performs slightly worse than $T_{18,2}$, whose solutions average at 82.7 moves.

T_6's histogram seems to have two humps. We believe that this is due to the fact that there are many very short macros for the second, third, fourth and fifth subgoals. If the cubies are in a "lucky" arrangement they will be fixed with significantly fewer moves than the average.

Tables 1 and 2 show the detailed statistics for obtaining macro tables $T_{18,1}$ and T_6. Table 1 also gives the combined results for those subgoals which were merged to form single subgoals in T_6. The entries in the first column are the individual subgoals. It is assumed that the cubies listed before the subgoal are fixed. For example, in Table 1, the first subgoal is to fix the cubie URF, the second subgoal is to fix the cubie URB while leaving the previously fixed cubies (namely URF) intact. For T_6 the first subgoal is to fix the entire upper face (the 8 cubies listed in the first row and first column of Table 2). The second column entries are the number of macros needed for the subgoal. For example, the number of macros needed for subgoal URB in $T_{18,1}$ is 21 (second row, second column) because cubie URB can occur in 21 different places and orientations once the previous subgoals are fixed. For T_6, the first subgoal would require 96,282,624 macros, which we do not store or pre-calculate. The third column lists the longest of the macros for the subgoal and column four gives the average. The fifth column is the total number of states expanded to calculate these macros. Table 1 has rows with label total, which are simply the totals for the subgoals just above. These can be directly compared to the rows of Table 2, because they total those subgoals which are merged to form single subgoals in T_6. For example, for the three subgoals LF, LB and DL in Table 1, the total number of macros is 42, the total of the longest macros is 25 and the total of the average of macro lengths is 15.7 moves. The corresponding subgoal in Table 2 is $\{LF, LB, DL\}$. For the composite subgoal, the number of macros needed is 2,688. The longest of these macros is 11 and the average macro length is 8.84 moves. The grand total column for the tables show the totals for all subgoals. The projected average performance of $T_{18,1}$ (grand total row, fourth column in table 1) is 101.6 moves and it is 58.07 moves for T_6. These are longer than the experimentally obtained averages. The reason is the path post-processing we described earlier.

$T_{18,1}$ has 258 macros of which 18 are trivial. T_6 has $2,902$ macros stored of which only 5 are trivial. A trivial macro has length 0 and corresponds to an already fixed subgoal. We counted these as well, because it can happen that a subgoal is fixed by chance and therefore should be included in the averages.

Both the projected and the experimentally determined worst case for T_6 (74 and 68) are much better than the average performance of $T_{18,1}$ (and $T_{18,2}$). The improvement in the average solution length is 44%. These reductions speak for themselves, however we must also consider at what cost they were achieved.

First we consider memory used to obtain the macro tables. It took 13 different pattern databases with 15 million entries stored altogether to build the macros for $T_{18,1}$. At any time there were no more than three pattern databases in memory with 5 million entries combined. We needed 11 pattern databases to build T_6 and similarly, we never used more than three of these at a time. All macros were obtained by IDA* [8], hence no memory additional to the pattern databases was required during the searches. Therefore we can conclude that memory requirements are roughly equivalent. In comparison to the partial-match, bi-directional search method this is big savings in memory usage. The longest macros are of length 13. For these, a bi-directional search must reach level 6, where the number of states in the search tree is over 10 million. Keeping in mind that the search frontier must be in memory and that for finding each macro the search trees are different, heuristic search with reusable pattern databases is a clear winner. To obtain the 258 macros of $T_{18,1}$, a total of 108 million states were expanded, while 2 billion states were expanded to build the $2,902$ macros of T_6. Building $T_{18,1}$ took an hour of CPU time, while over a day of CPU time was needed to build T_6.

Table 1. Macro table $T_{18,1}$: Statistics

subgoal	# of macros	longest macro	average macro	states expanded
URF	24	2	1.54	200
URB	21	3	2.05	8,300
ULB	18	4	2.22	40,400
ULF	15	6	3.87	117,000
UF	24	8	5.33	187,200
UL	22	8	5.27	171,600
UR	20	8	5.40	156,000
UB	18	8	5.22	142,000
total:	**162**	**47**	**30.90**	**822,700**
LF	16	9	5.50	128,000
LB	14	9	5.92	122,400
DL	12	7	4.33	92,600
total:	**42**	**25**	**15.70**	**344,000**
RF	10	9	6.40	91,200
RB	8	10	6.75	141,600
total:	**18**	**19**	**13.15**	**232,800**
DF	6	7	5.33	46,800
DB	7	11	7.00	286,600
total:	**13**	**18**	**12.33**	**333,400**
DRF	12	12	8.25	6,117,600
DRB	9	12	8.22	6,081,000
total:	**21**	**24**	**16.47**	**12,198,600**
DLF	2	13	13.00	94,303,000
grand total:	**258**	**146**	**101.6**	**108,234,500**

Table 2. Macro table T_6: Statistics

subgoal	# of macros	longest macro	average macro	states expanded
$URF, URB,$ $ULB, ULF,$ UF,UL,UR,UB	96,282,624 *not stored!*	~ 13	9.30	$\sim 250,000$ *for each solution!*
LF,LB,DL	2,688	11	8.84	109,524,000
RF,RB	80	12	8.45	5,526,200
DF,DB	24	12	7.75	3,875,000
DRF,DRB	108	13	10.73	1,914,102,800
DLF	2	13	13.00	94,303,000
grand total:	**2,902**	**74**	**58.07**	**2,127,331,000**

The memory required to obtain a solution with $T_{18,1}$ is to store the 258 macros. This is negligible. On the other hand, T_6 uses two pattern databases with a combined size of 300,000 entries to search for the first subgoal. It also has more macros to store for the rest of the subgoals. However, we believe that even these requirements are negligible with modern computers.

With respect to the speed of obtaining a solution, $T_{18,1}$ and $T_{18,2}$ are the clear winners. It takes a constant number of operations to derive a solution and the post processing is linear in the number of moves of the solution. T_6 performs a heuristic search to fix the 8 cubies and this on average takes 250,000 states to expand. While this search takes about a second with our implementation, it is orders of magnitudes slower than $T_{18,1}$ and $T_{18,2}$.

Our primary goal, however, was to significantly reduce the solution lengths. We believe that the additional time required to build the macros and the initial search to fix the first subgoal are well worth the effort.

From Tables 1 and 2, we can also determine where the savings come from. The first 8 subgoals combined in $T_{18,1}$ are represented by a single search in T_6. The projected worst case for these subgoals is 47 seven moves and the average is 30.9 moves without post processing. We conjecture that it would take no more than 13 moves to fix the eight subgoals together (we can prove a very pessimistic 15), the average is 9.3 moves. The difference in the predicted average is 21 moves and hence this one big subgoal merge accounts for almost 50% of the total savings alone. Then we merged 3 subgoals (*LF*, *LB* and *DL*) into one and effectively increased the number of macros needed to calculate 64 times (from 42 to 2,688). The projected expected savings is 7 moves (from 15.7 to 8.84). The rest of the subgoal combinations show similar ratios, except there is less of an explosion in the number of macros.

There are two other methods we can compare our approach to. The two extremes of the scale are the algebraic solutions calculated by the Schreier-Sims method and the optimal solutions obtained by Richard Korf. Our implementation of the Schreier-Sims method needs only 8 minutes to build a stabilizer chain[2] (the Group Theory equivalent of macro tables). The average solution length is around 455 moves. A path improvement, suggested by Philip Osterlund in a private communication, shrinks these paths to an average of 89 moves, but is also much costlier than obtaining the original solution.

The optimal solutions obtained by Korf [10] required expanding 3 billion states for optimal solutions of length 16 and close to a trillion states for optimal solutions of length 18. He used three pattern databases with 172 million entries combined. The long solutions take days of CPU time individually. In essence, any one of the optimal searches, even for the short solutions, require expanding many more states and much more memory than obtaining all macros in both macro tables combined and solving the 10,000 test instances.

---

[2] This was implemented in the interpreted language MIT Scheme, while our macro implementation is in C++

6 Future Work and Conclusion

In this paper we demonstrated that macro operators can be found efficiently with automatically generated heuristics. The speedup due to heuristic search over uninformed techniques also allows us to reduce the number of subgoals by merging consecutive ones. This results in dramatically reduced solution lengths at reasonable additional cost. On our test problem, the Rubik's Cube, we achieved 44% improvement in solution length. Unlike bi-directional techniques, our method does not require invertibility of operators and can run within user defined memory limits. We are currently investigating whether the order of subgoals have an impact on performance. Different encodings of the same problem will give rise to different types and number of subgoals. However, once a subgoal sequence is defined, our method of merging consecutive subgoals and using heuristic search with automatically generated heuristics can improve the solution lengths at the expense of calculating and storing more macros.

References

1. G. Butler. *Fundamental Algorithms for Permutation Groups*. Lecture Notes in Computer Science. Springer-Verlag, 1991.
2. J. C. Culberson and J. Schaeffer. Searching with pattern databases. *Advances in Artificial Intelligence (Lecture Notes in Artificial Intelligence 1081)*, pages 402–416, 1996.
3. I. T. Hernádvölgyi and R. C. Holte. PSVN: A vector representation for production systems. Technical Report TR-99-04, School of Information Technology and Engineering, University of Ottawa, 1999.
4. I. T. Hernádvölgyi and R. C. Holte. Experiments with automatically created memory-based heuristics. In *Abstraction, Reformulation and Approximation*, volume 1864 of *Lecture Notes in Artificial Intelligence*, pages 281–290, 2000.
5. R. C. Holte and I. T. Hernádvölgyi. A space-time tradeoff for memory-based heuristics. *Proceedings of the Sixteenth National Conference on Artificial Intelligence (AAAI-99)*, pages 704–709, 1999.
6. R. E. Korf. *Learning to Solve Problems by Searching for Macro-Operators*. PhD thesis, Canegie-Mellon University, 1983.
7. R. E. Korf. Operator decomposability: A new type of problem structure. *Proceedings of the National Conference on Artificial Intelligence (AAAI-83)*, pages 206–209, 1983.
8. R. E. Korf. Depth-first iterative-deepening: An optimal admissible tree search. *Artificial Intelligence*, 27:97–109, 1985.
9. R. E. Korf. Macro-operators: A weak method for learning. *Artificial Intelligence*, 26:35–77, 1985.
10. R. E. Korf. Finding optimal solutions to Rubik's Cube using pattern databases. *Proceedings of the Fourteenth National Conference on Artificial Intelligence (AAAI-97)*, pages 700–705, 1997.
11. A. E. Prieditis. Machine discovery of effective admissible heuristics. *Machine Learning*, 12:117–141, 1993.
12. C. C. Sims. Computational methods in the study of permutation groups. *Computational Problems in Abstract Algebra*, pages 169–183, 1970.

Solving Multiple-Instance and Multiple-Part Learning Problems with Decision Trees and Rule Sets. Application to the Mutagenesis Problem

Yann Chevaleyre and Jean-Daniel Zucker

LIP6-CNRS, University Paris VI,
4, place Jussieu,
F-75252 Paris Cedex 05, France
{Yann.Chevaleyre,Jean-Daniel.Zucker}@lip6.fr

Abstract. In recent work, Dietterich et al. (1997) have presented the problem of supervised multiple-instance learning and how to solve it by building axis-parallel rectangles. This problem is encountered in contexts where an object may have different possible alternative configurations, each of which is described by a vector. This paper introduces the multiple-part problem, which is related to the multiple-instance problem, and shows how it can be solved using the multiple-instance algorithms. These two so-called "multiple" problems could play a key role both in the development of efficient algorithms for learning the relations between the activity of a structured object and its structural properties and in relational learning. This paper analyzes and tries to clarify multiple-problem solving. It goes on to propose multiple-instance extensions of classical learning algorithms to solve multiple-problems by learning multiple-decision trees (ID3-MI) and multiple-decision rules (RIPPER-MI). In particular, it suggests a new multiple-instance entropy function and a multiple-instance coverage function. Finally, it successfully applies the multiple-part framework on the well-known mutagenesis prediction problem.

1 Introduction

Supervised learning can be seen as the search for a function h, a set of objects O towards a set of results R that will be a good approximation of a function f for which the result is only known for a certain number of objects of O, the examples of f (Dietterich [5]). This problem consists in inducing the description of h from a set of pairs $(description(object_i), result_i = f(object_i))$ - the learning examples - and criteria - learning bias - that enable a space of functions of O towards R to be chosen and one function to be preferred to another. The description of $object_i$ is often referred to as an instance of $object_i$. Recent research has shown that this traditional framework could be too limited for complex learning problems [6,11, 2,1]. This is particularly the case when several descriptions of the same object are associated with the same result, baptized a multiple-instance problem (MIP) by Dietterich et al. [6]. Thus the term multiple-instance characterizes the case

E. Stroulia and S. Matwin (Eds.): AI 2001, LNAI 2056, pp. 204–214, 2001.

where the result $f(object_i)$ is associated not with one instance but with a set of instances $\{instance_{i,1}, instance_{i,2}, \ldots instance_{i,\sigma_i}\}$.

Chemistry is a domain *par excellence* where these multiple-instance problems are to be found. Dietterich et al. present the task of classifying aromatic molecules according to whether or not they are "musky" [6]. Several steric configurations of the *same* molecule can be found in nature, each with very different energy properties. In this way it is possible to produce several descriptions of the different configurations - instances - of this molecule. These descriptions correspond to measurements obtained in each of the different configurations. To simplify, let us say that a molecule is said to be musky if, in one of its configurations, it binds itself to a particular receptor. The problem of learning the concept "musky molecule" is one of multiple-instance learning. Maron and Lozano-Perez [9] consider other possible applications, such as learning a simple description of a person from a series of images.

Dietterich et al. have proposed different variations of a learning algorithm where the concepts are represented by axis-parallel rectangles (APR). They observed that "*a particularly interesting issue is how to design multiple-instance modifications for decision trees, neural networks and other popular machine learning algorithms*" [6]. This paper will analyze the difficulties raised by multiple-instance problems in general. It will show the link between this problem and the multiple-part problem (MPP), in which instances are not necessarily alternative descriptions of the object but may be descriptions of different parts of the object. "Multiple-extensions" will be proposed for classical algorithms in order to handle MIP and MPP problems by learning decision trees and rule-based systems. The main reasons that motivate us for finding such algorithms are that MPPs play a central role in learning structure-activity relations. This is the problem that was solved in the REMO learning system (Zucker and Ganascia [11]), and in the REPART (Zucker, Ganascia et al. [12]) Inductive Logic Programming system. Section 2, which is a more formal presentation of the MIP problem, shows how it is linked to the MPP problem and explains how in the two cases problem solving comes down to learning special concepts called multiple ones. Section 3 proposes extensions to classical algorithms in order to solve the multiple-problems and in particular suggests an entropy function and a multiple-instance coverage function. Section 4 presents the results of predicting mutagenecity with the multiple-part framework.

2   Multiple-Instance and Multiple-Part Problems

2.1   Definition of Multiple-Instance Problems

For the sake of clarity, let us consider the case where f is a function with boolean values - a concept - the value of which is known for a subset $\{object_i\}$ of O. Thus $f(object_i) = TRUE$ (positive example) or $FALSE$ (negative example) - depending on whether or not $object_i$ belongs to the concept. We shall note $instance_{i,j}$ the jth description of object $object_i$. We shall call X the representation space for instances and co-instances of $instance_{i,k}$, the other instances of the example $object_i$, i.e. the set $\{instance_{i,j \neq k}\}$. Function h, which we are trying to learn and must be a good approximation of f, is a function which associates a boolean value with a subset of the parts of X, which can be noted by h: $2^X \rightarrow \{TRUE, FALSE\}$. A learning example in the multiple-instance framework is represented in the following form: $(\{instance_{i,1}, \ldots, instance_{i,j}, \ldots, instance_{i,\sigma i}\}, f(objet_i))$ It should be added that the number σi can vary depending on $object_i$ and that the suffix j of 1 to σi given to instances $instance_{i,j}$ is purely arbitrary. Note that in the limited theoretical research that has been done on the PAC-learnability of this problem, the number σi is equal to a constant r [2,3]. In the multiple-instance framework, Dietterich et al. [6] suggest that if the result of f is positive for an $object_i$ it is because *at least one of its instances has produced this result*. If the result is negative it means that none of its instances can produce a positive result. The researchers support this hypothesis by the fact that in the domain of molecular chemistry they are studying this is precisely the case. Here, this hypothesis will be called *the linearity hypothesis*. If we use the vocabulary introduced above, the multiple-instance problem presented by Dietterich et al. [6] in their seminal paper can be defined as follows:

Definition 1 (MIP). *The multiple-instance learning problem consists in learning a concept from examples that are represented by bags of instances that describe them, on the linearity hypothesis.*

2.2 Representation Shifts for MIPs

The function h to be learned is more complex to learn than a traditional concept since it takes its values from the set 2^X of the parts of X which has a cardinal that increases exponentially with that of X. Today, no algorithm exists that is capable of solving this problem directly. A possible approach to too complex a problem would be to try to change the representation in order to find a representation where learning would be less complex (Giordana and Saitta [7]). Using the linearity hypothesis, it is possible to introduce a boolean concept rv_f which no longer applies to sets of instances but instead to one single instance of these sets. An instance belongs to this boolean concept if "the instance has produced the result". This representation shift of a concept defined on 2^X by a concept defined on X can be said to be isomorphic (Korf [8]) in that it changes the structure of the problem but not the amount of information. The concept thus defined will be called a "multiple-concept". Following on from the linearity hypothesis, h is therefore defined as a disjunction of the multiple-concept applied to the different instances of an object:

$$f(objet_i) = rv_f(instance_{i,1}) \vee \ldots \vee rv_f(instance_{i,\sigma i})$$

Property 1. The problem of multiple-instance learning of a concept f comes down to the mono-instance learning of a concept rv_f. The description of f is given as the logical OR of the values of rv_f on the different instances of an object.

Concept rv_f can be read as "responsible for the value of f". The multiple-instance problem can be reformulated with respect to this new function. Figure 1 gives Property 1 in graphic form. If defining MIP is relatively easy, understanding and solving it are far less simple. To illustrate the problem intuitively, let us consider the problem we have decided to call the simple jailer problem. Let there be a locked door and a set of N bunches of keys containing a variable number of keys such that N+ of the bunches of keys are labeled "useful" and N- are labeled "useless" (not useful). A bunch of keys is said to be useful if at least one of its keys opens the door, otherwise it is considered useless. The concept of usefulness could be represented by two classes: that of useful bunches of keys and that of useless bunches of keys. Learning the concept "useful bunch of keys" is a MIP problem. Starting from a set of positive and negative examples of f (here, useful and useless bunches of keys), the concept rv_f must be learned, which characterizes the keys which open the door. This problem is said to be "simple" as it presumes the linearity hypothesis to hold, i.e. at least one key per useful bunch of keys is sufficient to open the door.

2.3 The Multiple-Part Problem and How It Is Linked to the Multiple-Instance Problem

In work done before the development of MIP problems, researchers have introduced a problem that was apparently similar to the MIP and that was baptized a reformulated problem (Zucker and Ganascia [11]) but which, for reasons of clarity, will henceforth be called the *multiple-part problem* (MPP). Informally, the MPP characterizes concept learning from the description of parts of examples.

In MPP as in MIP, each example is represented by a bag of instances. In MIP, an instance is a snapshot of the entire object, whereas in MPP, an instance is a small part of the object. LetÕs consider, for example, the application of MIP and MPP to chemistry. Has shown before, in MIP, the bag of instances related to a molecule would be measurements on various configurations of this molecule. In MPP, we would have to cut a molecule in small parts, each of which would become an instance. Of course, these parts will have to be homogenous. Putting the description of a single atom, or even of a pair of bonded atoms in each instance would both be valid MPP representations. In the first case, the example would be represented by a bag of attribute-value descriptions of each atom. In the second case, each possible pair of bonded atoms of a molecule will

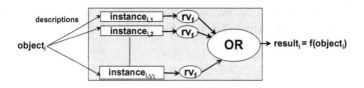

Fig. 1. Multiple instance learning of f and mono instance learning of rv_f

become an instance of that molecule. We can see now that the jailer problem mentioned above is more a MPP problem than a MIP problem. In fact, the keys are seen as parts of the same bunch and each of the instances describes one of the keys.

As seen above, there can be many valid MPP representation of the same data, depending on the size of the chosen parts. The linearity hypothesis, stating that a single instance can be used to identify the belonging of an example to the studied concept, depends here on the representation. For example, if we know that the presence of a carbon linked to a nitrogen atom makes a molecule highly active, it will then be impossible to predict such an activity by examining atoms individually. Hence, the MPP representation for which an instance corresponds to an single atom wonÕt respect linearity hypothesis, whereas the one for which an instance corresponds to a pair of bonded atoms will.

Choosing the appropriate representation in MPP, and moreover shifting between representations is a crucial problem which is deeply studied in (Zucker and Ganascia [11]). In their article, they propose an algorithm called REMO which chooses such an appropriate representation dynamically. Starting with a very simple representation, it generates increasingly complex representations on which a MIP learner is launched, until an accurate enough hypothesis is obtained. In fact, if the linearity hypothesis does not hold on a simple representation, the MIP learner will not perform well and REMO will shift towards more complex representations, until the linearity hypothesis is recovered.

The following sections will focus on designing multiple-instance learners, which as shown here are needed to solve both MIP and MPP.

2.4   Multiple-Concept Learning

As presented in sections 2.1 and 2.3, MIP problems and MPP problems can be reduced to multiple-concept mono-instance learning (rv_f). Once learned, such concepts can be used to characterize the initial concept that is looked for. One of the difficulties of multiple-concept learning comes from the fact that we don't know any examples of these multiple-concepts in the traditional meaning of the term. All we know is whether the disjunction of the rv_f applied to co-instances is positive or negative. Intuitively, we can say that ignoring the specificities of the problem will not help to learn multiple-concepts satisfactorily. Ignoring a multiple-problem means that we consider that all the instances of the same example are from the same class as the example. In the jailer problem, this comes down to considering that all the keys on a bunch of keys open the door if the bunch is useful. A classical learning algorithm that is applied without any modifications to multiple-problems would thus fail to learn an accurate description of the target concept.

3   Adapting Concept Learning Algorithms to Learn Multiple-Concepts

As demonstrated informally in section 2, the learning of multiple-concepts comes down to the mono-instance learning of multiple-concepts. Moreover, it has been shown that the difficulty of learning such multiple-concepts is that there are no learning examples as classically used in the mono-instance framework. There exists a large number of algorithms that solve the mono-instance concept learning problem. The most popular ones are top-down inductive systems. They may be separated into two categories: divide-and-conquer approaches and cover-and-differentiate ones: The divide-and-conquer algorithms generally represent hypotheses as decision trees (ID3, C4.5, etc.) and many use a heuristics based on a variant of the entropy function to build the tree iteratively. The cover-and-differentiate algorithms generally represent hypotheses as sets of if-then rules (AQ, RIPPER [4], etc.). Many use a heuristics based on the number of examples covered by the rules. To date, the main approach for solving the multiple-instance problem is to learn APR. This section proposes extensions to classical concept learning algorithms in order to solve the multiple-problems, in particular through a multiple entropy function and a multiple coverage function.

3.1   Representing Multiple-Concepts and Classifying Multiple-Instances

It is assumed that the basic notions of decision trees as defined in ID3 or C4.5 (Quinlan [10]) and those of IF-THEN rules as defined in AQ or RIPPER [4] are familiar to the reader . A decision tree used to represent a multiple-concept rv_f will be called multiple-decision tree for the sake of clarity. Similarly, a rule set used to represent multiple-concepts will be called a multiple-ruleset. Multiple-decision trees and multiple-rulesets have the same structure as a classical decision trees and rule sets. In fact, multiple-classifiers differ from traditional classifiers in the way they are used to classify a new bag and in the way they are learned. To classify a new object in the MIP where the concept rv_f is represented as a multiple-tree, the entire bag of instances is passed through the tree. If (or as soon as) one positive leaf is reached by one of the instances, the object is classified positive, negative otherwise. Similarly, to classify an object in the MIP with a multiple-ruleset, each instance is passed through each rule. If at least one instance fires a rule, then the entire bag is classified positive, negative otherwise. Figure 2 uses the jailer problem to illustrate these notions.

3.2   Learning Multiple Decision-Trees and Rules

Both MIP and mono-instance framework use attribute-value representation. In addition, classical learning tools use generate-and-test algorithms, exploring a search space which is as suitable for mono-instance as for MIP. Hence, only the test part of the algorithm will have to be modified. We will therefore describe the MIP adaptation of heuristics used in mono-instance learners.

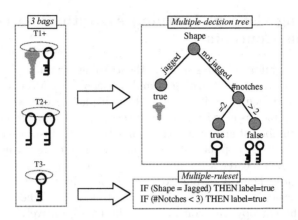

Fig. 2. Two useful bunches of keys T1+ and T2+ and a useless bunch T3- are used to induce a multiple-decision tree and a multiple-ruleset. All three bags are correctly classified by both classifiers

3.3 Multiple-Instance Entropy and Coverage for Multiple-Concept Learning

Classically, the growing of a decision tree is guided by a heuristics based on entropy or a related criterion. Given a collection S containing p positive instances and n negative instances of some target concept, the entropy of S relative to this boolean classification is : $Info_{mono}(S(p,n)) = -\frac{p}{p+n}\log_2\left(\frac{p}{p+n}\right) - \frac{n}{p+n}\log_2\left(\frac{n}{p+n}\right)$ The information gain $Gain(S,A)$ of an attribute A relative to a collection of instances S is defined as: $Gain(S(p,n),A) = Info(S) - \sum_{v \in Values(A)} \frac{|S_v|}{|S|} \times Info(S_v)$. Let us define an extension to both the entropy of S and the gain of an attribute w.r.t. S in the multiple-instance framework. In this context, let us consider a set S containing p positive instances of the concept rv_f and n negative instances of the concept. Let us introduce two functions π and ν that, given a set of instances S, return the number of different positive examples and negative examples that the elements of S are instances of respectively. The entropy that characterizes the (im)purity of an arbitrary collection of examples ought to be redefined here so as to take into account the fact that one example is represented by several instances.

In multiple-problems, the goal is to learn a concept for discriminating examples and not instances. Therefore, the (im)purity ought not to be measured by p and n, the number of positive or negative instances of the concepts rv_f but using $\pi(S)$ and $\nu(S)$, which represent the number of examples that have representatives in S. The multiple- instance entropy and gain may therefore be defined as:
$$Info_{multi}(S(p,n)) = -\frac{\pi(S)}{\pi(S)+\nu(S)}\log_2\left(\frac{\pi(S)}{\pi(S)+\nu(S)}\right) - \frac{\nu(S)}{\pi(S)+\nu(S)}\log_2\left(\frac{\nu(S)}{\pi(S)+\nu(S)}\right)$$
$$Gain_{multi}(S(p,n),A) = Info_{multi}(S) - \sum_{v \in Values(A)}\frac{\pi(S_v)+\nu(S_v)}{\pi(S)+\nu(S)} \times$$

$Info_{multi}(S_v)$ This multiple-instance entropy directly implemented in a decision tree learner will result in overly complex trees. Let us illustrate this drawback with an example. Suppose that only the root node of the tree has been induced. Suppose that one of the positive bags from the training set contains two instances, the first one following the left branch of the root node, and other one following the right branch. If the left subtree being induced succeeds in classifying positively the first instance of this positive bag, then trying to correctly classify the other instance during the induction of the right subtree is useless. Nevertheless, a learner such as ID3 extended with the multiple-instance entropy will try to classify both instances correctly, which will lead to an overly complex tree.

To avoid this drawback, the induction process has to be modified as follows: when an instance from a positive bag is correctly classified by the tree being induced, remove *all* its co-instances from the training set. In our example, as soon as a subtree attached to the root node correctly classifies an instance of the positive bag, the other instance is immediately removed. Note that this drawback is specific to separate-and-conquer algorithms. Based on the multiple entropy measure and this algorithmic modification, ID3-MI has been built as a multiple version of the well known ID3 decision tree learner.

3.4 Learning Multi-rules

This section focuses on ruleset learners that are based on a coverage measurement. The growing procedure of the set of rules used in such kinds of algorithms relies on the notion of coverage. To learn multiple-rules, it is necessary to redefine this very notion of coverage. In a classical framework, an instance x is covered by a generalization G (noted $COVER(G, x)$) if G is more general than x. To measure the degree of generality of a generalization w.r.t. a set of examples, this notion should be refined. In the multiple instance framework, a generalization G "multi-covers" an $object_i$ if it covers at least one of its instances: $COVER_{multi}(G, Object_i) \leftarrow \exists j / COVER(G, instance_{i,j})$. The number of covered bags is thus : $COVERAGE_{multi}(G) = |\{object_i \, COVER_{multi}(G, object_i)\}|$. Based on this measure, RIPPER-MI has been built as a multiple-instance extension of Cohen's efficient rule learner RIPPER [4]. In the next section, various experiments will be done using this algorithm.

4   Predicting Mutagenecity Using MPP Framework

The prediction of mutagenecity problem is considered as a typical benchmark for first-order induction tools. In fact, The highly structured nature of molecules prohibits the straightforward use of propositional representation. The learn goal is here to generate a theory which, provided a given molecule, will best predict its mutagenic activity. The available database consist of 230 chemical compounds. In the following, a subset of 188 molecules known as being *regression-friendly*

Table 1. Accuracy measured with a tenfold validation of various learners on the 188 compounds of the *regression-friendly* set

Learner	Accuracy with $\mathcal{B}_0$	Accuracy with $\mathcal{B}_2$
RIPPER-MI on individual atoms	0.75 (0.04)	0.90 (0.02)
RIPPER-MI on pairs of bonded atoms	0.78 (0.02)	0.90 (0.02)
PROGOL	0.79	0.86
FOIL	0.61	0.83

will be used. For each molecule, the available background knowledge provides several description levels. At the atomic level, two predicates describe the atoms and the bonds. At the molecular level, global informations concerning the entire molecule are given, such as the hydrophobicity and the lowest molecular orbital of a molecule. The dataset restricted to the atomic description level is often refered to as $\mathcal{B}_0$, whereas the $\mathcal{B}_2$ refers to the dataset including both atomic and molecular informations.

Together with RIPPER-MI, the REMO [11] algorithm was used to generate various multiple-instance representations from $\mathcal{B}_0$ and $\mathcal{B}_2$. Using $\mathcal{B}_0$, REMO began by generating a multiple-instance dataset in which each bag contains attribute-value descriptions of individual atoms. During the next run, REMO generated a dataset in which each instance of each bag represents a pair of bonded atoms. Using $\mathcal{B}_2$, the two first datasets generated were the same as for $\mathcal{B}_0$, except that molecular attributes were added to each instance. Table 1 displays the accuracy of RIPPER-MI measured with a tenfold cross validation, on these four MPP-datasets, as well as the accuracy of two popular relational learners. PROGOL and FOIL.

The best accuracy was obtained using the simple representation $\mathcal{B}_2$ with individual atoms. Using pairs of bonded atoms in this case does not lead to an increase of the accuracy. In fact, the global molecular features available in $\mathcal{B}_2$ are highly correlated with the activity of the molecule. Hence, taking into account pairs of atoms does not bring much more information than using only individual atoms. On the contrary, using $\mathcal{B}_0$, the accuracy of RIPPER-MI significantly increases when using pairs of bonded atoms instead of just individual atoms.

Despite the fact that RIPPER-MI uses a greedy-search algorithm, it is competitive in terms of predictive accuracy, with respect to other learners. In addition, it is much faster: using the dataset which represents individual atoms and global molecular properties, rules sets are generated in an average times of 2.6 seconds. In addition, the induced hypotheses are concise, as they contain an average of six rules. The following is an example of rule generated by our learner: `active` $\leftarrow$ `(type1 = 1)` $\wedge$ `(ch1 < 0.288)` $\wedge$ `(ch2 < -0.404)`. It indicates that if a molecule has a pair of bonded atoms such that the first one is of type 1 and has a partial charge lower than 0.288 and that the second one has a partial charge lower than -0.404, then the molecule is mutagenic.

The results obtained on this real-world problem show that the multi-instance paradigm, sort of Òmissing linkÓ between propositional and first order representation, is very promising for a wide range of future learning problems.

5   Conclusion

The problem of supervised multiple-instance learning is a recent learning problem which has excited interest in the learning community. The problem is encountered in contexts where an object may have several alternative vectors to describe its different possible configurations. This paper has shown that the problem is subsumed by the multiple-part problem, which can play a key role in relation-learning algorithms and in inductive logic programming (Zucker et al.[12]). Multiple-instance learning were first applied to the prediction of drug activity. Very recently, Maron et Lozano-Perez [9] have proposed a framework called *Diverse Density* for solving multiple-instance problems. Solving multiple-problems using classical algorithms raises important subtle issues that have been analyzed here. The paper has shown how these problems can be solved using multiple-concept mono-instance learning algorithms. Extensions to classical algorithms have been proposed to solve these problems by learning decision trees and decision rules. They are based on two notions: multiple- instance entropy and multiple-instance coverage. Thanks to these modifications it was possible to implement the learners ID3-MI,RIPPER-MI. Our experiments on the mutagenesis problem show that our approach performs well, and that MIP algorithms can handle numeric as well as symbolic data. It also suggests efficient multiple-instance algorithms could be of primary interest for relational learning tasks.

References

1. Alphonse, E., Rouveirol, C. 1999. Selective Propositionalization for Relational Learning. Principles and Practice of Knowledge Discovery in Databases.
2. Auer, P. 1997. On learning from multi-instances examples. Empirical evaluation of a theoretical approach. 14th International Conference on Machine Learning.
3. Blum, A. and A. Kalai 1997. A note on learning from multiple-instances examples. Machine Learning .
4. Cohen, W. 1995. Fast Effective Rule Induction. International Conference on Machine Learning.
5. Dietterich, T. 1990. Inductive Learning from Preclassified Training Examples. Readings in Machine Learning: 45-56.
6. Dietterich, T., R. Lathrop, et al. 1997. Solving the Multiple-Instance Problem with Axis-Parallel Rectangles. Artificial Intelligence 89(1-2): 31-71.
7. Giordana, A. and L. Saitta 1990. Abstraction: a general framework for learning. AAAI Workshop on Automated Generation of Approximations and Abstraction.
8. Korf, R. E. 1980. Towards a Model for Representation Change. Artificial Intelligence 14: 41-78.
9. Maron, O. and T. Lozano-PŽrez. 1998. A Framework for Multiple-Instance Learning. Neural Information Processing Systems

10. Quinlan, J.-R. 1986. Induction of Decision Trees. Machine Learning(1): 81-106.
11. Zucker, J.-D. and J.-G. Ganascia 1996. Changes of Representation for Efficient Learning in Structural Domains. International Conf. in Machine Learning.
12. Zucker, J.-D., J.-G. Ganascia, Bournaud. I. 1998. Relational Knowledge Discovery in a Chinese Characters Database.Applied Artificial Intelligence Journal, Special Issue on KDD in Structural Domains.

Stacking for Misclassification Cost Performance

Mike Cameron-Jones and Andrew Charman-Williams

University of Tasmania, Launceston, Australia
Michael.CameronJones@utas.edu.au, A.CharmanWilliams@utas.edu.au

Abstract. This paper investigates the application of the multiple classifier technique known as "stacking" [23], to the task of classifier learning for misclassification cost performance, by straightforwardly adapting a technique successfully developed by Ting and Witten [19,20] for the task of classifier learning for accuracy performance. Experiments are reported comparing the performance of the stacked classifier with that of its component classifiers, and of other proposed cost-sensitive multiple classifier methods – a variation of "bagging", and two "boosting" style methods. These experiments confirm that stacking is competitive with the other methods that have previously been proposed. Some further experiments examine the performance of stacking methods with different numbers of component classifiers, including the case of stacking a single classifier, and provide the first demonstration that stacking a single classifier can be beneficial for many data sets.

1 Introduction

Whilst the field of machine learning addresses a wide range of tasks, one of the most common is that of learning a classifier from flat attribute-value descriptions of items for which the class is known, with the aim of predicting well the classes of new items from their attribute values. The usual notion of predicting well is that of accuracy – making few mistakes.

However in many circumstances different forms of mistake are considered to be of different levels of importance, e.g. some systems of criminal justice are based upon a view that it is a greater mistake to punish the innocent than to fail to punish the guilty. In the case of many commercial classification-style decisions, the different costs of different forms of misclassification will be estimated and will influence the decision-making process. There is current interest in the topic of classifier learning for situations with misclassification costs, as evidenced at ICML 2000 in papers e.g. [10], and at the workshop on cost-sensitive learning organised by Margineantu, (notes available at http://www.cs.orst.edu/~margindr/ Workshops/CSL-ICML2k/worknotes.html). Some work [22] has also considered other costs, such as the cost of measuring the values of attributes, e.g. in medical diagnosis it may not be considered worth conducting an expensive test in some circumstances. Here we consider only misclassification costs, hereafter referred to simply as costs, but unlike some authors e.g. [11], we do not restrict ourselves to the two class case.

E. Stroulia and S. Matwin (Eds.): AI 2001, LNAI 2056, pp. 215–224, 2001.

Many different forms of classifier, and different forms of classifier learning method have been investigated in machine learning, and recently there has been considerable interest in learning classifiers that combine the predictions of component classifiers. The two types of multiple classifier method that have been most commonly investigated are "bagging" (bootstrap aggregating) due to Breiman e.g. [4], and "boosting" developed by Freund and Schapire e.g. [12]. Both of these have been adapted to multi-class problems with costs, e.g. bagging (in work involving one of us) [5] and boosting style methods (hereafter simply referred to as boosting) by Ting and Zheng [21], and by Quinlan in C5, his commercial (http://www.rulequest.com) successor to C4.5 [16].

In this paper we look at an application of "stacking", a general idea due to Wolpert [23], successfully applied by Ting and Witten [19,20], to the problem of learning classifiers for accuracy performance. The basic concept of stacking is that the classifier consists of levels of classifiers (or "generalisers"), with the outputs from each level being inputs to the level above. (Stacking can be seen to some extent as a generalisation of the sort of architecture typical in neural networks.) Ting and Witten developed a successful two level approach, with three classifiers of different types at the lower level. Their experiments showed that an important aspect of the success was producing probability-style estimates, not just class predictions, from the lower level, and their successful higher level generalisers also produced probability-style estimates. Good probability estimates enable good cost-based decisions, hence this paper follows up their work by adapting it to the cost context. Experiments are conducted to evaluate and compare the performance of some stacking variations against each other, their component classifiers, and other multiple classifier techniques for problems with costs.

The paper continues with a description of the stacking method used, then the experiments and results, and ends with conclusions and further work.

2   Stacking with Costs

When altering multiple classifier methods to make use of cost information one possible approach is to make the individual component classifiers take the costs into account, and then combine categorical predictions from these cost-sensitive classifiers, as was considered for bagging in [5]. However, here we take the approach of delaying the use of the cost information, using stacking to generate probability estimates from which the expected cost of each possible classification decision can be estimated, and the decision with least expected cost chosen. (Using p_i to stand for the estimated probability that an item is of class i, and c_{ij} to stand for the cost of predicting class j when the actual class of the item is i, the expected cost of predicting class j is estimated as $\sum_i p_i c_{ij}$). As most of the implementation for estimating the probabilities was intended to follow that of Ting and Witten, much of the description below follows theirs.

2.1   Learning Stacked Classifiers

As stated in the Introduction the stacked classifiers considered here consist of two levels. The lower, "level-0", contains individual classifiers that have been learned from the training data as they would normally be learned for use as single classifiers, e.g. one of the classifiers is a decision tree produced by the application of Quinlan's C4.5 [16] to the training data. When the stacked classifier is used to classify an item, the level-0 classifiers are given the values of the attributes for the item, as they would be if they were going to be used as single classifiers, but produce class probability estimates rather than a categorical class prediction, hence the term "generaliser" is more appropriate than classifier. The stacked classifier's output is produced by the generaliser in the higher level, "level-1", which takes the outputs from all the lower level generalisers as its inputs, estimating the class probabilities from these.

While the process of learning the lower level generalisers is standard, the higher level has a less standard task in that while it predicts items' class probabilities, as the lower does, the "attributes" that describe items to the higher level are the probability estimates from the lower. Further, its training data should not be generated by simply using the lower level generalisers that were learned from all the training data, as the higher level generaliser would then be learning only from probability estimates made by generalisers that had seen the items for which they were making the estimates. Such estimates could be of very different accuracy to those produced by the lower level when classifying unseen items – the circumstance for which the higher level is being learned. Ting and Witten generated the training data for the higher level by 10-fold cross-validation (CV). The training data is divided into 10 equal (or near equal) parts. Then for each of these 10 parts, higher level training data is created by training the lower level generalisers on the other 9 parts, and producing their probability estimates for the items in this part. The 10 parts of higher level training data are then combined to learn the higher level generaliser.

2.2   The Lower Level Generalisers

The experiments reported here use three different types of lower level generaliser, as per Ting and Witten.

The instance-based approach (IB) used was a modification of the Waikato Environment for Knowledge Analysis (WEKA) reimplementation of Aha's IB1 [1]. (WEKA has been developed by Witten's group at Waikato, and a more recent version can be obtained from http://www.cs.waikato.ac.nz/~ml.) The WEKA implementation does distance weighted class probability estimation – the weight of each classifying instance is the reciprocal of its distance from the item to be classified, and the estimated probabilities are normalised to sum to 1. Following Ting and Witten, only the three nearest neighbours were used to estimate the class probabilities, and the distance measure was modified to use Cost and Salzberg's Modified Value Difference Metric [8] for discrete attributes.

The naive Bayesian (NB) approach used was that from WEKA, using Laplace style (m-) estimation of probabilities for discrete attributes, and normal distribution assumptions for continuous attributes. Again the normalised probability estimates were used.

The decision tree method used was a modification of C4.5 [16], which was modified as per [19,20] to use a form of Laplace estimate for the class probability estimates at a leaf. Using M for the number of items of the most frequent class at this leaf, and N for the total number of items at the leaf, the probability estimated for the most frequent class is: $\frac{M+1}{N+2}$, and the probabilities of the other classes are proportional to their frequency, such that the sum of the class probabilities is 1.

2.3   The Higher Level Generalisers

Ting and Witten used two main types of higher level generaliser, but found that one, an instance-based approach was generally inferior, and our experiments on this method have shown it to be almost always worse then their other approach, and are not reported here. Their more successful type of higher level generaliser was a weighted sum method. At classification time this method estimates the probability of each class separately, as a weighted sum of the probability estimates from the lower level generalisers. Using p_{ij} for the probability estimated by lower level generaliser j for class i, the higher level generaliser estimates the probability of class k as $\sum_i \sum_j \alpha_{ijk} p_{ij}$, where the coefficients, α_{ijk}, are learned from the training data generated through CV. Ting and Witten experimented with some alternative methods for learning the coefficients, and here we use their suggestion of restricting the coefficients to be non-negative, and learning the coefficients separately for each predicted class minimising the sum of the squares of the training errors, using Lawson and Hanson's NNLS routine [13]. In addition to considering the general case in which the weighted sum estimating the probability for one class includes terms that are the lower level generalisers' probability estimates for other classes (as in [19]), we also report results here for the approach in which the weighted sum estimating the probability of a class only includes terms that are the lower level generalisers' probability estimates for the class being predicted (as in [20]). The latter will be referred to as the "no off-diagonals" case, as it corresponds to zeroing off-diagonal coefficients in a view of the relevant coefficient arrays.

The way in which the final probability estimate are used to make a misclassification cost based decision is such that the accuracy of the ratio of the estimates may be more important than the accuracy of their differences, so a higher level generaliser based upon minimising the log loss of probabilities may be preferable to one minimising the square loss. Hence, in addition to the previously used higher level generalisers, we have also used the parallel update logistic regression method of [7] which learns weighting coefficients to minimise training log loss. Similarly to the main form of the weighted sum method, the probabilities for each class are estimated independently, from all lower level class probability estimates. The logistic is applied to a weighted sum of inverse logistics of the lower level estimates. (The use of the inverse logistic was suggested by Rob Schapire subsequent to the original version of the paper.) Based on heuristic considerations, the coefficients were updated 30 × number of classes times.

3 Experiments

This section presents the results of the experiments on the stacking and other methods. The number of data sets publically available with true commercial misclassification costs is very small as such costs are usually commercially confidential. Hence our experiments here follow the example of some previous misclassification cost work, e.g. [21], in using a range of generated misclassification cost matrices for each data set, so as to enable use of a broad range of commonly accessible data sets.

The 16 data sets used for the experiments were chosen to have a variety of numbers of instances, classes, and discrete and continuous attributes, while favouring data sets that had been used before in previous multiple classifier and cost work. With one exception, the data sets were simply used as obtained either direct from the UCI repository [3], as generated from the programs at the UCI repository, or as obtained in the WEKA distribution. The exception was the "mushroom" data set in which a class stratified sample of one tenth (rounded up) of the full data set is used, as the full data set would pose an uninterestingly easy problem for the learning methods. The data sets will be recognisable by name to those in machine learning, but a few brief notes are needed to clarify which versions of some data sets are used: Heart Disease Cleveland (5 classes), Hypothyroid and Sick Euthyroid (3772 instances, 4 classes and 2 classes respectively), LED-24 (200 instances), Waveform-40 (300 instances).

All experimental results reported are average costs per instance, (for accuracy results from our earlier experiments see [6], and for alternative suggestions on what to report see e.g. [15] and Holte's paper in the ICML 2000 workshop, but note that some of the alternatives may only be practicable for two class problems). Each average cost reported is an average over ten experiments. Each experiment consists of randomly generating ten cost matrices and determining the performance of each learning method on each cost matrix using a ten-fold CV. The same splits of the data and cost matrices were used for all learning methods. (The outer CVs to assess the performance of learning methods are distinct from the inner CVs used in stacking, which is learning from the same training data as the other learning methods.)

The random cost matrices were generated in a manner similar to that of [21]. All the diagonal elements, which correspond to correct predictions, are given costs of 0, one other element is chosen at random to have cost 1, and the remaining elements are assigned (uniformly) random integer costs from 1 to 10 inclusive. (Cost matrices thus generated cannot be degenerate in the sense introduced by Margineantu at the ICML 2000 workshop.) We permit uniform cost matrices, which were deliberately excluded in [21] for the two class case – the only one in which they are likely to arise.

Table 1 shows the average misclassification costs per instance of each of the three types of lower level generaliser (IB, NB and DT), each making cost-sensitive

Table 1. Cost results for lower level generalisers and some combined methods

Data set	IB	NB	DT	Vote	PSum	Cheap	Stack	PBag	C5	CB
abalone	1.634	1.606	1.600	1.447	1.408	1.505	1.344	1.341	1.588	1.359
colic	0.418	0.543	0.417	0.392	0.363	0.424	0.351	0.348	0.370	0.406
credit-a	0.383	0.640	0.341	0.330	0.330	0.347	0.323	0.279	0.293	0.296
credit-g	0.582	0.488	0.518	0.457	0.450	0.453	0.427	0.441	0.447	0.452
diabetes	0.529	0.483	0.495	0.430	0.423	0.479	0.415	0.409	0.442	0.432
heart	1.994	1.919	2.370	1.942	1.882	1.955	1.714	1.886	2.070	1.905
hypothyroid	0.491	0.234	0.021	0.193	0.162	0.021	0.020	0.018	0.018	0.020
led	1.587	1.643	1.901	1.543	1.504	1.636	1.636	1.565	2.018	1.616
mushroom	0.004	0.131	0.016	0.011	0.029	0.007	0.005	0.004	0.009	0.012
sick	0.064	0.130	0.029	0.038	0.051	0.029	0.027	0.020	0.019	0.025
sonar	0.280	0.913	0.689	0.423	0.324	0.280	0.290	0.388	0.317	0.492
soybean	0.260	0.514	0.384	0.265	0.267	0.261	0.226	0.320	0.309	0.435
splice	0.197	0.175	0.261	0.162	0.157	0.175	0.145	0.212	0.199	0.232
tumor	2.932	2.358	2.899	2.483	2.464	2.361	2.440	2.649		2.689
vowel	0.100	1.569	1.044	0.473	0.439	0.100	0.098	0.481	0.378	0.755
waveform	1.077	0.779	1.414	0.832	0.803	0.785	0.733	0.789	0.724	0.814
Rel	2.28	2.35	1.00	1.32	1.30	0.76	0.69	0.73	0.76	0.85
W/L	3/13	1/15	0/16	1/15	1/15	3/13	0/0	8/8	4/11	4/12

predictions in accordance with its probability estimates, voting amongst the three cost-sensitive generalisers (Vote), averaging the probability estimates from the three lower level generalisers then making a cost-sensitive prediction (PSum), selecting the lowest cost of the three cost-sensitive lower level generalisers on the basis of a ten-fold CV on the training data (Cheap), cost-stacking using the three lower level generalisers with the weighted sum higher level generaliser using all lower level probability estimates (Stack), making cost-sensitive predictions on the basis of probabilities estimated by our implementation of Bauer and Kohavi's "p-bagging" [2] (using 30 rounds) with unpruned trees and "backfitting" as suggested (PBag), using C5 boosting (for 30 rounds) with cost-sensitivity (C5), and using our implementation of Ting and Zheng's Cost Boosting [21] (for 30 rounds) switching for uniform cost matrices to our implementation of the version of AdaBoost in [2] (using 30 rounds) as Cost Boosting does not boost on uniform cost matrices (CB). (The use of 30 classifiers in bagging and boosting is for approximately fair comparability of computational effort in training with stacking's 10-fold CV across 3 classifiers.) The results for C5 on the tumor data set are missing because the early version of C5 being used did not report misclassification cost results for data sets with so many classes. (Quinlan has confirmed that more recent versions do report such results.)

There is no universally accepted approach to the comparison across different data sets of the performance of different learning methods. Here we provide two forms of summary result. The first, Rel, is the average relative cost over the data sets, where a method's relative cost for a data set is its cost divided by that of the cost-sensitive decision tree method (DT) for the same data set. DT was chosen as the basis for this calculation because the main multiple classifier methods that we are interested in comparing are based on decision tree methods that are in some respect cost-sensitive. The other form of summary result, W/L, is the method's "win/loss" performance relative to that of the Stack method, i.e. for how many data sets the reported results are better than those of Stack and for how many they are worse. This is reported as Stack is the main novel approach to the cost context that we are advocating. Both forms of summary result are calculated from figures less truncated than those shown in the tables. The summary figures for C5 exclude the tumor data set. (Stack's average relative cost performance excluding the tumor data set is 0.68.)

The results show that Stack has the best average relative cost performance of all the methods in table 1, and is ahead of all methods except p-bagging (with which it ties) in terms of the win/loss performance. Interpreting the win/loss performance in terms of the corresponding level of significance treating each performance as an individual one-tailed paired sign test, the results would all be significant at the 95% level, except for the comparison with C5 and with bagging. Thus Stack's summary performance is substantially better than that of all its constituent lower level generalisers, the simpler methods of combining them, and our implementation of Cost Boosting, better than that of C5, and similar to that of bagging. Given the reported general superiority of boosting over bagging in accuracy terms e.g. [17], the results here (and some smaller scale comparisons in [14]) raise the question as to whether the adaptations of boosting to the cost situation can be further improved, and additional experiments implementing a form of the two-class-only AdaCost [11] and Adaboost' [18] have shown more similar performance to bagging in the two class case.

As a referee has commented, it should be noted that a better average cost for a data set does not imply being better on every cost matrix tested, e.g. examining the results for the 4 data sets on which bagging and stacking perform most similarly, shows that out of the 400 random cost matrix draws, the method better on average is better on 227, tied on 19, and worse on 154. (In the 4 data sets in which they perform least similarly, the method better on average is better on 399 and tied on 1.)

Table 2 shows the average costs per instance for stacking each of the individual classifiers and using costs (IBSt, NBSt, DTSt), stacking pairs of classifiers (IBNBSt, IBDTSt, NBDTSt), stacking all three as before (Stack), stacking all three using weighted sums with no off-diagonals, (StNO), and stacking all three using the log loss based high level (StLog).

If the stacked individual classifiers are compared with their non-stacked versions, it can be seen that all three are better in terms of their average relative performance, and further all three stacked methods are better in terms of win/loss performance comparing directly against their non-stacked version, particularly the NB. Thus it seems that even stacking individual classifiers is generally beneficial, something which has not been previously demonstrated on such a variety of data sets. When the effect of increasing the number of stacked classifiers is examined, the average relative cost results show the desirable trend that each two classifier stacking technique has better performance than either of the two corresponding stacked individual classifiers, and the three classifier

Table 2. Cost results for different stacking methods

Data set	IBSt	NBSt	DTSt	IBNBSt	IBDTSt	NBDTSt	Stack	StNO	StLog
abalone	1.389	1.395	1.401	1.353	1.362	1.362	1.344	1.398	1.345
colic	0.414	0.465	0.417	0.404	0.359	0.363	0.351	0.351	0.359
credit-a	0.390	0.463	0.350	0.363	0.330	0.303	0.323	0.321	0.321
credit-g	0.479	0.437	0.480	0.430	0.460	0.429	0.427	0.447	0.439
diabetes	0.477	0.415	0.448	0.412	0.435	0.409	0.415	0.420	0.422
heart	1.835	1.696	1.959	1.718	1.826	1.713	1.714	1.844	1.716
hypothyroid	0.372	0.231	0.021	0.230	0.021	0.020	0.020	0.020	0.021
led	1.618	1.672	1.958	1.572	1.668	1.669	1.636	1.572	1.558
mushroom	0.004	0.114	0.016	0.004	0.005	0.016	0.005	0.005	0.006
sick	0.065	0.091	0.030	0.062	0.028	0.028	0.027	0.027	0.028
sonar	0.290	0.468	0.465	0.301	0.278	0.442	0.290	0.288	0.274
soybean	0.252	0.415	0.393	0.238	0.235	0.286	0.226	0.228	0.221
splice	0.195	0.174	0.262	0.149	0.185	0.156	0.145	0.145	0.139
tumor	2.622	2.356	2.788	2.364	2.611	2.430	2.440	2.366	2.382
vowel	0.099	1.536	1.039	0.099	0.098	0.929	0.098	0.098	0.085
waveform	1.073	0.744	1.296	0.741	0.990	0.733	0.733	0.740	0.719
Rel	1.89	2.06	0.95	1.41	0.74	0.81	0.69	0.70	0.69
W/L	3/13	3/13	0/16	4/12	2/13	5/11	0/0	7/8	8/8

technique has better performance than any of the two classifier techniques. (Our preliminary experiments in [6] also show that adding a fourth classifier, a neural network method, had potential.)

The comparison between the stacking methods shows that the use or non-use of the off-diagonals in the weighted sum approach is very evenly balanced consistent with Ting and Witten's results for accuracy performance. However, there is an aspect worth noting to the use or non-use of the off-diagonals, namely that the two data sets on which not using them seems noticeably beneficial are the LED and tumor data sets, which both have a low ratio of number of instances to number of off-diagonal coefficients, hence are cases where problems of overfitting are likely to be observed for the more complex model. Overall the log loss method performs similarly to the weighted sum.

4   Conclusions and Further Work

This paper has proposed the use in the misclassification cost context of some stacking methods for combining different types of underlying classifier, and experimentally compared (using 16 data sets) the cost performance of these methods against their constituent parts, against other methods of combining the same constituent parts, and against other cost-sensitive multiple classifiers that use bagging or boosting style methods. In these experiments the main stacking method's summary performance has been superior to that of nearly all the non-stacking alternatives considered and similar to that of the bagging approach. The issue of overfitting with the main method when there are too many coefficients relative to the amount of data has been raised for two data sets. The possibility of using a log loss based higher level generaliser has been shown. The performance of bagged decision trees has been generally slightly superior to that of boosted decision trees, against the typical trend reported for performance in terms of accuracy. Experiments involving different numbers of constituent classifiers have shown that stacking can improve the performance of even a single classifier, and that performance generally improves with additional constituent classifiers.

The experimental results on stacking are generally encouraging, showing that the version considered here can be competitive with other previously proposed methods. By comparison with the bagging and boosting methods here, the stacking method has the benefit of using different types of constituent classifier, but the bagging and boosting methods can have the benefit of using more classifiers (of the same type) at classification time, e.g. 30 bagged decision trees versus one each of three types of classifier. Dieterich [9] has investigated the relative performance of bagging and boosting on decision trees in terms of the accuracy of the constituent classifiers produced and their diversity in terms of how much they differ in their mistakes, as such difference is essential to gaining a benefit from multiple classifier methods. It might be interesting to compare the diversity of different types of classifier with that of classifiers of the same type produced from boosting and bagging, to see how these compare.

While this paper has proposed and successfully demonstrated the potential of stacking in the misclassification cost context, there is much left to study, from the suggestion above involving investigating the current methods, through attempting to improve them, to the possibility of combining stacking with other methods to improve upon both.

Acknowledgements. This paper was completed while the first author was on study leave at AT&T Labs Research, whom the author wishes to thank, particularly Rob Schapire and Michael Collins. Thanks are also due to the UCI repository maintainers, and the contributors, e.g. R. Detrano for the Cleveland data, and M. Zwitter and M. Soklic for the primary tumour data which was obtained from the University Medical Centre, Institute of Oncology, Ljubljana, Yugoslavia.

References

[1] D.W. Aha, D. Kibler, and M.K. Albert. Instance-based learning algorithms. *Machine Learning*, 6:37–66, 1991.

[2] E. Bauer and R. Kohavi. An empirical comparison of voting classification algorithms: Bagging, boosting, and variants. *Machine Learning*, 36:105–139, 1999.

[3] C. Blake, E. Keogh, and C.J. Merz. *UCI Repository of Machine Learning Databases*. University of California, Department of Information and Computer Science, Irvine, California, 1998.
http://www.ics.uci.edu/~mlearn/MLRepository.html.

[4] L. Breiman. Bagging predictors. *Machine Learning*, 24:123–140, 1996.

[5] M. Cameron-Jones and L. Richards. Repechage bootstrap aggregating for misclassification cost reduction. In *PRICAI'98: Topics in Artificial Intelligence – Fifth Pacific Rim International Conference on Artificial Intelligence*, pages 1–11. Springer Verlag, 1998.

[6] A. Charman-Williams. Cost-stacked classification, 1999. Honours thesis, School of Computing, University of Tasmania.

[7] M. Collins, R.E. Schapire, and Y. Singer. Logistic regression, adaboost and bregman distances. In *Proceedings of the Thirteenth Annual Conference on Computational Learning Theory*, pages 158–169. Morgan Kaufmann, 2000.

[8] S. Cost and S. Salzberg. A weighted nearest neighbor algorithm for learning with symbolic features. *Machine Learning*, 10:57–78, 1993.

[9] T.G. Dietterich. An experimental comparison of three methods for constructing ensembles of decision trees: Bagging, boosting and randomization. *Machine Learning*, 40:139–157, 2000.

[10] C. Drummond and R.C. Holte. Exploiting the cost (in)sensitivity of decision tree splitting criteria. In *Proceedings of the Seventeenth International Conference on Machine Learning (ICML-2000)*, pages 239–246. Morgan Kaufmann, 2000.

[11] W. Fan, S.J. Stolfo, J. Zhang, and P.K. Chan. Adacost: Misclassification cost-sensitive boosting. In *Machine Learning: Proceedings of the Sixteenth International Conference (ICML '99)*, pages 97–105, 1999.

[12] Y. Freund and R.E. Schapire. A decision-theoretic generalization of on-line learning and an application to boosting. *Journal of Computer and System Sciences*, 55:119–139, 1997.

[13] C.L. Lawson and R.J. Hanson. *Solving Least Squares Problems*. SIAM, 1995.

[14] M.G. O'Meara. Investigations in cost boosting, 1998. Honours thesis, School of Computing, University of Tasmania.

[15] F. Provost, T. Fawcett, and R. Kohavi. The case against accuracy estimation for comparing induction algorithms. In *Machine Learning: Proceedings of the Fifteenth International Conference (ICML'98)*. Morgan Kaufmann, 1998.

[16] J.R. Quinlan. *C4.5: Programs for Machine Learning*. Morgan Kaufmann, 1993. The Morgan Kaufmann Series in Machine Learning.

[17] J.R. Quinlan. Bagging, boosting and c4.5. In *Proceedings of the Thirteenth American Association for Artificial Intelligence National Conference on Artificial Intelligence*, pages 725–730. AAAI Press, 1996.

[18] K.M. Ting. A comparative study of cost-sensitive boosting algorithms. In *Proceedings of the Seventeenth International Conference on Machine Learning (ICML-2000)*, pages 983–990. Morgan Kaufmann, 2000.

[19] K.M. Ting and I.H. Witten. Stacked generalization: when does it work? In *Proceedings of the Fifteenth International Joint Conference on Artificial Intelligence*, pages 866–871. Morgan Kaufmann, 1997.

[20] K.M. Ting and I.H. Witten. Issues in stacked generalization. *Journal of Artificial Intelligence Research*, 10:271–289, 1999.

[21] K.M. Ting and Z. Zheng. Boosting trees for cost-sensitive classifications. In *Machine Learning: ECML-98: Proceedings of the Tenth European Conference on Machine Learning*, pages 190–195. Springer-Verlag, 1998.

[22] P.D. Turney. Cost-sensitive classification: Empirical evaluation of a hybrid genetic decision tree induction algorithm. *Journal of Artificial Intelligence Research*, 2:369–409, 1995.

[23] D.H. Wolpert. Stacked generalization. *Neural Networks*, 5:241–259, 1992.

Stratified Partial-Order Logic Programming

Mauricio Osorio[1] and Juan Carlos Nieves[2]

[1] Universidad de las Americas
CENTIA
Sta. Catarina Martir,
Cholula, Puebla
72820 Mexico
`josorio@mail.udlap.mx`
[2] Universidad Tecnologica de la Mixteca
Instituto de Electronica y Computacion
Huajuapan de Leon, Oaxaca
69000 Mexico
`jcnieves@nuyoo.utm.mx`

Abstract. The stable semantics has become a prime candidate for knowledge representation and reasoning. The rules associated with propositional logic programs and the stable semantics are not expressive enough to let one write concise optimization programs. We propose an extension to the language of logic programs that allows one to express optimization problems in a suitable well. In earlier work we defined the declarative semantics for partial order clauses. The main contribution of our paper is the following: First, we define the language of our extended paradigm as well as its declarative semantics. Our declarative semantics is based on translating partial order clauses into normal programs and the using the stable semantics as the intended meaning of the original program. Second, we propose an operational semantics for our paradigm. Our experimental results show that our approach is more efficient than using the well known system SMODELS over the translated program.

1 Introduction

The stable semantics has become a prime candidate for knowledge representation and reasoning. The rules associated with propositional logic programs and the stable semantics are not expressive enough to let one write concise optimization programs. We propose an extension to the language of logic programs that allows one to express optimization problems in a suitable well. Furthermore, our proposal allows some degree of integration between logic and functional programming. We use partial order clauses as the functional programming ingredient and disjunctive clauses as the logic programming ingredient.

Partial-order clauses are introduced and studied in [11,10], and we refer the reader to these papers for a full account of the paradigm. In comparison with traditional equational clauses for defining functions, partial-order clauses offer better support for defining recursive aggregate operations. We illustrate with an

E. Stroulia and S. Matwin (Eds.): AI 2001, LNAI 2056, pp. 225–235, 2001.
© Springer-Verlag Berlin Heidelberg 2001

example from [11]: Suppose that a graph is defined by a predicate edge(X,Y,C), where C is the non-negative distance associated with a directed edge from a node X to node Y, then the shortest distance from X to Y can be declaratively specified through partial-order clauses as follows:

$$\text{short(X,Y)} \leq \text{C :- edge(X,Y,C)}$$
$$\text{short(X,Y)} \leq \text{C + short(Z,Y)   :- edge(X,Z,C)}$$

The meaning of a ground expression such as short(a,b) is the *greatest lower bound* (smallest number in the above example) of the results defined by the different partial-order clauses. In order to have a well-defined function using partial-order clauses, whenever a function is circularly defined (as could happen in the above example when the underlying graph is cyclic), it is necessary that the constituent functions be monotonic. We refer to this paradigm as *partial-order programming*, and we have found that it offers conciseness, clarity, and flexibility in programming problems in graph theory, optimization, program analysis, etc. Partial-order program clauses are actually a generalization of subset program clauses [7,8].

The declarative semantics of partial-order clauses is defined by a suitable translation to normal clauses. We have studied this approach in full detail in [14]. However, this is the first time that we consider the use of the stable semantics [5]). Since the stable semantics is defined for disjunctive clauses and constraints, we obtain a paradigm that allows the integration of partial-order programs with disjunctive programs. We have solved some optimization problems (taken from the archive of the ACM programming contest) in this paradigm and we claim that the use of partial-order clauses were suitable in this respect.

The operational semantics of our language combines a general form of dynamic programming with the *SMODELS*[1] algorithm (proposed in [15]). We compute all the stable models of the program by dividing the program in modules, computing the models of the lower module, reducing the rest of the program with respect of each model found and iterating the process. When we need to compute the stable models at a given module, we have two cases: In the first case the module consists of partial-order clauses. We use dynamic programming to compute the (exactly one) model of such module. In the second case the module consists of normal clauses. We use *SMODELS* to obtain all the stable models. If there are no stable models the entired program is inconsistent. The rest of this paper is organized as follows: Section 2 provides a basic background on partial-order programming. We also define our class of legal programs. In section 3 we present the declarative semantics of our language. In section 4 we present the operational semantics of our full language. The last section presents our conclusions and future work. We assume familiarity with basic concepts in logic programming[2].

---

[1] *SMODELS* is a system available in : http://www.tcs.hut.fi/Software/smodels/

[2] A good introductory treatment of the relevant concepts can be found in the text by Lloyd [9]

2   Background

Our language includes function symbols, predicate symbols, constant symbols, and variable symbols. A *f-p* symbol is either a function symbol or a predicate symbol. A *term* is a constant symbol or a variable symbol. *Function atoms* are of the form $f(t_1, \ldots, t_n) = t$, where $t, t_1, \ldots, t_n$ are terms and f is a function symbol of arity n. *Inequality atoms* are of the form $f(t_1, \ldots, t_n) \leq t$, where $t, t_1, \ldots, t_n$ are terms and f is a function symbol of arity n. *Predicate atoms* are of the form $p(t_1, \ldots, t_n)$, where $t_1, \ldots, t_n$ are terms and p is a predicate symbol of arity n. A *f-p* atom is either a function atom or a predicate atom. A *f-p* literal is a *f-p* atom or a negated *f-p* atom.

A program P is a pair $< PO, DA >$ where PO is a set of partial-order clauses and DA is a set of disjunctive clauses. Partial-order clauses are of the form:

$$f(terms) \leq expression :- lit_1, \ldots, lit_k$$

where each lit_i (with $1 \leq i \leq k$) is a *f-p* literal. By *terms* we mean a list of terms. The syntax of *expression* is given below:

expression ::= *term* | *f(exprs)*

exprs ::= *expression* | *expression* , *exprs*

The symbol f stands for a function symbol, also called user-defined function symbol. A disjunctive clauses is of the form: $head_1 \vee \ldots \vee head_n :- l_1 \ldots l_k$, where $n \geq 0$, $k \geq 0$, each $head_i$ is an atom, and each l_j is a *f-p* literal. When $n = 0$ the clause is called a constraint. Our lexical convention in this paper is to begin constants with lowercase letters and variables with uppercase letters. We assume that our programs use only $\leq$ clauses. Since we assume complete lattices, the $\geq$ case is dual and all the results hold immediately.

We now present several examples that are naturally expressed in our paradigm.

Example 2.1 (Data-flow Analysis). Partial-order clauses can be used for carrying out sophisticated flow-analysis computations, as illustrated by the following program which computes the *reaching definitions* and *busy expressions* in a program flow graph. This information is computed by a compiler during its optimization phase [1]. The example also shows the use of monotonic functions.

```
reach_out(X) ≥ reach_in(X) - kill(X).
reach_out(X) ≥ gen(X).
reach_in(X)  ≥ reach_out(Y) :- pred(X,Y).
```

In the above program, kill(X) and gen(X), are predefined set-valued functions specifying the relevant information for a given program flow graph and basic block X. We assume an EDB pred(X,Y), that defines when Y *is predecessor of* X. The set-difference operator (-) is monotonic in its first argument, and hence the program has a unique intended meaning as it is shown in [1]. A general result that explains this fact can be found in [11]. Our operational semantics behaves exactly as the algorithm proposed in [1] to solve this problem. We consider this fact as a main evidence that our operational semantics is efficient.

Example 2.2 (Shortest Distance). The formulation of the shortest-distance problem is one of the most elegant and succinct illustrations of partial-order clauses:

```
short(X,Y) ≤ C :- edge(X,Y,C)
short(X,Y) ≤ C + short(Z,Y) :- edge(X,Z,C)
```

The relation `edge(X,Y,C)` means that there is a directed edge from X to Y with distance C which is non-negative. The function `short(X,Y)` = C means that a shortest path (in terms of costs) from node X to node Y has cost C. The + operator is monotonic with respect to the numeric ordering, and hence the program is well-defined. The *logic* of the shortest-distance problem is very clearly specified in the above program.

This problem can be solved using dynamic programming, that corresponds in this case to Floyd's algorithm. Our operational semantics behaves exactly as Floyd's algorithm and hence this is again a main evidence that supports that our approach is suitable.

Suppose we wanted to return both the shortest distance as well as the shortest paths corresponding to the shortest distance. We then can include the following code to our program:

```
path(X,Y)    ∨ complement(X,Y) :- edge(X,Y,C).
             :- node(X), ini(A), path(X, A).
             :- node(X), fin(D),path(D,X).
             :- node(X), node(Y), node(Y1), path(X,Y),
             path(X,Y1), neq(Y,Y1).
             :- node(Y), node(X), node(X1), path(X,Y),
             path(X1,Y), neq(X,X1).
r(X)         :- ini(X).
r(X)         :- num(C), node(X), node(Y), r(Y),path(Y,X).
k(Y)         :- node(X), node(Y), path(X,Y).
             :- node(D), k(D), not r(D).
             :- fin(D), not r(D).
cost(X,Y,C)  :- node(X), node(Y),num(C),path(X,Y), edge(X,Y,C).
cost(X,Y,C)  :- node(X), node(Y), node(Z), num(C),num(C1), num(C2)
             ,path(X,Z), edge(X,Z,C1), cost(Z,Y,C2), C = C1 + C2.
             :-num(C), num(C1), ini(A), fin(D), cost(A,D,C),
             short(A,D) = C1, C > C1.
```

The meaning of the constraint `:- node(X), ini(A), path(X, A)` is that the initial node of the graph is of indegree zero. In a similar way, the meaning of the second constraint `:- node(X), fin(D),path(D,X)` is that the final node of the graph is of outdegree zero. The idea of the third and fourth constraints, is that every node of the path must be of indegree (and outdegree) less or equal to one. The relation `r(X)` defines the nodes that are possibly reachable since the initial node. The relation `cost(X,Y)` defines the cost of the partial paths and the total path to reach the final node.

The declarative semantics defines as many models as shortests paths. In each model, `path` defines such shortest path.

Example 2.3 (Matrix Chain Product). [16]
Suppose that we are multiplying n matrices $M_1,...M_n$. Let `ch(J,K)` denote the

minimum number of scalar multiplications required to multiply $M_j, ...M_k$. Then, ch is defined by the following inequalities:

```
ch(I,I) ≤ 0 :- size(N), 1≤I, I≤ N
ch(J,K) ≤ ch(J,I)+ch(I+1,K) + r(J)*c(I)*c(K) :- J≤I, I≤ K-1
```

where we encode the size of matrix M_i by r(I), number of rows, and c(I), number of columns, and we suppose that c(I)=r(I+1). The functions r and c have been omitted in the above code.

In order to capture the ⊤-as-failure assumption, we assume that for every function symbol f, the program is augmented by the clause: f(X) $\leq$ ⊤.

3 Declarative Semantics

In the following we assume that our programs are free-head cyclic, see [2]. We adopt this assumption for two reasons. First, we have never found an interesting example where this condition does not hold. Second, free-head cyclic programs can be translated to normal programs such that the stable semantics agree. In this case *SMODELS* is a very fast tool to compute stable models.

We now explain how to translate a disjunctive clause into a set of normal clauses.

Definition 3.1. *Let P be a program such that P :=< PO, DA >. We define the map of DA to a set of normal clauses as follows: Given a clause C ∈ DA where C is of the form $p_1(terms) \vee \ldots \vee p_n(terms) : -body$, we write dis-nor(C) to denote the set of normal clauses:*

$$p_i(terms) : -body, \neg p_1(terms), \ldots, \neg p_{i-1}(terms), \neg p_{i+1}(terms), \ldots, \neg p_n(terms)$$

where $1 \leq i \leq n$.
We extend this definition to the set DA as follows. Let dis-nor(DA) denote the normal program:

$$\bigcup_{C \in DA} dis - nor(C)$$

From now on we may assume that every disjunctive clause of the program has been translated as before. We also get rid of the constraints as follows: Replace every constraint clause *:- RHS* by *new :- RHS,* ¬ *new.*

Where *new* is a propositional symbol that does not appears at all in the original program.

Definition 3.2. *A program P is stratified if there exists a mapping function, level : $F \cup Pr \rightarrow \mathcal{N}$, from the set F of user-defined (i.e., non-constructor) function symbols in P union the set Pr of predicates symbols of P to (a finite subset of) the natural numbers $\mathcal{N}$ such that all clauses satisfy:*

(i) For a clause of the form

$$f(term_1) \leq term_2 : -RHS$$

where RHS is a conjunction of f-p atoms then level(f) is greater than level(p) where p is any f-p symbol that appears in RHS.
(ii) For a clause of the form

$$f(term) \leq g(expr) : -RHS$$

where f and g are user-defined functions, and RHS is as before then level(f) is greater or equal to level(g), level(f) is greater than level(h), level(f) is greater than level(p), level(g) is greater to level(p), where p is any f-p symbol that appears in RHS and h is any user-defined function symbol that occurs in expr.
(iii) For a clause of the form

$$f(terms) \leq m(g(expr)) : -RHS$$

where RHS is as before and m is a monotonic function then, level(f) is greater than level(m), level(f) is greater or equal to level(g), level(f) is greater than level(h), level(f) is greater than level(p), where p is any f-p symbol that appears in RHS and h is any function symbol that occurs in expr.
(iv) For a clause of the form

$$p(term) : -RHS$$

where RHS is as before, if f is a f-p symbol that appears in RHS then level(p) is greater than level(f).
(v) No other form of clause is permitted.

Although a program can have different level mappings we select an image set consisting of consecutive natural numbers from 1. In addition we select the level mapping such that $level(p) \neq level(f)$ where p is a predicate symbol and f is a function symbol. In the above definition, note that f and g are not necessarily different. Also, non-monotonic "dependence" occurs only with respect to lower-level functions. We can in fact have a more liberal definition than the one above: Since a composition of monotonic functions is monotonic, the function m in the above syntax can also be replaced by a composition of monotonic functions, except that we are working with functions rather than predicates.

Considering again our shortest path example, a level mapping could assign: All predicate symbols of the EDB have level 1. The function symbol + has level 2. The function symbol **short** has level 3. The rest of the predicates have level 4.

Our next step is to *flatten* the functional expressions on the right-hand sides of the partial-order clauses [3,6]. We illustrate flattening by a simple example:

Assuming that f, g, h, and k are user-defined functions the flattened form of a clause $f(X,Y) \geq k(h(Y,1))$ is as follows:

$f(X,Y) \geq Y2 :- h(Y,1) = Y1, k(Y1) = Y2.$

In the above flattened clause, we follow Prolog convention and use the notation $:-$ for 'if' and commas for 'and'. The order in which the basic goals are listed on the right-hand side of a flattened clause is the *leftmost-innermost* order for reducing expressions.

3.1   Translating a Partial Order Program into a Normal Program

The strategy here is to translate a stratified program to a standard normal program and then to define the semantics of the translated normal program as the semantics of the original program. We work in this section with the *normal form* of a program. This form is obtained from the flattened form by replacing every assertion of the form $f(t) = t1$ by the atom $f_=(t, t1)$ and every assertion of the form $f(t) \leq t1$ by $f_\leq(t, t1)$. Except for minor changes, the following four definitions are taken from [13]. Just to keep the notation simple we assume that functions accept only one argument.

Definition 3.3. *Given a stratified program P, we define P' to be as follows: Replace each partial-order clause of the form*
$\quad E_0 :- condition, E_1, \ldots, E_k, \ldots, E_n$
by the clause
$\quad E_0 :- condition, E_1, \ldots, E_k^*, \ldots, E_n$
where E_0 is of the form $f_\leq(t_1, X_1)$, E_k is of the form $g_=(t_k, X_k)$, E_k^* is of the form $g_\leq(t_k, X_k)$ and f and g are (not necessarily different) functions at the same level^P. Note that it is possible that $k = n$.

Definition 3.4. *Given a program P, we define head(P) to be the set of head function symbols of P, i.e., the head symbols on the literals of the left-hand sides of the partial-order clauses.*

Definition 3.5. *Given a program P, a predicate symbol $f_\leq$ which does not occur at all in P, we define $ext_1(f)$ as the following set of clauses:*
$f_=(Z, S) :- f_\leq (Z, S), \neg f_{better}(Z,S)$
$f_{better}(Z, S) :- f_\leq(Z, S1), S1 < S$
$f_\leq(Z, S) :- f_\leq(Z, S1), S1 < S$
$f_\leq (Z, \top)$
$f_\leq(Z, C) :- f_\leq(Z, C_1), f_\leq(Z, C_2), glb(C_1, C_2, C).$

We call the last clause, the *glb* clause, and it is ommited when the partial order is total, $glb(C_1, C_2, C)$ interprets that C is the greatest lower bound of C_1 and C_2. Symmetric definitions have to be provided for $f_\geq$ symbols.

Definition 3.6. *Given a stratified program P, we define*

$ext_1(P) := \bigcup_{f \in head(P)} ext_1(f)$, *and*

$transl(P) := P' \cup ext_1(P)$, *where P' is as the definition 3.3.*

As an example of the translation we use program **Short** given in example 2.2

```
short≤(X,Y,⊤).
short≤(X,Y,C) :- edge(X,Y,C).
short≤(X,Y,C) :- edge(X,Z,C1), short≤(Z,Y,C2), C = C1 + C2.
short≤(W,W1,X) :- short≤(W,W1,X1), X1 < X.
short<(W,W1,X) :- short≤(W,W1,X1), X1 < X.
short=(W,W1,X) :- short≤(W,W1,X), ¬short<(W,W1,X).
```

Definition 3.7. *For any stratified program P, we define $D(P)$, as the set of stable models for $transl(P)$.*

Definition 3.8. *For any stratified program P, we define $level(P) = max\{n : level(p) = n$, where p is any f-p symbol $\}$*

Lemma 3.1. *Given any program P of level n greater than 1, there exists P_1 such that the following holds:*

1. *$Level(P_1) < n$,*
2. *Every f-p symbol p in the head of every clause in $(P \setminus P_1)$ is of level n.*
3. *All clauses in $(P \setminus P_1)$ are partial-order clauses or all clauses in $(P \setminus P_1)$ are disjunctive clauses.*
4. *If M_i for $1 \leq i \leq k > 0$ are all the stable models of P_1 then $stable(P) = \{M|M \in stable((P \setminus P_1)^{M_i}), 1 \leq i \leq k\}$. Moreover, if $(P \setminus P_1)$ consists of partial-order clauses then $SEM((P \setminus P_1)^{M_i})$ has exactly one model. (Here we understand P^M, where P is a program and M an interpretation of P, as reducing P w.r.t. M. A formal definition is given in [4].*

Proof. (Sketch) We actually select P_1 as the program that consists of every clause where the level of the head is less than n. Therefore 1, 2 and 3 are immediate. To prove 4 we note that each M_i is a candidate to be completed as a stable model of P. Moreover the stable semantics satisfies reduction, see [4]. Also, if M is a stable model of P then exists $M' \subset M$ over the language of P_1 that is a stable model of P_1. Therefore, exists i such that $M_i = M'$.

A naive idea to obtain the semantics of a program would be to translate a program and use the SMODELS system. However this could be very inefficient. We have in fact tried several examples where SMODELS got the answer in several minutes while in our current implementation we got an answer in less than one minute[3].

---

[3] Both systems ran in C++ under a SUN SPARC station

4   Operational Semantics

We discuss the operational semantics of our language. We assume that our lattice is finite. Our lemma of the last section is one of the notions that we use to define our operational semantics. Based on this notion, computing the operational semantics of a program reduces almost[4] to compute the operational semantics of a program of level 1. Here, we have two cases:

First, when the program consists only of normal clauses where the body of every clause is free of function atoms. Then, we can use the algorithms that are used by the well known systems: *SMODELS* and *DLV*[5]. We have successfully tried this process with several program examples, meaning that it is possible to handle programs that after instantiating them they contain hundreds of thousands of rules.

Second, when the program consists only of partial-order clauses. Then we can use dynamic programming to compute the *glb* among the fix-points of the program, see [11]. The precise formulation of the operational semantics of a program is the following. Let *Fix-Point-Semantics(P)* be the fix-point semantics defined in [12]. Let *SMODELS(P)* be the operational semantics for normal programs (with constraints) given in [15]. Let *reduce(P,M)* be P^M (already defined). Our operational semantics is then *OP(P, n)* where n is the level of P.

$$
\begin{aligned}
&\textit{Function OP(P, n)} \\
&\quad \textit{if } n = 1 \qquad \textit{return(One\_level(P))}; \\
&\quad \textit{else} \\
&\quad \{ \\
&\qquad \textit{let } M_S = OP(P, n-1); \\
&\qquad \textit{if } M_S = \emptyset \qquad \textit{return } \emptyset; \\
&\qquad \textit{else} \\
&\qquad \{ \\
&\qquad\quad M' = \emptyset; \\
&\qquad\quad \textit{for each } M \in M_S \\
&\qquad\qquad P' = reduce(P, M); \qquad M' = M' \cup One\_level(P'); \\
&\qquad\quad return(M'); \\
&\qquad \} \\
&\quad \} \\
\\
&\textit{Function One\_level(P)} \\
&\quad \textit{if P is a partial-order program} \qquad \textit{return(Fix-Point-Semantics(P))}; \\
&\quad \textit{else} \qquad \textit{return(SMODELS(P))};
\end{aligned}
$$

The correctness of our algorithm follows immediately by induction on the level of our program, lemma 3.1, proposition 3 in [12] and the well known correctness of the *SMODELS* algorithm.

---

[4] We also need to reduce the program w.r.t. the semantics of a lower module

[5] DLV is a system available in : http://www.dbai.tuwien.ac.at/proj/dlv/

5   Conclusion and Related Work

Partial-order clauses and lattice domains provide a concise and elegant means for programming problems involving circular constraints and aggregation. Such problems arise throughout deductive databases, program analysis, and related fields. Our language allows some degree of integration between logic and functional programming. We use partial order clauses as the functional programming ingredient and disjuntive clauses as the logic programming ingredient. We use the Stable smantics to take care of the relational component. We also discuss an operational semantics that integrates dynamic programming with the algorithm used in *SMODELS*.

References

1. Alfred V. Aho, Ravi Setvi, and Jeffrey D. Ullman. *Compilers Principles, Techniques, and Tools*. Addison Wesley, 1988.
2. Rachel Ben-Eliyahu and Rina Dechter. Propositional Semantics for Disjunctive Logic Programs. In K. R. Apt, editor, *LOGIC PROGRAMMING: Proceedings of the 1992 Joint International Conference and Symposium*, pages 813–827, Cambridge, Mass., November 1992. MIT Press.
3. D. Brand. Proving theorems with the modification method. *SIAM Journal*, 4:412–430, 1975.
4. Gerd Brewka, Jürgen Dix, and Kurt Konolige. *Nonmonotonic Reasoning: An Overview*. CSLI Lecture Notes 73. CSLI Publications, Stanford, CA, 1997.
5. Michael Gelfond and Vladimir Lifschitz. The Stable Model Semantics for Logic Programming. In R. Kowalski and K. Bowen, editors, *5th Conference on Logic Programming*, pages 1070–1080. MIT Press, 1988.
6. D. Jana and Bharat Jayaraman. Set constructors, finite sets, and logical semantics. *Journal of Logic Programming*, 38(1):55–77, 1999.
7. Bharat Jayaraman. Implementation of subset-equational programs. *Journal of Logic Programming*, 11(4):299–324, 1992.
8. Bharat Jayaraman and K. Moon. Subset logic programs and their implementation. *Journal of Logic Programming*, 41(2):71–110, 2000.
9. John W. Lloyd. *Foundations of Logic Programming*. Springer, Berlin, 1987. 2nd edition.
10. Bharat Jayaraman Mauricio Osorio and J. C. Nieves. Declarative pruning in a functional query language. In Danny De Schreye, editor, *Proceedings of the International Conference on Logic Programming*, pages 588–602. MIT Press, 1999.
11. Bharat Jayaraman Mauricio Osorio and David Plaisted. Theory of partial-order programming. *Science of Computer Programming*, 34(3):207–238, 1999.
12. Mauricio Osorio. Semantics of partial-order programs. In J. Dix and L.F. del Cerro andU. Furbach, editors, *Logics in Artificial Intelligence (JELIA '98)*, LNCS 1489, pages 47–61. Springer, 1998.
13. Mauricio Osorio and Bharat Jayaraman. Aggregation and WFS$^+$. In J. Dix, L. Pereira, and T. Przymusinski, editors, *Nonmonotonic Extensions of Logic Programming*, LNAI 1216, pages 71–90. Springer, Berlin, 1997.
14. Mauricio Osorio and Bharat Jayaraman. Aggregation and negation-as-failure. *New generation computing*, 17(3):255–284, 1999.

15. P. Simons. Towards constraint satisfaction through logic programs and the stable model semantics. Technical Report 47, Helsinki University of Technology, Digital Systems Laboratory, August 1997.
16. D.R. Stinson. *An introduction to the Design and Analysis of Algorithms*. The Charles Babbage Research Centre, Winnipeg, Canada, 1987.

The Importance of Being Discrete: Learning Classes of Actions and Outcomes through Interaction

Gary King and Tim Oates

Computer Science Department, LGRC
University of Massachusetts, Box 34610
Amherst, MA 01003-4610
gwking@cs.umass.edu, oates@ai.mit.edu
(413) 577-0669

Abstract. A robotic agent experiences a world of continuous multivariate sensations and chooses its actions from continuous action spaces.
Unless the agent is able to successfully partition these into functionally
similar classes, its ability to interact with the world will be extremely limited. We present a method whereby an unsupervised robotic agent learns
to discriminate discrete actions out of its continuous action parameters.
These actions are discriminated because they lead to qualitatively distinct outcomes in the robot's sensor space. Once found, these actions can
be used by the robot as primitives for further exploration of its world.
We present results gathered using a Pioneer 1 mobile robot.

1 Introduction

To live sucessfully in a world, robotic agents must be able to derive meaning from
continuous state spaces and select actions from continuous ranges of possibility.
In order to thrive agents must be able to find discrete classes of states and actions
that enable them to achieve their goals. For example, the Pioneer 1 mobile robot
has a pair of independent drive wheels and a variety of sensors including seven
sonars and a CCD camera. To move, the robot must select a speed for its right
and left wheels from an infinite range of possible parameters. While it acts, the
values returned from its sonars, camera and other sensors will transition through
a subset of an infinite number of states. As far as the robot can tell, every one of
its possible wheel speed settings is a different action and every one of its distinct
sensor readings is a different state. If the robot had to use these as primitives,
it would be unable to understand the world or determine what actions to take
in any reasonable amount of time.

Of course, many of these wheel speed settings lead to qualitatively similar
outcomes. The robot will go forward, backwards, turn left or right or not move
at all. We can examine the robot's behavior and categorize its actions because *we*
have already categorized these continuous domains into discrete chunks. However, providing a robot with knowledge of our categories by hand-coding primi-

E. Stroulia and S. Matwin (Eds.): AI 2001, LNAI 2056, pp. 236–245, 2001.

tive actions and states is tedious, error prone, and must be tuned to each particular model of robot. Lastly, since the robot's sensing and effecting abilities are not equivalent to our own, we may be unable to provide distinctions which are optimally effective for the robot as it attempts to interact with and control its environment.

The problem of learning action models for the purpose of planning is studied in a variety of forms. Much of this work focuses on simulated domains and assumes discrete state and action spaces and deterministic outcomes of actions [5,15], though some allows for the possibility of probabilistic outcomes [2,9]. One notable exception is [11], which describes a method for learning action models given continuous state and action spaces for a simulated robot with noisy sensors. Though [16] and others explore the discovery of regimes in time series, their regimes are approximated by normal distributions and their method does not address the case where the time series are (at least partially) caused by an agent.

In stochastic domains with continuous states and discrete actions, reinforcement learning methods can learn reactive control policies [7], and recent work in this area addresses the case in which both the state and action spaces are continuous [13]. Reinforcement learning has also proven to be effective both in simulated domains and with physically embodied robots. Our work differs from these approaches in that the goal is to learn a declarative action model suitable for use by symbolic planning algorithms (and other cognitive tasks such as natural language generation and understanding [10]), not opaque, non-symbolic policies.

Our representation of outcomes as prototypical time series is based on earlier work on clustering time series [8]. Several other recent approaches to identifying qualitatively different regimes in time series data include [1,3,6].

Below, we present a method whereby an unsupervised robotic agent can learn qualitively distinct regions of the parameters that control its actions. In our model, the robot begins with a finite number of distinct controllers, each of which is parameterized over zero or more dimensions. Using our method, a robot will be able to learn for itself which regions of the parameter spaces of its controllers lead to what sensory outcomes. These regions can then become the discrete primitive actions which the robot can use to plan. The layout of the paper is as follows: we first describe our robotic agent–the Pioneer 1 mobile robot–and the primitive controllers we created for it; then we describe our method and the experimental results that validate it. Lastly, we discuss the future work involved in turning the prototype actions discovered by our algorithm into planning operators.

2 Method

We can view the sensor data collected by the robot as being generated by distinct activities or processes. For example, a process may involve the robot going forward, turning to the right, spinning sharply left or doing nothing at all. Our problem falls into two pieces. The first is to take the set of continuous multivariate time series generated by the robot and discover the distinct activities which created it and which activity generated which time series. In essence we want to discover how many different kinds of things the robot did and which thing goes with which time series. The second problem is to use this information to divide the parameter space(s) of the controller(s) that generated each activity into possibly overlapping regions. These regions build upon the robot's innate controllers and we use them to form the robot's primitive actions.

2.1 Framework

Although the method we propose is quite general, we explicate it in the context of our experimental work with the Pioneer mobile robot. We provide a robot with three distinct controllers:

- $\Psi_{RL}(r, l)$–a left-right wheel speed controller. By varying r and l, the robot sets its right and left wheel speeds.
- $\Psi_\emptyset$–a null controller that sets all the robots effectors to their resting states. Though perhaps perverse, this 'controller' lets the system differentiate action from inaction.
- Ψ_{OS}–a controller designed to seek out and move the robot towards open space. It does this by rotating to find the direction with the least amount of sonar clutter, moving in that direction and then orienting towards a randomly chosen heading.

We then let the robot randomly select controllers and parameters and execute them for a brief time–typically between 10 and 20 seconds. The data recorded by the robot during each experience is saved along with the controller type and its parameters, if any. We call the complete set of robot experiences $\mathcal{E}$. Note that qualitatively distinct controller/parameter settings should generate trajectories of qualitatively distinct sensor readings as outcomes. For example, going forward will typically cause the forward facing sonar's distances to go down, the sizes of objects in the visual field to grow and the translational velocity to be positive. Other actions will produce very different readings. The next section describes how we can learn which of these sensor time series are associated with the different kinds of activities in which the robot engages.

2.2 Learning Distinctive Outcomes for a Controller

Given $\mathcal{E}$, we search for distinctive outcomes by first uniformly sampling fixed length subsequences of length L, called L-sequences, from the data. We then form k clusters from the L-sequences via hierarchical agglomerative clustering using Dynamic Time Warping (DTW) [12] to measure the distance between each sequence. DTW is a generalization of classical algorithms for comparing discrete sequences (e.g. minimum string edit distance [4]) to sequences of continuous values. The k centroids of the clusters found, C_i, partition the space of L-sequences, with each centroid standing in for all of the L-sequences that are most similar to it. In effect, the centroids discretize the continuous sensor space and form an alphabet which can be used to tokenize any other experience.

We next divide $\mathcal{E}$ into two sets for each controller: one set contains experiences that occurred while the controller was running; the other experiences that occurred while some other controller was running. For each centroid, we can determine the probability that C_i occurred when the controller was running, $p(C_i|\Psi)$, and the probability that C_i occurred when the controller was not running, $p(C_i|\overline{\Psi})$. If $p(C_i|\Psi)$ is significantly different from $p(C_i|\overline{\Psi})$ then the centroid is *distinctive* for Ψ. Centroids that occur more frequently than by chance (under the null hypothesis that the occurrence does not depend on the controller) are called positively distinctive centroids for Ψ and are denoted by $\Psi(C_i)^+$. Centroids that occur less frequently are negatively distinctive centroids and are denoted by $\Psi(C_i)^-$. Centroids which are neither positively nor negatively distinctive are said to be neutral with respect to the controller. As positively distinctive centroids occur more often in the presence of Ψ, we infer that Ψ causes them: that the sensor trajectories similar to $\Psi(C_i)^+$ are the outcomes of running Ψ. Typically, the inference that a causes b requires that a and b covary, that a occurs before b and that other potential causes of b are controlled [14]. As our method does not account for the last item, some of the causal inductions will be incorrect and further effort will need to go into resolving them.

2.3   From Distinctive Outcomes to Distinctive Actions

For each centroid in $\Psi(C_i)^+$, we examine the experiences in $\mathcal{E}$ and see if the centroid occurs more frequently than by chance. We accomplish this by comparing the number of occurrences of L-sequences similar to the centroid in the experience to that expected given the overall population density of the centroid in $\mathcal{E}$. If C_i occurs frequently in an experience, then we say that the experience is distinctive for the centroid. The set of distinctive experiences for each centroid is $\mathcal{E}_{C_i}$. We will denote the parameters of the distinctive experiences for a centroid as P_{C_i}. We can plot P_{C_i} for each controller colored by the centroid. For example, figure 1 shows one particular division of Ψ_{RL}'s parameter space. This plot shows left and right wheel speed parameters associated with data collected from the Pioneer-1 while running Ψ_{RL}. Each of these robot experiences is labeled with one of six distinctive centroids. For example, the experiences labeled with the small x's all have wheel speeds that are generally below zero. The center portion of the plot is empty because our method did not find any distinctive outcomes for these experiences. Notice that each of the prototypical centroids is associated with a subset of the entire parameter space and that the subsets appear to be well separated.

In general, there are several possible outcomes for the distributions of controller parameters derived from individual centroids C_i and from pairs of centroids C_j and C_k. We first list the possibilities and then provide intuitions for their meanings:

1. P_{C_i} has a uniform distribution across the entire parameter space.
2. P_{C_i} has a non-uniform distribution–some parameter values lead to C_i more frequently than others. This distribution may be uni-modal, bimodal or more complex.

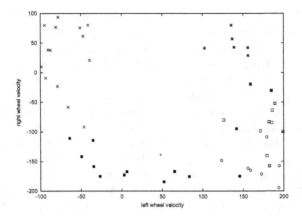

Fig. 1. Scatter-plot of Left and Right wheel velocities labeled by their centroid or distinctive outcome.

3. P_{C_j} and P_{C_k} are well separated (note that this can only occur if the individual distributions are non-uniform to begin with).
4. P_{C_j} and P_{C_k} overlap significantly.

We will formalize these notions below but the intuitions should be clear. In the concrete terms of $\Psi_{RL}(r, l)$, item 1 indicates that although the outcome occurs more frequently when Ψ_{RL} is running, it does not depend on the parameters of Ψ_{RL}. Item 2 indicates that the occurrence of the centroid depends on r and l. If the distribution is uni-modal, then only one range of r and l leads to this outcome; if it is more complex, then two or more ranges lead to it. This corresponds to a different regions of the parameter space having the same outcome.

Items 3 and 4 both require that the outcomes C_j and C_k depend on the choice of r and l. If the parameter ranges for the two outcomes overlap significantly, then this corresponds to a single action leading to two (or more) different outcomes. This may be due to the context in which the two action occurs.

2.4 Knowing When an Action Is Discrete

Given a distribution P_{C_i}, we must ask whether it is significantly different from that expected by random chance. We can divide the parameter space of a controller into uniform cells and create a histogram of the number of occurrences of P_{C_i} in a cell. We can create a similar histogram of the total number of experiences with parameters in a cell regardless of centroid. We can use these histograms to form a discrete probability distribution of the probability that a given range of parameters leads to the distinctive outcome (C_i). The null hypothesis is that the parameter values have no effect on the outcomes and that the distribution obtained from P_{C_i} is uniform. We can test H_0 for each C_i by building a sampling distribution of the Kullback-Leibler distances between randomly generated distributions of the number of experiences containing C_i. elements and the true uniform distribution. The discrete Kullback-Leibler distance or average variance measures how much one probability distribution differs from another:

$$d(p_1, p_2) = -\sum_x p_1(x) ln \frac{p_1(x)}{p_2(x)}$$

Once we have obtained the distribution of the distance measures, we can use randomization testing to see if the actual distribution derived from P_{C_i} is significant.

If P_{C_i} is significantly different from the non-uniform distribution, then we can use randomization testing again on each of the cells in the distribution. In this case, we build the sampling distribution for the cells of the histogram using the Kullback-Leibler distance of the probability value in each cell as compared to the uniform probability distribution. We then look for cells whose Kullback-Leibler score is significantly different from that expected under H_0. These cells are the ones who contribute highly to P_{C_i}'s significance. They define the discrete action which leads to outcome C_i.

2.5 Summary of the Method

In summary, our method is as follows. Given a set of parameterized controllers for a mobile robot and a set of sensors:

1. Randomly select a controller and run it with randomly selected parameters. While it is running, record the data that it generates and save this along with the type of controller and its parameter values.
2. Sample fixed length subsequences uniformly from the data generated and form clusters.
3. For each cluster centroid, C_i, and controller, Ψ, determine if the probability of the centroid occurring while Ψ is running, $p(C_i|\Psi)$, differs significantly from the probability of the centroid occurring while Ψ is *not* running, $p(C_i|\overline{\Psi})$.
4. Determine the distinctive experiences for each of Ψ's positively distinctive centroids. Use these to create probability distributions for P_{C_i}, the parameters of the experiences that lead to outcome C_i.
5. Use randomization testing and the discrete Kullback-Leibler distance to find centroids that are dependent on the parameters of Ψ and the regions of the parameter-space that lead to the centroid.

The regions found are ranges of parameter values that typically result in specific outcomes of sensory trajectories. They are candidates for primitive actions of the mobile robot.

3 Experiment

3.1 Method

We collected 120 experiences using $\Psi_{RL}(r, l)$ (96-experiences), $\Psi_\emptyset$ (12-experiences) and Ψ_{OS} (12-experiences). The distribution was weighted towards

Ψ_{RL} as this controller was the focus of our experiment. The r and l parameters for Ψ_{RL} were uniformly sampled between -100 and 200 so as to obtain more forward-moving experiences than backward-moving experiences. The robot operated in a convex space containing numerous small objects with which it could interact. Intervention was required once during the data collection when the robot became stuck on power conduit lines attached to one of the walls of the space.

In the analysis that follows we used the following subset of sensors: heading, right-wheel-velocity, left-wheel-velocity, translational-velocity and rotational-velocity. The Pioneer keeps track of its heading and assumed position by dead reckoning. It determines its right and left wheel velocities, translational and rotational velocities via proprioceptive feedback from its wheel encoders. The values of its sensors are recorded every 10-milliseconds.

3.2 Results

The algorithm described above found several statistically significant ($p < 0.01$) regions of the parameter space of $\Psi_{RL}(r, l)$ including ones that we would label roughly as "forward", "backwards", "hard-left", "slow-left" and so forth. Figure 2 below demonstrates several probability distributions linking particular setting of left and right wheel speeds and their distinctive outcomes (C_i). In this experiment, each distribution was decidedly non-uniform (corresponding to item 2 in the taxonomy above) and demarcated a single contiguous region of the parameter space. The regions are relatively large, however, and several overlap each other. Our assumption is that this is due in part to the small size of our data set and in part to the fact that different actions can result in the same qualitative outcome. Further experiments are underway to clarify this.

Each plot in figure 2 shows the action associated with a particular distinctive outcome. These plots are based on clusters of the data from the original 120-trials. The darker cells of each plot indicate the range of parameters that define the action. The first plot shows the action defined by high values of left and right wheel speeds and with the right wheel speed generally higher than the left wheel speed–with what we would label forward motion and turning to the right. Investigation of the distinctive centroid associated with the plot confirms this interpretation. The second plot shows actions with right wheel speeds below zero and the third shows actions with high left wheel velocities and low right wheel velocities. We might label these activities as "backwards to the left" and "forward left turn" respectively. Of course, each atomic action discovered by our method ranges over a large portion of the controller's parameter space. This is due in part to the limited amount of data collected and in part to the noisy environment in which the robot runs. We expect that additional data would allow the atomic actions to become more precise.

We have shown that our method allows an unsupervised mobile robot to interact with its environment and learn discrete actions over the parameter spaces of its controllers.

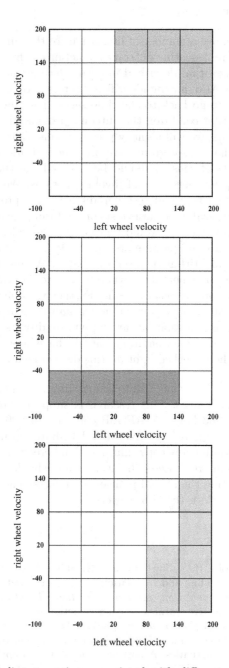

Fig. 2. Examples of discrete actions associated with different distinctive outcomes. They corresponds roughly to "going forward"; "going backwards or turning left"; and "turning to the left".

4   Future Work

Future work will remove a number of limitations of the current method. In particular, rather than representing outcomes of actions as fixed-length prototypes, we will apply the algorithm described in [8] to identify and represent outcomes of variable duration. Also, having identified discrete actions and their outcomes, it becomes possible to go back to the time series data and search for features of the environment that condition the outcome probabilities. In terms of classical planning operators, we will identify preconditions. Another limitation of the current method is that sensor groups are pre-specified. Ideally, the robot would determine which sets of sensors should be grouped together because patterns in those sensors capture outcomes of invoking actions. We plan to explore the utility of a simple generate and test paradigm to this problem, with the test phase involving statistical hypothesis tests of the form previously described. Another extension to this method would be to apply active learning techniques by letting the robot choose its parameters rather than selecting them at random. Finally, the current algorithm runs only in batch. We intend to move towards a completely online implementation whereby the robot will continuously find, test and improve its prototypical actions. Further work also needs to be done to investigate the scalability of our approach and to deal with non-stationary time series. Indeed, as the robot's learning will modify its interactions, we are prima facie in a non-stationary environment. We have hopes that the continuous on-line version will help to shed light on this developmental problem.

Acknowledgments. We would like to thank our anonymous reviewers for their helpful comments and ideas. This research is supported by DARPA contract DASG60-99-C-0074 and DARPA/AFOSR contract F49620-97-1-0485. The U.S. Government is authorized to reproduce and distribute reprints for governmental purposes notwithstanding any copyright notation hereon. The views and conclusions contained herein are those of the authors and should not be interpreted as necessarily representing the official policies or endorsements either expressed or implied, of the DARPA or the U.S. Government.

References

1. R. Agrawal, K. Lin, H. S. Sawhney, and K. Shim. Fast similarity search in the presence of noise, scaling and translation in time series databases. In *Proceedings of the 21st International Conference on Very Large Databases*, 1995.
2. Scott Benson. Inductive learning of reactive action models. In *Proceedings of the Twelfth International Conference on Machine Learning*, pages 47–54, 1995.
3. Paul R. Cohen, Marco Ramoni, Paola Sebastiani, and John Warwick. Unsupervised clustering of robot activities: A bayesian approach. To appear in *Proceedings of the Fourth International Conference on Autonomous Agents*, 1999.
4. Thomas H. Cormen, Charles E. Leiserson, and Ronald L. Rivest. *Introduction to Algorithms*. The MIT Press, 1990.
5. Yolanda Gil. *Acquiring Domain Knowledge for Planning by Experimentation*. PhD thesis, Carnegie Mellon University, 1992.

6. Eamonn Keogh and Michael J. Pazzani. An enhanced representation of time series which allows fast and accurate classification, clustering and relevance feedback. In *Working Notes of the AAAI-98 workshop on Predicting the Future: AI Approaches to Time-Series Analysis*, pages 44–51, 1998.

7. Sridhar Mahadevan and Jonathan Connell. Automatic programming of behavior-based robots using reinforcement learning. *Artificial Intelligence*, 55(2–3):189–208, 1992.

8. Tim Oates. Identifying distinctive subsequences in multivariate time series by clustering. In *Proceedings of the Fifth International Conference on Knowledge Discovery and Data Mining*, pages 322–326, 1999.

9. Tim Oates and Paul R. Cohen. Searching for planning operators with context-dependent and probabilistic effects. 1996.

10. Tim Oates, Zachary Eyler-Walker, and Paul R. Cohen. Toward natural language interfaces for robotic agents: Grounding linguistic meaning in sensors. In *Proceedings of the Fourth International Conference on Autonomous Agents*, pages 227–228, 2000. Extended abstract.

11. David M. Pierce. *Map Learning with Uninterpreted Sensors and Effector*. PhD thesis, University of Texas, Austin, 1995.

12. David Sankoff and Joseph B. Kruskal, editors. *Time Warps, String Edits, and Macromolecules: Theory and Practice of Sequence Comparisons*. Addison-Wesley Publishing Company, Reading, MA, 1983.

13. J. C. Santamaria, R. S. Sutton, and A. Ram. Experiments with reinforcement learning in problems with continuous state and action spaces. *Adaptive behavior*, 6(2):163–218, 1998.

14. Patrick Suppes. *A Probabilistic Theory of Causality*. North Holland, Amsterdam, 1970.

15. Xuemei Wang. Learning by observation and practice: An incremental approach for planning operator acquisition. In *Proceedings of the Twelfth International Conference on Machine Learning*, 1995.

16. Andreas S. Weigend, Morgan Mangeas, and Ashok N. Srivastava. Nonlinear gated experts for time series: discovering regimes and avoiding overfitting. *Int J Neural Syst*, 6:373–399, 1995.

User Interface Aspects of a Translation Typing System

Philippe Langlais, Guy Lapalme, and Sébastien Sauvé

RALI-DIRO, Université de Montréal
C.P. 6128, Succ Centre-Ville
Montréal, Québec, Canada H3C 3J7
{felipe,lapalme,sauvese}@iro.umontreal.ca

Abstract. This paper describes the user interface design and evaluation of TRANSTYPE, a system that watches over the user as he or she types a translation and repeatedly suggests completions for the text already entered. We show that this innovative approach to a translation tool, both unobtrusive and very useful, can be very productive for the translators.

1 Introduction

TRANSTYPE is a project set up to explore an appealing solution to the problem of using *Interactive Machine Translation* (IMT) as a tool for professional or other highly-skilled translators. IMT first appeared as part of Kay's MIND system [6], where the user's role was to help the computer analyze the source text by answering questions about word sense, ellipsis, phrasal attachments, etc. Most later work on IMT, such as Brown [2], has followed in this vein, concentrating on improving the question/answer process by having less questions, more friendly ones, etc. Despite progress in these endeavors, systems of this sort are generally unsuitable as tools for skilled translators because the user serves only as an advisor, with the MT components keeping the overall control over the translation process.

TRANSTYPE originated from the conviction that a better approach to IMT for competent translators would be to shift the focus of interaction from the *meaning* of the source text to the *form* of the target text. This would relieve the translator of the burden of having to provide explicit analyses of the source text and allow him to translate naturally, assisted by the machine whenever possible. In this approach, a translation emerges from a series of alternating contributions by human and machine. In all cases, the translator remains directly in control of the process: the machine must work within the constraints implicit in the user's contributions, and he or she is free to accept, modify, or completely ignore its proposals.

The core of TRANSTYPE is a completion engine which comprises two main parts: an *evaluator* which assigns probabilistic scores to completion hypotheses and a *generator* which uses the evaluation function to select the best candidate for completion. The evaluator is a function $p(t|t', s)$ which assigns to each target-text unit t an estimate of its probability given a source text s and the tokens

E. Stroulia and S. Matwin (Eds.): AI 2001, LNAI 2056, pp. 246–256, 2001.

t' which precede t in the current translation of s. We use a linear combination of separate predictions from a language model $p(t|t')$ and a translation model $p(t|s)$. Our linear combination model is fully described in [8] but can be seen as follows:

$$p(t|t',s) = \underbrace{p(t|t')\ \lambda(\Theta(t',s))}_{\text{language}} + \underbrace{p(t|s)\ [1 - \lambda(\Theta(t',s))]}_{\text{translation}}$$

where $\lambda(\Theta(t',s)) \in [0,1]$ are context-dependent interpolation coefficients. $\Theta(t',s)$ stands for any function which maps t',s into a set of equivalence classes. Intuitively, $\lambda(\Theta(t',s))$ should be high when s is more informative than t' and low otherwise. For example, the translation model could have a higher weight at the start of sentence but the contribution of the language model can become more important in the middle or the end of the sentence.

The language model is an interpolated trigram [5] trained on the Hansard corpus (about 50 million words), with 75% of the corpus used for relative-frequency parameter estimates, and 25% used to reestimate interpolation coefficients.

Our translation model is a slight modification of an IBM model 2 [1] in which we account for invariant entities such as English forms that almost invariably translate into French either verbatim or after having undergone a predictable transformation e.g. numbers or dates. These forms are very frequent in the Hansard corpus.

TRANSTYPE is a specialized text editor with a non intrusive embedded Machine translation engine as one of its components. In this project we had to address the following problems: how to interact with the user and how to find appropriate multi-word units for suggestions that can be computed in real time. The former has been described by Langlais [9] but this article focuses on the latter.

2   The TransType Model

2.1   User Viewpoint

Our interactive translation system is illustrated in figure 1 for an English to French translation. It works as follows: a translator selects a sentence and begins typing its translation. After each character typed by the translator, the system displays a proposed completion, which may either be accepted using a special key or rejected by continuing to type. This interface is simple and its performance may be measured by the proportion of characters or keystrokes saved while typing a translation. Throughout this process, TRANSTYPE must continually adapt its suggestions to the translator's input. This differs from the usual machine translation set-ups where it is the machine that produces the first draft which then has to be corrected by the translator.

TRANSTYPE mode of interaction requires a synchronization between the user interface module and the translation engine in order to maintain a coherent state:

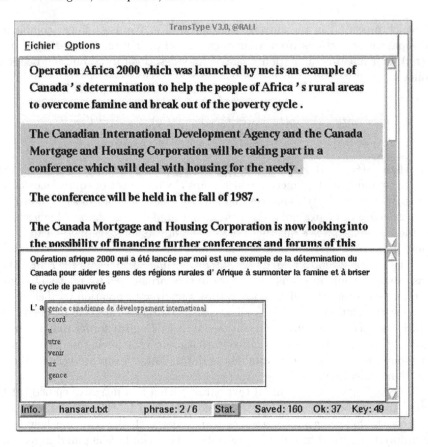

Fig. 1. Example of an interaction in TRANSTYPE with the source text in the top half of the screen. The target text is typed in the bottom half with suggestions given by the menu at the insertion point. Unlike the version used in the evaluation, the current prototype which offers unit completion is illustrated here.

the translation engine must be aware of the sentence the translator is working on and continuously keep track of the part of the sentence that precedes the cursor. The synchronization must always be kept even in the case of cursor movements with the mouse or in the case of cut and paste operations.

3   Development of the User Interface Elements

A major part of the TRANSTYPE project went into the design of a real-time translation engine fast enough to respond after each action of the user. This work was first described by Foster [4] and was implemented with a rudimentary line-oriented interface. The user was presented suggestions one at a time and control keys were used to cycle through them and to select one. This prototype showed the feasibility of the underlying translation engine but was not really "usable" by translators.

We then defined the following objectives for a better user-interface:

- hide the inner workings of the translation engine
- provide an adequate display for the user showing both the source text and appropriate suggestions
- embed the engine in a more convenient and intuitive text editor similar to the usual working environment of a translator.

We developed a first version of the editor in order to find the best way to display the text and the suggestions: we tried to display the text and its translation side by side but it seems that a synchronized display of the original text and its translation one over the other is better; we also tried displaying suggestions in a separate window but we finally chose the set-up shown in Figure 1 where the seven best suggestions are shown as a floating menu positioned at the cursor. In the first version, editing was limited at going from left to right. The only way to correct what had been typed was by hitting the backspace key. This reflected the left to right working of the translation engine. But we quickly saw that this was too rigid (users could not even move the cursor with the arrow keys) and that the results would not be meaningful. Even though, our goal was only to prove the feasibility of our translation engine, we found that these interface limitations would hide the usefulness of TRANSTYPE to the translators.

So we decided to invest more time in a translator friendlier interface that allows a free movement of the cursor either with the mouse or arrow keys. We also allowed all usual editing such as cut and paste of arbitrary selections of text. This implied a synchronization mechanism between the user interface and the translation engine of TRANSTYPE in order to follow these cursor movements and to update in real-time the context of the engine. We also added easier means of dealing with suggestions which can either be cycled through using PageUp or PageDown keys; the current element of the menu always appear at the same level of the text to ease reading and can be accepted using either the Tab or the Return key. A user can also click directly any suggestion of the menu using the mouse.

User preferences can tailor some aspects of the interface dealing with:

- relevance of suggestions: mixing coefficients of the language and translation models, minimal score for a suggestion to be given;
- number of suggestions displayed, prefix length before a suggestion is made (currently 0) and the minimum number of letters that a suggestion must have before being shown.

We have not done a systematic comparison of all these parameters but we chose a set of what seemed to be the most adequate settings for the purpose of our evaluation if this tool really supported a more productive way of producing translations.

This interface was implemented using a text widget in Tcl/Tk linked with our translation engine written in C++. The text widget is limited to the edition of plain character files and thus is not a full featured text editor such as Microsoft Word which allows for formatting of characters using bold and italics, for paragraph indenting and centering and for creating figures and tables.

As we wanted to only test the speed of typing translations of isolated sentences, we did not need a full text processor but one that we could customize. We instrumented the interface to keep track in a file of all user actions. This file was then analyzed off-line to deduce measurements about the behavior of the user.

4   User-Interface Evaluation

We first defined a theoretical evaluation of TRANSTYPE on a word completion task, which assumes that a translator carefully observes each completion proposed by the system and accepts it as soon as it is correct. Under these optimistic conditions, we have shown that TransType allows for the production of a translation typing less than a third of its characters, see Langlais et al [11] for more details.

The goal of the evaluation was two-fold: first to see if this behavior of a hypothetical user is similar to the one of a human translator while composing a translation; second to gauge if TRANSTYPE could help in other ways such as giving ideas for translations for terms for which there is some hesitation. As the suggestions of TRANSTYPE are correctly spelled, their selection insures that there are less misspellings; this is particularly useful for completed proper nouns or numbers which must always be carefully transcribed and are often error prone.

4.1   User Protocol

We asked ten translators with various work years of experience and areas of expertise, to try TRANSTYPE in a controlled setting. We took for granted that the translations were correct because we wanted to evaluate our system and not the translators themselves. All translators were given the same sentences to translate; these sentences were chosen arbitrarily from our corpus.

The protocol consisted of three steps:

1. **6 minutes without TransType** to reassure the translators that our text editor was quite conventional for typing texts: the usual keys for deletion, motion, cutting and pasting are present. There is no provision for formatting though. This step measures the "natural" typing speed of each translator, i.e. their speed of thinking and typing a translation in our text editor but without TRANSTYPE activated.

2. **25 minutes with TransType** in which the user types a translation while being able to select suggestions given by the system. At about the middle of the experiment, we stopped and gave the translator some advice on trying

an alternate way of using TRANSTYPE in order to make a better use of the facilities of the system. We soon realized that this intervention was more of an annoyance than a help but we kept it in order to have comparable results.

3. **6 minutes with longer suggestions** that were inspired by the work of Langé [7], we wanted to check if some longer suggestions that we called *briskels* (bricks and skeletons) could be useful. Briskels were presented to the user as soon as a user selected a sentence. The briskels were determined by hand for the sentences of our experiment but Langlais [10] has shown that is possible to automatically compute units longer than one word.

Table 1. Number of characters typed, automatically by accepting the suggestions of TRANSTYPE, erased, the number of acceptations and the number of characters finally present in the text produced at Step 2 of our protocol. The last column shows the proportion of characters manually typed over the number of characters in the final text. The last line indicates the mean.

	typed	auto	erased	accept.	final	% typed
1	223	748	33	117	938	40%
2	578	1469	118	238	1929	48%
3	281	746	64	129	963	49%
4	887	985	124	152	1748	67%
5	817	1446	143	228	2120	56%
6	189	505	92	82	602	60%
7	669	885	85	151	1469	62%
8	588	820	201	119	1207	75%
9	222	962	93	166	1091	44%
10	405	1156	155	198	1406	54%
	486	972	111	158	1347	55%

5   Results

5.1   Comparison with the Theoretical Evaluation

As we have discussed in section 3, the theoretical gain in the number of keys saved using TRANSTYPE is about 0.45 if a user does not change his mind once something has been typed, does not move the cursor with the mouse and does not erase whole words or parts of the text.

Table 1 shows the number of characters that were typed during step 2 of the protocol. We observe that on average a translation can be obtained by typing only about a third for the characters. This figure roughly agrees with our theoretical user performance which had been used in developing our translation engine.

The number of suggestions that were accepted was quite high which shows the usefulness of TRANSTYPE.

5.2 Productivity

We define productivity as the ratio of the number of characters in the final text over the time it took to produce the text. Interviews with the translators had shown that almost all of them thought that TRANSTYPE had improved their productivity. Unfortunately Table 2 on the left does not corroborate this favorable impression because on the average raw productivity went down by 35%!

Table 2. Table on the left gives the raw productivity of the translators at each step of the protocol; Table on the right gives the corrected productivity rate not taking into account inactivity periods. The last line indicates the mean for all translators.

	Step 1	Step 2	Gain	Step 3	Gain
1	67.2	54.9	-18 %	83.7	25 %
2	143.9	85.0	-41 %	102.4	-29 %
3	79.3	60.0	-24 %	89.3	13 %
4	87.7	86.5	-1 %	98.5	12 %
5	131.9	92.6	-30 %	90.4	-32 %
6	70.0	34.9	-50 %	38.2	-45 %
7	141.7	84.3	-40 %	131.1	-7 %
8	116.8	45.9	-61 %	79.3	-32 %
9	77.1	46.4	-40 %	63.7	-17 %
10	101.6	58.5	-42 %	69.4	-32 %
	101.7	64.9	-35 %	84.6	-14 %

	Step 1	Step 2	Gain	Step 3	Gain
1	123.4	128.4	4.1 &	194.0	57%
2	155.6	112.8	-28 %	137.2	-12%
3	118.0	107.7	-8.7 %	147.2	25%
4	138.6	189.4	37 %	221.8	60%
5	148.1	127.5	-14 %	145.1	-2%
6	115.5	105.4	-8.7 %	84.0	-27%
7	156.9	127	-19 %	193.6	23%
8	156.0	126.4	-19 %	185.9	19%
9	138.5	188.9	36 %	163.5	18%
10	131.3	97.1	-26 %	153.5	17%
	138.2	131.1	-5 %	162,6	17%

This can be attributed to the learning process involved in using a new tool: some users did not hit the right keys to accept the suggestion, stopped for some periods or were stunned by some suggestions given by TRANSTYPE. Interestingly enough, translator 4 who managed to get the most out of TRANSTYPE used mainly the mouse to enter the translation. This means that the right suggestions almost always appeared in the menu. Some translators would have liked to temporarily deactivate TRANSTYPE for reformulating some sentences that seemed to have "gone on the wrong track". We did not want to burden our voluntary translators for more than an hour although some of them would have liked to bring TRANSTYPE home to use it regularly.

In order to partially take into account some of these factors we removed all inactivity periods of more than five seconds from the productivity computation. After these corrections, we see (Table 2 on right) that three translators managed to improve their productivity in step 2. But in step 3 where larger suggestions (briskels) were proposed, then 7 translators managed to improve their productivity. This prompted us to develop further work in computing longer suggestions than only one word [10].

5.3 Saved Effort

Another useful measure is the effort saved by TRANSTYPE in producing a translation. Effort is defined as the number of actions (key press and mouse clicks) done in a unit of time. An ideal tool would increase productivity while redirecting the effort by inserting more characters with the least number of actions.

Figure 2 shows the relation between the effort and productivity at each step of our protocol. The diagonal corresponds to a ratio of one action for each character and would be observed by a translator who would type correctly all the text on the first try. This line roughly corresponds to the underlying assumption made in the theoretical evaluation.

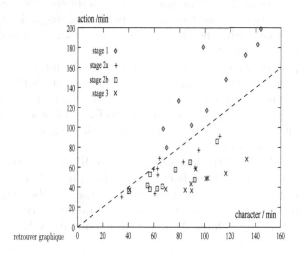

Fig. 2. Productivity versus effort of each subject over each stage of the protocol. The x-axis indicates the productivity, that is: the number of characters produced by unit of time (here a minute). The y-axis (the effort) indicates the number of keystrokes (or mouse clicks) produced on average each minute.

We see that actions of Step 1 of the protocol are over the diagonal and that the points of steps 2 and 3 are under the diagonal which means that each action produced more than one character.

We define efficiency as the ratio of productivity over effort. For example, an efficiency of 0.6 means that a user only produces 60 characters for 100 actions. Table 5.3 shows that the efficiency for all translators increases with each step of use of TRANSTYPE.

5.4 Qualitative Evaluation

All our testers (except one) were enthusiastic about this concept of translation typing tool even though our prototype was far from being perfect. They liked

Table 3. Average productivity, effort and efficiency of all subjects for each stage of the protocol.

stage	productivity	effort	efficiency
1	102.1	139.1	0.7
2	72.4	56.4	1.3
3	91.1	47.0	1.9

the idea that they could work at their own pace either accepting or ignoring TRANSTYPE suggestions, contrarily to other translating tools that are always there even when they are not needed. The translators appreciated the fact that they did not have to check for the correct spellings of suggestions. Most of them were confident that with time they would become more proficient at making a better use of TRANSTYPE.

The translators had more mixed feelings about the influence of TRANSTYPE on the literary quality of their translations: some were under the impression that TRANSTYPE induced a literal mode of translation. But they also noticed that it could have a positive effect because TRANSTYPE allowed them to easily get the "long formulation" of a translation in cases where they would probably have typed an abbreviated form.

Translators also liked the idea of "false briskels" because they are long suggestions. But as it takes more effort to read them, it is often not easy to think about them at the right moment. This reinforces the idea that longer suggestions that would pop up at the appropriate moment would be very useful. We plan on evaluating this aspect later. More details about this evaluation are given by Sauvé [12].

6   Related Work

It is hard to compare TRANSTYPE with other systems because it is unique thanks to the statistical translation engine that drives it.

Although the style of text prediction proposed in TRANSTYPE is novel, there are numerous precedents for text prediction in a unilingual setting. Many programs such as *GNU Emacs* and *tcsh* offer built-in word or command completion features, and word-completion add-ons are also available for standard word processing environments. For example the "small floating yellow windows" that Microsoft Word pops up when a prefix of a unique known word in a special table is recognized. In this case, the strings to be suggested were determined either when Word was compiled or they were painstakingly added by the user. Word only suggests one possibility while TRANSTYPE determines many suggestions at run-time depending on the contexts of both the target and the source texts.

Dynamic completions also occur in the field of *alternative and augmentative communication* (AAC), which deals with communication aids for the disabled such as the *Reactive Keyboard* [3]. The system then tries to guess what the user wants to type next. In this case, the suggestions or choices only depend on what has already been typed. In TRANSTYPE, it is possible to vary the relative contributions of both the language and translation models; so in principle, we could set it up so that only the language model is used but we have not done any experiment with this.

Translation memories such as the one implemented in the Translator's workbench of Trados [13] also address the problem of speeding up the typing of translations. A translation memory is an interface to a database of pairs of sentences and their associated translations. Within a text editor, the translation memory manager first checks if the current sentence can be found in the database of previous translations and if so, it proposes its previous translation that can either be accepted or modified by the translator. This environment can be quite efficient in the case of repetitive texts or for revisions of already translated texts. Although some "fuzzy matches" are allowed for finding close enough sentences (for example sentences can vary by dates or numbers) this approach is not as flexible as the dynamic suggestions of TRANSTYPE. Another drawback is the fact that once a user operates in the context of a translation memory, it is often awkward to stop it from proposing new sentences even if they are not relevant or to go around them. TRANSTYPE on the other side is a silent helper whose suggestions can be quietly ignored when the translator already knows what is to be typed.

7   Conclusion

Although some drawbacks have been identified, this user evaluation was very useful to show the interest of the innovative TRANSTYPE concept in a real setting. It is thus possible to develop computer aided translation tools that can help to improve the efficiency of translators who are more and more in demand in the new global economy.

Acknowledgements. TRANSTYPE is a project funded by the Natural Sciences and Engineering Research Council of Canada. We thank the Machina Sapiens company for its support in this project. We are greatly indebted to Elliott Macklovitch and Pierre Isabelle for the fruitful orientations they gave to this work.

References

1. Peter F. Brown, Stephen A. Della Pietra, Vincent Della J. Pietra, and Robert L. Mercer. The mathematics of machine translation: Parameter estimation. *Computational Linguistics*, 19(2):263–312, June 1993.
2. Ralf D. Brown and Sergei Nirenburg. Human-computer interaction for semantic disambiguation. In *Proceedings of the International Conference on Computational Linguistics (COLING)*, pages 42–47, Helsinki, Finland, August 1990.
3. John J. Darragh and Ian H. Witten. *The Reactive Keyboard*. Cambridge University Press, 1992.

4. George Foster, Pierre Isabelle, and Pierre Plamondon. Target-text Mediated Interactive Machine Translation. *Machine Translation*, 12:175–194, 1997.
5. Frederick Jelinek. Self-organized language modeling for speech recognition. In A. Waibel and K. Lee, editors, *Readings in Speech Recognition*, pages 450–506. Morgan Kaufmann, San Mateo, California, 1990.
6. Martin Kay. The MIND system. In R. Rustin, editor, *Natural Language Processing*, pages 155–188. Algorithmics Press, New York, 1973.
7. Jean-Marc Langé, Éric Gaussier, and Béatrice Daille. Bricks and Skeletons: Some Ideas for the Near Future of MAHT. *Machine Translation*, 12:175–194, 1997.
8. Philippe Langlais and George Foster. Using context-dependent interpolation to combine statistical language and translation models for interactive machine translation. In *Computer-Assisted Information Retrieval*, Paris, April 2000.
9. Philippe Langlais, George Foster, and Guy Lapalme. Unit completion for a computer-aided translation typing system. *to appear in Machine Translation*, page 25 p., Dec 2000.
10. Philippe Langlais, George Foster, and Guy Lapalme. Unit completion for a computer-aided translation typing system. In *Applied Natural Language Processing 2000*, page 10 pages, Seattle, Washington, May 2000.
11. Philippe Langlais, Sébastien Sauvé, George Foster, Elliott Macklovitch, and Guy Lapalme. Evaluation of transtype, a computer-aided translation typing system: A comparison of a theoretical- and a user- oriented evaluation procedures. In *Conference on Language Resources and Evaluation (LREC)*, page 8 pages, Athens, Greece, June 2000.
12. Sébastien Sauvé. L'évaluation d'un logiciel de traduction interactive: l'usager tiret-il profit de transtype ? Internal report, Université de Montréal, avril 2000.
13. Trados Translator's Workbench 2, product description. URL: www.trados.com/workbench/index.html, 1998.

A Hybrid Approach to Making Recommendations and Its Application to the Movie Domain

Shawn Grant[1] and Gordon I. McCalla[2]

[1]DolphinSearch, Inc., Ventura, California, U.S.A.
shawn@dolphinsearch.com

[2]ARIES Laboratory, Department of Computer Science, University of Saskatchewan,
Saskatoon, Saskatchewan, Canada
mccalla@cs.usask.ca

Abstract. There are two main techniques used to capture an individual's personal preferences in order to make recommendations to them about various items of interest: feature-based and clique-based. In this paper we present an approach that can use either technique or a hybrid of the two. Features are captured in the granularity knowledge formalism, giving the feature-based approach more representational power than in most systems. But, the most novel feature of the approach is its ability to use a hybrid technique, which aims to combine the advantages of both feature-based and clique-based approaches while minimising the disadvantages. The hybrid technique also allows for the construction of a personalised explanation to accompany the recommendation. A prototype for the movie domain, MovieMagician, has been developed. A formative evaluation of this prototype has been undertaken in all of its modes: feature-based, clique-based, and hybrid. Other evidence of effectiveness has also been gathered.

1 Introduction

The glut of unorganised information on the Web has led to the advent of commercial services such as Alta Vista and Lycos, using information filtering (IF) and information retrieval (IR) techniques to help a user satisfy short term information needs (Steinberg 1996). The need to satisfy long term information needs has initiated the appearance of systems to model a user's preferences and recommend items of interest to the user. Such systems have been called *recommender systems* (Resnick & Varian 1997). Application domains have included recommending movies, music, books, online news articles, web pages, and even mates. Our work investigates the development of a personal preference system called MovieMagician, designed for the movie domain.

Recommender systems draw their techniques from many sources, including IR/IF, intelligent agents, and expert systems. The most common approach is clique-based filtering, also called collaborative filtering (Goldberg et al. 1992) or social information filtering (Shardanand & Maes 1995) by the IR/IF community. Clique-based filtering

E. Stroulia and S. Matwin (Eds.): AI 2001, LNAI 2056, pp. 257–266, 2001.

uses a group of similar-minded people as indicators of a user's interests. The other approach is feature-based filtering, also termed content-based filtering (Oard 1997). The presence of preferred (or disliked) features in a new item can be used to form a judgement of whether the user will like or dislike it.

An advantage of the clique-based approach is that it doesn't require data about the item or the extraction of features from the data. A disadvantage is that there is no way to construct a recommendation for an item just introduced to the system and not rated by any users. Moreover, the coverage of ratings may be sparse if the user base is small, resulting in an insubstantial or inappropriate clique, and the method is slow to adapt to changing user goals or to respond to fine-grained preference distinctions. Finally, as Pennock et al (2000) have shown, there may be theoretical limits on finding optimal preference combinations, at least without using other information. The feature-based approach has no problems with the size of the user base and it can take advantage of empirically proven IR techniques. However, it can have severe disadvantages. Frequently, only a shallow analysis of the content is possible. Also, feature identification procedures must often deal with natural language issues within the text (for example recognising synonyms or disambiguating multiple meanings).

The recommender system we have developed can use either feature-based or clique-based techniques, but can also use a hybrid of the two approaches. Such a hybrid encapsulates the intuition that you receive better advice about item m from people who share your tastes about items similar to m in style and content. For example if you like action movies, you will be more likely to listen to advice on whether to see a new action movie from somebody who likes that kind of movie than from somebody who doesn't. A proof of concept prototype system for the movie domain, MovieMagician, has been implemented. A formative evaluation, aimed at comparing the three approaches, and especially at giving insight into the power and useability of the hybrid approach, has been carried out.

2 A Hybrid Model

The methodology behind the incorporation of a hybrid feature-based/clique-based technique for the prediction of movie ratings can be described with the help of the two Venn diagrams shown in Figure 1.

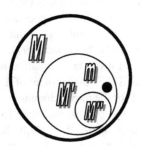
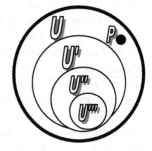

Fig. 1. Venn diagrams of model

Person p is a user who is requesting a movie rating prediction for movie m. The set M represents all movies in the system's library. M' is the subset of movies that are similar to movie m (in a sense that will be defined shortly). M" is the subset of movies that are similar to m and that person p has seen. The set U represents the set of all registered users. U' is the subset of users who have seen the movie m. U" is the subset of users who have seen m and who also have seen "all of" or "some of" the similar movies M". Finally, U''' is the subset of users who "feel the same as" or "agree with" p concerning the similar movies M".

The method used to rate a movie for a user, p, involves selecting a clique of similar users. Clique members are deemed to be similar based on previously viewed movies about which p and the clique feel the same way (based on similar ratings), and which at the same time are similar to the movie m (based on similar features). Once this clique is formed (corresponding to U'''), the rating of each clique member for the movie m can be used to form a predicted rating for p. This method creates *relativistic cliques*, that is cliques of people who feel the same way as p relative to movies similar to m (even though they may feel quite differently about other kinds of movies).

This hybridisation of feature-based and clique-based methods has the potential to realise the advantages of both. The features of the movies can be used to relativise the cliques, filter out irrelevant movies, allow categorisations of types of movies, annotate preferences about various features, and generate explanations for a movie. Using cliques, the subjective judgement of humans is naturally factored into the recommendation process. Also, cliques allow a holistic view of the movies to be captured, based upon the opinions of other human beings, whose ability to understand a movie as a "whole" cannot be replicated by today's AI systems.

2.1 Capturing and Using Features

The features of a movie are captured in a granularity hierarchy (McCalla et. al 1992), used extensively in intelligent tutoring systems and more recently information filtering (McCalla et al, 1996) and software engineering applications (Palthepu et al 1997). Granularity allows the representation and recognition of domain knowledge and concepts at many levels of detail (or grain sizes) along the two orthogonal dimensions of aggregation and abstraction. In the movie domain, standard features of movies (genre, actors, directors, etc.) are represented in a *generic* granularity hierarchy that is independent of a particular movie. A simple version of a generic hierarchy can be seen in Figure 2. *S-objects*, denoted by rectangles in Figure 2, are the primary objects in a granularity hierarchy and represent high-level conceptual knowledge. S-objects are allowed to have child objects connected along either or both the aggregation and abstraction dimensions. *Observers*, denoted in Figure 2 by ovals, are active objects that perceive features of the domain (in this case looking through a database of movie information for particular features of relevance to each observer). They thus act as the interface between the representation scheme and the real world. Any specific movie is an *instantiation* of this hierarchy. Each individual movie has a different instantiation hierarchy and thus is uniquely defined. However, the degree to which the instantiation hierarchies of two movies overlap also defines their similarity, an important aspect of granularity for our purposes, as discussed below.

The instantiation process is carried out automatically, using the recognition engine that is part of the granularity-based reasoning system. Instantiation takes observed characteristics of the movie and propagates this recognition through relevant portions of the hierarchy. Characteristics are observed from a database of movie information, such as the Internet Movie Database (IMDb), which provides detailed information about thousands of movies. The result is a library of instantiated hierarchies.

Similarity between two movies is determined by the degree of overlap between their instantiation hierarchies. This process is comparable to the techniques used in case-based reasoning for information retrieval based on the knowledge of similar cases, where a new problem is solved by finding similar cases and reusing them in the new problem situation (Daniels & Rissland 1995). An instantiated hierarchy will thus be called a *case* and the collection of such cases will be deemed a *case library*. The subset M' of similar movies for any movie m need be constructed only once, at the time m is instantiated and added to the library. It is saved as a *similarity list*.

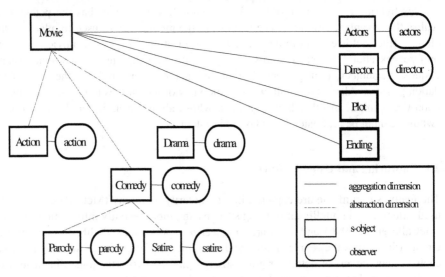

Fig. 2. A sample generic granularity hierarchy for the movie domain

2.2 User Interaction

The more the system knows about a user, the better it should perform. Following this idea, it is desirable to have a new user rate as many previously viewed movies as possible, and make updates frequently. A user rates a movie by annotating appropriate parts of the movie's instantiation hierarchy, accessible through an interface incorporated into MovieMagician. The user must supply an overall rating on a 7-point scale of $+3 \geq x \geq -3$ corresponding to the terms {Excellent, Very Good, Good, Indifferent,

Mediocre, Poor, Terrible}. Using this rating scheme, the user can give an overall rating for a movie and also rate particular features such as the genre, actors, and plot. The collection of annotated instantiation hierarchies for movies seen by a user constitute a *user model* for that user, and is used to refine the feature matching when forming the relativistic cliques.

The case library and user model can be used together to make recommendations regarding a particular (unseen) movie for a particular user. As an example, suppose user Alice has not seen the movie Pulp Fiction and requests a recommendation. M″ (the set of movies similar to Pulp Fiction that have been seen by Alice) is easily found by comparing the list of movies that Alice has seen with the similarity list for Pulp Fiction, resulting in the list shown in Table 1. Similarly, it is straightforward to find U″, the users who have seen Pulp Fiction as well as the other movies in M″. At this point, the system can select a clique from U″ using feature matching to find the users who feel the same about the M″ movies as Alice. To do this, the annotations for each movie in M″ are compared for Alice versus each of the U″ users. The matches are summed for all the movies, and a ranking of the U″ users is produced. The top ranked users are selected to form the clique U‴ (the users who feel the same way about the similar movies as does Alice). The annotations for the Overall Rating node are then averaged across the clique members and presented to Alice as the predicted rating. In this example, the results of the similarity matching are listed in Table 1. Frank, David and Carol, the highest ranking clique candidates, are chosen as the clique. The annotation values {-1, 0, -1} of the corresponding movie ratings {"Mediocre", "Indifferent", "Mediocre"} for the three clique members are averaged, and Alice is presented with a predicted rating of "Mediocre" (-1) for Pulp Fiction. This example demonstrates the ability of the hybrid model to use feature matching to select appropriate movies and cliques, and clique matching to select an appropriate rating as a prediction.

Table 1. An example of clique selection

M″ for Pulp Fiction	U″ for Pulp Fiction	Ranking of similarity to Alice	Rating for Pulp Fiction (annotation values)
1. GoodFellas	Bob	5	Excellent (2)
2. Jackie Brown	Carol	3	Mediocre (-1)
3. Die Hard	David	2	Indifferent (0)
4. Face/Off	Earl	4	Good (1)
	Frank	1	Mediocre (-1)

It should be noted that there are a huge variety of possibilities for the matching of users using the feature annotations and "cutoff" heuristics during clique selection. Numerous matching algorithms were tested to discover the better performing ones. The experimental results in the next section are based on the best algorithms found.

3 Experiments and Results

An array of experiments has been carried out to allow an internal comparison of the feature-based, clique-based, and hybrid models within the MovieMagician framework, as well as an external comparison of these models to the predictive skills of a professional movie reviewer, and to an existing online movie recommendation system. The results were also compared to the published evaluations of other personal preference systems in the movie domain.

Two data sets were used to test the predictive ability of MovieMagician: a data set, collected locally at the University of Saskatchewan; and a data set created from movie ratings available on-line from the DEC Research Systems Center[1]. To create the *UofS data set*, 54 test subjects were given access to 562 movies in the case library and were asked to rate the movies they had seen, providing both an overall rating as well as annotating features of each of the movies that had impacted them either negatively or positively. A total of 8260 ratings were made, with an average of 153 movies per subject. There were 306 movies in common between the UofS data set and the movies available from DEC. The overall ratings of these 306 movies by 1276 DEC users formed the *DEC data set*, containing a total of 24728 movie ratings. While much larger than the UofS data set, the DEC data set does not contain user annotations of specific movie features, only an overall rating of each movie.

In each experiment, a comparison was made between the predicted movie ratings of the MovieMagician system and the users' actual ratings. We used the common information retrieval metrics of precision and recall. In the context of our experimentation, *precision* is the percentage of predictions where the actual rating was at least as good for a liked movie (or conversely, at least as bad for a disliked movie) as the predicted rating. *Recall* is the percentage of the number of movies correctly predicted as "liked" to the total number of movies "liked". The final metric used involves calculating the Pearson correlation coefficient of the predicted ratings and actual ratings of a test subject. The results for the internal testing of the feature-based, clique-based, and hybrid techniques in MovieMagician are shown in Table 2.

Table 2. Summary of experimental results

Technique	Data set	Precision (%)	Recall (%)	Correlation
Feature-based	UofS	62	72	0.19
Clique-based	UofS	62	62	0.47
	DEC	68	62	0.61
Hybrid	UofS	63	64	0.40
	DEC	65	66	0.44

Although it performed more poorly according to the correlation measure, the feature-based technique, usually considered the underdog to clique-based techniques,

---

[1] http://www.research.digital.com/SRC/

compared favourably to the two other approaches in the UofS data set on precision and recall measures. The clique-based and hybrid techniques performed relatively well, considering the user population was quite small in the UofS data set and the annotations were only of the movies overall, not specific features, in the DEC data set. Thus, any of the approaches could be used where appropriate: the feature-based technique in situations with small user populations but lots of information about the movies, the clique-based technique in situations with more users but less information about the movies, and the hybrid technique in any situation.

Moving to the external examination of performance, MovieMagician was compared to a representative professional reviewer, Roger Ebert. MovieMagician outperformed Ebert (that is, if users simply accepted Ebert's recommendation without question). Using the Pearson correlation coefficient, the experiment revealed an average correlation of each user's actual rating to Ebert's rating of 0.26 for the UofS data set and 0.28 for the DEC data set. These values are much lower than those retrieved for any of the MovieMagician techniques in Table 2.

The final experiment conducted using the test data involved submitting the movie ratings of a typical test subject to a functional online recommendation system in order to compare the results with those of MovieMagician. The system selected for comparison was *MovieLens*[2], a clique-based system with tens of thousands of users. A total of 100 movie ratings were entered into *MovieLens* for the test subject. The results are shown in Table 3. MovieMagician, despite its small user and movie base, compared favourably (sometimes surpassing) *MovieLens*.

Table 3. Comparison of results using MovieMagician and MovieLens

Methodology	Precision (%)	Recall (%)	Correlation
MovieMagician Feature-based	61	75	0.36
MovieMagician Clique-based	74	73	0.58
MovieMagician Hybrid	73	56	0.51
MovieLens	66	74	0.48

The performance of MovieMagician can also be compared to the performance of movie recommendation systems reported in the literature. Alspector et al. (1997), using a neural net employing feature-based techniques, were able to obtain an average correlation of 0.38 between the predicted and actual ratings of users. Clique-based techniques achieved an average correlation of 0.58. The correlation with a professional movie reviewer, Leonard Maltin, was found to be 0.31. These numbers are comparable to ours, and further support our findings that on the correlation measure, the clique-based technique performs better than the feature-based technique and a professional movie reviewer. Unfortunately, this is the only metric available for com-

---

[2]http://movielens.umn.edu/

parison with Alspector et al. (1997). Another clique-based system, MORSE (Fisk, 1996), obtained exceptional results where 95.28% of the recommendations were found to be "satisfactory" by the users. This is very good performance, but this measure does not directly compare to any of our measures, making it difficult to draw any firm conclusions about the relative performance of MORSE and MovieMagician.

The hybrid system of Basu et al. (1998) is the closest in both methodology and measurement to MovieMagician. Using slightly different measures of precision and recall, the Basu et al system achieves a precision of 83%, while maintaining a recall of 34%. These results are impressive, yet when comparing them to MovieMagician we must consider that a prediction was not made for every movie as in our study, but instead a list of recommended movies was returned to each user from which the results were calculated. Their approach placed much emphasis on obtaining a high precision for each movie returned in the list, at the expense of recall. Thus, their higher precision values are counterbalanced by our higher recall values.

So, in all of its external comparisons, MovieMagician performs well, especially considering its small user and movie base which put both the clique and hybrid approaches at a disadvantage. In internal comparisons among the three approaches, we had expected our hybrid model to clearly perform better than the feature-based and clique-based methods. We feel the reasons it does not stand out as definitely superior stems mostly from restrictions within the experiments rather than any specific shortcoming in the design of the model.

One final capability of MovieMagician, not found in other systems, should be mentioned: the ability to automatically generate a (currently still quite crude) personalised movie review based on the user's feature preferences extracted from the clique used to predict the user's rating of the movie. An example of such a review is shown in Figure 3.

> The MovieMagician feels you will probably like the movie Mrs. Doubtfire. Overall, you will likely think it is Very Good. You will very likely feel the actor Robin Williams (Daniel Hillard/Mrs. Doubtfire) is Excellent. You also will probably feel the realization of the genre Comedy is Good. Finally, you will probably feel the plot is Good.

Fig. 3. Personalised movie review

4 Related Work

We discuss here research into hybrid techniques. Alspector et al (1997), while not building a hybrid system, were the first to formally compare feature-based and clique-based approaches. Recently, there have been a number of other hybrid approaches. Fab (Balabanović& Shoham 1997) is a system that provides users with personalized web page recommendations. In Fab feature-based filtering is used to select web pages that correspond to the topic designated to a collection agent, and after a user rates a page highly, clique-based filtering is used to pass the URL to the user's nearest neighbours based on the profile maintained by the selection agents. Basu et al. [1998] also employ a hybrid technique, where an inductive learning system draws on collaborative features (such as the set represented by users who like movie m or movies liked by user u) and content features (the features of the movies such as actor and genre) to make a recommendation. PTV (Cotter & Smyth, 2000) is a recent, but widely used system that produces personalised TV listings for its users. PTV provides the user with a list combining two types of recommendations: content-based (feature-based), generated essentially from the program descriptions as mapped to each user's interests, and collaborative (clique-based), generated from evaluations provided by other users with similar overall program preferences.

While all of these systems are hybrids in that they use both feature-based and clique-based approaches, in none of them are the two approaches integrated in the sense of MovieMagician, where all the cliques in the hybrid technique are indexed by feature preferences. Moreover, in these other systems, features are merely an unstructured list, as opposed to the more powerful granularity-based representation scheme in MovieMagician. Thus, MovieMagician has the potential to capture features more deeply, and to explore more subtle cliques, relativised by user preferences applied to this deep feature representation.

5 Conclusions

Overall, our experiments shed new light on feature-based vs. clique-based techniques for personal preference systems, and show that there is still promise for feature-based techniques, both in how well they can perform and in their incorporation into feature/clique hybrids. Indeed, we have proposed one such hybrid technique that combines the advantages of both feature-based and clique-based techniques. The formative evaluation showed that the hybrid system worked, but not its superiority to other approaches. The asymptotic behaviour of the hybrid system as data sets grow larger will only be possible through widespread web deployment.

The use of granularity-based reasoning in recommender systems is also a contribution. The hybrid and feature-based approaches gain much of their power from their use of a granularity-based representation of features. In fact, the movie domain is perhaps not the best domain to show these techniques to their best advantage, since the representation of the domain makes relatively little use of many of the most powerful features of granularity. Text retrieval, for example, may be a richer domain for exploring the feature-based and hybrid techniques investigated in this paper. McCalla et al (1996) have already explored the use of granularity for "similarity-based" text retrieval; and Woods (2000) shows how a powerful granularity-style subsumption hierarchies can be used to enhance text retrieval. Future investigations into building MovieMagician-style recommender systems for these feature-richer domains would likely prove profitable

Acknowledgements. We would like to thank the Natural Sciences and Engineering Research Council of Canada for its financial support for this research.

References

Alspector, J., Koicz, A., and Karunanithi, N. (1997). Feature-based and Clique-based User Models for Movie Selection: A Comparative Study. User Modeling and User-Adapted Interaction, **7**, 279-304.

Balabanović M., and Shoham, Y. (1997). Fab: Content-Based Collaborative Recommendation. Communications of the ACM, **40**(3), 66-72.

Basu, C., Hirsh, H., and Cohen, W. (1998). Recommendation as Classification: Using Social and Content-Based Information in Recommendation. Proc. AAAI 98, 714-721.

Cotter, P. and Smyth, B. (2000). PTV: Intelligent Personalised TV Guides. Proc. AAAI-00, 957-964.

Daniels, J.J., and Rissland, E.L. (1995). A Case-based Approach to Intelligent Information Retrieval. In, Proc. SIGIR '95, 238-245.

Fisk, D. (1996). An Application of Social Filtering to Movie Recommendation. BT Technology Journal, **14** (4), 124-132.

Goldberg, D., Nichols, D., Oki, B.M., and Terry, D. (1992). Using Collaborative Filtering to Weave an Information Tapestry. Communications of the ACM, **35**(12), 61-70.

McCalla, G. I., Greer, J. E., Barrie, J. B. and Pospisil, P. (1992). Granularity Hierarchies. International Journal of Computers and Mathematics, Special Issue on Semantic Networks, **23**(2-5), 363-376.

McCalla, G.I., Searwar, F., Thomson, J., Collins, J., Sun, Y., and Zhou, B., Analogical User Modelling: A Case Study in Individualized Information Filtering, Proc. User Modeling Conference, 1996, 13-20.

Oard, D.W. (1997). The State of the Art in Text Filtering. User Modeling and User-Adapted Interaction, **7**(3), 141-178.

Palthepu, S., Greer, J.E. and McCalla, G.I. Cliche Recognition in Legacy Software: A Scalable Knowledge-Based Approach. Proc. 4th Working Conference on Reverse Engineering (WCRE'97), 1997, 94-103.

Pennock, D.M., Horvitz, E., and Giles, C. L. (2000). Social Choice Theory and Recommender Systems: Analysis of the Axiomatic Foundations of Collaborative Filtering. Proc. AAAI-00, 729-734.

Resnick, P., and Varian, H.R. (1997). Recommender Systems. Communications of the ACM, **40**(3), 57-58.

Shardanand, U., and Maes, P. (1995). Social Information Filtering: Algorithms for Automating „Word of Mouth". Proc. CHI '95, 210-217.

Steinberg, S.G. (1996). Seek and Ye Shall Find (Maybe). Wired, **4**(5), 108-114.

Woods, W.A. (2000). Conceptual Indexing: Practical Large-Scale AI for Efficient Information Access. Proc. AAAI-00, 1180-1185.

Agents with Genders for Inventory Planning in E-Management

Hanh H. Pham[1] and Van-Hop Nguyen[2]

[1] Department of Computer Science, State University of New York at New Paltz
75 S. Manheim Blvd. Suite 6, New Paltz, NY 12561, USA.
pham@mcs.newpaltz.edu

[2] Industrial Systems Engineering Program, School of Advanced Technologies
Asian Institute of Technology
P.O. Box 4, Klong Luang, Pathumthani 12120, Thailand
vanhop@s-t.au.ac.th

Abstract. This paper studies an integration of agents and genetic algorithms for inventory management. It involves multistage planning for distributed business components. In order to avoid local optimums in a large and multi-level search space we propose an agent-based management model where agents cooperate with each other to implement a genetic *gender-based* algorithm. We introduce *agent gender* concept and use it to abstract search levels. Agent gender represents characteristics of an agent at a time. Based on agent gender maps we can skip obvious non-optimal generations and therefore reduce planning complexity and time. This hybrid model also makes distributed units more adaptive to changes and local requirements and is suitable for E-management.

1 Introduction

Agent-based systems are efficient models for distributed management. They can use distributed data, support interaction and autonomously adjust to local requirements and changes. On the other hand, genetic algorithms are known as tools to achieve global optimization avoiding local optimums. However, agent-based models require coordination of actions, which could be fairly complicated when the systems are large, and genetic algorithms require long computation time.

In order to cope with these obstacles while combining agents and genetic algorithms, we propose a hybrid agent-genetic architecture with a special concept called agent gender. This approach is described through a particular solution for a case study in inventory management within an E-business environment. The proposed architecture, which takes advantages of the two mentioned AI techniques and the agent gender concept, breaks down the given management problem into local tasks while satisfying global requirements thanks to agent teamwork cooperation. This method also increases the autonomous control of business units and makes the management become more adaptive to dynamic changes of the business units and of the market.

E. Stroulia and S. Matwin (Eds.): AI 2001, LNAI 2056, pp. 267–276, 2001.
© Springer-Verlag Berlin Heidelberg 2001

In order to test the proposed approach we examine a specific problem in inventory management, the lot-sizing problem for multistage production [1,4,16]. Nowadays, business and manufacturing units of modern corporations are decentralized and multistage production is dominating [9]. Inventory planning in these systems is complicated not only because of the multilevel flow of inventory and products but also because the data are distributed at different locations and could be changed dynamically while units are interacting with each other. In order to manage inventory for a company which spreads over large territories, e-management is essential [3]. However, in e-management where orders are defined and transmitted electronically and automatically, it is difficult to manage business units so that it coordinates distributed data, satisfies local requirements and achieves global optimization. This paper proposes a way to deal with those obstacles by integrating agents, a gender concept, and genetic algorithms.

The rest of this paper is organized as follows. A case study, inventory planing and particularly lot-sizing problem in multistage production, is examined in section 2. Then, we describe the agent-based architecture as a solution for breaking down the complexity of the given problem in section 3. The combination of this model with another AI technique: genetic algorithm is proposed, and the agent gender concept, which helps to reduce search space, is introduced in section 4. Next, we discuss advantages and disadvantages of the proposed solution compared with the existing ones in section 5. Finally, conclusions and future work's direction are given in section 6.

2   Multistage Inventory Planning in E-Management

A multistage production could be described as the following. A company produces Y products and has X business units which includes: P procurement units; M manufacturing units; and S selling units, X=P+M+S. Procurement units are responsible for buying materials and distribute them to manufacturing units. Selling units are responsible for collecting final products and sell them. A manufacturing unit may use raw materials or middle products produced by other units. Outputs of a manufacturing unit could be inputs for the other units. Each unit can participate in producing several products. All units which involve in producing a product form a product line. We may have W product lines:$\{PL_1, PL_2, .., PL_W\}$. In a product line, the units and their connections are defined by its product schemata $SCHEM(PL_i)$, i=1..W. Hence, the production structure of a company is represented by:

❑   The set of business units:
- Procurement: $\{PU_1, PU_2, .. , PU_P\}$;   (1)
- Manufacturing: $\{MU1, MU2, .. , MU_M\}$;
- Selling: $\{SU_1, SU_2, .. , SU_S\}$.

❑   The product line configuration: $SCHEM(PL_1), SCHEM(PL_2), .. , SCHEM(PL_W)$.

Lot-sizing optimization is a key issue in inventory management. In general, this is to define lot sizes for inventory supplies and movements from one unit to the others so that it minimizes average-per-period transferring cost and holding cost. This problem may have various forms[2,9,18]. We will study the following lot-sizing problem:

A production structure is given as in (1). Assume that for each unit U_i, $i=1..X$, which participates in W_i product lines, we have a set of inputs $INP_{i,k}$ which we will call local materials, a set of outputs $OUT_{i,k}$ which we will call local products, and a set of production functions F_i^k, $k=1..W_i$, which defines the amount of products $PRO_{i,k}$ needed to be produced by the given unit. The unit U_i virtually has its own e-warehouse with V_i items including local materials and local products of all W_i product lines. The costs for holding items are defined by functions $G_{i,k}(v_{i,k})$, where $v_{i,k}$ is the subtotal items for product PL_k, $k=1..W_i$. The costs for transferring local products from U_i to the others are defined by $H_{i,k}(R_{i,k},U_j)$, where $R_{i,k}=OUT_{i,k}$, $k=1..W_i$, and U_j is the destination unit. Assume that the production process is carried out by a series of time moments: $\{1,2, ...,T\}$. Then, in order to satisfy the given production plan we have:

$$V_i(t) = V_i(t-1) + \sum_{k=1}^{W_i} INP_i^{\ k}(t) - \sum_{k=1}^{W_i} OUT_i^{\ k}(t) \qquad (2)$$

The lot-sizing problem in this case is to define a schedule of holding and transferring local materials and products for each of X units. For each time moment t, where $t=1..T$, a unit should receive a planed number $INP_{i,k}(t)$ of materials, and produce a planned number $PRO_{i,k}(t)$ of products, and output a planned number of its products $OUT_{i,k}(t)$ so that the total cost of storing $V_{i,k}(t)$ and transferring $R_{i,k}(t)$ was minimized.

In other words, the given problem can be stated as follows:

Given:
- X business units: $\{PU_1, PU_2, ..., PU_P\}$, $\{MU_1, MU_2, ..., MU_M\}$, $\{SU_1, SU_2, ..., SU_S\}$.
- Production rules described in (2) and production configuration for W product lines given in: $SCHEM(PL_1), SCHEM(PL_2), .., SCHEM(PL_W)$ **(3)**
- Estimated market demands, i.e. the amounts of products that can be sold at S selling units: $OS_1(t), OS_2(t),..., OS_S(t)$, where $t=1..T$. (3)

Requirements:
Define a schedule for holding and transferring products, i.e. define the non-negative elements of matrix $R[1..X][1..X][1..T]$ for transferring and the non-negative elements of matrix $V[1..X][1..T]$ for holding for each time moment t, $t=1..T$, so that:

(*1) $INP_{i,k} \geq 0$, and $OUT_{i,k} \geq 0$, $i=1..X$, $k=1..W_i$, when (1),(2), and (3) apply, *and*

(*2) $\displaystyle\sum_{l=1}^{W} \left(\sum_{1}^{T} \sum_{i=1}^{X} V[i][t] + \sum_{t=1}^{T} \sum_{j=1}^{X} \sum_{i=1}^{X} R[i][j][t] \right) \rightarrow MIN$ (4)

Notice that in order to satisfy (4) we need to calculate and verify (4) for each of W product lines. Hence, the matrix R has four-dimension (T*X*X*W) and solving this problem is extremely time-consuming. If elements in matrixes V range in a domain of Dv values and elements in R range within Dr values and assume that max(Dv,Dr)=Z, then, the time complexity of the given problem is $Z^{(T*X*X*W)}$ since indeed elements of matrix V could be defined knowing all elements of R. This is for the simplest case, without discounts and other trade factors.

3 Multi-agent Configuration

We propose to use agents in building the production management system in the given problem to reduce its complexity. In our agent-based model (Fig.1), each agent represents a business unit U_i, i=1..X, in one product line PL_k, k=1..W_i. Thus, if the given unit U_i participates in W_i product lines it would have W_i agents. Then, in total we would need N agents to support X units:

$$N = \sum_{i=1}^{X} W_i$$

Assume that the given production requirements are defined by (1),(2), and (3). All of data concerning inputs, output, warehouse, and production of the given unit are stored locally and are managed by local agents, one per product, instead of being stored and managed by a centralized center of the company.

The architecture of an agent with its data flow is zoomed-in in Fig.2. Within an agent A_i, i=1..N, at a time moment t, there is $C_i(t)$ amount of local materials comes in and there is $E_i(t)$ amount of local product goes out. Each agent has two main components: e-warehouse and e-manufacture (Fig.2). The e-warehouse stores $IA_i(t)$ amount of intermediate and $OA_i(t)$ amount of a product. The e-manufacture component needs $QA_i(t)$ amount of local materials to produce $PA_i(t)$ amount of local product items. Thus, the initial lot-sizing problem for the whole company is broken down into N identical and much less complicated sub-problems for single agent as follows.

Given production rules which are described in (1) and the configuration for W product lines: SCHEM(PL_1), SCHEM(PL_2), .., SCHEM(PL_W), we can define the configuration of the agent-based model for production management as in Fig.1. Then, knowing the market demands: $OS_1(t)$, $OS_2(t)$,…, $OS_S(t)$, where t=1..T, and the agent configuration (Fig.2) we can backtrack $PA_i(t)$ for each agent A_i, i=1..N, at each time moment t=1..T. From production functions F_x^k, k=1..W_x for each unit U_x, x=1..X, we can easily infer the production ratio FA_i for each agent A_i, i.e:

$$PA_i(t) = FA_i(QA_i(t)) \text{ or } QA_i(t) = FA^*_i(PA_i(t)).$$

Next, the conditions for satisfying these production requirements for agents can be described as:

$$\begin{cases} IA_i(t) = IA_i(t-1) - QA_i(t) + C_i(t) \geq 0 \\ \qquad \forall t = 1..T, i = 1..N \\ OA_i(t) = OA_i(t-1) + PA_i(t) - E_i(t) \geq 0 \\ \qquad \forall t = 1..T, i = 1..N \end{cases} \tag{5}$$

The requirement for agent lot-sizing is to define $E_i(t)$, i=1..N, t=1..T so that:

$$\sum_{t=1}^{T} \sum_{i=1}^{N} (VA_i(IA_i(t) + OA_i(t)) + RA_i(E_i(t))) \tag{6}$$

was minimum.

Notice that, from $E_i(t)$, $i=1..N$, $t=1..T$ and using agent configuration (Fig.2) we can define $C_i(t)$, $i=1..N$, $t=1..T$ since output of an agent forms input of other agent. Then, as $PA_i(t)$ and $QA_i(t)$ are also known, we can recursively define $IA_i(t)$ and $OA_i(t)$ using the equations in (5). Thus, we can check (5) and (6) recursively by time and in parallel by agents. The complexity of lot-sizing problem *for each agent* is now reduced to $Z^{(T*N)}$, compared with $Z^{(T*X*X*W)}$ in the standard model. We will estimate the overall complexity in section 5. In order to solve the lot-sizing problem for each agent, that is to find a proper set of $E_i(t)$, $i=1..N$, $t=1..T$, we build a genetic algorithm and will describe it in the next section.

This agent-based model (Fig.2) is proposed for the general case. In order to build a particular team of agents for a specific scenario with a specific priority, for instance adaptation or real-time constraints, we can use frameworks proposed in [7,15] for distributed adaptation to dynamic changes, in [17] to address real-time requirements, in [12] for scheduling, and in [14] for communication between agents. When the data is known in incomplete forms caused by dynamic and contiguous changes we can use interval techniques described in [10,13]. In order to test the performance of the agent-based management, which is proposed in this paper, we need to separate it from the other techniques. Therefore, we do not use any of the mentioned techniques in the simulation experiments which are described in section 5.

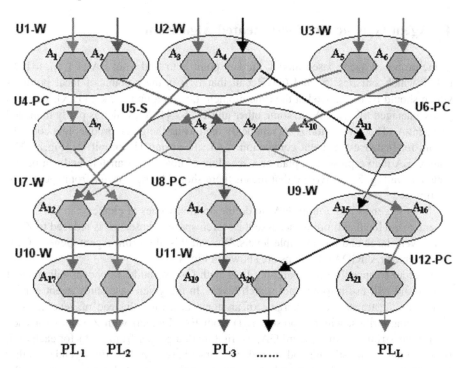

Fig. 1. Agent-Based Model for Inventory Management. W=Workstations; PC= Personal Computer; S=Server machine. U1-W means Unit 1 runs on a Workstation.

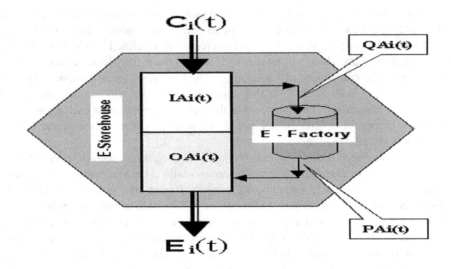

Fig. 2. Agent Configuration and its Data Flow.

4   Agent Genetic Gender-Oriented Algorithm

In the proposed agent-based model, the key point is to find a set EA of $E_i(t)$, i=1..N, t=1..T which satisfies (5) and (6). Recall that $E_i(t)$ is the amount of local products which should be transferred at the time moment t, from a unit U_k, k $\in$ [1..X], which is partly managed by agent A_i, to some other unit U_h, h $\in$ [1..X], which is partly managed by agent A_j. The connection A_i-A_j can be defined using the given product line configuration, for instance the agent connection A_6-A_{12} from unit U_5 to unit U_7 (Fig.1). The matrix EA then represents a plan or a schedule of inventory transfers and can be depicted as in Fig. 3.a. If $E_i(t)$=0 that means there should be no transfer from agent A_i at the time t.

We use genetic algorithm (GA) to define optimal values of elements in EA so that we can avoid local optimums, because the search space, whose size is reduced to $Z^{(T*N)}$, is still very large and has multiple levels. We call this algorithm Agent Genetic Gender-Oriented (AGGOA). Its steps are shown in Fig. 4.

In order to speed up the searching time with GA we build a concept called agent gender and will use it to abstract search levels. In the given case study agent gender represents the transfer characteristic of an agent at a time. Instead of generating or reproducing strings, which represent $E_i(t)$ from EA (Fig.3.a) with Z values for each digit in the strings, as in standard GA, we first mark a gender from {0,1} for each digit (Fig.3.b) and then estimate and reproduce strings based on their digit genders rather than on their values. Anytime when a replenishment is needed for an agent A_j the gender of the previous agent A_i should be "1", if gender of A_i is "0" that means there should not be any transfer at the given time t. Recall that A_i and A_j forms an agent connection in the agent chain of the given product line.

	1	2	...	T
A_1	$E_1(1)$	$E_1(2)$	...	$E_1(T)$
A_2	$E_2(1)$	$E_2(2)$	...	$E2(T)$
...	...	...	...	...
A_N	$E_N(1)$	$E_N(2)$	...	$E_N(T)$

(a) Full schedule represented by EA matrix

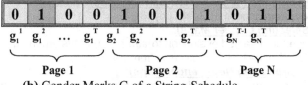

0	1	0	0	1	0	0	1	0	1	1

g_1^1 g_1^2 ... g_1^T g_2^1 g_2^2 ... g_2^T ... g_N^{T-1} g_N^T

Page 1   Page 2   Page N

(b) Gender Marks G of a String-Schedule

Fig. 3. Formation of Code Strings in AGGOA.

This modification of GA using the gender concept simplifies the string format and reduces the complexity of agent local task from $Z^{(T*N)}$ to $2^{(T*N)}$. Now we can work with the gender map of string EA, which is an abstract image of a string, rather than the string itself. Using this abstract notation we can skip obvious non-optimal generations and therefore reduce planning time. The gender map $G[N,T]=\{\{g_1^1, g_1^2, ..., g_1^T\}, \{g_2^1, g_2^2, ..., g_2^T\}, \{g_N^1, ..., g_N^{T-1}, g_N^T\}\} = \{0,1,0,0, ... 0,0,1,1\}$ has N*T binary digits while the full-schedule string $EA=\{E_1(1), E_1(2), .., E_1(T), .., E_N(1), .., E_N(T)\}$ would have $N*T*Log_2(Z)$ binary digits. The full schedule of inventory replenishments EA can be defined using its gender map G. Notice that the gender map $G[N,T]=\{g_1^1, g_1^2, ..., g_1^T, g_2^1, .. g_2^T, .., g_N^{T-1}, g_N^T\}$ tells us: (i) *when* (by t, t=1..T) and (ii) *where* (by i, i=1..N) the replenishments are made without specifying what is the amount of a replenishment for each agent. However, this hidden data can be calculated recursively as follows. Starting from time 0, assume that the first "1" in the gender map G is g_K^R. This "1" represents the first transfer of the corresponding agent A_K and it can be defined as the subtotal accumulated amount of local products that the given agent A_K has produced from time 0 to time R. Similarly, we can define the amounts of the first transfers for other agents by the positions of their first "1"s in each page (Fig.3b) of the gender map G. After each transfer, products are accumulated again and are passed to the next agent in the product chain. Therefore, we have:

$$OA_i(t) = OA_i(t-1) + PA_i(t) - E_i(t) = 0$$

Thus, for each next transfer of $G[N,T]=\{0,1,0,0, ... 0,0,1,1\}$, we can recursively find the corresponding transfer amount as the following:

$$E_i(t) = OA_i(t-1) + PA_i(t) \qquad (7)$$

Then, we can evaluate the total cost or the efficiency of this full schedule or the given gender map by (6). Thus, GA mutation and crossover operations are performed over the map of agent genders rather than over the string-values of the full schedule.

Step-1(Representing Agent Genders):
   we represent the full schedule $E_i(t)$, i=1..N, t=1..T, where $E_i(t)$ can have one among Z values, by a gender-map string G of $N*T$ digits $\in \{0,1\}$: "1" means to transfer all of available products to the next agent in the given product line; "0" means no transfer, i.e. $OA_i(t)=0$.
Step-2(Generating Gender Maps):
   generate a population of H strings $G_h[N*T]$, h=1..H, for each string $G_h[N*T]$:
      + WHILE ((5) for $G_h[N*T]$ is false) DO **generate** new $G_h[N*T]$
Step-3(Evaluating the generated Gender Maps):
      + **evaluate** fitness of $G_h[N,T]$ by (6);
Step-4(Selecting Gender Maps):
      + use the obtained evaluation to **select** K parents among given H strings $G_h[N*T]$, h=1..H by a given **schemata**.
Step-5(Reproducing New Gender Maps):
   use **crossover** and **mutation** operators of GA to **reproduce** a new population (generation) of H strings $G'_h[N*T]$, h=1..H. from K parents. Then, for each new-born string $G'_h[N*T]$ go back to Step-3 and then Step-4.
Step-6(Checking Age):
   based on a life counter LC go back to *Step-3* or **stop.**

Fig. 4. Genetic Gender-Oriented Algorithm with Agents.

5 Analysis and Estimation

The complexity of the given problem for each agent using the gender concept is $2^{(T*N)}$. The total complexity of this approach is the sum of agent's complexity and the overhead of sending data from one agent to the other in a product line. The overhead depends on the product line configurations, especially their lengths, and on the data transmission speeds via networks. In theory, with an assumption that the data transmission time is zero, it is $MaxL*2^{(T*N)}$ where MaxL is the maximal length of product lines and may range in [1,N]. However, this theoretical estimation on complexity may not show the real picture because the data transmission time is not zero.

In order to estimate the performance of the proposed agent-based genetic method AGGOA we simulate and compare it with a standard lot-sizing method (SM) which uses step-down allocation mechanism [9] and a standard genetic algorithm SGA without agents. We use two criteria : (i) computation time Tc to evaluate performance and (ii) response time Trp to evaluate quality of service. We measure the computation times of the methods when they achieve the same quality of solution, i.e. approximately the same cost of holding and transferring calculated by (6). The results are shown in Fig.5a, the time differences between AGGOA and SGA are recorded while Z, the size of the domain, is varying from 1 to 10 values. The simulation results (Fig.5a) show us that AGGOA can find a inventory schedule of the same quality as by SGA for a significantly less time. The more Z is the more this tendency shows.

In evaluating the quality of service we measure how quickly a new plan of inventory management is found when there is a change in production configuration or in market demands. The response time Trp is the period of time which is needed for each method to modify the existing inventory management plan since the change occurs. Response times of AGGOA and SM are recorded while the number of time moments T is varying from 1 to 12 slices. The simulation results (Fig.5b) show us that AGGOA can modify its plans for less time than SM can. This trend continues when the number of time slice is more than 12.

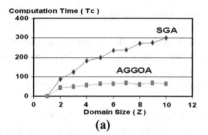 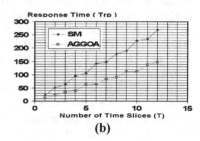

(a)   (b)

Fig. 5. Simulation Results.

The obtained results in Fig.5a can be explained by the fact that the standard genetic algorithm SGA heavily depends on Z since it represents a transfer plan by a full-schedule string $EA=\{E_1(1),E_1(2),..,E_1(T),.., E_N(1), ..,E_N(T)\}$ as usual, using values of the amounts to be transferred. Meanwhile, AGGOA's computation time does not change while Z increases. That is because AGGOA uses gender marks of agents to represent transfer plan and therefore does not depend on Z. We also obtain better results with AGGOA in term of response time (Fig.5b) because when there is a change, either in production configuration or in market demands, only agents which participate in the given product line modify their data, not all the agents in the system. On the other hand, the proposed method AGGOA will not be better than SGA or SM for the problems with unstructured search space where the gender concept can not be applied. This is because in unstructured search problems where the distribution is random heuristics do not work and a standard GA would be the best solution.

6 Conclusion

We have combined agents and a genetic algorithm in a solution for a planning problem in distributed and multistage production. The use of agents breaks the initial search problem with a complexity of four dimensions into identical smaller search tasks for each agent with two dimensions. A concept of *agent genders* is introduced and used to abstract search levels and therefore reduces the searching time for an optimal plan. That is why we can gain significant time cuts as shown in simulation results. This approach can also deal better with updating data or responding to dynamic changes in large-scale E-business environment. The proposed model can be applied for solving other management or search problems in other areas. In the future we will work on generalizing the gender concept for other problems.

Acknowledgment. This work is supported by the Research and Creative ProjectAward 00-01 of SUNY New Paltz.

References

1. Ben-Daya, M. and Rahim, A.,. Multi-stage Lot Sizing Models with Imperfect Processes and Inspection Errors. *Production Planning and Control*, 10, 2, (1999) 118-126.
2. Chyr, F., Huang, S.T. and Lai, S.D.,. A Dynamic Lot-sizing Model with Quantity Discount. *Production Planning & Control*, 10, 1, (1999) 67-75.
3. Elofson G. and Robinson W., Creating a Custom Mass-Production Channel on the Internet, ACM Communications, March (1998) 56-62.
4. Hariga, M.A.,. Comparision of Heuristic Procedures for the Inventory Replenishment Problem with a Linear Trend in Demand. *Computers and Industrial Engineering*, 28, 2, (1995) 245-258.
5. Janin K, and Singh M. Agents for Process Coherence in Virtual Enterprises, *ACM Communication*, Vol.42 N3, (1999) 62-80.
6. Ma Moses. Agents in E-commerce, ACM Communications , March (1999) 79-80.
7. Nguyen V. Hop, Pham H. Hanh, A Self-Guiding Derandomized Genetic Algorithm for Setup Problem in PCB Assembly, proceeding of the *International Conference on Artificial Intelligence* (IC-AI 2000), (2000) 493-499.
8. Nissen M and Mehra A., Some Intelligent Supply Chain Agents, *Proceeding of Autonomous Agents '99*, (1999) 374-375.
9. Pfeiffer, T., Transfer Pricing and Decentralized Dynamic Lot-sizing in Multistage, Multi-product Production Processes. *European Journal of Operational Research*, 116, (1999) 319-330.
10. Pham H. Hanh, " Processing Intervals For Search Control Under Incomplete Data, at *AAAI Spring Symposium on " Search Techniques for Problem Solving under Uncertainty and Incomplete Information "* at Stanford University - USA, March 1999.
11. Pham H. Hanh, Nguyen Hien, Nguyen V.Hop, Environment and Means for Cooperation and Interaction in E-commerce Agent-based Systems, proceeding of the *International Conference on Internet Computing* (IC'2000), Las Vegas, (2000) 253-259.
12. Pham H. Hanh, Simonenko V., Objective-Oriented Algorithm for Job Scheduling in Parallel Heterogeneous Systems, in *Lecture Notes in Computer Science* (LNCS), Springer-Verlag Pub., Vol. 1291, (1997) 193-214.
13. Pham H. Hanh, Thitipong Tanprasert, and Do Q. Minh, "Fuzzy Adaptive Controller for Ordering Concurrent Actions in Real –Time Systems", in the Proceeding of the 8th *IEEE International Conference FUZZ '99*, Seoul, South Korea, August - 1999.
14. Pham H. Hanh, Tran C. Son, Round-Table Architecture for Communication in Multi-Agent Softbot Systems, (to appear) in *Lecture Notes in Artificial Intelligent* (LNAI), Springer-Verlag Pub. (2000).
15. Pham H. Hanh, Worasing R. , and Thanadee U., "Distributed Multi-level Adaptation for Dynamic Multi-Agent Systems", in the Proceeding of *22nd IEEE Conference on Systems, Man, and Cybernetics* (SMC'99), (1999) 6.
16. Silver, E.A., Pyke, F.D. and Peterson, R.,. Inventory Management and Production Planning and Scheduling, *John Wiley & Sons* (1998).
17. Soto Ignacio, Garijo Mercedes, Iglesias Carlos A. and Ramos Manuel , An agent architecture to fulfill real-time requirements, *Autonomous Agents '2000*, Spain, (2000) 475 - 482.
18. Wagner, H. and Whitin, T.M.,. Dynamic Version of the Economic Lot Size Model. *Management Science*, 5, 1, (1958) 89-96.

Évaluation d'un Système pour le Résumé Automatique de Documents Électroniques

David Nadeau et Nicole Tourigny

Département d'informatique, Pavillon Adrien-Pouliot, Université Laval
Ste-Foy (Québec), Canada, G1K 7P4
{danad0, tourigny}@ift.ulaval.ca

Résumé. Cet article présente une évaluation de la fonction de résumé du système *Extractor*. Quatre attributs de qualité ont été considérés, soit la cohérence et la balance des résumés produits ainsi que la polyvalence et la performance du système. Notre démarche a pour but d'évaluer les deux premiers attributs, représentant des problèmes bien connus en résumé automatique, pour procéder à leur amélioration tout en minimisant la dégradation des deux autres attributs, purement quantitatifs. Notre évaluation diffère de ce qui a été fait en ce sens qu'elle se concentre sur le contexte propre à l'activité résumante d'*Extractor*. Notre travail tire profit de l'abondante documentation qui s'organise autour des approches pour le résumé automatique et des méthodes d'évaluation des systèmes.

1 Introduction

Le moteur de recherche Google [8] répertorie 1,346 millions de pages web, une forte proportion de celles-ci véhiculant de l'information en langage naturel. Devant cette masse d'information, le résumé automatique a été proposé comme solution viable à plusieurs reprises. En effet, on retrouve désormais plusieurs systèmes dédiés à cette tâche. Par exemple, Copernic.com a mis au point l'assistant de lecture *Copernic Summarizer* [5], basé sur le système *Extractor* de Peter D. Turney [26]; nStein [19] a mis au point *NewsEmailer* pour le résumé d'articles de journaux; Inxight [11] propose un environnement de développement nommé *Summarizer SDK*.

Dans cet article, nous présentons une évaluation du système *Extractor* dans son contexte d'utilisation comme outil de résumé automatique. Le but recherché est de déterminer les lacunes afin de procéder à des améliorations, ce qui est en cours de réalisation. La section qui suit introduit les approches du résumé automatique et les métriques utilisées dans notre évaluation. La section 3 présente l'évaluation du système *Extractor*. Enfin, les sections 4 et 5 présentent respectivement une discussion des résultats et la conclusion.

2 Fondements Théoriques

Afin d'être en mesure de caractériser le système *Extractor*, les sections 2.1, 2.2 et 2.3 présentent trois approches importantes en résumé automatique: l'approche en surface

E. Stroulia and S. Matwin (Eds.): AI 2001, LNAI 2056, pp. 277-286, 2001.

(*surface-level*), l'approche en profondeur (*entity-level*) et l'approche basée sur le discours (*discourse-level*). Les métriques que nous avons utilisées pour l'évaluation du système sont présentées par la suite.

2.1   L'approche en Surface

L'approche classique utilisée pour le résumé automatique consiste à traiter le texte source en surface [14]. Le traitement en surface est issu du calcul statistique et du repérage d'indices explicites. Il ne demande que peu de connaissances linguistiques et est donc peu dépendant du langage et peu coûteux (temps de calcul, espace mémoire). Le début des travaux remonte à 1958, avec la méthode de Luhn qui consiste à extraire les phrases contenant les unités textuelles revenant le plus fréquemment dans le texte source [13]. Puis, Baxendale ajoute que la position ordinale des phrases est un bon indice de la représentativité de celles-ci [4]. Edmundson met en évidence l'importance des mots contenus dans les titres [7] et introduit la méthode des indices, exploitant la présence de mots positifs (comparatifs, superlatifs, adverbes de conclusion) et de mots négatifs (expressions anaphoriques, expressions péjoratives). Cette méthode est reprise par plusieurs auteurs [10,18]. Plus tard, d'autres contributions s'ajoutent, comme les travaux sur les mots commençant par une majuscule [1,12] et les travaux sur les phrases indicatrices suivant des patrons prédéfinis [21]. Bon nombre de systèmes découlent de ces travaux, la plupart produisant des résumés par extraction de phrases (*extract*) par opposition aux systèmes faisant la génération de langage naturel (*abstract*).

2.2   L'approche en Profondeur

L'approche en profondeur présuppose un formalisme de représentation des connaissances qui permet de mettre en évidence la corrélation entre les mots ou la progression thématique. Certains systèmes procèdent à une analyse syntaxique pour étiqueter les mots du texte source (nom, adjectif, verbe) [6]. D'autres proposent une décomposition chronologique et sémantique du texte en segments. [23]. L'étude des liens entre les segments leur permet de caractériser la structure du texte. D'autres encore exploitent une base de connaissances associant chaque sujet au vocabulaire le plus fréquemment utilisé pour en traiter [10]. Une autre approche pour le traitement en profondeur consiste à transformer le texte en un graphe où chaque phrase est un sommet et où les liens conceptuels entre les phrases sont les arêtes [25]. Il existe alors un lien conceptuel entre deux phrases distinctes si elles font référence à un même concept ou à un concept sémantiquement voisin. Enfin, une approche consiste à appliquer le raisonnement par cas pour associer le texte à un thème archivé dans la base de cas et en réutiliser les connaissances pertinentes [22]. Un résumé peut alors être produit en présentant les points saillants du thème dont il est question.

2.3   L'approche Basée sur le Discours

L'approche basée sur le discours regroupe des techniques reconnues pour augmenter la cohérence et la cohésion d'un résumé produit par extraction de phrases [14]. Par exemple, certains systèmes capturent le discours de l'auteur dans une structure appelée chaîne lexicale [3]. Les chaînes lexicales sont des séquences de concepts séparés des relations de cohésion textuelle (synonymes, antonymes, expressions anaphoriques). D'autre systèmes portent sur la structure argumentative du texte source et ont pour base commune la théorie des structures rhétoriques de Mann et Thompson (*Rhetorical Structure Theory* – RST [16]). On y retrouve entre autres les travaux de Ono, Sumita et Miike [20] et de Marcu [15].

2.4   Les Métriques d'Évaluation

Les quatre attributs de qualité que nous utilisons sont les suivants :

La **cohérence** définit la structure d'un discours en terme de relations entre les segments de texte. Un résumé cohérent laisse une impression de complétude [15,16,17].

La **balance** exprime le rapport entre l'importance d'un sujet dans le texte source et l'importance accordée dans le résumé [17].

La **performance** mesure le nombre de mots qu'il est possible de traiter par unité de temps.

La **polyvalence** est ici le nombre de langues dans lesquelles le système peut résumer.

Les deux premiers attributs sont bien connus en résumé automatique mais aucune méthode ne permet de les mesurer précisément. Les deux autres sont strictement quantitatifs, donc facilement mesurables. Ils sont présentés ici pour discuter de l'impact négatif que pourrait avoir l'ajout de connaissances linguistiques au système *Extractor*.

3   Évaluation d'*Extractor*

Le système *Extractor* de Peter D. Turney [26] est basé sur l'approche en surface. Il permet d'extraire de 3 à 30 concepts d'un texte source. Turney les appelle *KeyPhrase* car il s'agit en fait de groupes de 1,2 ou 3 mots. Dans ce papier, nous utiliserons le terme « concept » pour référer aux *Keyphrases* sans toutefois référer à la notion de concepts définis dans une hiérarchie. Les techniques utilisées pour extraire et classer les concepts en ordre d'importance sont basées sur l'information de surface suivante :

1. **La fréquence d'apparition du concept** : plus un concept est utilisé fréquemment dans le texte, plus il est important.
2. **Le nombre de mots dans le concept** : plus un concept contient de mots (jusqu'à concurrence de 3), plus il est important.
3. **La position du concept dans le texte** : les concepts en début et en fin de texte sont plus importants que ceux dans le corps du texte.

Une dizaine d'indices sont associés à ces informations et servent à bonifier l'importance des concepts, par exemple : bonus pour les concepts en début de texte, bonus pour les concepts en fin de texte, bonus pour les concepts de 2 mots, bonus pour les concepts de 3 mots, etc. Ces indices varient selon la longueur du texte source et ont été ajustés par entraînement préalable dans *GenEx,* un algorithme génétique maximisant la correspondance entre les concepts générés par *Extractor* et ceux déterminés par un expert humain pour un même texte source. En sortie, un utilisateur peut obtenir la liste des concepts les plus saillants ou un résumé de longueur variable produit par extraction des phrases contenant ces concepts. Notre objectif est d'évaluer la qualité de ces résumés.

Il est important de souligner que le taux de contraction des résumés d'*Extractor* est variable. En effet, il est fonction du nombre de concepts extraits et de la densité de concepts à l'intérieur des phrases. Ainsi, si une phrase contient trois concepts, elle les représentera tous trois au sein du résumé. Comme le nombre de concepts extraits varie de 3 à 30, le nombre de phrases représentatives attendues varie quant à lui de 1 à 30.

La qualité des concepts produits par *Extractor* a été évaluée par son auteur. Sa démarche a été de comparer les concepts extraits et ceux qu'il considère comme attendus [26]. De plus, Barker et Cornacchia ont procédé à deux expériences consistant à comparer les concepts extraits à ceux choisis par des experts humains [2]. Ce type de comparaison mène à des résultats intéressants au niveau de la qualité des concepts, mais n'apporte aucune information quant à la qualité des résumés. Notre évaluation diffère de ce qui a été fait en ce sens qu'elle se concentre sur le contexte propre à l'activité résumante d'*Extractor,* présenté à la section suivante. Par la suite, nous décrivons notre corpus et les méthodes d'évaluation utilisées pour chaque attribut.

3.1   Le Contexte de l'Activité Résumante

La notion de contexte a été introduit par Karen Sparck Jones [24]. Nous l'utilisons ici pour déterminer le rôle du résumé pour l'utilisateur du système. Tout d'abord, *Extractor* est utilisé dans le logiciel *Copernic Summarizer,* un assistant de lecture de documents électroniques. Le but premier du logiciel est que les résumés soient compréhensibles sans la lecture du texte source. Il doit permettre de traiter des documents de formats divers et de niveaux de langage différents : groupe de discussion, article journalistique, publication scientifique. Il doit fournir au lecteur un condensé représentatif du sujet principal du document, mais doit aussi traiter l'ensemble des sujets pour, au besoin, permettre au lecteur de raffiner son résumé. Dans le contexte de l'Internet, le système doit supporter plusieurs langues et être très rapide pour effectivement accélérer la navigation.

Le choix des attributs de qualité a été fait de façon à évaluer précisément la qualité des résumés d'*Extractor* dans le contexte de *Copernic Summarizer.*

3.2   Le Corpus

Le corpus est composé de 100 articles de journaux tirés des quotidiens le Devoir [http://www.ledevoir.com] et le Soleil [http://www.lesoleil.com]. Les articles ont une longueur variant entre 450 et 2000 mots. Le fait de ne disposer que d'un seul type de document électronique biaise nos résultats mais l'ajout de documents en d'autres langues, formats et longueurs est en cours.

3.3   Évaluation de la Cohérence

Nous avons évalué la cohérence des résumés au niveau des liens entre les phrases. Une incohérence survient lorsqu'une phrase laisse une impression d'incomplétude. Par exemple, une unité textuelle commençant par l'expression « D'une part » doit être suivie d'un autre débutant par « D'autre part », à défaut de quoi le propos est incomplet. Pour mesurer la cohérence, nous avons tout d'abord posé l'hypothèse de Mann et Thompson, à savoir que deux segments de textes sont reliés de telle sorte que l'un joue un rôle spécifique par rapport à l'autre. Le segment le plus essentiel à la compréhension du propos de l'auteur est dénommé noyau et le segment qui sert d'appui (contraste, cause, concession, etc.) est dit le satellite [16]. Puis, nous avons reproduit l'expérience de Marcu [15], qu'il appelle *cue-phrase-based approach,* et n'avons considéré que les liens entre les phrases débutant par un marqueur de relation et celles qui les précèdent. Nous nous sommes limités à une soixantaine de marqueurs de relation. Par conséquent, les phrases n'ont pas toutes été exprimées en termes de noyau ou de satellite. La figure 1 donne un exemple de lien pour le marqueur « Car ». À la lecture, on peut reconnaître que la phrase (b) est la cause de l'action délibérée décrite en (a) et donc que l'essentiel du propos de l'auteur se trouve en (a).

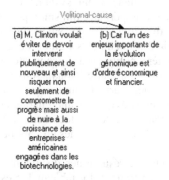

Fig. 1. Les phrases (a) et (b) sont liées par le marqueur de relation « Car ».

Nous avons analysé les résumés d'*Extractor* pour l'ensemble du corpus et identifié les noyaux et les satellites tels que mis en évidence par les marqueurs de relation. Les résumés ont été produits pour une extraction de dix (10) concepts. La figure 2 présente le nombre de satellites isolés et de satellites en présence de leur noyau. Selon les hypothèses posées ci-haut, un résumé cohérent et minimal ne devrait présenter que les noyaux des argumentations.

Les deux situations sont interprétées comme suit: (1) un satellite seul dénote une incohérence; (2) un satellite et son noyau préservent la cohérence mais ne constituent pas un extrait minimal. Un incohérence a donc été relevée dans 26% des résumés. Et un extrait cohérent mais non minimal a été relevé dans 21% des résumés. Nous n'émettons pas de jugement quant à la qualité du système *Extractor* mais soulignons que le traitement de la cohérence peut améliorer 36% des résumés, compte tenu que les situations (1) et (2) ont été remarquées en même temps dans 11% des cas.

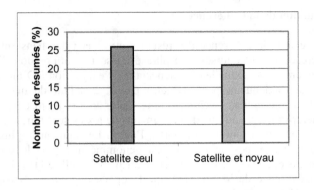

Fig. 2. Nombre des résumés présentant un satellite seul et un satellite et son noyau.

3.4   Évaluation de la Balance

Pour produire des résumés balancés, un système doit pouvoir diviser les sujets abordés dans le texte source. L'expérience qui suit a pour but de montrer qu'*Extractor* ne permet pas de faire de divisions entre les sujets. Nous avons combiné les articles du corpus de façon à avoir des documents traitant de 2, 3 et 4 sujets différents. Par exemple, un texte à caractère politique a été concaténé à un texte portant sur les technologies et à un texte d'art culinaire. Nous avons ainsi produit une vingtaine de nouveaux documents de tailles variant entre 300 et 5000 mots. Pour obtenir un document de taille désirée, nous avons résumé chaque article à l'aide d'*Extractor* et les avons mis bout à bout. Par exemple, un document de 1000 mots traitant de 4 sujets est en fait un groupement de 4 articles résumés en 250 mots.

Nous avons ensuite produit le résumé des documents et associé à chaque sujet le pourcentage de phrases qui en traitent. Le tableau 1 présente un exemple de résultat sur les documents de 1000 et de 5000 mots.

Pour les documents de taille variant entre 400 et 900 mots, nous avons remarqué un bon équilibre dans la proportion du résumé associée à chaque sujet. Cependant, à partir de 1000 mots, on remarque une dégradation de la balance. Par exemple, pour les documents à 4 sujets, le premier occupe toujours plus de 38% du résumé alors que le dernier n'occuper au mieux que 7%.

3.5   Évaluation de la Polyvalence

Extractor permet de produire des résumés pour des textes sources en cinq langues: anglais, français, allemand, japonais et espagnol. Les connaissances linguistiques sont divisées en modules pour chaque langage et permettent d'identifier: les mots vides de sens (*stop words*), les verbes, les abréviations, les pronoms et la racine des mots, pour fins d'analyse morphologique.

Tableau 1. Balance entre les sujets pour des documents de 1000 mots et de 5000 mots.

Nombre de sujets :	Document de 1000 mots			Document de 5000 mots		
	2	3	4	2	3	4
Sujet 1 (%)	71	59	38	82	81	55
Sujet 2 (%)	29	24	44	18	11	34
Sujet 3 (%)		17	12		8	4
Sujet 4 (%)			6			7

3.6   Évaluation de la Performance

Pour évaluer la performance, nous avons groupé les articles du corpus de façon à avoir des documents de taille variant entre 500 et 100 000 mots. Nous avons remarqué que le temps de traitement a une tendance linéaire. Cela vient du fait que le temps de lecture du texte augmente linéairement et que l'algorithme d'extraction se limite à 30 concepts quelle que soit la taille du texte source. Typiquement, *Extractor* permet de traiter 25000 mots à la seconde. Cette mesure n'est prise qu'à titre indicatif et servira de référence lors de l'amélioration du système.

4   Discussion

L'objectif de notre expérimentation était d'évaluer le système d'extraction de concepts *Extractor* dans le contexte de l'assistant de lecture *Copernic Summarizer* afin de déterminer ses points faibles et d'apporter des améliorations.

L'étude du système nous a permis de remarquer des lacunes au niveau de la qualité des résumés, en particulier au niveau de la cohérence entre les phrases extraites (figure 2) et de la balance entre les sujets abordés (tableau 1).

Au niveau de la cohérence, on remarque qu'un résumé de petite taille présente souvent des phrases secondaires au propos de l'auteur et laisse une impression d'incomplétude. Cette lacune peut être corrigée, du moins partiellement, en associant un poids plus fort aux phrases du noyau de l'argumentation. Pour ce faire, nous avons implémenté la méthode des indices de Marcu [15] (*cue-phrase-based approach*). Pour l'instant, nous avons recensé plus d'une soixantaine de marqueurs de relation fréquemment utilisés en début de phrase pour le français et une quarantaine pour l'anglais. Pour préserver la polyvalence, la méthode devra être étendue aux autres langues supportées par *Extractor*. Les travaux comme celui de Ono, Sumita et Miike [19] semblent confirmer que la méthode s'applique aussi bien aux langues romaines (français, anglais, espagnol, allemand) qu'au japonais. En ce qui concerne la performance, on peut remarquer que le traitement de la cohérence ralentit *Extractor* (figure 3), mais d'un point de vue empirique, le temps de traitement nous paraît a priori acceptable.

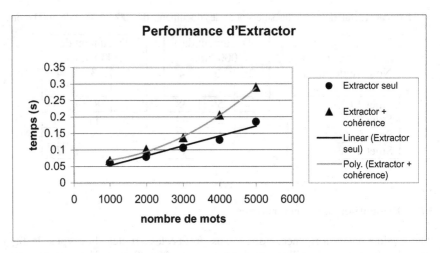

Fig. 3. Performance d'*Extractor* seul et performance du prototype de cohérence pour des textes de 1000 à 5000 mots.

En ce qui concerne la balance, nos observations indiquent que le système produit de bons résumés pour des textes de taille variant entre 400 et 900 mots. En deçà de cette taille, il est clair que le résumé est trop court pour aborder chaque thème. Pour les textes de plus de 900 mots, il est important d'ajuster la sélection des phrases pour assurer la balance. À cette fin, le texte pourrait être segmenté en unités thématiques et résumé par segment. L'algorithme de Hearst [9] semble approprié pour cette tâche et nous travaillerons dans cette direction afin de déterminer le sujet principal des textes ainsi que les sujets secondaires. Idéalement, ces connaissances devraient permettre à l'utilisateur de raffiner le résumé en choisissant un ou plusieurs concepts (*query based summarization*).

5   Conclusion

Le but de cet article était d'évaluer le système *Extractor* au niveau de son activité résumante. Après avoir présenté les fondements théoriques permettant de caractériser l'approche utilisée par un système de résumé automatique, nous avons décrit quatre attributs de qualité. Ceux-ci ont été utilisés pour évaluer *Extractor* et lui apporter des améliorations. La suite de nos travaux consistera donc à poursuivre ces améliorations et évaluer d'autres systèmes utilisés dans le même contexte.

Remerciements. Nous remercions le Conseil de Recherche en Science Naturelles et en Génie (CRSNG) pour le support financier (155387-00).

6   Bibliographie

1. C. Aone, J. Gorlinsky, B. Larsen et M.E. Okurowski, "A trainable summarizer with knowledge acquired from robust NLP techniques", *Advances in Automatic Text Summarization,* ed. I. Mani et M.T. Maybury, M.I.T. Press, 1999, pp. 71-80.
2. K. Barker, N. Cornacchia, "Using noun phrase heads to extract document keyphrases", *Advances in Artificial Intelligence,* Eds. H.J. Hamilton, New York, (Lecture notes in computer science : Lecture notes in artificial intelligence 1822), 2000.
3. R. Barzilay et M. Elhadad, "Using lexical chains for text summarization", *Advances in Automatic Text Summarization,* ed. I. Mani et M.T. Maybury, M.I.T. Press, 1999, pp. 111-121.
4. P.B. Baxendale, "Machine-made index for technical literature – an experiment", *IBM Journal,* octobre, 1958, pp.354-361.
5. Copernic.com, *Copernic Summarizer,* http://www.copernic.com, 2001.
6. L.L. Earl, "Experiments in automatic extracting and indexing", *Inf. Stor, Ret.,* 6 (6), 1970, pp.313-334.
7. H.P. Edmundson, "New methods in automatic extracting", *Journal of the association for computing machinary,* 16, 2, 1969, pp.264-285.
8. Google, http://www.google.com, 2001
9. M. A. Hearst et C. Plaunt, "Subtopic structuring for full-length document access", in proc. SIGIR, Pittsburg, 1993.
10. E. Hovy et C.-Y. Lin, "Automated text summarization in SUMMARIST", *Advances in Automatic Text Summarization,* ed. I. Mani et M.T. Maybury, M.I.T. Press, 1999, pp. 81-94
11. Inxight, *Summarizer SDK,* http://www.inxight.com, 2001.
12. J. Kupiec, J. Pedersen, F. Chen, {kupiec,pedersen,fchen}@parc.xerox.com, « A Trainable Document Summarizer », rapport de recherche, 1995, URL : http://www.inxight.com/News/Research_Papers.html.
13. 13.H.P. Luhn, "The automatic creation of litterature abstracts", *IBM Journal of Research and Development,* 2 (2), 1958, pp.159-165.
14. I. Mani et M.T. Maybury, *Advances in Automatic Text Summarization,* M.I.T Press, Massachusetts, 1999.
15. Daniel Marcu, "The Theory and Practice of Discourse Parsing and Summarization", The MIT Press, 2000, 248 p.
16. W.C. Mann et S.A Thompson, Rhetorical Structure Theory: toward a functional theory of text organization. *Text,* 8(3):243-281, 1988.
17. N. Masson, *Méthodes pour une génération variable de résumé automatique : vers un système de réduction de texte,* Thèse de doctorat en informatique, Université Paris XI, 1998.
18. S.H. Myaeng et D.H. Jang, "Development and evaluation of a statistically-based document summarization system", *Advances in Automatic Text Summarization,* ed. I. Mani et M.T. Maybury, M.I.T. Press, 1999, pp. 61-70.
19. nStein, *NewsEmailer,* http://www.nstein.com, 2001.
20. K. Ono, K. Sumita et S. Miike, "Abstract generation based on rhetorical structure extraction", *Proceedings of the 15th International Conference on Computational Linguistics (COLING-94),* Japon, 1994, volume 1, pp. 344-348.
21. C.D. Paice, "Constructing litterature abstracts by computer : techniques and prospects", *Information Processing and Management,* 26, 1990, pp.171-186.
22. E. Riloff, "A corpus-based approach to domain specific text summarization", *Summarizing Text for Intelligent Communication,* ed. B. Endres-Niggemeyer, J. Hobbs et K.S. Jones, 1995, pp. 69-84.

23. G. Salton, A. Singhal, C. Buckley et M. Mitra. "Automatic text decomposition using text segments and text themes", *Proceedings of the Seventh ACM Conference on Hypertext*, Washington D.C., 1996.

24. K. Sparck Jones, "Automatic summarizing: factors and directions", *Advances in Automatic Text Summarization,* ed. I. Mani et M.T. Maybury, M.I.T. Press, 1999, pp. 1-14.

25. E.F. Skorokhod'ko, "Adaptive method of automatic abstractiong and indexing", *Information Processing*, 71, North Holland, 1972.

26. P. D. Turney, "Learning algorithm for keyphrase extraction", *Information Retrieval*, 2 (4), 2000, pp.303-336.

On Obligations, Relativised Obligations, and Bilateral Commitments

Maria Fasli

Department of Computer Science, University of Essex
Wivenhoe Park, Colchester CO4 3SQ, UK
mfasli@essex.ac.uk

Abstract. This paper presents a formalisation of obligations for BDI agents. Although a lot of effort has been put into studying the properties of B(elief)D(esire)I(ntention) logics, little has been done to incorporate a deontic component into such logics. We identify two broad categories of obligations: general obligations which express normative statements that ought to be the case for all agents, and relativised obligations which have an explicit bearer and a counterparty. We present a formal analysis of general obligations and *relativised-to-one* obligations from a bearer to a single counterparty. We also discuss how *relativised-to-one* obligations arise as a result of bilateral commitments, and finally we examine obligations and *relativised-to-one* obligations in the context of different notions of realism for BDI agents.

1 Introduction

Agents are obviously highly complicated systems and formal theories that describe and predict their behaviour have attracted considerable attention within the Artificial Intelligence community. One of the most well known theoretical frameworks, the BDI paradigm, describes agents as having three propositional attitudes: beliefs, desires and intentions. Although a lot of effort has been devoted to the study of BDI logics, little work has been done in incorporating and studying obligations. However, since agents are required to act and interact in an increasingly complex environment, rules and norms may be adopted in order to facilitate the means for basic social interaction and as a way of regulating the agents' behaviour. Multi-agent environments in which agents are required to cooperate and negotiate need some means of regulating their behaviour in order to avoid disruption and to ensure smooth performance, fairness and stability. For instance consider an agent that desires to participate in an auction because it desires to acquire an item. If the agent is allowed to register and participate in the auction by the auction house, then this creates the obligation that in case the agent wins the item it has to pay the price of the winning bid to the auctioneer. Moreover we can extend the example and consider that the agent may decide to violate its obligation if it is offered the same good by another agent at a considerably lower price. This violation of its obligation may have consequences for the agent, perhaps the agent will be blacklisted by the particular auction house

E. Stroulia and S. Matwin (Eds.): AI 2001, LNAI 2056, pp. 287–296, 2001.

and it may not be allowed to participate in auctions any more. But if the agent weights its gains and decides that it is to its benefit to violate the obligation, it may do so. Although the agent's desires and intentions can be formalised in the BDI framework, a deontic component expressing obligations and their relations to beliefs, desires and intentions is missing.

In this paper we provide a formalisation of obligations in the BDI framework. We identify two broad categories of obligations: general and relativised obligations. The former express normative states that ought to be the case for all agents, whereas the latter express obligations which explicitly involve a bearer and one or more counterparty agents. Here we concentrate on relativised-to-one obligations where the counterparty is a single agent. Such obligations seem to result from bilateral commitments and the adoption of roles. We discuss a definition of bilateral commitments which involves among other things the adoption of a relativised-to-one obligation. The adoption of roles and their relation to relativised-to-one obligations although discussed, are not formally analysed. The paper is organised as follows. In the following section we present our extended logical framework which is based upon the classical BDI paradigm. Next we discuss the deontic concepts of obligation and relativised obligation and how they arise. Then we present a formal analysis of general obligations and relativised-to-one obligations, as well as how relativised-to-one obligations result from bilateral commitments. Finally, we discuss relativised-to-one obligations in the context of the three notions of realism for BDI agents. The paper ends with a summary of the main results, a discussion of related work, and a pointer to future work.

2   The Logical Framework

The BDI framework [7],[8] is a theoretical formalism in which an agent's information state is described in terms of beliefs, its motivational state in terms of desires (or goals), and its deliberation state in terms of intentions. Our logical framework is based on the BDI paradigm and it is a many-sorted first order modal logic which enables quantification over various sorts of individuals such as individual agents and groups of agents. The language includes apart from the usual connectives and quantifiers, three modal operators B, D, and I for expressing beliefs, desires and intentions respectively. There are three sorts: *Agents*, *Groups* of agents, and *Other* which indicates all the other objects/individuals in the universe of discourse. Although space does not allow to present all the technical details, in order to make this paper self-contained we provide a brief and compact account of the syntax of the language $\mathcal{L}$ in Table 1.

Semantics is given in terms of possible worlds. A model for the logical language $\mathcal{L}$ is a tuple $M = <W, U, \mathcal{B}, \mathcal{D}, \mathcal{I}, \pi>$ where W is a set of worlds, U is the universe of discourse which is a tuple itself $U = <U_{Agents}, U_{Groups}, U_{Other}>$, $\mathcal{B}$ is the belief accessibility relation, $\mathcal{B} : U_{Agents} \to \wp(W \times W)$, and $\mathcal{D}$ and $\mathcal{I}$ are similarly the desire and intention accessibility relations. Finally π interprets the atomic formulas of the language. Satisfaction of formulas is given in terms of a model M, a world w, and a mapping v of variables into elements of U:

$M_{v,w} \models P(\tau_1, ...\tau_k)$ iff $<v(\tau_1), ..., v(\tau_k)> \in \pi(P^k, w)$
$M_{v,w} \models \neg\phi$ iff $M_{v,w} \not\models \phi$

Table 1. The Syntax of $\mathcal{L}$

<agent-term>	::=	<agent-var> | <agent-const>
<group-term>	::=	<group-var> | <group-const> |
		{<agent-term>,..,<agent-term>}
<other-term>	::=	a variable or constant standing for any other
		individual in the universe of discourse
<term>	::=	<agent-term> | <group-term> | <other-term>
Pred	::=	<Pred-symbol> (<term>,...,<pred-symbol>)
var	::=	any element of the set V of all variables
<wff>	::=	<Pred-symbol>(<term>,...,<term>)
		B(<agent-term>,<wff>) | D(<agent-term>,<wff>)
		I(<agent-term>,<wff>) | (<term>=<term>)
		(<agent-term>∈<group-term>)|
		¬ <wff> | <wff> ∧ <wff> | ∀ <var><wff> | true

$M_{v,w} \models \phi \wedge \psi$ iff $M_{v,w} \models \phi$ and $M_{v,w} \models \psi$

$M_{v,w} \models \forall x\phi$ iff for all d in U, $M_{v[d/x],w} \models \phi$

$M_{v,w} \models B(i,\phi)$ iff $\forall\, w'$ such that $\mathcal{B}_i(w,w')$, $M_{v,w'} \models \phi$

$M_{v,w} \models (\tau_1 = \tau_2)$ iff $\parallel \tau_1 \parallel = \parallel \tau_2 \parallel$

$M_{v,w} \models (i \in g)$ iff $\parallel i \parallel \in \parallel g \parallel$

By imposing restrictions on the accessibility relations we can capture different axioms for the respective modalities [3]. Thus, $\mathcal{B}$ is taken to be serial, transitive and symmetric, $\mathcal{I}$ is serial, and no particular restrictions are imposed on $\mathcal{D}$. Thus for belief we adopt the K, D, S4, and S5 axioms and the Nec rule, for desires the K axiom and Nec rule, and for intentions the K and D axioms and the respective Nec rule. We illustrate with the axioms for belief:

K. $B(i,\phi) \wedge B(i,\phi \Rightarrow \psi) \Rightarrow B(i,\psi)$ (Distribution Axiom)

D. $B(i,\phi) \Rightarrow \neg B(i,\neg\phi)$ (Consistency axiom, seriality)

S4. $B(i,\phi) \Rightarrow B(i,B(i,\phi))$ (Positive Introspection axiom, transitivity)

S5. $\neg B(i,\phi) \Rightarrow B(i,\neg B(i,\phi))$ (Negative Introspection axiom, symmetry)

Nec. if $\vdash \phi$ then $\vdash B(i,\phi)$ (Necessitation Rule)

The K axiom and the Necessitation rule are inherent of the possible worlds approach and they hold regardless of any restrictions that we may impose on the accessibility relations. Thus the agents are logically omniscient [3] with respect to their beliefs, desires and intentions. Temporal and action components such as those of [7], [8] can be incorporated in a straightforward way; due to lack of space we chose not to do so in the current exposition.

2.1 Notions of Realism

It is reasonable to assume that an agent's beliefs affect its desires and intentions as well as the course of actions that it is going to take in order to achieve them. There are two ways of examining the relations between the three attitudes: (i) by imposing conditions between the sets of the belief, desire, and intention-accessible worlds and (ii) by imposing restrictions on the structural relationships

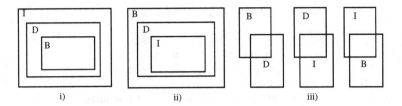

Fig. 1. i) Strong Realism, ii) Realism, iii)Weak Realism

Table 2. Axioms for the Notions of Realism

Strong Realism	Realism	Weak Realism
$I(i,\phi) \Rightarrow D(i,\phi)$	$B(i,\phi) \Rightarrow D(i,\phi)$	$I(i,\phi) \Rightarrow \neg D(i,\neg\phi)$
$D(i,\phi) \Rightarrow B(i,\phi)$	$D(i,\phi) \Rightarrow I(i,\phi)$	$I(i,\phi) \Rightarrow \neg B(i,\neg\phi)$
		$D(i,\phi) \Rightarrow \neg B(i,\neg\phi)$

between worlds if a temporal component is included. These constraints are called notions of realism and the interesting and meaningful ones can be characterised semantically and captured axiomatically. In [8] three such notions which suggest ways in which the propositional attitudes could be related to each other yielding different types of agents were suggested. Here we will present the axioms that ensue by considering conditions between the sets of accessible worlds. These set relations between the belief-, desire- and intention-accessible worlds are shown in Figure 1. Since set containment corresponds to logical implication, and intersection of sets corresponds to consistency Table 2 presents the axioms for each of the three notions of realism In the absence of a temporal component some of the axioms that are presented such as $I(i,\phi) \Rightarrow B(i,\phi)$ may appear unintuitive. Such formulas should be read as "if agent i intends ϕ, then it believes it to be possible (achievable) some time in the future".

2.2   Mutual Beliefs

Apart from adopting modal operators for expressing an individual agent's attitudes we will also consider modal operators describing group attitudes. We extend our language to include two more modal operators $EB(g,\phi)$ and $MB(g,\phi)$ which are read as "Everybody in a group of agents g believes ϕ" and "ϕ is a mutual belief among the agents in group g" respectively. Following [3]:

$EB(g,\phi) \equiv_{def} \forall i \in g \Rightarrow B(i,\phi)$

Intuitively everybody in a group of agents believes ϕ if and only if every agent i agent in this group believes ϕ. Then a proposition ϕ is mutually believed among a group of agents if everyone believes it, and everyone believes that everyone else believes it, and everyone believes that everyone believes..., and so on:

$MB(g,\phi) \equiv_{def} EB^k(i,\phi)$ for k=1,2,....

As Fagin et al. showed [3] this definition of mutual belief (they use common knowledge instead), semantically requires the notion of reachability which involves paths of arbitrary finite length. Given a set of accessibility relations, a world w' is reachable from w with respect to the given set, iff there is a sequence of worlds starting from w and ending in w' such that each pair of worlds in the sequence is in one of the given accessibility relations. A group g has mutual belief of ϕ in a world w if there is a world w' such that there is a path in the graph from w to w' whose edges are labelled by members of g. Thus:

$M_{v,w} \models EB^k(g, \phi)$ iff $M_{v,w'} \models (\phi)$ $\forall w'$ that are g-reachable from w in k steps.
$M_{v,w} \models MB(g, \phi)$ iff $M_{v,w'} \models (\phi)$ $\forall w'$ that are g-reachable from w.

Using the second condition the following axiom and rule can be added:

$MB(g, \phi) \Leftrightarrow EB(g, \phi \wedge MB(g, \phi))$

From $\phi \Rightarrow EB(g, \psi \wedge \phi)$ infer $\phi \Rightarrow MB(g, \psi)$ (Induction Rule)

3   Obligations

Deontology is in principle the study of norms and associated concepts such as obligations and permissions for human agents [4]. In the same sense it seems natural to use obligations to express what is ought to be the case for artificial agents. Obligations seem to be external to agents, usually obligations are being imposed by another agent or perhaps a larger body, such as a group of agents, an organisation or society. We can identify two broad categories of obligations: general obligations and relativised obligations. In [5] what we have termed relativised obligations are called special obligations, our use of the word "relativised" instead of "special" will become clearer later. General obligations express what is ought to be the case for all agents. These obligations are impersonal, that is no explicit reference is being made to a particular agent. They express normative sentences for all agents and can be seen as rules that provide the minimal means of social interaction and coordination among agents.

Apart from general impersonal obligations, individual agents may hold obligations towards another specific individual or a group of other agents. We distinguish between relativised-to-one obligations which are obligations of one agent towards another agent, and relativised-to-many obligations which are obligations of an agent towards a group of other agents. Relativised-to-one obligations can be the result of bilateral commitments. Thus if agent A commits to deliver a piece of work to agent B, this bilateral commitment implies among other things, the creation of a relativised-to-one obligation of A towards B. Although related, bilateral commitments and relativised obligations seem to be different in the following sense: if an agent commits to another agent to bring about a certain state, then this involves not only a relativised obligation on behalf of the bearer towards the counterparty, but an intention (a personal commitment) of the bearer to bring about that state of affairs. On the other hand a relativised obligation may not necessarily mean that the bearer is personally committed to bring about the state of affairs. Thus, if A is obliged to deliver a piece of work to B this does not necessarily mean that A has committed itself by adopting an individual intention to do so. If however, A makes a promise that he is going to deliver it, then A is declaring that he has made a personal commitment, an intention to do so. Another way that relativised-to-one obligations arise is via the adoption of roles. If A adopts the role of the supervisor towards B, then this creates certain obligations for the two agents. B has the obligation to submit draft chapters of the thesis and A has the obligation to provide feedback on B's chapters. As an extension of relativised-to-one obligations we have relativised-to-many obligations of an agent, the bearer, towards a group of other agents, the counterparty. These obligations arise as a result of social commitments on behalf of the bearer, or as a result of the adoption of social roles. So if an agent A makes a social commitment to group g of agents that he will bring about x this creates an obligation on behalf of agent A towards the group g. If agent A adopts the role of a teacher towards a group of students g then this creates certain relativised-to-many obligations such as for instance an obligation to teach them adequately a particular subject, while at the same time it creates relativised-to-one obligations on behalf of the students towards the teacher.

The following subsections discuss a formalisation of general obligations, and relativised-to-one obligations and their relation to bilateral commitments. The issue of how such relativised-to-one obligations result from the adoption of roles is a subject of current research and will be treated separately. Relativised-to-many obligations will not be dealt with at this stage.

3.1   Formal Analysis

Deontic logic attempts to represent a set of norms or obligations that an agent conforms to. In standard propositional deontic logic (SDL), an obligation operator O prefixes propositions $\phi, \psi, \ldots$ to create formulas of the form $O(\phi)$. Such a formula is read "It is ought to be the case that ϕ". In a statement like $O(\phi)$ there is no explicit reference to the individual agent for whom ϕ ought to be the case. Since the standard obligation operator takes only one argument it cannot capture relativised to one obligations of an agent towards another agent. Intuitively another operator $O(i, j, \phi)$ relativised to two agents is needed in order to describe such obligations of an agent i towards another agent j. In order to be able to express general and relativised obligations in our framework we extend our language to include two modal operators $O(\phi)$ and $O(i, j, \phi)$. $O(\phi)$ is read as "It ought to be the case that ϕ", and $O(i, j, \phi)$ as " Agent i ought to bring about ϕ for agent j". The model for the language needs to be extended as well. Thus $M = <W, U, \mathcal{B}, \mathcal{D}, \mathcal{I}, \pi, \mathcal{O}, \mathcal{O}^* >$ where $\mathcal{O}$ is the accessibility relation for general obligations and $\mathcal{O}^* = \{\mathcal{O}_{ij} | \forall i, j \in U_{Agents} \wedge i \neq j\}$ is the accessibility relation for relativised obligations between pairs of agents. $\mathcal{O}$ is considered to yield the deontically ideal worlds relative to a world w [2]. Semantics is as follows:

$M_{v,w} \models O(\phi)$ iff for all w' such that $\mathcal{O}(w, w')$, $M_{v,w'} \models \phi$

$M_{v,w} \models O(i, j, \phi)$ iff for all w' such that $\mathcal{O}_{ij}(w, w')$, $M_{v,w'} \models \phi$

The axiomatisation for general obligations is provided below:

$O(\phi) \wedge O(\phi \Rightarrow \psi) \Rightarrow O(\psi)$

$O(\phi) \Rightarrow \neg O(\neg \phi)$

if $\vdash \phi$ then $\vdash O(\phi)$

The accessibility relation $\mathcal{O}$ for general obligations is required to be serial and this in turn yields property D. Intuitively D states that there may not be deontic conflicts, that is not both ϕ and $\neg\phi$ ought to be the case. Furthermore a permission operator is defined as the dual of the general obligation operator:

$P(\phi) \equiv_{def} \neg O(\neg\phi)$

Although general obligations express what is ought to be the case for all agents, it does not necessarily mean that what is ought to be the case is going to be the case as well. Thus the principle of veracity $O(\phi) \Rightarrow \phi$ is rejected. We do not impose any restrictions on the accessibility relation for relativised obligations $\mathcal{O}_{ij}$. In particular we do not impose seriality; in other words deontic conflicts are allowed for relativised obligations. Thus, for the relativised obligations operator we adopt the K axiom and the respective necessitation rule:

$O(i, j, \phi) \wedge O(i, j, \phi \Rightarrow \psi) \Rightarrow O(i, j, \psi)$

if $\vdash \phi$ then $\vdash O(i, j, \phi)$

One way in which relativised-to-one obligations seem to arise is as a result of bilateral commitments. The term commitment intuitively means "promise". Commitments are often the result of promises. The basic idea behind our theory is that bilateral commitments involve the creation of obligations as well as individual commitments on behalf of the bearer (intentions). We will explicate this idea via an example: Agent A agrees to rent a house from B and commits himself to paying a monthly rent. Since A has made a commitment to B, this seems to have created an obligation now towards B to pay the monthly rent. A's commitment expressed his intention to do so. Moreover, his obligation and intention have now become a mutual belief among A and B. In other words bilateral commitments create relativised obligations and personal intentions. To express our ideas formally we adopt an operator $BCom(i, j, \phi)$ defined as follows:

$BCom(i, j, \phi) \equiv_{def} O(i, j, \phi) \wedge I(i, \phi) \wedge MB(\{i, j\}, (O(i, j, \phi) \wedge I(i, \phi)))$

3.2   Further Properties

It seems reasonable to suggest that if something is a general obligation then each of the agents believes that this is the case ($g0$ denotes the set of all agents):

$\forall(i \in g0) \Rightarrow (O(\phi) \Rightarrow B(i, O(\phi)))$

In other words if ϕ ought to be the case then each agent i believes that it ought to be the case. This axiom requires the following semantic condition:

$\forall i \in U_{Agents}, \forall w, w', w'' \ \mathcal{O}(w, w') \wedge \mathcal{B}_i(w', w'') \Rightarrow \mathcal{O}(w, w'')$

Since general obligations ought to be believed by all agents we also derive:

$O(\phi) \Rightarrow MB(g0, O(\phi))$

This means that normative statements are mutually believed (ideally) by all agents. For instance driving to the left is a statement mutually believed by all agents in UK. Further axioms for relativised-to-one obligations will now be examined. It seems reasonable to suggest that if such an ought-to relation between an agent (counterparty) and another agent (bearer) is in place, both of them should be aware of it, or in other words, they should believe that this is the case:

$O(i, j, \phi) \Rightarrow B(i, O(i, j, \phi))$

$O(i, j, \phi) \Rightarrow B(j, O(i, j, \phi))$

Moreover we can accept the stronger axiom that such a relativised-to-one obligations is mutual belief between the bearer and the counterparty:

Table 3. Theorems of Obligations and Relativised Obligations in BDI Agents

Strong Realism	Realism	Weak Realism
$O(\phi) \Rightarrow \neg D(i, \neg O(\phi))$	$O(\phi) \Rightarrow D(i, O(\phi))$	$O(\phi) \Rightarrow \neg D(i, \neg O(\phi))$
$O(\phi) \Rightarrow \neg I(i, \neg O(\phi))$	$O(\phi) \Rightarrow I(i, O(\phi))$	$O(\phi) \Rightarrow \neg I(i, \neg O(\phi))$
$O(i,j,\phi) \Rightarrow \neg D(i, \neg O(i,j,\phi))$	$O(i,j,\phi) \Rightarrow D(i, O(i,j,\phi))$	$O(i,j,\phi) \Rightarrow \neg D(i, \neg O(i,j,\phi))$
$O(i,j,\phi) \Rightarrow \neg I(i, \neg O(i,j,\phi))$	$O(i,j,\phi) \Rightarrow I(i, O(i,j,\phi))$	$O(i,j,\phi) \Rightarrow \neg I(i, \neg O(i,j,\phi))$
$O(i,j,\phi) \Rightarrow \neg D(j, \neg O(i,j,\phi))$	$O(i,j,\phi) \Rightarrow D(j, O(i,j,\phi))$	$O(i,j,\phi) \Rightarrow \neg D(j, \neg O(i,j,\phi))$
$O(i,j,\phi) \Rightarrow \neg I(j, \neg O(i,j,\phi))$	$O(i,j,\phi) \Rightarrow I(j, O(i,j,\phi))$	$O(i,j,\phi) \Rightarrow \neg I(j, \neg O(i,j,\phi))$
$O(i,j,\phi) \Rightarrow B(j,\phi))$	$O(i,j,\phi) \Rightarrow I(j,\phi))$	$O(i,j,\phi) \Rightarrow \neg I(j, \neg\phi))$
$O(i,j,\phi) \Rightarrow \neg I(j, \neg\phi))$	$O(i,j,\phi) \Rightarrow \neg B(j, \neg\phi))$	$O(i,j,\phi) \Rightarrow \neg B(j, \neg\phi))$

$$O(i,j,\phi) \Rightarrow MB(\{i,j\}, O(i,j,\phi))$$

Another plausible principle connects a relativised-to-one obligation with the desires of the counterparty. Thus if an agent i ought to bring about the state of affairs ϕ for agent j, then at least j should desire that state of affairs:

$$O(i,j,\phi) \Rightarrow D(j,\phi)$$

This in turn requires the following semantic restriction to be put in place between the relativised-to-one and the desire accessibility relations:

$$\forall j \in U_{Agents}, \forall w, w', w'' \quad \mathcal{O}_{ij}(w,w') \wedge \mathcal{D}_j(w',w'') \Rightarrow \mathcal{O}_{ij}(w,w'')$$

Each notion of realism assumes different relations between the three basic sets of accessible worlds $\mathcal{B}$, $\mathcal{D}$, and $\mathcal{I}$. In strong realism we have $D(j,\phi) \Rightarrow B(j,\phi)$. This in combination with the axiom that connects relativised-to-one obligations and the counterparty's desire entails $O(i,j,\phi) \Rightarrow B(j,\phi)$. In realism desires are related to intentions with the axiom $D(j,\phi) \Rightarrow I(j,\phi)$. This in combination with the axiom relating a counterparty's desires to a relativised-to-one obligation gives us $O(i,j,\phi) \Rightarrow I(j,\phi)$. This may initially seem peculiar, but this formula can be understood as stating that if agent i is obliged to bring about ϕ for agent j, then j intends to bring about ϕ (perhaps by encouraging i to commit to bring about ϕ). In weak realism the consistency axioms between desires and beliefs and desires and intentions yield the following theorems:

$$O(i,j,\phi) \Rightarrow \neg B(j, \neg\phi)$$
$$O(i,j,\phi) \Rightarrow \neg I(j, \neg\phi)$$

Table 3 summarises the theorems regarding obligations and relativised-to-one obligations in the three notions of realism for BDI agents.

4   Concluding Remarks

The research presented in this paper has been motivated by the need to formalise obligations in the context of the classical BDI paradigm. The paper discussed general obligations and relativised obligations. In particular a formal analysis of general obligations and relativised-to-one obligations was presented. One way in which relativised-to-one obligations arise as a direct result of bilateral commitments undertaken by agents was discussed and formalised. Finally the particulars of the formal analysis of general obligations and relativised-to-one obligations with respect to the three notions of realism for BDI agents were also presented.

Obligations and their relevance to Multi-agents systems were discussed in [5]. Krogh distinguishes between general and special obligations. A special obligations operator $_iO$ expresses the fact that an agent i has an obligation, without reference to a counterparty agent. Another operator O_i is adopted which expresses what is ideal from the perspective of agent i. The basic idea is that the O_i operator captures that a state or action is beneficial for agent i and it can be viewed as being by an agent's goals states. Another praxiological operator $_iEA$ is adopted and is read as "i sees to it that A", where A indicates an action. Finally special obligations with a bearer and a counterparty agent is defined as $_iO_j(_iEA) \equiv_{def} {_iO(_iEA)} \wedge O_j(_iEA)$. Our approach is simpler than Krogh's since we only adopt two modal operators. Although no action component has been presented the incorporation of such a component is straightforward. Furthermore, in this paper we have accepted that obligations are external to the agent, they are either imposed by another agent or by a larger body. Even in the case of general obligations, the obligations stem from the environment in which the agent acts and interacts in. The omission of the $_iO$ operator under this assumption does not seem to reduce expressiveness. The O_i operator in our framework can be thought as replaced by the D operator which expresses in what states the agent would like to be in, i.e. the ideal states for the agent.

Another recent approach involving obligations and BDI agents is [6]. The authors offer an alternative to the BDI logic, in which the primitive modalities are beliefs, desires and obligations, whereas intention is not a primitive modality but an obligation of an agent towards itself. Thus beliefs and desires are individual modalities but obligations are defined as social modalities. An operator $OBL(x, y, \phi)$ similar to our $O(i, j, \phi)$, expresses that an agent x has an obligation towards agent y to bring about ϕ. The definition of an intention as an obligation of an agent towards itself seems unintuitive. Intentions express the individual agent's commitments to itself to bring about certain states of affairs. Obligations on the other hand express what ought to be the case and this sense they are weaker. Defining intentions as obligations of an agent towards itself we think unnecessarily deprives intentions of their strong character of personal commitment. Moreover BDO logic is only able to capture agents as the ones described by the strong realism constraints. An attempt to describe any other notion of realism for BDO agents fails because of the following axioms and the way in which intentions are defined as obligations:

$DES(x, \phi) \Rightarrow BEL(x, \phi)$

$OBL(x, y, \phi) \Rightarrow DES(x, \phi)$

$INT(x, \phi) \Rightarrow OBL(x, x, \phi)$

We will now revisit and sketch the reasoning in the auction example (Section 1):

$D(i,\text{participate-in-auction})$

$D(i,\text{acquire-item})$

$BCom(i, j,\text{pay}(j)) \Rightarrow O(i, j, \text{pay } (j)) \wedge I(i, pay(\text{j})) \wedge$
$$MB(i, j, O(i, j,\text{pay}(j)) \wedge I(i,\text{pay}(j)))$$

The first two formulas express that agent i desires to participate in an auction and acquire an item. The third formula expresses the bilateral commitment that is created after the agent has been registered in the auction. This bilateral commitment gives rise to a relativised-to-one obligation and a personal commitment (intention) on behalf of i. We can now imagine that the agent wins the auction and thus is required to pay the auctioneer (j). However, if i is offered the same good by another provider at a lower price it may decide to drop its intention to pay j and thus break its bilateral commitment and relativised-to-one obligation. In a BDI architecture we can assume that a decision procedure compares the loss from violating one's obligations with that of achieving one's desire at a lower cost. If i considers its reputation to be more important than a short-term gain from a lower price it may keep its commitment, otherwise it may decide to break it. That will depend on the agent's design and priorities. Conditions for punishment for breaking one's commitments are yet to be formalised.

There are a number of possible avenues for future development of the approach presented here. Firstly, incorporating a temporal and an action component such as the ones in [7] and [8] is straightforward. Secondly, work under way is dealing with the formalisation of roles and the bilateral adoption of roles by agents as well as the relativised-to-one obligations entailed by the adoption of such roles. Although some work on agents and roles has been done [1], this has not been associated with obligations but rather with the goals that the adoption of roles entails. A farther goal is to formalise relativised-to-many obligations and their relation to social commitments and the adoption of social roles. Yet another direction is to define conditions for decommitment, as well as punishment if an agent chooses to violate a commitment or an obligation.

References

1. L. Cavedon and L.Sonenberg (1998). On Social Commitments, Roles and Preferred Goals. In Proceedings. of the 3rd Int. Conference on Multi-Agent Systems, pp:80-87
2. B.F.Chellas (1980). *Modal Logic.* Cambridge University Press
3. Fagin *et.al.* (1995). *Reasoning about Knowledge.* Cambridge Mass.: The MIT Press
4. R.Hilpinen (ed.)(1971) *Deontic Logic: Introductory and Systematic Readings.* Reidel Publishing Company
5. C. Krogh(1995). Obligations in Multi-Agent Systems. In Proceedings of the 5th Scandinavian Conference on Artificial Intelligence
6. G.Ma and C.Shi (2000). Modelling Social Agents on BDO Logic. *Proceedings of the 4th Int. Conference on Multi-Agent Systems.* IEEE Computer Society. pp. 411-412
7. Rao A. and Georgeff M. (1991). Modeling Rational Agents within a BDI-Architecture. *Proceedings of the 2nd Int. Conf. on Principles of Knowledge Representation and Reasoning,* San Mateo, Calif.: Morgan Kaufmann Publishers
8. Rao A. and Georgeff M. (1998). Decision Procedures for BDI Logics. *Journal of Logic and Computation,* 8(3):293-343

Question Answering Using Unification-Based Grammar*

Vlado Kešelj

Department of Computer Science, University of Waterloo,
Waterloo, ON N2L 3G1, Canada,
vkeselj@cs.uwaterloo.ca,   http://www.cs.uwaterloo.ca/~vkeselj

Abstract. The problem of Question Answering (QA) as used in
TREC [13] can be formulated as follows:

> Given a collection of natural-language (NL) documents find an
> answer to given NL query that is a short substring of one of the
> documents, and it is found in a relevant context.

We present a novel approach to the problem based on unification-based
grammars for NL.

Keywords: question answering, stochastic unification-based grammars.

1   Introduction

The traditional approach to the problem of QA assumes existence of a knowledge
base, which is used to produce answers to NL questions. The problem, defined
in this way, is too difficult for the current state of the art in natural language
processing (NLP). Schwitter *et al.* [11] argue that even an easy comprehension
test performed on a simple story of three paragraphs, titled "How maple syrup
is made," is a too difficult task.

We use an easier version of QA, in which the system returns only a short
document substring that contains an answer. This problem formulation is used in
the TREC competition, where the QA track is introduced in 1999. Some authors
(Mollá *et al.* [8]) call this version of QA *Answer Extraction,* which is probably a
more precise name of the task.

There are four related NL-based retrieval tasks:

- classical information retrieval (IR)—the task of retrieving relevant documents from a collection,
- information extraction (IE)—the task of collecting specific content data,
- QA or answer extraction (AE)—the task of locating an answer, and
- classical QA—the task of providing an intelligible answer to a question using
  a knowledge base.

---

* This work is supported by NSERC and OGS.

E. Stroulia and S. Matwin (Eds.): AI 2001, LNAI 2056, pp. 297–306, 2001.

Let us give more details about the TREC-8 QA task, which is the testbed for our approach. TREC-8 included 198 questions. All questions can be successfully answered by relatively short strings—the longest minimal answer has length of 35 bytes. The participants can submit a run of 50-byte or a run of 250-byte strings. Five ranked strings are submitted for each question. A submission is ranked according to the *reciprocal answer rank* (RAR); i.e., 1 mark is given if a correct answer is found in the first string, otherwise 1/2 marks are given for a correct answer in the second string, 1/3 for third string, 1/4 for the fourth string, or 1/5 for a correct answer in the fifth string. Only the highest ranked answer is taken into consideration. Zero mark is given for not having an answer. The final evaluation score for one run is the *mean reciprocal answer rank* (MRAR); i.e., the average of the per-question scores.

Here are three examples from TREC-8.[1] The first example is the first TREC-8 question, the second example is the question with the longest minimal answer, and the third example is an example for which our "classical" IR system could not find an answer:

1. Who is the author of the book, "The Iron Lady: A Biography of Margaret Thatcher?" (*Young*)
2. Why did David Koresh ask the FBI for a word processor?
   (*To record his revelations*)
3. When was London's Docklands Light Railway constructed? (*1987*)

A typical approach to QA consists of two phases: First, some relevant passages are extracted using a standard IR technique. Second, the fine-grained answer extraction is done using a shallow NLP technique. This NLP technique incorporates a shallow semantic representation of the text and the query. We describe a novel approach to QA based on a unification-based grammar.

2   Related Work

QA has received a lot of attention recently. The commercial site AskJeeves [1] offers a service where users can ask NL questions. If an answer is not found, the system offers similar questions for which it knows the answer. We have tried an example session with the question: "When did Beethoven die?" The question is interesting since it appeared in TREC-8, and it is a general question. The system could not find an answer, but it suggested a list of about dozen questions for which it knew some answers. Some of them were:

- Where can I find albums with the music of Beethoven?
- Where can I buy a biography of Beethoven on video or DVD?
  . . .
- How can I make my end of life wishes known?
- How will I die?

---

[1] After this paper was submitted, the TREC-9 data and results became available. It will be used in our future evaluations.

AskJeeves represents a case-based approach where case problems are question instances and solutions are associated answers. A similar case-based approach is used in FAQ Finder (Burke *et al.* [2]). FAQ Finder uses shallow NLP with a simple lexical semantic method based on WordNet. Given a question, FAQ Finder uses the classical SMART system to retrieve FAQ files relevant to the question, and then using a combination of statistical IR and semantic matching, the relevant question-answer pairs are extracted.

Shallow lexical semantics is also used in the method of *predictive annotation* (Radev *et al.* [9]) used in TREC-8. In this approach, the questions and the collection documents are annotated with *QA-tokens*, like DATE$ and PLACE$. For example, in question "Where did *smth* happen?" the words 'Where' is crucial for answering the question; however, a classical IR system would remove it as a stop word. By replacing the word 'Where' with the QA-token PLACE$, the removal can be prevented, and the token gets even a high weight. Pattern matching is used to annotate queries. The documents are also annotated with QA-tokens. The two-phase approach is used, consisting of the first IR phase and the second answer-selection phase.

Deeper semantic processing is applied in the system ExtrAns (Mollá *et al.* [8]). ExtrAns is a QA system for Unix man pages, implemented in Prolog. Horn clauses are used for semantic representation of the query and the text. Finding an answer to a query is modeled as "proving" the query using the facts from the text. For example, the sentence

cp copies the contents of *filename1* onto *filename2*.

is translated into the following set of facts:

```
holds(e1)/s1. object(cp,o1,x1)/s1.
object(command,o2,x1)/s1.    evt(copy,e1,[x1,x2])/s1.
object(content,o3,x2)/s1.    object(filename1,o4,x3)/s1.
object(file,o5,x3)/s1.       of(x2,x3)/s1.
object(filename2,o6,x4)/s1. object(file,o7,x4)/s1.
onto(e1,x4)/s1.
```

The question "Which command copies files?" is translated into the query:

```
object(command,_,X)/S,
(evt(copy,E,[X,Y])/S; evt(duplicate,E,[X,Y])/S),
object(file,_Y)/S)
```

The answer is located by the standard Prolog resolution procedure.

This QA approach is brittle, so a multi-level fall-back strategy for graceful degradation is introduced. If the system cannot find an answer, then some contraints are made weaker and the procedure is repeated. If an answer is not found again, more constraints are weakened or removed, and so on. Finally, a keyword-based approach is applied at the last level of the strategy.

In section 4 we present a novel unification-based approach to QA, which is based on the work in unification based-grammars [12]: in particular, the HPSG grammars [10] and attribute-value logic [3].

3   Performance of a Classical IR System

As in most other approaches (e.g., [9] and [2]), we also use two phases in QA. Processing the whole document collection would be too expensive for NLP, so in the first phase we rely on the MultiText retrieval engine (Cormack *et al.* [4]). The MultiText engine retrives a ranked list of 25 relevant 2000-byte passages for each question. The middle part of each passage most likely contains an answer, so a simple solution to QA is extraction of the middle part of each passage.

In order to later evaluate our system, we first measure the performace of this simple extraction method. The evaluation results are presented in figure 1. The x-axis represents answer lengths in bytes, and y-axis represents the score

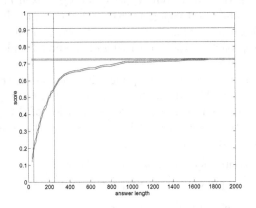

Fig. 1. Simple extraction method

(MRAR). The answer length varies from 35 bytes, which was the shortest minimal answer on TREC-8, to 2000 bytes. Two answer lengths accepted at TREC-8 are emphasized: 50 bytes and 250 bytes.

If we merge all 25 passages for each question, and return this large 50000-byte passage as an answer, the score of the run would be 0.91. This is represented by the first horizontal line on the figure. This is an upper bound on the performance of the NLP part, since the passages returned by the search engine do not contain answers to 18 questions ($\frac{1 \times 180 + 0 \times 18}{198} \approx 0.91$).

The next lower horizontal line ($y = 0.83$) is obtained by merging first 5 passages for each question (10000 bytes) and treating this as an answer. The significant difference between this line and the previous line shows that a significant number of answers is not located in the first 5 passages, so all 25 passages are important for our task.

The next two lower horizontal lines (0.73 and 0.72) are the scores obtained by submitting all and the first five 2000-byte passages as answer strings, respectively. The difference between the numbers is not big since even when the first correct answer is below the 5th submitted passage, its reciprocal rank adds less then $0.2 = 1/5$ marks. A significant difference between the 50 000-byte line (0.91) and these lines implies that the performance can be significantly improved just by a better ranking of the passages.

Below these horizontal lines, there are two monotonically increasing curves, which represent the scores of the strings submitted by the simple extraction method. The lower curve is for the first 5 strings and the higher curve is for all 25 strings. The score for the first five strings is 0.187 for 50-byte run, and 0.549 for the 250-byte run. If we compare this to the results reported on TREC-8, we can see that the 50-byte result is between 13th and 14th among 17 50-byte runs with scores from 0.071 to 0.660; and the 250-byte result is between 1st and 2nd among 24 of the 250-byte runs with scores from 0.060 to 0.646.

The conclusion of this analysis is: The NLP part could improve the results obtained from the search engine by:

1. re-ranking the passages (0.18 gain), and
2. locating more precisely the candidate string ($0.543 = 0.73 - 0.187$ gain for 50-byte run, and $0.181 = 0.73 - 0.549$ gain for the 250-byte run).

4   QA Using Unification-Based Grammars

A description of unification-based grammars for NL can be found in Shieber [12]. We rely on a more specific kind of unification-based grammar called *Head-driven Phrase Structure Grammar* (HPSG) (Sag and Wasow [10]). The HPSG grammar formalism is described in Carpenter [3]. We use the formalism as defined in Kešelj [6], which also describes the Java parser Stefy [5] for HPSGs used in our experiments.

Let us give a short and informal introduction to unification-based grammars. The unification-based NL formalisms use a data structure called *attribute-value matrix* (AVM) or *typed feature structure*. An AVM can be regarded as the standard record data structure in programming languages. An example of a simple AVM is AVM (1):

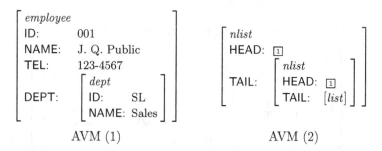

less then $0.2 = 1/5$

One specific and important feature of AVMs is *re-entrancy,* or *structure sharing.* For example, in AVM (2) the symbol ① denotes the elements that are the same, i.e., shared. Furthermore, we allow AVMs to be cyclic in a sense illustrated by

AVM (3):

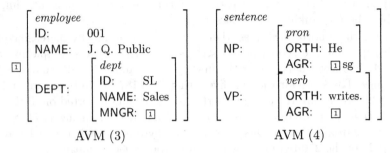

$$
\boxed{1}\begin{bmatrix} employee \\ \text{ID:} \quad 001 \\ \text{NAME:} \quad \text{J. Q. Public} \\ \text{DEPT:} \begin{bmatrix} dept \\ \text{ID:} \quad \text{SL} \\ \text{NAME: Sales} \\ \text{MNGR:} \boxed{1} \end{bmatrix} \end{bmatrix}
\qquad
\begin{bmatrix} sentence \\ \text{NP:} \begin{bmatrix} pron \\ \text{ORTH: He} \\ \text{AGR:} \boxed{1}\,sg \end{bmatrix} \\ \text{VP:} \begin{bmatrix} verb \\ \text{ORTH: writes.} \\ \text{AGR:} \boxed{1} \end{bmatrix} \end{bmatrix}
$$

AVM (3) 　　　　　AVM (4)

AVM (3) represents an employee, who is a member of the "Sales" department, who is additionally the manager of the department. AVM (4) illustrates how the AVMs are used to describe NL syntax. It shows how we can enforce number agreement in the sentence 'He writes.' using AVMs and structure sharing.

Beside syntax, AVMs are also used to represent semantics in HPSGs, which has the following advantages: First, it improves parsing disambiguation since we can use semantics to prune some alternatives. And second, we have a uniform representation of syntax and semantics, which makes the grammar easier to maintain.

Let us use the query "When did Beethoven die?," which appeared in TREC-8, to illustrate how we represent question semantics in a unification-based grammar. The grammar has three rules:

$$
\begin{bmatrix} Q \\ \text{SEM:} \begin{bmatrix} \text{SELECT:} \boxed{3} \\ \text{WHERE:} \boxed{2}\,[\text{DATE:}\boxed{3}] \end{bmatrix} \end{bmatrix} \rightarrow \text{When did } \boxed{1}\,[\,NP\,] \begin{bmatrix} V \\ \text{S:} \quad \boxed{1} \\ \text{SEM:} \boxed{2} \end{bmatrix}
$$

$$
\begin{bmatrix} V \\ \text{S:} \quad \boxed{1}\,[\,person\,] \\ \text{SEM:} \begin{bmatrix} \text{EVENT: die} \\ \text{SUBJ:} \quad \boxed{1} \end{bmatrix} \end{bmatrix} \rightarrow \text{die}
$$

$$
\begin{bmatrix} person \\ \text{NAME: Beethoven} \end{bmatrix} \rightarrow \text{Beethoven}
$$

The result of the query parsing is the following AVM:

$$
\begin{bmatrix} Q \\ \text{SEM:} \begin{bmatrix} \text{SELECT:} \boxed{1} \\ \text{WHERE:} \begin{bmatrix} \text{EVENT: die} \\ \text{SUBJ:} \begin{bmatrix} person \\ \text{NAME: Beethoven} \end{bmatrix} \\ \text{DATE:} \boxed{1} \end{bmatrix} \end{bmatrix} \end{bmatrix}
$$

The attributes names SELECT and WHERE are inspired by the SQL query language.

The relevant passage containing the answer contains the following excerpts:

If Beethoven felt... after finishing his monumental Ninth in early 1824... (he would die of jaundice and ascites on March 26, 1827), ...

A part of the semantic representation of the above text is the following AVM:

$$\begin{bmatrix} \text{EVENT:} & \text{die} \\ \text{SUBJ:} & \text{Beethoven} \\ \text{DATE:} & \text{March 26, 1827} \end{bmatrix}$$

which is easily matched to the query.

We will now describe how we use a unification-based grammar in QA. The parser Stefy [6] uses a chart parsing algorithm. Three charts are constructed in the process of parsing: a passive chart, an active chart, and a context chart. Figure 2 illustrates the use of those charts. We do not discuss basics of chart parsing

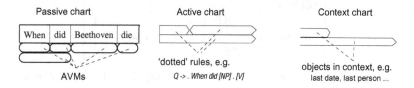

Fig. 2. Charts

here, but we will just briefly describe three charts used in our approach.[2] The passive chart is used to store finished edges. The active chart stores unfinished edges, which are analogous to the dotted rules in the Earley's parsing algorithm. The context chart stores objects in context in form of unfinished edges. The edges in the context chart are used for anaphoric resolution.

The result of parsing the question is an AVM that represents the question—its syntax and semantics. For each passage relevant to that question, we apply chart parsing on the whole passage. As a result, we obtain many edges within the passage representing semantics (and syntax) of various parts of passages (sub-sentence parts, sentences, and even some inter-sentence links). Finally, we locate the answer by finding the AVM in the passage chart that is best-matched to the question AVM. This is illustrated in figure 3.

Ideally, the matching procedure finds an AVM in the passage chart whose semantic part unifies with the 'WHERE' part of the question AVM so that the 'SELECT' variable from question AVM becomes instantiated; and the answer is found by tracing the 'SELECT' variable. However, this assumes perfect parsing of the query and the passage, which is not a realistic assumption. To solve the problem, we apply a unification matching procedure (similar to graded unification [7]). The procedure unifies AVMs at the same feature names, and calculates a matching score for features appearing in only one AVM.

---

[2] Chart parsing is a well-known subject. [6] describes the approach used in Stefy.

Query:

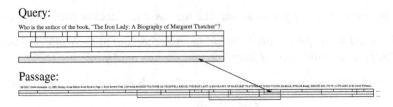

Passage:

Fig. 3. Matching AVMs

The approach is not perfected enough to be presented in a formal and complete form. We illustrate it on four examples from TREC-8, which were difficult for the classical IR method, but handled with our approach.

Example 1. The question "When was London's Docklands Light Railway constructed?" is represented as the following AVM:

$$
\begin{bmatrix}
\text{SELECT:} & \boxed{1} \\
\text{WHERE:} & \begin{bmatrix}
\text{EVENT:} & \text{construct} \\
\text{OBJ:} & \text{London's}\ldots\text{Railway} \\
\text{DATE:} & \boxed{1}
\end{bmatrix}
\end{bmatrix}
$$

A string containing the answer is "...the opening of the first 7 1/2 miles of the railway in 1987." and it is represented in this way:

$$
\begin{bmatrix}
\text{HEAD:} & \text{opening} \\
\text{OF:} & \text{the first...railway} \\
\text{DATE:} & 1987
\end{bmatrix}
$$

These two AVMs are matched using a lexical similarity measure between features ('HEAD' and 'EVENT', and 'OBJ' and 'OF'), atomic strings (keyword 'railway' and similarity between 'open' and 'construct'), and using the fact that 'SELECT' variable is instantiated. We see how simple syntactic analysis improves performance.

Example 2. The question "How much could you rent a Volkswagen bug for in 1966?" is represented by

$$
\begin{bmatrix}
\text{SELECT:} & \boxed{1} \\
\text{WHERE:} & \begin{bmatrix}
\text{EVENT:} & \text{rent} \\
\text{OBJ:} & \text{a Volkswagen bug} \\
\text{FOR:} & \boxed{1} \\
\text{DATE:} & 1966
\end{bmatrix}
\end{bmatrix}
$$

A relevant string is "...your could rent a Volkswagen bug for \$1 a day." which produces the following AVM:

$$
\begin{bmatrix}
\text{HEAD:} & \text{rent} \\
\text{OBJ:} & \text{a Volkswagen bug} \\
\text{FOR:} & \text{\$1 a day}
\end{bmatrix}
$$

which has a high matching score with the question AVM.

Example 3. The question "In what year did Ireland elect its first woman president?" is represented by:

$$
\begin{bmatrix}
\text{SELECT:} & \boxed{1} \\
\text{WHERE:} & \begin{bmatrix}
\text{EVENT:} & \text{elect} \\
\text{SUBJ:} & \text{Ireland} \\
\text{OBJ:} & \text{its first woman president} \\
\text{DATE:} & \begin{bmatrix} \boxed{1} \end{bmatrix}
\end{bmatrix}
\end{bmatrix}
$$

The following excerpts from a passage are relevant to answering the question:

> December 3, 1990, . . . Ireland The nation's first female president, Mary Robinson, was inaugurated today. . .

Using the context chart, we resolve the reference 'today', unify it with the date given at the beginning of the article ('December 3, 1990'), and obtain the following representation:

$$
\begin{bmatrix}
\text{EVENT:} & \text{inaugurate} \\
\text{OBJ:} & \text{The. . . first female president, Mary Robinson} \\
\text{DATE:} & \text{December 3, 1990}
\end{bmatrix}
$$

This example illustrates the importance of anaphoric resolution.

Example 4. The question "When did Beethoven die?" is represented as

$$
\begin{bmatrix}
\text{SELECT:} & \boxed{1} \\
\text{WHERE:} & \begin{bmatrix}
\text{EVENT:} & \text{die} \\
\text{SUBJ:} & \text{Beethoven} \\
\text{DATE:} & \boxed{1}
\end{bmatrix}
\end{bmatrix}
$$

The relevant parts of the passage are:

> If Beethoven felt. . . after finishing his monumental Ninth in early 1824. . . (he would die of jaundice and ascites on March 26, 1827), . . .

and the relevant AVM produced in the chart is:

$$
\begin{bmatrix}
\text{EVENT:} & \text{die} \\
\text{SUBJ:} & \text{Beethoven} \\
\text{DATE:} & \text{March 26, 1827}
\end{bmatrix}
$$

In this example, the resolution of the pronoun 'he' is important in solving the problem.

5 Conclusion and Future Work

In this paper, we present a novel approach to QA, based on a unification-based grammar. Although some unification-based approaches to QA are successfully implemented, we do not know of any previous use of unification-based NL grammars. We argue that the semantic representation obtained from such grammars is robust and easy to maintain.

The preliminary evaluation results show that the NL approach can significantly improve performance of a classical IR system. We have described our unification-based approach, and presented four preliminary examples. These simple examples use very shallow AVMs, which is a simplifying limitation, but not inherent to the approach. Currently, the matching procedure relies on manually encoded lexical similarity function between features, and between atomic strings. We expect that the use of WordNet will expand the coverage with a satisfiable performance.

The system is not evaluated on a larger scale, but its large-scale performance as a part of the MultiText QA system will be evaluated.

Acknowledgments. I wish to thank Dr. Nick Cercone for valuable discussions and comments regarding this work. I thank Dr. Charlie Clarke for providing me with the MultiText passages from TREC-8. I also thank anonymous reviewers for precise, useful, and encouraging comments.

References

1. Askjeeves. WWW, 2000. http://askjeeves.com/.
2. R. Burke, Hammond K., V. Kulyukin, S. Lytinen, Tomuro N., and S. Schoenberg. Question answering from frequently asked quest. files. *AI Mag.*, 18(2):57–66, 1997.
3. B. Carpenter. *The Logic of Typed Feature Structures*, volume 32 of *Cambridge Tracts in Theor. Comp. Sci.* Cambridge Univ. Press, 1992.
4. G. Cormack, C. Clarke, C. Palmer, and D. Kisman. Fast automatic passage ranking (MultiText experiments for TREC-8). In *Proc. of TREC-8*, 1999.
5. V. Kešelj. Stefy. WWW. http://www.cs.uwaterloo.ca/~vkeselj/stefy.html.
6. V. Kešelj. Stefy: Java parser for HPSGs, version 0.1. Technical Report CS-99-26, Dept. of Comp. Sci., Univ. of Waterloo, 2000.
7. A. Kim. Graded unification: A framework for interactive processing. In *Proc. ACL-32*, pages 313–315, 1994.
8. D. Mollá, J. Berri, and M. Hess. A real world implementation of answer extraction. In *Proc. of 9th Int. Conf. and Workshop on Database and Expert Sys. NLIS'98*.
9. D. Radev, J. Prager, and V. Samn. Ranking suspected answers to natural language questions using predictive annotation. In *Procóf the 6th Conf. on ANLP*, 2000.
10. I. Sag and T. Wasow. *Syntactic Theory: A Formal Introduction.* CSLI, 1999.
11. R. Schwitter, D. Mollá, R. Fournier, and M. Hess. Answer extraction: Towards better evaluations of NLP systems. In *Wshp. on Reading Comprehension Tests as Eval. for Comp.-Based Lang. Underst. Sys., ANLP-NAACL*, pages 20–27, 2000.
12. S. Shieber. *An Introduction to Unification-Based Approaches to Grammar.* Number 4 in CSLI Lecture Notes. CSLI, Stanford, CA, 1986.
13. E.M. Voorhees and D.M. Tice. The TREC-8 question answering track evaluation. In *Proc. of TREC-8*, 1999.

Solving the Traveling Salesman Problem Using the Enhanced Genetic Algorithm

Lixin Yang and Deborah A. Stacey

Department of Computing and Information Science,
University of Guelph, Guelph, Ontario, Canada N1G 2W1
{lyang, dastacey}@uoguelph.ca

Abstract. An extension to the Enhanced Genetic Algorithm (EGA) analysis of Gary W. Grewal, Thomas C. Wilson, and Deborah A. Stacey [1] is introduced and applied to the TSP. Previously the EGA had successfully handled constraint-Satisfaction problems, such as graph coloring. This paper broadens the application of the EGA to the specific NP-hard problem, the Traveling Salesman Problem (TSP). The first part of this paper deals with the unique features of the EGA such as running in an unsupervised mode, as applied to the TSP. In the second part, we present and analyze results obtained by testing the EGA approach on three TSP benchmarks while comparing the performance with other approaches using genetic algorithms. Our results show that the EGA approach is novel and successful, and its general features make it easy to integrate with other optimization techniques.

1 Introduction

This paper focuses on the enhancements that transform the traditional genetic algorithm into an effective mechanism for solving the Traveling Salesman Problem (TSP), especially the symmetric TSP, in which given a set of n nodes (cities) and distances for each pair (edge) of nodes, a roundtrip of minimal total length visiting each node exactly once will be found [2]. The distance from node i to node j is the same as from node j to node i. The path that the salesman takes is called a tour. There are two alternatives concerned by the researchers in optimization studies, especially with regard to the TSP: either to find near-Optimal or global-Optimal tours, or how quickly and efficiently to do so.

In most of the variant GA approaches, heuristic approaches have been the most important factors to be incorporated into the genetic algorithms used to solve the TSP. Often, heuristics about problems are incorporated into algorithms in the form of operators which iteratively perform local improvements to candidate solutions. Examples of such GA approaches focus on either employing highly specialized and problem-Specific operators such as famous crossover operators, including Order [3], PMX [4], Cycle [5], Edge Family [6], MPX [7], and Greedy crossover [8], or combining classical or recent local optimization improvement techniques such as 2-Opt, 3-Opt, hillclimbing, Lin-Kernighan, simulated annealing, etc. [7],[9],[10],[11],[12]. Although these GA approaches have presented satisfied results on many TSPs, they all have some overhead problems; there exists

E. Stroulia and S. Matwin (Eds.): AI 2001, LNAI 2056, pp. 307–316, 2001.
© Springer-Verlag Berlin Heidelberg 2001

an extremely time-Consuming process of fine-Tuning various parameters such as crossover and mutation rates and the running of the GA is expensive since the performance of these GA approaches largely relies on the employment of local improvement techniques. Also, there has been some research published on the effects of different selection strategies in this problem domain [15], [16]. Even so, some of this research inevitably falls into the category of requiring a fair amount of parameter fine-tuning. The EGA approach, however, concentrates on the GA theory itself and transforms the traditional GA to work in an unsupervised manner meanwhile maintaining high efficiency with low cost when applied to solving the TSP.

2   EGA Approach for the TSP

The basic goal of the EGA approach is to provide a general mechanism to quickly get close to a global optimum or reach the global optimum, which matches the major concern of current various researches on optimization problems including TSP. For the TSP problem, this paper shows that performance can be further improved when the EGA is used in conjunction with the recombination crossover operator on which most of the local improvement techniques have concentrated. The EGA employs three major enhancements with respect to the traditional GA: selection method, mutation method, and partial elitism policy. From Fig. 1, it can be seen that appropriate operator rates need not be determined a priori; crossover is always performed, while mutation is applied at appropriate times. These enhancements enable the EGA to run unsupervised. Details of the whole genetic search are introduced in the following sections.

2.1   Encoding

Permutation encoding is used, where each individual tour is simply the list of cities in the order the salesman has traveled. For example, assuming there are 5 cities (1, 2, 3, 4, 5), if a salesman goes from city 2, through city 1, city 3, city 5, city 4 and returns back to city 2, the individual tour in a population will be 2 1 3 5 4. Such an encoding method can be used in ordering problems, such as travelling salesman problem or the task ordering problem.

Each individual tour has a fitness value which is the sum of distances called Euclidean distances between every pair of cities in the tour. That is for the N cities TSP:

$$Fitness = \sum_{i=1}^{N} \sqrt{(x_i - x_{i-1})^2 + (y_i - y_{i-1})^2}$$

where x_i, y_i are the coordinates of city i and x_N, y_N equal x_0, y_0.

In TSP, the smaller the fitness value is, the better the tour. The global optimum tour is the tour with the smallest fitness value.

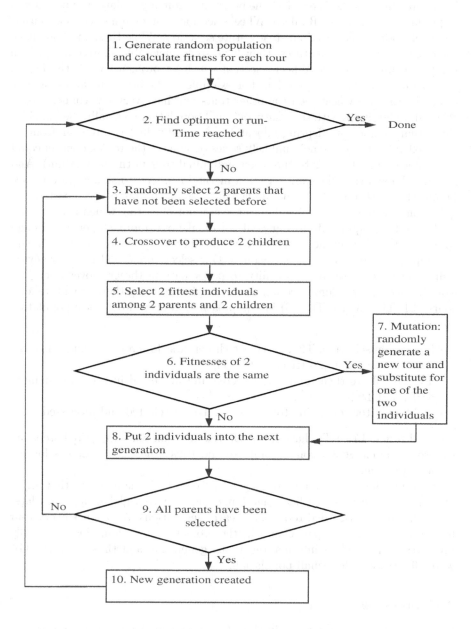

Fig. 1. Logical process of EGA approach

2.2   Selection Method

There are many methods to select the best tours from a population to be parents to produce offspring, e.g. Roulette Wheel selection, Boltzmann selection, tournament selection, rank selection, steady state selection. While these methods have their unique and good features, they have some inevitable shortcomings. The commonly used Roulette Wheel selection will have problems when the fitness differs greatly within a population. For example, if the best tour fitness is 90% of all the roulette wheel then the other tours will have very few chances to be selected. In addition, with the relatively small populations typically used in GAs, the actual number of offspring allocated to an individual is often far from its expected value (an extremely unlikely series of spins of the roulette wheel could even allocate all offspring to the worst individual tour in the population). And it is well known that the rank selection method can lead to slower convergence because the best individual tours do not differ so much from other ones and it is quite computational expensive due to the amount of sorting which is necessary.

In the EGA approach, as our goal is to make our approach general enough to extend to other applications, we consider that the selection method should be simple, low cost, but efficient enough. Our selection method is to give every individual tour an *equal* opportunity to participate in the crossover operation exactly once by a random selection. For example, assuming there are a total of 6 tours (T1, T2, T3, T4, T5, T6) in a population, in other words, the population size is 6:

  − by random selection, T2 and T6 are chosen first for crossover and finish the next steps after step 3 (refer to Fig. 1),
  − T1 and T3 are then randomly selected and processed in the same manner as T2 and T6 ,
  − and finally the remaining tours T4 and T5 are selected and processed.

Since all tours, T1 to T6, have been selected and finished all required steps, all the work for one generation is complete and thus a new generation is formed according to Fig. 1.

By using this selection method, a good potential schema in a tour that might unlikely be good at an earlier stage but could lead to a global optimum later on might not be discarded too soon in early generations. Also, since every tour has an opportunity to participate in the crossover operation, this maximally preserves various edges information in the generation and thus helps the GA work efficiently with a small population.

2.3   Crossover

Crossover is always performed in the EGA approach. Many effective crossover operators, which have been employed by GA researchers and other local optimization techniques for solving the TSP, can be plugged into the EGA approach. These crossover operators focus on producing validate child tours without missing any single city and without repetition of any single city, ensuring that city adjacencies are maximally preserved from the parents to the children, employing local improvement mechanism, or all of the above. The EGA approach does not restrict what kind of crossover operator should be used.

In this paper, we use the fifty-fifty greedy crossover of Victor *et al* [13] to demonstrate that performance is improved when solving three benchmark TSP problems with the EGA approach compared to the results produced by Victor *et al.* For further details about the comparison see Sect. 3. The following is an example to explain how the fifty-fifty greedy crossover works.

- assume there exist 2 tours 1 2 3 4 5 (parent 1) and 3 1 2 4 5 (parent 2)
- to generate a child, find a random city in parent1, let's say city 3 as the first current city of child 1: 3 ? ? ? ?
- then we find the adjacent edges of city 3 in parent1: (3, 2) and (3,4) and compare the distance of these two edges. If the distance of (3,4) is shorter, we select city 4 as the next city of child1: 3 4 ? ? ?
- then we find the adjacent edges of current city 4 in parent2: (4,2) and (4,5) and compare the distance of these two edges. If the distance of (4,2) is shorter, we select city 2 as the next city of child1: 3 4 2 ? ?
- then we find the adjacent edges of current city 2 in parent1: (2,1) and (2,3) and we select city 1 as the next city of child1: 3 4 2 1 ? since city 3 already appears in child1
- we find the adjacent edges of current city 1 in parent2: (1,3) and (1,2). Since both city 3 and city 2 already appear in child1, the closest city to city 1 from the number of remaining unattended cities is selected. In this example, only city 5 remains and so it is selected as the next city of child1: 3 4 2 1 5
- since all the cities are visited, child1 is formed. Other children can be created in the same way

2.4   Mutation Method

To prevent too many similar individuals from being in the same generation which leads to premature convergence and the danger of becoming stuck in a local optimum, the mutation operator is usually used. But the question is when, where and how it is used.

The EGA uses the mutation operator at appropriate times without determining a mutation rate in advance. As step 6 and step 7 in Fig. 1 illustrate, when *every* two offspring are ready to be put into the next generation, which is actually the time when mutation operator is used, the EGA checks whether these two individual tours have the same fitness value. If they do, a new randomly generated tour will replace one of them and is injected into the next generation with the other offspring. In this sense, a good tour never gets lost and meanwhile high diversity is always maintained in each generation. This is very important in the GA approach to the TSP and many other problems because high diversity is the basic criteria for the optimization search to find the global optimum. In addition, by introducing new edges (new pairs between two cities generated by randomization) into the population, it is possible for the EGA to solve the TSP using small populations.

Even though the mutation operator is traditionally considered untrustworthy and "dangerous", it has an important role in the EGA approach and is executed in an unsupervised manner at the appropriate time without losing any edge information from parents to offspring.

2.5 Partial Elitism Policy

Premature convergence is one of the major difficulties with the GA and in fact with most search algorithms. It is well known that this problem is also closely tied to the problem of losing diversity in the population and it makes it hard for the GA to find the global optimum. One source of this problem is that the occasional appearance of a "super-Individual" takes over the population in a few generations.

The partial elitism policy of the EGA is designed to avoid premature convergence while taking advantage of the appearance of super-Individuals. It is related to the whole selection procedure from step 3 to step 8 in Fig. 1. To emphasize the difference between the EGA's partial elitism and other elitist strategies used in genetic algorithms, we illustrate the select procedure from step 3 to step 8 again in a simpler form in Fig. 2(b).

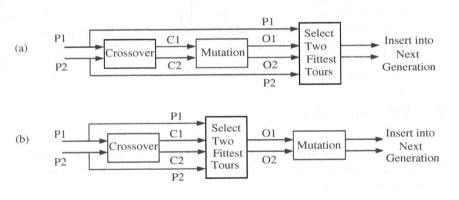

Fig. 2. (a) Elitism (b) Partial Elitism of EGA (C-Child, O-Offspring, P-Parent)

In Fig. 2(a), offspring are no longer guaranteed membership in the next generation, nor are parents forced to die after a single generation since mutation mostly produces worse tours so that O1 and O2 are less likely to survive than their parents P1 and P2. Therefore, it is easy to generate the premature convergence problem.

In Fig. 2(b), the EGA limits the scope of the elitist strategy to the crossover operator. The fitnesses of parents are compared with their children's fitnesses before mutation. Thus offspring O1 and O2 may include one of the parents and one of their children, or both parents, or both children because crossover usually produces better individuals. EGA mutation is then applied to the two fittest individuals O1 and O2 if they have the same fitness value. By postponing the application of EGA mutation, diversity is reintroduced into the next population, and the likelihood of premature convergence is reduced since the best individual is always maintained and propagated but never gets too much chance to dominate the population.

3   Experimental Results

The following experiments examine the effectiveness of the unsupervised EGA approach by applying it to three TSP benchmarks: Oliver (30 cities) [5], Eilon (50 cities) [14] and Eilon (75 cities) [14], and comparing the performance of the EGA approach to the performance produced by Victor *et al* who studied the same TSP problems but employed several fine-Tuning and pre-specified genetic operator rates (*mutation rate* = 0.3, *elite number* = 10) and the Roulette Wheel selection method. Their application was only tested using the population size of 20 (Details are contained in [13]).

All results are produced under the experimental environment illustrated in Table 1. The entire experiment consists of two parts. In part 1, a summary of experimental results for these three TSPs are contained in Table 2, in which the population size is 20 and 100 runs are executed for each problem. In part 2, the experiment presents one of the EGA's outstanding performances using an extremely small population to solve Eilon's 75-City TSP. The result of the experiment of part 2 is illustrated in Table 3.

Table 1. Experimental environment

Machine Model	Operating System	Programming language	Processor	Memory
IBM Aptiva E2U	Windows98	Java (JDK1.2)	AMD-K6-2/333	48MB

3.1   Part 1

In Table 2, the average generation when the optimum was found is calculated according to:

$$G = (\sum_{i=1}^{100} G_i)/100 \quad (G_i = Generation\ when\ optimum\ was\ found\ in\ each\ run)$$

Diversity is measured for each run when the optimum is found:

$$D_i = (Number\ of\ distinct\ individual\ tours)/(Population\ size) \times 100\%$$

so the resultant average diversity when the optimum was found in 100 runs is:

Table 2. Summary of results of all experiments

Three TSPs	Times Optimum Found	Average Generation When Optimum Found (G)	Average Diversity When Optimum Found (%) (D)	Average Running Time When Optimum Found (Seconds) (T)
30 cities	100	143	79	2
50 cities	100	2061	79	11
75 cities	100	1740	80	10

$$D = (\sum_{i=1}^{100}(D_i)/100$$

Average running time when the optimum was found is calculated according to:

$$T = (\sum_{i=1}^{100} T_i)/100 \quad (T_i = Running\ time\ of\ each\ run)$$

3.2   Part 2

The EGA approach was also tested on Eilon's 75-City TSP with an extremely small population size of 14. The EGA approach discovered the optimum in all 100 runs. Although the average generation when the optimum was found is greater, there is no significant performance difference from the result produced when the population size is 20 (refer to Table 3).

Table 3. Population size=20 versus population size=14 (Eilon's 75-City TSP)

Population Size	Times Optimum Found	Average Generation When Optimum Found (G)	Average Diversity When Optimum Found (%) (D)	Average Running Time When Optimum Found (Seconds) (T)
20	100	1740	80	10
14	100	2372	81	10

3.3   Advantages of the EGA Approach

As a result, the EGA approach outperforms in several ways:

1. High efficiency. As in solving these three TSPs, the EGA approach can always reach the optimum without showing obvious difficulty. In the experiment of Victor *et al*, there are still many local minima encountered. And only about 50% of the total runs can locate the optimum for Eilon's 50-City and Eilon's 75-City TSPs.

2. High diversity maintenance ability. From the experimental results, it can be seen that the population still maintains very high diversity even when the optimum has been reached. The mechanism of the EGA helps genetic search escape from local optima.
3. Good performance with extremely small populations.
4. No pre-specified parameters needed. The EGA approach runs in an unsupervised way.

4   Conclusion

We have introduced an enhanced genetic algorithm for solving the Traveling Salesman Problem. The enhanced combination mechanism of EGA selection method, mutation method and partial elitism allows the genetic search to maintain a very high diversity, and to run efficiently with a very small populations (14-20 individuals). The most important part of this EGA research is that not only does it improve the performance of the genetic algorithm on TSP problems, but it also enables it to run unsupervised without determining appropriate operator rates *a priori*. In this sense, the EGA approach is more worthwhile than other non-traditional GA approaches which focus on either fine-Tuning various types of parameters in order to get better results but have to undergo extremely expensive time-Consuming side-Effects, or borrowing some other computationally expensive local improvement mechanism to enhance the GA search.

Thus, unlike most non-traditional GA approaches, our approach is general and flexible and not limited to specific problem types. And its quick convergence but with high diversity features make the EGA suitable to act as the foundation to produce heuristic information for other optimization techniques. In future studies, more work will be done to apply the EGA approach to other problems in different domains and to categorize what kinds of problem are most suitable for solution by the EGA.

References

1. Gary W. Grewal, Thomas C. Wilson, Deborah A. Stacey: Solving Constraint Satisfaction Problems Using Enhanced Genetic Algorithms. Proc. of the Artificial Neural Networks in Engineering Conference (ANNIE'99), 1999.
2. http://ftp.zib.de/mp-testdata/tsp/tsplib/tsplib.html
3. Davis, Lawrence: Applying Adaptive Algorithms to Epistatic Domains. Proc. International Joint Conference on Artificial Intelligence, 1985.
4. Goldberg, D.E., Lingle, R.: Alleles, Loci, and the Traveling Salesman Problem. Proc. International Conference on Genetic Algorithms and their Applications, 1985.
5. I.M. Oliver, D.J. Smith, J.R.C. Holland: A Study of Permutation Crossover Operators On The Traveling Salesman Problem. Proc. of the Second Int. Conf. on Genetic Algorithms, 1987.
6. K. Mathias, D. Whitley: Genetic Operators, the Fitness Landscape and the Traveling Salesman Problem. In: Parallel Problem Solving from Nature-PPSN 2. R. Manner and B. Manderick, ed. Elsevier Science Publishers, 1992.

7. N. Ulder, E. Aarts, H. Bandelt, P. Laarhoven, E. Pesch: Genetic Local Search Algorithms for the Traveling Salesman Problem. In: Parallel Problem Solving In Nature. Springer/Verlag, 1990.

8. J.J. Grefenstette, R. Gopal, B.J. Rosmaita, D. Van Gucht: Genetic Algorithms for the Traveling Salesman Problem. Proc. Intern. Conf. of Genetic Algorithms and their applications, pp, 1985.

9. L. Eshelman: The CHC Adaptive Search Algorithms: How to Have Safe Search When Engaging in Nontraditional Genetic Recombination. In: Foundations of Genetic Algorithms. Morgan Kaufmann, 1991.

10. Jog P *et al*: The Effect of Population Size, Heuristic Crossover and Local Improvement on a Genetic Algorithm for the Traveling Salesman Problem. Proc. of the Third International Conf. on Genetic Algorithms, 1989.

11. B. Chandra, H. Karloff, C. Tovey: New Results on the Old K-Opt Algorithm for the TSP. In: Proceedings 5th ACM SIAM Symp. on Discrete Algorithms, Society for Industrial and Applied Mathematics, Philadelphia, 1994.

12. C. H. Papadimitriou: The Complexity of the Lin-Kernighan Heuristic for the Traveling Salesman Problem. SIAM J. Comput. 21, 1992.

13. Victor M. Kureichick, Victor V. Miagkikh, Alexander P. Topchy: Genetic Algorithm for Solution of the Traveling Salesman Problem with New Features against Premature Convergence.
http://www.ing.unlp.edu.ar/cetad/mos/TSPBIB_home.html

14. Whitley *et al*: Scheduling Problems and Traveling Salesman: The Genetic Edge Recombination Operator. Proc. of the Third Int. Conf. on Genetic Algorithms, 1989.

15. Thierens D., D.E. Goldberg: Elitist Recombination: An Integrated Selection Recombination GA. Proc. of IEEE World Congress on Computational Intelligence WCCI-94, Vol. 1, pp. 508-512, 1994.

16. Wiese, K., S.D. Goodwin: Keep-Best Reproduction: A Selection Strategy for Genetic Algorithms. Proceedings of the 1998 ACM Symposium on Applied Computing SAC'98, pp. 343-348,1998.

The Bottom-Up Freezing: An Approach to Neural Engineering

Ali Farzan[*] and Ali A. Ghorbani

Faculty of Computer Science
University of New Brunswick
Fredericton, NB, E3B 5A3
ghorbani@unb.ca

Abstract. This paper presents a new pruning method to determine a nearly optimum multi-layer neural network structure. The aim of the proposed method is to reduce the size of the network by freezing any node that does not actively participate in the training process. A node is not active if it has little or no effect to reduce the error of the network as the training proceeds. Experimental results demonstrate a moderate to nearly significant reduction in the network size and generalization performance. A notable improvement in the network's training time is also observed.

1 Introduction

The concept of neural engineering is defined as the process of designing an optimum neural network structure with respect to the problem. The process is also involves in the predetermination of some of the network's parameters with respect to the training data as well as the way to preprocess and present the training data to the network.

In recent years, many neural networks algorithms have been proposed by researchers to overcome the inefficiency of ANNs with predetermined architecture. They all address ANNs with dynamic structures where the learning algorithms not only search the weights space, but also modify the architecture of the network during the training. In other words, the proposed algorithms are mainly concerned with the issue of adapting the topology of a network as the training progresses and determine an optimum topology to obtain a desired generalization.

This paper presents a new pruning method. The proposed method, which we call Bottom-Up Freezing (BUF), alters and ultimately optimizes the network architecture as learning proceeds. The optimization process is carried out by freezing any node that has the smallest effect at further reducing the error of the network during the training process. The outline of the paper is as follows. In the next section the constructive neural networks learning algorithms are summarized. The BUF pruning algorithm for multi-layer neural networks is presented in Section 3. Subsequently, the experimental results are given. Finally, the conclusions of the present study are summarized.

---

[*] Presently at Azad university, Tabriz, Tehran, Iran

E. Stroulia and S. Matwin (Eds.): AI 2001, LNAI 2056, pp. 317–324, 2001.

2   Constructive Learning Algorithm

In multi-layer feedforward neural networks, the learning process is very sensitive to the size of the network. If the network is very large, the training of the network may only force the network to memorize the input patterns. While large size network may lead to over-generalization and poor performance, too small a network size cannot generalize and is unable to solve the problem. Usually, the structure of a network is decided in a trial-and-error manner. This approach which requires various ad hoc rules of thumb is very time consuming and is bound to failure.

Various researchers have investigated the alternative approaches to conventional trial-and-error scheme and have proposed constructive learning algorithms to automate the process of network design. Constructive algorithms are aimed at finding an *adequate* sized network for a given problem. They fall into two main categories. One involves the use of larger network architecture at the beginning and pruning it down to near optimum size. Learning algorithms using this general approach are called pruning. Examples include optimal brain damage[1], optimal brain surgeon[2], interactive pruning[3], and skeletonization[4]. See[5] and[6, chapter 13] for a good review of pruning algorithms. With the other approach, the training begins with a minimal network and ends with a satisfactory network size. The algorithms using this approach are referred to as growth or constructive methods. Examples include the cascade-correlation leaning architecture[7], upstart algorithm [8], and the tiling algorithm [9]. In multi-layer feedforward neural networks, a minimal network does not have any hidden layer.

3   Bottom-Up Freezing Algorithm

Pruning methods start with a large network that is over-parameterized and eliminate relatively unimportant nodes or connections. The pruning of selected nodes and/or connections is carried out during the training process until a (nearly) optimum network architecture is reached. The essential idea behind the weight removal technique such as optimal brain damage is to analytically determine the relative importance of weights in a multi-layer neural network using Taylor's series on the error function to second order in the weights. The optimal brain surgeon technique is the generalization of weight perturbation technique to sets of weights instead of individual weights (see [2] for details).

Another pruning approach involves the removal of (nearly) *irrelevant nodes*. The basic idea underlying the BUF algorithm is to evaluate the hidden nodes and isolate (freeze) those hidden nodes whose contribution to the convergence of the network falls below a certain threshold. When a node is frozen, it will not participate in the training process for a certain period of time or for a given number of training examples. When the freezing period of a node is over, it is returned to the network. The state of the node at the time of return will be the same as its state at the time of freezing.

Initially, a frozen node stays out of the training process temporarily, which we call *local freezing*. If a node freezes very often and the number of instances that a node was frozen exceeds a certain limit, the node is permanently removed from the network*pruning*. The pruning occurs when a node is found to be redundant and ineffective to the progress of learning a problem.

Artificial neural networks as learning models do not have to use the same structure from the beginning to the end of the training process. Using the same topology throughout the learning process imposes crucial limitations on the speed and convergence of the network. *The local freezing part of the BUF approach allows a network to change its underlying structure and adapt dynamically to the ever-changing problem space as the training proceeds.*

3.1   Local Freezing

Local freezing is the process of temporarily removing a node from the network. The process involves identifying those nodes that barely contribute to the reduction of the criterion function of the network, $\mathcal{E}$, measured over the entire training set. We use the error signal of a node, $e(t)$, measured over a single training pattern presented to a node at time t as the main criteria to evaluate the effectiveness of a node on the convergence of the network. The error signal of node i in layer l is defined as $e_i^l(t) = \sum_i (\Delta w_{ij})^2$, where w_{ij} represents the outgoing weight of node i. Since the calculation of Δw is embedded in the training algorithm for multi-layer neural networks, our choice of using the above criterion function in the freezing process will not impose any extra computation on the training process.

Let $\rho = \lambda \mathcal{S}$ represent an $\rho - approximation$, where $\mathcal{S}$ represent the size of the training set and λ is set by the user. A node is a candidate for local freezing if its error signal did not decrease in the last ρ consecutive presentations of the training examples. The freezing time of a node (i.e., the number of presentations that a node does not participate in the training process) is decided using the distribution of the errors of ρ consecutive increases in the error signals. Moreover, to be consistent with the behavior of gradient descent type algorithm, wherein the size of steps is getting smaller as the optimum point is approached, the magnitude of $\rho - approximation$ at any point should be decided based on the shape of the error surface as well as the position on the error surface relative to the optimum point. The error rate (i.e., the rate of increase of error signal) of node i in layer l at time t is defined as follows:

$$\gamma_i^l(t) = \left(\frac{e(t)}{e(t-1)} - 1 \right) * 100.$$

The distribution of the errors of κ consecutive increases in the error signal of node i in layer l is calculated by:

$$\mathcal{D}_i^l = \sum_{t=1}^{\rho} \frac{\gamma_i^l(t) - E\left[\gamma_i^l\right]}{\rho * E\left[\gamma_i^l\right]},$$

where $E[.]$ represents the mean. The magnitude of $\mathcal{D}_i^l$ shows the degree of poor behaviour of node i during the ρ consecutive presentations of the training examples. We use the magnitude of $\mathcal{D}$ as the freezing time, thus, a larger $\mathcal{D}$ means a longer freezing time. Freezing the insignificant nodes during the training process will speed up the convergence of BUF as compared to the standard backpropagation learning algorithm (see Section 4).

3.2   Relative Importance of a Node

The history of a hidden node (i.e., the number of times a node has been frozen, m) is used to approximate the *relative* importance of that node to the convergence of a network. The magnitude of m is a clear indication of the contribution of a node to reducing the error $\mathcal{E}$. The *relative* importance, $\mathcal{R}$, of a given node is defined as follows:

$$\mathcal{R}_i^l = \begin{cases} \frac{2+(m+1)}{2+m} & \text{if } node_i^l \text{ is freezing now} \\ 2+m & \text{otherwise} \end{cases}$$

The *relative* importance of a node is a decreasing function based on the magnitude of m. At the beginning of the training process it is set to the value 2. This initial setting will guarantee the decreasing nature of $\mathcal{R}$. The value 2 is calculated as follows:

$$\frac{m^{k+1}}{m^k} < m^k \implies \frac{m^k+1}{m^k} < m^k \implies m^k = 2.$$

where m^k represents the consecutive number of times a node was frozen at the time of presenting the kth training example. The *relative* importance of a set of nodes is represented by the vector $\underline{\mathcal{R}}$.

As the training proceeds, the number of frozen nodes as well as the number of times that a given node is frozen increases. Similarly, the variance of the values in $\underline{\mathcal{R}}$, $var\,[\underline{\mathcal{R}}]$, increases, whereas the mean of the values in $\underline{\mathcal{R}}$, $E\,[\underline{\mathcal{R}}]$, decreases. One of the key questions in the pruning algorithm is when is the proper time to remove a node from the network architecture. In BUF, the basic idea underlying the node removal is to analyze the freezing behaviour of a hidden node and remove the node if it freezes very frequently (i.e., when the freezing frequency becomes high). A node that freezes frequently is referred as node *trashing*.

3.3   Node Pruning

Let's assume that during the training of a network a node is frozen a relatively large number of times. If this node freezes one more time as the learning progresses, due to a small change in the magnitude of $\mathcal{R}$ (*relative* importance) of this node, the variance and the mean of relative importance of all nodes, $\underline{\mathcal{R}}$ of the network do not change significantly. However, when we inspect the difference between consecutive values of means, $\Delta\mu$, of *relative* importance of all nodes and their variances, σ_m^2, it is seen that the magnitude of the minimum value of all $\Delta\mu$s, $min\,[\,\underline{\Delta\mu}\,]$, decreases. $\Delta\mu$ and σ_m^2 of node i in layer l are defined as follows:

$$\Delta\mu = E\left[\mathcal{R}_i^l(t)\right] - E\left[\mathcal{R}_i^l(t-1)\right].$$

$$\sigma_m^2 = var\left[\mathcal{R}_i^l(t)\right] - var\left[\mathcal{R}_i^l(t-1)\right].$$

Thus, We can define the *pruning* time of a node as the time when the $min\left[\ \underline{\Delta\mu}\ \right]$ changes (reduces). However, this criteria is not suitable at the beginning of the training process when freezing frequency of a node is not high and a single freeze reduces the value of $min\left[\ \Delta\mu\ \right]$. To solve this problem, in addition to inspecting the value of $min\left[\ \Delta\mu\ \right]$ we also use the consecutive delta variances, $\Delta\sigma_m^2$ to determine a freezing candidate.

At the beginning of a training process, a single freezing of a node changes the magnitude of its $\mathcal{R}$ by a relatively large factor. Therefore, the differences between consecutive variances are high. However, as the learning progresses and a node shows ill-behaviour and its m gets larger, further freezing of such a node does not have any significant effect on its variance. In such a case, the delta variance remains nearly constant. We consider a delta variance constant if the variance of the last three σ_m^2s is less than 0.5. It is now possible to fully define the criteria to effectively prune a (nearly) *irrelevant* node. The training process is temporarily halted and the least important nodes are removed if the value of $min\left[\ \underline{\Delta\mu}\ \right]$ is changed and $var\left[\text{ last three } \sigma_m^2\ \right] < 0.5$.

In each step of the Bottom-Up Freezing algorithm, only one node with the highest trashing (i.e., largest m) is removed. After removing the least important node, the parameters are reset to their initial values (eg, the *relative* importance of nodes are set to 2).

Let n represent the number of nodes in a hidden layer. In a multi-hidden layer network, the pruning is done on a layer basis. The node pruning procedure starts with the first layer (bottom layer) and continues to remove the irrelevant nodes for n consecutive node freezing until none of the nodes in this layer is qualified to be removed from the network. The process then starts removing nodes from the second hidden layer and continues on with the next (higher level) hidden layer thereafter.

Generally speaking, a node in the lower hidden layers is considered to be of less significance compared to a node in the higher hidden layers. This is due to the fact that in the forward pass, the nodes in the lower hidden layers have relatively smaller effect in the production of the final output than those of the nodes in the higher hidden layers. Moreover, in the backward pass, the error signals calculated for such nodes are considered less accurate than those of the nodes in the higher hidden layers. Therefore, with less accuracy in their error signals, these nodes do not have as positive effect on the calculation of the weight updates and the networks convergence as the nodes in the higher hidden layers have. The basic idea behind bottom-up pruning is to remove nodes and possibly layers in the increasing order of their significance. Among all hidden layers, least significant nodes of the network are in the first hidden layer. The BUF algorithm identifies and removes as many unnecessary nodes as possible from the first hidden layer before moving on to the next layer. Moreover, the proposed pruning algorithm removes a relatively smaller number of nodes from the higher hidden layers as compared to the number of nodes removed from the lower hidden layers.

4   Experimental Results

The bottom-up freezing algorithm presented in the previous section has been tested on various artificial and real-world problems. The goal is to compare the performance of the BUF algorithm with that of the standard backpropagation algorithm. For each problem thirty trials were attempted, a few of which failed to reach the solution criteria. The statistics on the network size, number of pattern presentations, generalization and memorization rates include only those trials that were successful and reached optimum. The simulation results of the following problems are reported in this paper.

Sonar. The training and test sets each consists of 104 patterns. Each input pattern is a set of 60 numbers in the range of 0.0 to 1.0.

Two-spirals. This classic dataset pertains to a two-input, two-class classification problem. Each class contains data belonging to a separate spiral. The training set consists of 194 patterns (each spiral has 97 points). There is no test set for this problem to measure the generalization of the network, instead, we have measured the memorization capability of the network.

Iris. This is a four-input, three-class classification problem. The training and test sets each consists of 75 patterns.

Speech recognition. The training and test sets consists of 10 different words spoken by 10 female and 10 male at four different times during the day for a total of 20480 frames. The speech was sampled at 11025Hz.

Figure 1 compares the average network size, with and without pruning. Note that in the case of 'no pruning' (i.e., the conventional backpropagation algorithm), we have selected the architecture and network parameters that resulted in good performance. We have applied the BUF algorithm to the best possible network structure and it was able to further improve (in some cases substantially) network's structure, generalization and training time.

The experimental results for the above four problems are summarized in Table 1. It shows the percentage of savings in the number of pattern presentations, number of hidden nodes, and the degree of generalization. For the Spiral problem the degree of memorization is given. It is seen that the bottom-up freezing method not only eliminates the unnecessary nodes and improves networks generalization/memorization, it also reduces the number of pattern presentations.

5   Conclusion

In this paper, we have proposed a new pruning algorithm called Bottom-Up Freezing algorithm. The proposed algorithm consists of two main parts: (a) *local freezing* and (b) *node pruning*. The local freezing part of the BUF algorithm identifies and freezes those nodes that are unnecessary and (nearly) ineffective to the progress of learning the problem. This allows a network to change its underlying topology and continuously adapt itself to the problem space. The node pruning part of the BUF algorithm uses the past behaviour (freezing history) of a node to decide if a node is a good candidate to be removed from the network.

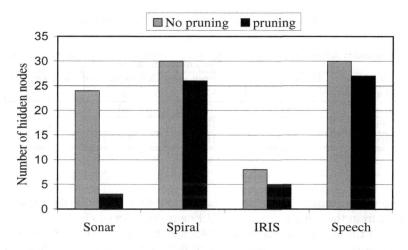

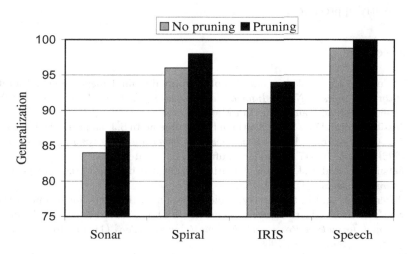

Fig. 1. Comparing network size and generalization with and without pruning.

The node pruning starts from the bottom (first) hidden layer and continues on with the next (higher) hidden layers.

In all the problems we have studied so far, the BUF algorithm has shown a moderate to significant degree of reduction in the number of hidden layers and improvement in the networks generalization/memorization. The computational cost of four benchmark problems reported in this paper, Sonar, Spiral, Iris, and Speech recognition problems are reduced by about 58%, 14%, 12%, and 12%, respectively. These improvement are considered significant given the fact that they are done on networks that have already been optimized using the trial-and-error technique to the fullest possible extent.

Table 1. Summary of the simulation studies.

Problems	Percentage of savings			
	Presentations	Hidden nodes	Generalization	Memorization
Sonar	57.5	87.5	3	—
Iris	13.8	37.5	3.3	—
Spiral	12.0	13.3	—	2.1
Speech	12.2	10.0	1.2	—

Acknowledgments. The second author gratefully acknowledges the partial support from the Natural Sciences and Engineering Research Council of Canada (NSERC) through grant RGPIN2277441-00. The support of the School of Computer Engineering, Iran University of Science and Technology, Tehran, Iran is also greatly appreciated.

References

1. Le Cun, Y., J.S. Denker, and S. A. Solla. Optimal brain damage. In D.S. Touretzky, editor, *Advances in Neural Information Processing Systems (Denver, 1989)* (2), pp. 598-605. Morgan Kaufmann, San Mateo, 1990.
2. Hassibi, B., and D.G. Stork. Optimal brain surgeon. In S.J. hanson, J.D. Cowan, and C.L. Giles, editors, *Advances in Neural Information Processing Systems (Denver, 1992)* (5), pp. 164-171. Morgan Kaufmann, San Mateo, 1993.
3. Sietsma, J., and R.J.F. Dow. Creating artificial neural networks that generalize. *Neural Networks* 4(1):67-79, 1991.
4. Mozer, M.C., and P. Smolensky. Skeletonization: A technique for trimming the fat from a network via relevance assessment. In D.S. Touretzky, editor, *Advances in Neural Information Processing Systems (Denver, 1988)* (1), pp. 107-115. Morgan Kaufmann, San Mateo, 1989.
5. Reed, R. Pruning algorithms - a survey," *IEEE transactions on Neural Networks*, 4(5):740-747, September 1993.
6. Reed, R., and R.J. Marks II. *Neural Smithing: Supervised Learning in Feedforward Artificial Neural Networks*, The MIT press, Cambridge, Massachusetts, 1999.
7. Fahlman, S.E., and C. Lebiere. The cascade-correlation architecture. In D.S. Touretsky, editor, *Advances in Neural Information Processing Systems (Denver, 1989)* (2), pp. 524-532. Morgan Kaufmann, San Mateo, 1990.
8. Frean, M. The upstart algorithm: a method for constructing and training feedforward neural networks. *Neural Computation* 2(2):198-209, 1990.
9. Mézard, M., and J.P. Nadal. Learning in feedforward layered networks: The tiling algorithm. *Journal of physics A* 22:2191-2203, 1989.

The Design and Implementation of an Electronic Lexical Knowledge Base

Mario Jarmasz and Stan Szpakowicz

School of Information Technology and Engineering
University of Ottawa
Ottawa, Canada, K1N 6N5
{mjarmasz, szpak}@site.uottawa.ca

Abstract. Thesauri have always been a useful resource for natural language processing. *WordNet*, a kind of thesaurus, has proven invaluable in computational linguistics. We present the various applications of *Roget's Thesaurus* in this field and discuss the advantages of its structure. We evaluate the merits of the 1987 edition of Penguin's *Roget's Thesaurus of English Words and Phrases* as an NLP resource: we design and implement an electronic lexical knowledge base with its material. An extensive qualitative and quantitative comparison of *Roget's* and *WordNet* has been performed, and the ontologies as well as the semantic relations of both thesauri contrasted. We discuss the design in Java of the lexical knowledge base, and its potential applications. We also propose a framework for measuring similarity between concepts and annotating *Roget's* semantic links with *WordNet* labels.

1 Introduction

WordNet [2, 14] is by far the most widely used electronic lexical semantic resource in natural language processing (NLP). The Coling-ACL '98 Workshop "Usage of WordNet in Natural Language Processing Systems" [4] demonstrates that many people adapt their research to this electronic database. Some 2000 citations to Miller's work [17] further substantiate the impact of *WordNet* on the computational linguistics (CL) community. And yet, at first it was not much more than a machine tractable thesaurus. Could a classical thesaurus, namely *Roget's Thesaurus*, also be such an invaluable resource if it were properly computerized?

We are not the first to wonder about the effectiveness of *Roget's Thesaurus* for NLP. Masterman [13] pioneered the use of *Roget's* in CL when the field was in its infancy. Many researchers have used *Roget's* with mixed success, working with the printed format or the electronic version of the 1911 edition [5]. Both of these resources have proven ineffective for large-scale computational work: the printed book for obvious reasons, the 1911 version for its dated vocabulary and methods of representing the richness of the *Thesaurus*. Several better known experiments will be discussed in this paper.

It is our opinion that *Roget's Thesaurus* has great potential for NLP research. We present the design and implementation of an electronic lexical knowledge base (ELKB) using the 1987 edition of Penguin's *Roget's Thesaurus of English Words and*

E. Stroulia and S. Matwin (Eds.): AI 2001, LNAI 2056, pp. 325–334, 2001.
© Springer-Verlag Berlin Heidelberg 2001

Phrases. We further discuss how the *Thesaurus* can be made machine-tractable in Wilks' sense of an electronic resource that is appropriate for further CL tasks [23]. Cassidy [1] as well as Sedelow and Sedelow [20] have attempted to formalize the *Thesaurus*, but they did not manage to implement effective software. We show how this can be done. We discuss the most challenging aspects: labeling implicit semantic relations in a manner similar to that of *WordNet*, and building a framework for calculating similarity between concepts. The availability of another ELKB can only benefit our research community.

2   A Brief History of Thesauri in NLP

Dictionaries and thesauri have been used in NLP ever since the problem of language understanding was first addressed. As Ide and Véronis [7] explain, machine-readable dictionaries (MRDs) became a popular source of knowledge for language processing during the 1980s. A primary research activity was to extract knowledge automatically from MRDs to construct large knowledge bases, yet *WordNet*, the only available resource of its kind, has been constructed by hand. We are now constructing an ELKB automatically not from a dictionary, but from a thesaurus. An overview of research done with *Roget's* presents its potential and limitations.

2.1   Early NLP Experiments

Early NLP work relied on available lexical material. One resource was *Roget's Thesaurus*, used by Masterman [13] to improve word-for-word machine translation (MT). Sparck Jones [21: 15] realized that the format of the *Thesaurus* must be adapted for MT. She wrote that an ideal MT dictionary "... has to be a dictionary in the ordinary sense: it must give definitions or descriptions of the meanings of words. It must also, however, give some indication of the kinds of contexts in which the words are used, that is, must be a 'semantic classification' as well as a dictionary". *Roget's* is a classification system that can be the basis for such a MT resource.

Morris and Hirst [16] used *Roget's International Thesaurus* for manual construction of lexical chains, a measure of a text's cohesiveness. Hirst and St-Onge [6] continued this experiment by automatically computing lexical chains using *WordNet*. Word sense disambiguation (WSD) might be the most popular use of *Roget's* in NLP, for example in the oft-quoted work of Yarowsky [25]. Other WSD experiments using *Roget's Thesaurus* are explained in [7].

2.2   Recent NLP Experiments

Many systems initially designed with *Roget's* in mind, for example lexical chains or WSD, were implemented using *WordNet*, perhaps only because *WordNet* is computerized. It has also been used for text classification, information extraction, text summarization and as the model for *Euro WordNet* [22]. And yet *WordNet* has weaknesses that *Roget's Thesaurus* does not have. For example, few links exist between different parts of speech, and proper nouns are not represented.

A current trend in NLP is to combine lexical resources to overcome their individual weaknesses. Mandala *et al.* [12] try to enrich *WordNet* with both proper nouns and relations between parts of speech from *Roget's*. Kwong [10] aligns word senses of a sample of the 1987 Penguin's *Roget's* with *WordNet*. Merely 30 nouns were matched *manually*, but the experiment does suggest that *WordNet* and *Roget's* can be combined. The author states: "In general we cannot expect that a single resource will be sufficient for any NLP applications. *WordNet* is no exception, but we can nevertheless enhance its utility". An electronic version of the *Thesaurus* will allow for large-scale combining and enhancing of both resources.

3   A Comparison of *Roget's Thesaurus* and *WordNet*

Roget's Thesaurus can be described as a reverse dictionary. It is "... a collection of the words it [the English language] contains and of the idiomatic combinations peculiar to it, arranged, not in alphabetical order as they are in a Dictionary, but according to the *ideas* which they express" [19]. This catalogue of semantically similar words is divided into nouns, verbs, adjectives, adverbs and interjections. The reader realizes implicit semantic relations between these groups. Here is an example of the way in which the lexical material is presented in the *Thesaurus*:

***Class one:** Abstract relations*
***Section five:** Number, **Category three:** Indeterminate*
Head: 102 Fraction: less than one
N. *fraction*, decimal fraction, *85 numerical element*; fractional part, fragment 53 *part*, 783 *portion*; shred 33 *small quantity*.
Adj. *fractional*, partial 53 *fragmentary*, 33 *small*.

Miller *et al.* [15] similarly describe *WordNet* as lexical information organized by word meanings, rather than word forms; nouns, verbs, adjectives and adverbs are organized into sets of near synonyms, each representing a lexicalized concept. Semantic relations serve as links between the sets. To contrast *WordNet's* structure with that of *Roget's*, here is one sense of the noun *fraction*, represented in *WordNet's* hyponym tree:

abstraction
   ⇒ measure, quantity, amount, quantum
     ⇒ definite quantity
       ⇒ number
         ⇒ complex number, complex quantity, imaginary number
           ⇒ real number, real
             ⇒ rational number
               ⇒ fraction

In this section we compare both resources: words and phrases, ontologies and semantic relations.

3.1 The Counts of Words and Phrases

The simplest way to compare *Roget's Thesaurus* and *WordNet* is to count strings. Table 1 shows the word and phrase counts for the 1987 Penguin's *Roget's Thesaurus*, divided among parts of speech. A sense is defined as the occurrence of a word or phrase within a unique semicolon group (see Section 3.2), for example, *{rising ground, rise, bank, ben, brae, slope, climb, incline}*. Table 2 presents the different counts for *WordNet 1.6* and the strings in common with *Roget's*. Here a sense is the occurrence of a string within a unique synset, for example, *{slope, incline, side}*.

Table 1. 1987 *Roget's Thesaurus* statistics

POS	Unique Strings	Paragraphs	Semicolon Groups	Senses
Noun	56967	2824	30658	99799
Verb	24788	1486	13865	47399
Adjective	21982	1488	12807	42460
Adverb	4254	491	1803	5500
Interjection	375	60	65	405
Totals	108366	6349	59198	195563

Table 2. *WordNet* 1.6 statistics. *Common* refers to strings both in *WordNet* and *Roget's*

POS	Unique Strings	Synsets	Senses	Common with *Roget's*	%
Noun	94474	66025	116317	25903	20.52
Verb	10319	12127	22066	7077	25.24
Adjective	20170	17915	29881	10197	31.46
Adverb	4546	3575	5677	1512	20.74
Interjection	0	0	0	0	0
Totals	121962	99642	173941	44689	24.07

The absolute sizes are similar. To calculate the overlap, we divide the number of common strings C by the number of unique strings in *both* resources minus C. Another way of viewing this would be to say that the common strings represent 41% of *Roget's* and 37% of *WordNet's* unique words and phrases. The surprisingly low 24% overlap may be due to the fact that *WordNet's* vocabulary dates to 1990, while *Roget's* contains a vocabulary that spans 150 years, since many words have been added to the original 1852 edition, but few have been removed. It is also rich in idioms: "The present Work is intended to supply, with respect to the English language, a desideratum hitherto unsupplied in any language; namely a collection of words it contains and of the idiomatic combinations peculiar to it …" [19]. Fellbaum [3] admits that *WordNet* contains little figurative language. She explains that idioms must appear in an ELKB if it is to serve NLP applications that deal with real texts where idiomatic language is pervasive.

3.2 The Ontologies

Roget's ontology is headed by six Classes. Three cover the external world: *Abstract Relations* deals with such ideas as number, order and time; *Space* is concerned with movement, shapes and sizes; *Matter* covers the physical world and humankind's perception of it. The remaining Classes deal with the internal world of human: the mind (*Intellect*), the will (*Volition*), the heart and soul (*Emotion, Religion and Morality*). There is a logical progression from abstract concepts, through the material universe, to mankind itself, culminating in what Roget saw as mankind's highest achievements: morality and religion [9]. Class Four, *Intellect*, is divided into *Formation of ideas* and *Communication of ideas*, and Class Five, *Volition*, into *Individual volition* and *Social volition*. In practice eight Classes head the *Thesaurus*.

A path in *Roget's* ontology begins with a Class. It branches to one of the 39 Sections, further divided into categories and then into 990 Heads. A Head is divided into paragraphs grouped by parts of speech: nouns, adjectives, verbs and adverbs, although not all parts of speech can be found in every Head [9]. A paragraph is divided into semicolon groups of semantically closely related words. These paths, variously interconnected, create a graph in the *Thesaurus*. A path has always 7 edges: Class, Section, Category, Head, POS, Paragraph, Semicolon Group, the word or phrase. *WordNet* took a different approach to constructing an ontology. Only nouns are clearly organized into a hierarchy. Adjectives, verbs and adverbs belong to various webs, difficult to untangle. This pragmatic decision was not based on theories of lexical semantics: "Partitioning the nouns has one important practical advantage: it reduces the size of the files that lexicographers must work with and makes it possible to assign the writing and editing of the different files to different people." [14] The noun hierarchies are organized around the following nine *unique beginners*:
{*entity, something*}, {*psychological_feature*}, {*abstraction*}, {*state*}, {*event*}, {*act, human_action, human_activity*}, {*group, grouping*}, {*possession*}, {*phenomenon*}.

A simple quantitative comparison of the two ontologies is difficult. Roget finds organizing words hierarchically useful: "In constructing the following system of classification of the ideas which are expressible by language, my chief aim has been to obtain the greatest amount of practical utility." [19]. Miller, on the other hand, feels that it is impossible to create a hierarchy for all words: "these abstract generic concepts [which make up the top levels of the ontology] carry so little semantic information; it is doubtful that people could agree on appropriate words to express them." [14]. The *Tabular synopsis of categories*, which represents the concept hierarchy, appears at the beginning of *Roget's*. In *WordNet* only the unique beginners are listed, and *only* in the documentation. Much more value was placed on the ontology in *Roget's*. We note that *WordNet's* ontology is entirely made up of synsets, whereas Roget's concept hierarchy is situated *above* semicolon groups.

WordNet's noun ontology is relatively shallow: it seems to have a limited number of levels of specialization, though in theory there is no limit to the number of levels in an inheritance system. Lexical inheritance, however, seldom covers more than 12 levels. Extreme examples usually contain technical distinctions not in the everyday vocabulary. For example, a Shetland pony is a pony, a horse, an equid, an odd-toe ungulate, a placental mammal, a mammal, a vertebrate, a chordate, an animal, an organism, and an entity: 12 levels, half of them technical [14].

3.3 The Semantic Relations

Roget's has a rich set of implicit semantic relations that should be made explicit if the ELKB is to be useful. Two types of explicit relationships are present at the word level. *Cross-reference* is a link between Heads via the syntactic form of a word. For example, the Heads **373** *Female* and **169** *Parentage* are linked by the Cross-reference 169 maternity. The word is present within the group *{ mother, grandmother 169 maternity }* in the Head **373** *Female* and is the first word of a paragraph in the head **169** *Parentage*. *See* refers the reader to another paragraph within the same Head, where the idea under consideration is dealt with more thoroughly. For example a general paragraph such as *killing* in Head **362** *Killing: destruction of life* is followed by more specific paragraphs *homicide* and *slaughter*. The *See* relationship appears thus: *{ murder, assassination, bumping off (see homicide) }*.

WordNet has 15 semantic relations [15, 2], the most important of which is synonymy. We note that synonymy is the only relation between words. All others are between synsets. For example, the synsets *{ car, auto, automobile, machine, motorcar }* and *{ accelerator, accelerator pedal, gas pedal, gas, throttle, gun }* are linked by the meronym (has part) relation, whereas the nouns *car* and *auto* are linked by synonymy. *WordNet* stretches the concept of synonymy by placing immediate hypernyms in synsets. Table 3 summarizes the semantic relations.

4   From a Machine Readable to a Machine Tractable Form

Our work is the first to transform the text files of the 1987 Penguin's *Roget's Thesaurus* into a machine tractable form. Our goal is to maintain the information available in the printed *Thesaurus* while also labeling implicit semantic relations and calculating weights for paths between two *semicolon groups*. Going from machine readable to machine tractable involves cleaning up and re-formatting the original files, deciding what services the ELKB should offer and implementing them.

4.1   Preparation of the Lexical Material

The source of the 1987 *Roget's* is divided into files with the text of the *Thesaurus* and files with its index. The 200,000 word Text File and the 45,000 entries Index File, both about 4 MB in size, are marked up using codes devised by Pearson Education.

Certain space-saving conventions are used. Where consecutive expressions use the same word, repetitions may be avoided using "*or*", as in "drop a brick *or* clanger", "countryman *or* –woman". The repeated word may also be indicated by its first letter, followed by a full stop: "weasel word, loan w., nonce w.," [9]. In the Index, " – " represents the first word of an entry, for example "narrow, – down, – the gap". All such abbreviations must be expanded before the lexical material is loaded into the ELKB. A Perl script was written to do this as well as to replace the Pearson codes by HTML-like tags, easier to process automatically. Other programs validated the expansion errors mostly due to noise in the original material.

Table 3. The semantic relations in *WordNet*

Semantic relation	Comments (*Cx* stands for *concept x*)	Part of speech			
		N	V	Adj	Adv
Synonym	C1 means exactly or almost C2.	×	×	×	×
Antonym	C1 is opposite in meaning to C2.	×	×	×	×
Hypernym	C1 is a superordinate of C2.	×	×		
Hyponym	C1 is a subordinate of C2.	×	×		
Substance meronym	C1 is a substance of C2.	×			
Part meronym	C1 is a part of C2.	×			
Member meronym	C1 is a member of C2.	×			
Substance of holonym	C1 has as substance C2.	×			
Part of holonym	C1 has as part C2.	×			
Member of holonym	C1 has as member C2.	×			
Cause to	C1 is the cause of a result.		×		
Entailment	C1 involves unavoidably a result.		×		
Troponym	C1 is a particular way to do C2.		×		
Pertainym	C1 relates to a noun.			×	×
Attribute	C1 is the value of a noun.	×			
Value	C1 has an adjective for a value.			×	

4.2 The Java Design of the ELKB

We have implemented in Java all functionality of the printed version of *Roget's*. Our system locates a semicolon group by looking its words up in the Index, or directly in the Text via the classification system. *Roget's* lattice of concepts will be used to measure the semantic distance between two words and to access all semantically related concepts; we discuss these extensions in Section 5.1.

Performance and memory use have been our main concerns. We have methods to access a semicolon group in near constant time. The ELKB occupies 45 MB of RAM. The Index is stored in a HashMap, Java's implementation of a hashtable. A list of references is stored for every entry. References point directly to one of the 990 Heads from which the paragraph and semicolon group containing the word or phrase looked up in the Index can be quickly found. The top part of the ontology (Classes, Sections, Categories, Heads) is stored in a separate Ontology object. The material in the *Thesaurus* can therefore be accessed via the Index, the Heads or the Ontology.The ELKB is implemented as a library of Java methods, a program that can be used to execute batch scripts and as a browser with a graphical user interface (GUI). A GUI is being designed now. It will allow easy navigation through the web of related words and phrases.

4.3   Immediate Applications of the ELKB

Computerizing the *Thesaurus* allows us to study and analyze all its aspects. We do not have to limit ourselves to small, labour-intensive experiments using the printed text. The most immediate application of this electronic resource is to perform a mapping between *Roget's* and *WordNet*. This will help enrich both resources, although our focus is on completing the ELKB. The mapping procedure is discussed in Section 5.2. An ambitious project would be to reorganize the lexical information in *WordNet* by classifying it using *Roget's* ontology. We have not performed any experiments yet, but, once the ELKB is complete, it could be used for many NLP applications. In fact, there is no reason why programs using *WordNet* could not be adapted to use this machine-tractable *Roget's*, although we cannot speculate on the quality of the results.

5   Discussion and Future Work

Roget's Thesaurus and *WordNet* are very different: a universal classification system versus a network of synonym sets. Wilks [24] argues that both types of thesauri are useful for NLP. Only proper computerization of *Roget's* can prove its usefulness. Once an ELKB has been constructed, a variety of NLP tasks will have to be attempted. Test applications include word sense disambiguation using Yarowsky's algorithm [25] and automatic construction of lexical chains [16]. Having done the original construction with a printed version of *Roget's,* Morris and Hirst [16] write: "Automation was not possible, for lack of a machine-readable copy of the thesaurus. Given a copy, implementation would clearly be straightforward".

Future work includes two major improvements, implementing a similarity measure for concepts and labeling semantic relations, which will help unlock this treasure of the English language.

5.1   A Similarity Measure for Concepts

Distance between concepts is central to many NLP applications. Those that use *WordNet* may import synsets using all semantic relations, not caring about any particular one. Problems arise because there is no subtle measure of semantic proximity. The number of edges traversed proves not to be an effective measure, because paths in *WordNet* are of varying lengths. For example, two senses of the noun *joint* in WordNet are:

- **Sense 1** : *{ joint, articulation, articulatio}*
- **Sense 6** : *{ joint, marijuana cigarette, reefer, stick }*

The third hypernym of these two senses are respectively:

- **Sense 1** : *{ entity, something }*
- **Sense 6** : *{ tobacco, baccy }*

{ entity, something } is a unique beginner while *{ tobacco, baccy }* is still six levels away from the top of the hierarchy.

We propose a solution that uses *Roget's Thesaurus*. All paths from Class to Semicolon Group are of length 6, and the ontology is already known explicitly. It is therefore possible to create a table of weights for calculating the cost of a path. Shorter paths via references will also be calculated. Edges for the same level of the ontology will have a given cost, with penalties when Class, Section, Category, Head or Paragraph boundaries are crossed. McHale [11] states that traditional edge counting works surprisingly well with *Roget's* taxonomy, with the results almost as good as those of human judges. This leads us to believe that it will be possible to come up with a precise measure for calculating the semantic similarity of semicolon groups.

5.2 Explicit Semantic Relations

It is a common misconception that the *Thesaurus* is simply a book of synonyms. The intention is to offer words that express every aspect of an idea, rather than to list synonyms [9]. The groups of words found under a Head form a logical sequence. Systematic semantic relations, such as IS-A and PART-OF, are not required between the semicolon groups and the Head. For example, both *restaurant* and *have brunch* are found under the same Head **301** *Food: eating and drinking*. Although native English speakers easily identify such relations they are hard to discover automatically. This is a challenge, since we do not know what criteria the lexicographers used to form the groups.

WordNet and *Roget's* have only a 24% overlap, but we hope to use *WordNet* to label some relations in the *Thesaurus*. We must map as many semicolon groups as possible onto synsets. Kwong [10] proposes an algorithm for aligning *WordNet* senses with those of *LDOCE* [18] and *Roget's Thesaurus*. We believe it to be possible to align *WordNet* and *Roget's* senses without having to use *LDOCE*. This alignment algorithm is explained in Jarmasz and Szpakowicz [8].

Acknowledgements. We thank Sylvain Delisle and Ken Barker for comments. This research would not have been possible without the help of Pearson Education, the owners of the 1987 Penguin's *Roget's Thesaurus of English Words and Phrases*; Steve Crowdy and Martin Toseland helped obtain this lexical resource and answered our many questions. Partial funding for this work comes from the Natural Sciences and Engineering Research Council of Canada.

References

1. Cassidy, P. (1996). "Modified Roget Available", http://www.hit.uib.no/corpora/1996-2/0042.html, May 28
2. Fellbaum, C. (ed.) (1998a). *WordNet: An Electronic Lexical Database*. Cambridge: MIT Press.
3. Fellbaum, C. (1998b). "Towards a Representation of Idioms in WordNet" In Harabagiu (1998), 52-57.
4. Harabagiu, S. (ed.) (1998). *Proc COLING/ACL Workshop on Usage of WordNet in Natural Language Processing Systems*. Montreal, Canada, August.
5. Hart, M. (1991). *Project Gutenberg Official Home Site*. http://www.gutenberg.net/

6. Hirst, G. and St-Onge, D. (1998). "Lexical Chains as Representations of Context for the Detection and Correction of Malapropisms". In Fellbaum (1998a), 305-332.
7. Ide, N. and Véronis, J. (1998). "Introduction to the Special Issue on Word Sense Disambiguation: The State of the Art." *Computational Linguistics. Special Issue on Word Sense Disambiguation,* 24(1), 1-40.
8. Jarmasz, M. and Szpakowicz, S. (2001). *Roget's Thesaurus as an Electronic Lexical Knowledge Base.* In W. Gruszczynski and D. Kopcinska (eds.) "NIE BEZ ZNACZENIA. Prace ofiarowane Profesorowi Zygmuntowi Saloniemu z okazji 40-lecia pracy naukowej", Bialystok (to appear).
9. Kirkpatrick, B. (1998). *Roget's Thesaurus of English Words and Phrases.* Harmondsworth, Middlesex, England: Penguin.
10. Kwong, O. (1998). "Aligning WordNet with Additional Lexical Resources". In Harabagiu (1998), 73-79.
11. Mc Hale, M. (1998). "A Comparison of WordNet and Roget's Taxonomy for Measuring Semantic Similarity." In Harabagiu (1998), 115-120.
12. Mandala, R., Tokunaga, T. and Tanaka, H. (1999). "Complementing WordNet with Roget and Corpus-based Automatically Constructed Thesauri for Information Retrieval" *Proc Ninth Conference of the European Chapter of the Association for Computational Linguistics,* Bergen, 94-101.
13. Masterman, M. (1957). "The Thesaurus in Syntax and Semantics". *Mechanical Translation,* 4(1-2), 35-43.
14. Miller, G. (1998). "Nouns in WordNet". In Fellbaum (1998a), 23-46.
15. Miller, G., Beckwith, R., Fellbaum, C., Gross, D. and Miller, K. (1990). "Introduction to WordNet: an on-line lexical database.". *International Journal of Lexicography,* 3(4), 235-244.
16. Morris, J. and Hirst, G. (1991). "Lexical Cohesion Computed by Thesaural Relations as an Indicator of the Structure of Text." *Computational Linguistics,* 17:1, 21-48.
17. NECI Scientific Literature Digital Library, http://citeseer.nj.nec.com/cs
18. Procter, P. (1978). *Longman Dictionary of Contemporary English.* Harlow, Essex, England: Longman Group Ltd.
19. Roget, P. (1852). *Roget's Thesaurus of English Words and Phrases.* Harlow, Essex, England: Longman Group Ltd.
20. Sedelow, S. and Sedelow, W. (1992). "Recent Model-based and Model-related Studies of a Large-scale Lexical Resource [Roget's Thesaurus]". *Proc 14ᵗʰ International Conference on Computational Linguistics (COLING-92).* Nantes, France, August, 1223-1227.
21. Sparck Jones, K. (1964). *Synonymy and Semantic Classification.* Ph.D. thesis, University of Cambridge, Cambridge, England.
22. Vossen, Piek (1998). *EuroWordNet: A Multilingual Database with Lexical Semantic Networks.* Kluwer Academic Publishers, Dordrecht
23. Wilks, Y., Slator, B. and Guthrie, L. (1996). *Electric Words : Dictionaries, Computers, and Meanings.* Cambridge : The MIT Press.
24. Wilks, Y. (1998). "Language processing and the thesaurus". Proc National Language Research Institute. Tokyo, Japan.
25. Yarowsky, D. (1992). "Word-Sense Disambiguation Using Statistical Models of Roget's Categories Trained on Large Corpora" *Proc 14ᵗʰ International Conference on Computational Linguistics (COLING-92).* Nantes, France, August, 454–460.

Towards a Temporal Extension of Formal Concept Analysis

Rabih Neouchi, Ahmed Y. Tawfik, and Richard A. Frost

School of Computer Science, University of Windsor, Windsor,
Ontario N9B 3P4, Canada
{neouchi, atawfik, richard}@cs.uwindsor.ca

Abstract. This article presents a method for analyzing the evolution of concepts represented by concept lattices in a time stamped database, showing how the concepts that evolve with time induce a change in the concept lattice. The purpose of this work is to extend formal concept analysis to handle temporal properties and represent temporally evolving attributes.

1 Introduction

Formal concept analysis (FCA) [2, 7, 14] is a mathematical tool for analyzing data and formally representing conceptual knowledge. FCA helps forming conceptual structures from data. Such structures consist of units, which are formal abstractions of concepts of human thought allowing meaningful and comprehensible interpretation. FCA is a mathematical discipline whose features include:
- Visualizing inherent properties in data sets,
- Interactively exploring attributes of objects and their corresponding contexts, and
- Formally classifying systems based on relationships among objects and attributes through the concept of mathematical lattices.

FCA automatically generates hierarchies called concept lattices that characterize the relationships among objects and their attributes.

Concepts change and evolve with time. In fact, change seems to be constant in a continuously changing world. In many domains such as science, medicine, finance, population, and weather patterns, change is noticeable from one time to another. The extension of concepts (set of objects) and their intensions (set of related attributes) may change, affecting how the entities are related. As a consequence, the concept lattice characterizing the relationships among a set of entities (objects and attributes) evolves over time. Temporal concept lattice metamorphosis is the change in the concept lattice over time.

The rest of this section introduces some basic FCA definitions, terminology and states some assumptions. Section 2 presents temporal lattices and the evolution of concept structures in these lattices. Section 3 identifies the importance and applications of this work. In Section 4, the extension of FCA is developed and techniques for identifying temporal evolution patterns are presented. Section 5 discusses the problem of inferring temporal properties.

E. Stroulia and S. Matwin (Eds.): AI 2001, LNAI 2056, pp. 335-344, 2001.

1.1 Terminology

Definition 1. A formal (or dyadic) context• = < G, M, I > is a triple consisting of two sets G and M and a relation I (also called dyadic relation) between G and M. The elements of G and M are called the formal objects and the formal attributes respectively. The relationship is written as gIm or $(g, m) \in I$ and is read as 'the formal object g has the formal attribute m'. A formal context can be represented by a cross table that has a row for each formal object g, a column for each formal attribute m and a cross in the row of g and the column of m if gIm.

Definition 2. Let < G, M, I > be a context. The set of all formal attributes of a set $A \subseteq G$ of formal objects is denoted by A' and defined by: $A' = \{m \in M \mid gIm$ for all $g \in A\}$. Similarly, the set of all formal objects of a set $B \subseteq M$ of formal attributes is denoted by B' and defined by: $B' = \{g \in G \mid gIm$ for all $m \in B\}$. Note that if $A = \{\emptyset\}$ then $A' = A$. Similarly, if $B = \{\emptyset\}$ then $B' = B$.

Definition 3. A formal (or dyadic) concept c of the context < G, M, I > is the pair (A, B) with $A \subseteq G$, $B \subseteq M$, $A' = B$ and $B' = A$. A is called the extent (denoted by Ext(c)) and B is called the intent (denoted by Int(c)) of the formal concept c := (A, B).

Definition 4. Let $c_1 := (A_1, B_1)$ and $c_2 := (A_2, B_2)$ be two concepts of a formal context < G, M, I >. The formal concept c_1 is a formal subconcept of the formal concept c_2 if $Ext(c_1) \subseteq Ext(c_2)$ (or $A_1 \subseteq A_2$), which is equivalent to $Int(c_2) \subseteq Int(c_1)$ (or $B_2 \subseteq B_1$), and we write $c_1 \leq c_2$ (or $(A_1, B_1) \leq (A_2, B_2)$). In this case c_2 is a formal superconcept of c_1, and we write $c_2 \geq c_1$ (or $(A_2, B_2) \geq (A_1, B_1)$). It follows from this definition that a formal concept c_1 is formal subconcept of the formal concept c_2 if c_1 has fewer formal objects and more formal attributes than c_2. Similarly, a formal concept c_1 is formal superconcept of the formal concept c_2 if c_1 has more formal objects and fewer formal attributes than c_2.

Definition 5. The set of all formal concepts of the formal context < G, M, I > is denoted by ß(G, M, I). The relation $\leq$ is a mathematical order relation called the hierarchical order (or simply order) of the formal concepts. It is also called formal conceptual ordering on ß(G, M, I). A concept lattice of the formal context < G, M, I > is the set of all formal concepts of < G, M, I > ordered in this way and is denoted by ß̲(G, M, I).

Definition 6. An ordered set (or partially ordered set) is a pair (M, $\leq$), with $\leq$ being a set and $\leq$ an order relation on M.

1.2 Assumptions

In extending FCA over time, we prefer to index an object with a time variable, e.g. Obj_{t_i}, rather than having time itself as an attribute for that object. The conventions we assume are as follows:

- Obj_{t_i} represents object Obj at time t_i, where t is the time variable and i is an integer, and read as 'Object Obj at time t i'
- t_i precedes t_j if $i < j$ for any two integers i and j
- Given all the time intervals $t_{i \in n}$, where i is an integer and n is the number of observations made on a particular object over time, they form a partial order

To define the hidden evolution patterns that the concepts exhibit in a time stamped database, we assume the following:
- The database is fairly complete; that is, there is no missing stage in the evolution patterns for all individual objects.
- We start with the patterns that have more stages. Then we fit individual objects that do not show the complete evolution stages to these patterns using temporal matching [13].
- As we do not have a reliable way to distinguish among stages that could be missed and stages that have happened in reality but are missing in the dataset for some object, we assume here the latter. This assumption may be unreasonable in some domain and we propose treating such cases as defaults in nonmonotonic reasoning that should be retracted to resolve conflicts. Such conflicts may occur if persistence or causation properties are violated. As this may involve a complex knowledge engineering tasks, the knowledge engineer should critically examine the validity of this assumption.

2 Temporal Lattices

To handle the evolution phenomenon of concept structures and analyze temporal metamorphosis, a temporal extension of FCA is developed. This temporal extension involves the study of persistence, and other temporal properties implied by the data and concept lattices.

As an example, consider the simple database in Table 1, where some attributes change over time (juvenile, adult, senior) while others persist (dead). It can be easily seen from the concept lattice how the concepts manifest a change over different times (figure 1). Note that in our notation, t represents the time variable and t_i precedes t_j if $i < j$ for any two integers i and j. In addition, t_i and t_j form partial order.

To represent temporal evolutions in a concept lattice, we use two types of edges: temporal edges and non-temporal edges. The temporal edges allow the evolution of a particular object to be followed over time. A temporal precedence relation "$<$" is defined over time points. The direction of the arrow indicates this precedence. Non-temporal edges are undirected, as they are not governed by the temporal precedence. In fact, non-temporal edges describe a concept at a particular point in time.

The temporal concept lattice in Figure 1 shows that there are transient attribute and persistent ones. For example, juvenile is a transient attribute as a juvenile becomes an adult but dead is a persistent attribute.

Table 1. Human context database

Objects/Attributes	Juvenile	Adult	Senior	Dead	Male	Female
Adam$_{t1}$	X				X	
Adam$_{t2}$		X			X	
Steve$_{t1}$		X			X	
Steve$_{t2}$			X		X	
Nancy$_{t1}$			X			X
Nancy$_{t2}$				X		X
Mary$_{t1}$				X		X
Mary$_{t2}$				X		X

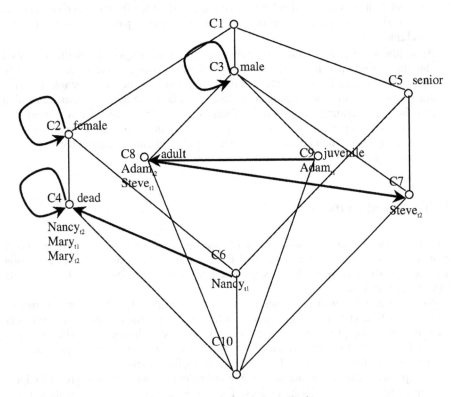

Fig. 1. Human context concept lattice

3   Importance and Applications

Understanding concept evolutions can be useful in many applications including data mining, planning, and decision support systems. The application that motivated this work in particular is identifying the evolution of a set of concepts and related vocabulary for speech recognition in the Speech Web [6] as a conversation evolves.

In discovering useful patterns from a database researchers are increasingly relying on data visualization to complement data mining in the knowledge discovery process. Visualization helps developing insights and deduces the hidden regularities in the data. Animation seems to provide proper visualization for temporal evolution. However such animations can be easily generated from the proposed lattices. Moreover, the concept hierarchies provide a new tool for the study of the relationships between an interval and its subintervals.

FCA has been applied to static domains such as assessing the modular structure of legacy code [11] in software engineering, text analysis from different sources [4] in information retrieval, designing and exploring conceptual hierarchies of conceptual information systems [12] in knowledge acquisition, transforming object class hierarchies into normalized forms [10] in databases, performing structure-activity relationships [1] in environmental/chemical applications, structuring the design interface of some educational applications [5], analyzing individual preference judgments [9] in decision making tasks, implementing the TOSCANA system [8] in natural-language, improving the accuracy of speech recognizers [15] in speech recognition, and using medical-discharge summaries as training data sets [3] in medicine.

Adding further notations to FCA's representation is important to extend it over time. The suggested extension opens up new areas of applications to FCA such as representing the course of infection for a disease, the life cycle of a software project, the evolution of social, economic, and population trends.

4   Classification of Temporal Patterns

4.1   Unconditional Evolution Patterns

Unconditional patterns are any kind of a change in the attributes of an object over time that always happens in one unique direction. For example, during the process of getting older in humans, a person always evolves from being a child to an adult and then to a senior.

4.2   Conditional Evolution Patterns

Conditional patterns are any kind of change in the attributes of an object over time that might happen in more than one direction depending on a certain condition that controls the order of the changing attributes. For example, depending on the external temperature, a piece of ice might evolve from being solid to liquid or vice versa. Note that both conditional and unconditional patterns are forms of evolution and that some unconditional patterns become conditional once the data set has enough information about causes and effects.

4.3 Persistence

Persistence is a state in which an object maintains its attributes throughout its lifetime without any change in these attributes. For example, once a person is born male, he will always remain male. We say that gender is a persistent property.

4.4 Transitions

As opposed to persistence, transitions are any kind of change in the attributes of an object over time that does not follow any specific direction. For example, a person might eat then sleep, or sleep then eat. In this case, we say that eating and sleeping are transient properties. Note that transitions do not constitute evolution patterns for our purpose here.

5 Inferring Temporal Properties

Let B be the set of formal attributes, and b_j be the attribute number j, where i and j are integers.

Definition 7. The intension of an object Obj at time t_i is the set of all attributes of that particular object at time t_i. It is written as:

$$i\{Obj_{ti}\} = \{b_j \in B\} . \tag{1}$$

Definition 8. An evolution of an object, $Ev(Obj)$, is an ordered set of sets containing all the intensions that this particular object from an arbitrary initial time t_0 to a certain time t_i. The intension of the object at time t_{i+1} is added to the resulting evolution set when we consider the evolution up to time t_{i+1}:

$$\forall t < t_i, i\{Obj_{ti}\} \in Ev_{t0-ti}(Obj) . \tag{2}$$

For example, according to Table 1 above, we describe the evolution of *Adam* to be:

$$Ev(Adam) = \{\{male, juvenile\}, \{male, adult\}\} . \tag{3}$$

Definition 9. The evolution interval (the subscript of the evolution) of an object, $Ev_{t0-ti}(Obj)$, specifies an interval from time t_0 to time t_i, where t_0 is the time at which the observation of the object started and t_i is the time at which the observation ended. In other words, the evolution depends on the interval we allow for the object to change. For example, according to Table 1, we describe the evolution of *Adam* at time t_i to be:

$$Ev_{t0-t1}(Adam) = \{\{male, juvenile\}\} . \tag{4}$$

Definition 10. An evolution pattern of an object, *EvPat(Obj)*, is an ordered set containing the elements of the conditional or unconditional patterns that this particular object might exhibit throughout its lifetime. For example, according to Table 1, we describe the evolution pattern of *Adam* to be:

$$\text{EvPat(Adam)} = \{\text{juvenile, adult}\} . \tag{5}$$

One way to determine the evolution pattern is to examine the intensions of a particular object over different points in time. For example, suppose that the intension of *Ann* includes at time t_1 the *child* attribute, at time t_2 the *adult* attribute, and at time t_3 the *senior* attribute, such that $t_1 < t_2 < t_3$ and $<$ is a precedence relation that defines a partial order. That is

$$i\{\text{Ann}_{t1}\} \supset \{\text{child}\} . \tag{6}$$

$$i\{\text{Ann}_{t2}\} \supset \{\text{adult}\} .$$

$$i\{\text{Ann}_{t3}\} \supset \{\text{senior}\} .$$

Then an evolution pattern from *child* to *adult* to *senior* exists. Usually we are interested in evolution patterns that are consistent for all the objects or for a class of objects. For example, the pattern of evolution from child to adult to senior is applicable to any object x of type *person* in the database. This evolution is written as:

$$\forall \text{ person}(x \in G), \exists \text{ EvPat}(x) = \{\text{child, adult, senior}\} . \tag{7}$$

To determine if such a pattern holds, we form a temporal matching problem [13]. Temporal matching can be formulated as a special constraint satisfaction problem that tries to find a consistent assignment of states such as child, adult, and senior to individuals whose state is only known at particular points in time. This assignment has to be consistent with temporal constraints representing the persistence properties of each state.

Definition 11. A persistent property of an object, *Persist(Obj)*, is a set containing all that object's attributes that persisted in all of the intension sets of that object over time, including its evolution set if that object happened to have an evolution. For example, according to Table 1, we describe the persistent property of *Adam* to be:

$$\text{Persist(Adam)} = \{\text{male}\} . \tag{8}$$

To determine the persistent property, we examine the intensions of a particular object over different points in time. For example, if the intension of *John* includes at times t_1, t_2 and t_3 the *male* attribute then *male* is a persistent property of *John* in particular and to all objects x of type *person* in the database, such that x has the *male* property:

$$i\{\text{John}_{t1}\} \supset \{\text{male}\} . \tag{9}$$

$$i\{\text{John}_{t2}\} \supset \{\text{male}\} .$$

$$i\{\text{John}_{t3}\} \supset \{\text{male}\} .$$

$$\forall t \ (person(x \in G) \land male(x)), i\{x\} \supset \{male\} \ . \tag{10}$$

Similarly, the *female* property is persistent to all objects *y* of type p*erson* in the database, such that *y* has the *female* property:

$$\forall \ t(person(x \in G) \land female(x)), i\{x\} \supset \{female\} \ . \tag{11}$$

Definition 12. A transient property of an object, *Transient(Obj)*, is a set containing all that object's attributes that exhibited a change in all of the intension sets of that object over time, including its evolution set if that object happened to have an evolution. For example, according to Table 1, we describe the transient property of *Adam* to be:

$$Transient(Adam) = \{juvenile, adult\} \ . \tag{12}$$

Note that a change that happens in any order is not considered to be an evolution pattern. For example, suppose that the intension of *Bob* includes at time t_1 the *eating* attribute, at time t_2 the *sleeping* attribute while the intension of *Sam* includes at time t_1 the *sleeping* attribute, at time t_2 the eating attribute. That is:

$$i\{Bob_{t1}\} \supset \{eating\} \ . \tag{13}$$

$$i\{Bob_{t2}\} \supset \{sleeping\} \ .$$

$$i\{Sam_{t1}\} \supset \{sleeping\} \ .$$

$$i\{Sam_{t2}\} \supset \{eating\} \ .$$

Then no evolution pattern from *eating* to *sleeping*, or from *sleeping* to *eating* exists, and that this rule is applicable to any object *x* of type p*erson* in the database.

$$\forall \ person(x \in G), \ !\exists \ EvPat(x) = \{eating, sleeping\} \ . \tag{14}$$

$$\forall \ person(x \in G), \ !\exists \ EvPat(x) = \{sleeping, eating\} \ .$$

Note also that the transient property set of an object is not always identical to its evolution pattern set. For example in the case we just mentioned about *Bob* and *Sam*, the evolution pattern set of both *Bob* and *Sam* would be empty, while it is not the case for the transient property set of either one:

$$EvPat(Bob) = \{\varnothing\} \ . \tag{15}$$

$$EvPat(Sam) = \{\varnothing\} \ .$$

$$Transient(Bob) = \{eating, sleeping\} \ .$$

$$Transient(Sam) = \{sleeping, eating\} \ .$$

Note that the temporal matching exercise detects such transients as failure to match.

6 Conclusion

In artificial intelligence, there is a great need to represent temporal knowledge and to reason about models that capture change over time. Since changing the time variable causes a change in the intension (attributes) of concepts, we end up having different concept lattices representing the same context at different times, which we call a temporal concept lattice metamorphosis. Finding the order of the changing attributes therefore defines the evolution itself in the concept lattice.

References

1. Bartel, H.-G., Bruggemann, R. 1998. Application of Formal Concept Analysis to Structure-Activity Relationships. Fresenius Journal of Analytical Chemistry (5 Jan.), vol. 361, no. 1. Springer-Verlag, Berlin, Germany, 23-28
2. Birkhoff, G. 1948. Lattice Theory. American Mathematical Society Colloquium Publications, Vol. XXV, Second (Revised) Edition. Providence, Rhode Island, Library of Congress Catalog Card Number 66-23707
3. Cole, R., Eklund, P. W. 1999. Scalability in Formal Concept Analysis. Computational Intelligence (Feb.), vol. 15, no. 1. Blackwell Publishers, USA, 11-27
4. Eklund, P. W., Wille, R. 1998. A Multimodal Approach to Term Extraction Using a Rhetorical Structure Theory Tagger and Formal Concept Analysis. In Proceedings of the 2nd International Conference on Multi-modal Communication, CMC/98, (Tilburg). 171-175, ISBN 90-9011386-X
5. Fernandez-Manjon, B., Fernandez-Valmayor, A. 1998. Building educational tools based on formal concept analysis. Education and Information Technologies (Dec.), vol. 3, no. 3-4. Kluwer Academic Publishers, Netherlands, 187-201
6. Frost, R. A., Chitte, S. 1999. A New Approach for Providing Natural-Language Speech Access to Large Knowledge Bases. In Proceedings of the Pacific Association of Computational Linguistics Conference, PACLING'99. University of Waterloo, Canada, August 1999, 82-89
7. Ganter, B., Wille, R. 1999. Formal Concept Analysis: Mathematical Foundations. Springer-Verlag, Berlin, Heidelberg, New York. 284 pp. ISBN 3-540-62771-5
8. Groh, B., Strahringer, S., Wille, R. 1998. TOSCANA-Systems Based on Thesauri. Conceptual Structures: Theory, Tools and Applications. In Proceedings of the 6th International Conference on Conceptual Structures, ICCS'98, (Montpellier, France, 10-12 Aug.). Lecture Notes in Artificial Intelligence, no. 1453. Springer-Verlag, Berlin, Germany, 127-38
9. Luksch, P., Wille, R. 1988. Formal Concept Analysis of Paired Comparisons. Classification and Related Methods of Data Analysis. In Proceedings of the 1st Conf. on the Intl. Federation of Classification Societies, IFCS, (Aachen, West Germany, 29 June-1 July 1987). North-Holland, Amsterdam, Netherlands, 567-75
10. Schmitt, I., Conrad, S. 1999. Restructuring Object-Oriented Database Schemata Using Formal Concept Analysis. Informatik Forschung und Entwicklung, vol. 14, no. 4. Springer-Verlag, Germany, 218-26
11. Snelting, G. 2000. Software Reengineering Based on Concept Lattices. In Proceedings of the Fourth European Conference on Software Maintenance and Reengineering (Zurich, Switzerland, 29 Feb.-3 March). IEEE Comput. Soc, Los Alamitos, CA, USA, 3-10

12. Stumme, G. 1999. Acquiring Expert Knowledge for the Design of Conceptual Information Systems. In Proceedings of the 11th European Workshop on knowledge Acquisition, Modeling, and Management, (Dagstuhl, 26-29 May), (submitted). Lecture Notes in Artificial Intelligence, no. 1621. Springer-Verlag, Berlin-Heidelberg, 271-286
13. Tawfik, A. Y., Scott, G. 2001. Temporal Matching under Uncertainty. In Proceedings of the Eighth International Workshop on Artificial Intelligence and Statistics.
14. Wille, R. 1982. Restructuring Lattice Theory: An Approach Based on Hierarchies of Concepts. Ordered Sets. D. Reidel Publishing Company, Dordrecht-Boston, 445-470
15. Willett, D., Neukirchen, C., Rottland, J., Rigoll, G. 1999. Refining Tree-Based State Clustering by Means of Formal Concept Analysis, Balanced Decision Trees and Automatically Generated Model-Sets. In Proceedings of the IEEE International Conference on Acoustics, Speech, and Signal Processing, ICASSP99, (Phoenix, AZ, USA, 15-19 March), vol. 2. IEEE, Piscataway, NJ, USA, 565-8

Adaptive Representation Methods for Reinforcement Learning

Stuart I. Reynolds

School of Computer Science, The University of Birmingham,
Edgbaston, Birmingham, B15 2TT, England
sir@cs.bham.ac.uk
http://www.cs.bham.ac.uk/~sir

Overview of Planned Thesis

The aim of my PhD. is to investigate the use of adaptive representation methods in reinforcement learning (RL). Reinforcement learning algorithms attempt to learn a policy which maximises a reward signal. In turn, this policy is directly derived from long-term return estimates of state-action pairs (Q-values). However, in environments with real-valued or high-dimensional state-spaces, it is impossible to enumerate the value of every state-action pair. This necessitates the use of function approximation in order to infer state-action values from similar states. However, traditional systems of this kind are typically bound to the parameters and resources with which they are initially provided. If the chosen representation is too fine then learning proceeds to slowly to be practical, while representations which are too coarse may result in poor policies. Furthermore, even if adequate *uniformly* detailed representations can be decided upon, these typically provide more detail than is necessary in most of the state-space. Again, this can have severe negative effects on the rate of learning in some tasks.

The thesis will discuss several methods to manage this tradeoff by adaptively and *non-uniformly* increasing the resolution of the Q-function based upon a variety of different criteria and within a variety of RL setting (model-based, model-learning and model-free). In addition to this, it will examine the interaction between Q-function and policy representations and the RL algorithms used to generate them.

Recursive Partitioning

One method to improve the Q-function representation is to begin learning with a coarse, discrete representation and recursively sub-divide it in areas of interest. Because the initial representation is coarse, Q-value estimates can quickly be generated for most of the state-space and useful initial policies can be generated.

We note that in most RL problems, representing an optimal policy is easier than representing the optimal Q-function, and in many continuous state problems an optimal policy representation may consist of just a few boundaries separating the space into areas of the same optimal action(s).

For example, consider the mountain-car task shown in Figure 1. The learner has the task of driving a car to the top of a steep hill in the shortest time

E. Stroulia and S. Matwin (Eds.): AI 2001, LNAI 2056, pp. 345–348, 2001.

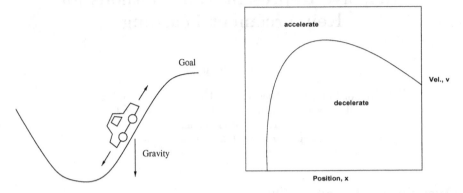

Fig. 1. *(left)* The mountain-car task. *(right)* An optimal policy for this task can be represented by dividing the space into 2 partitions.

possible by applying either an acceleration or deceleration to the car. The car is under-powered and must first reverse to gain enough momentum to propel it to the goal. An optimal solution to this problem may be found by dividing the state-space into just two partitions; one where the car should accelerate and one where it should decelerate.

We exploit this with the decision boundary partitioning algorithm [5] which refines the Q-function representation by subdividing the state-space at boundaries where the currently recommended actions differ. In the areas between the boundaries, the optimal action(s) are easy to choose and remain coarsely represented (see Figure 2). The algorithm also partitions the space less finely at decision boundaries where the estimated gain for being able to accurately choose the best action is small.

Experiments have shown that the final policies achieved can be better and are reached more quickly than with fixed uniform representations. This is especially true in problems requiring fine control in a relatively small part of the entire state-space. In addition, compared to traditional function approximation techniques, relatively little prior knowledge is required about the configuration of the function approximator.

The partitioning of the state-space is achieved with a kd-tree. The root node of the tree represents a hyper-rectangle covering the entire space, each branch of the tree divides the space into two smaller subspaces along a single dimension and the leaves of the tree store the actual data. However, this method is currently only suitable for use in low dimensional state-spaces (as are most grid based approximation methods) since even a single division along each dimension causes an exponential growth in the number of grid cells. Future work will examine ways to adapt this approach to use sparse instance-based function approximation.

Related Work

A number of other researches have also employed kd-trees to recursively partition state-spaces for reinforcement learning. Munos and Moore [3] have independently developed the same heuristic of refining the Q-function around areas of policy

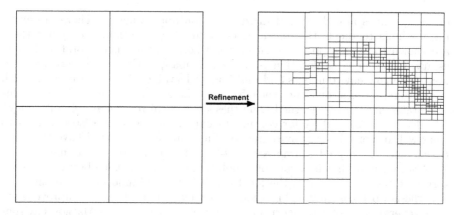

Fig. 2. *(left)* An initial coarse representation of the mountain-car state-space. *(right)* The representation after refinement. The highest resolutions areas are found along decision boundaries where there is the greatest loss for taking an incorrect action.

difference. A key difference is that their method requires a model of the environment to be provided in advance. As such, it is a method for planning and cannot, at present, be used for learning on-line with experience, but has been found to successfully find near optimal policies for complex 6 dimensional problems.

In an earlier paper, the Parti-Game algorithm [2] and a later version of it [1], *kd*-trees were also employed for adapting resolution. Although the method has been shown to work in problems of up to 9 dimensions, it is limited by its applicability: the goal must be known in advance, general reinforcement functions may not be used, local controllers need to be provided and the state-transitions must be deterministic.

Another independent model-free approach to this problem has also recently been proposed. *kd-Q*-Learning [9] starts with a *kd*-tree that is fully partitioned to a given resolution. *Q*-values are kept and maintained at *all* levels of the tree. The method improves upon other multi-resolution methods, such as the CMAC [7], as it can select *Q*-values from different resolutions; it chooses the level whose *Q*-value it is most confident of. In addition, maintaining *Q*-values at several levels in less wasteful of experience than the method presented here. However, it is important to note that although the method reduces learning cost it still suffers from the kind of state explosion experienced by fixed resolution methods. As such, the method is restricted to problems where it is possible to keep the fully partitioned tree from the outset.

Learning with Adaptive Representations

Almost all RL algorithms rely upon the Markov property to maintain their guarantees of convergence. Where this property is violated, as it typically is when function approximation is used, the effects of naively applying the learning algorithms can be unpredictable. This is particularly true of 1-step RL algorithms, such as *Q*-learning [10] and dynamic programming [8], which make heavy use of the Q-values already stored in the function approximator. There are existing methods to tackle this (such as eligibility trace methods [4,8]) but these are known to behave poorly in situations where continuous exploration is necessary. Continuous exploration is needed in many different RL settings (e.g. non-stationary environments and multi-agent learning), including learning with adaptive representations since the effects of taking actions in new higher resolution states needs to be learned. The thesis work will present novel "off-policy" RL algorithms that allow for continuous exploration and are also expected to work well in non-Markov environments. These are also expected have the same convergence-to-optimal guarantees as Q-learning in Markov environments.

Also, we note that in a variable resolution system, the time between the observed states depends upon the local density of the Q-function representation. The thesis work has provided methods which exploit this to make improvements to a general class of RL algorithms that work better in non-Markov environments. These employ *temporal abstraction* [6] at a granularity defined by the local density of the representation in order to reduce the problems associated with losing the Markov property. The result is a reinforcement learning system which employs both spatial abstraction (through function approximation) and temporal abstraction (through the learning algorithm) simultaneously.

References

1. M. A. Al-Ansari and R. J. Williams. Efficient, globally-optimized reinforcement learning with the parti-game algorithm. In *Advances in Neural Information Processing Systems 11*. The MIT Press, Cambridge, MA, 1999.
2. A. W. Moore and C. G. Atkeson. The parti-game algorithm for variable resolution reinforcement learning in multidimensional state-spaces. *Machine Learning*, 21:199–233, 1995.
3. Rémi Munos and Andrew Moore. Variable resolution discretization for high-accuracy solutions of optimal control problems. In *Proceedings of the 16th International Joint Conference on Artificial Intelligence*, pages 1348–1355, 1999.
4. J. Peng and R. J. Williams. Technical note: Incremental Q-learning. *Machine Learning*, 22:283–290, 1996.
5. Stuart I. Reynolds. Decision boundary partitioning: Variable resolution model-free reinforcement learning. In *Proceedings of the 17th International Conference on Machine Learning (ICML-2000)*, San Fransisco, 2000. Morgan Kaufmann.
6. R. Sutton, D. Precup, and S. Singh. Between MDPs and Semi-MDPs: A framework for temporal abstraction in reinforcement learning. *Artificial Intelligence*, 112:181–211, 1999.
7. Richard S. Sutton. Generalization in reinforcement learning: Successful examples using sparse coarse coding. In David S. Touretzky, Michael C. Mozer, and Michael E. Hasselmo, editors, *Advances in Neural Information Processing Systems 8*, pages 1038–1044. The MIT Press, Cambridge, MA., 1996.
8. Richard S. Sutton and Andrew G. Barto. *Reinforcement Learning: An Introduction*. The MIT Press, Cambridge, MA., 1998.
9. Hans Vollbrecht. kd-Q-learning with hierarchic generalisation in state space. Technical Report SFB 527, Department of Neural Information Processing, University of Ulm, Ulm, Germany., 1999.
10. C.J.C.H. Watkins. *Learning from Delayed Rewards*. PhD thesis, King's College, Cambridge, UK, May 1989.

Imprecise and Uncertain Engineering Information Modeling in Databases

Z.M. Ma[1,2], W.J. Zhang[1], and W.Y. Ma[2]

[1] University of Saskatchewan,
57 Campus Driver, Saskatoon, SK S7N 5A9, Canada
mezminma@cityiu.edu.hk
Chris_Zhang@engr.USask.Ca
[2] City University of Hong Kong,
83 Tat Chee Avenue, Kowloon, Hong Kong SAR, China
mewma@cityiu.edu.hk

1 Introduction

Engineering information modeling involves database systems and modeling tools. Currently, there are no existing database systems and modeling tools that support imprecise and uncertain engineering information. Information imprecision and uncertainty exist in almost all aspects of engineering applications. Constructing intelligent manufacturing systems (IMS) has imposed great challenge to current database technologies in modeling engineering data with imprecise and uncertain information.

Information modeling in databases should be implemented at two levels, i.e. conceptual data modeling and logical database modeling. In our research, imprecise and uncertain engineering information is identified and represented by null values, partial values (including interval values), fuzzy values, and probabilistic values. A particular emphasis is on fuzzy data. Several major logical database models are first extended for fuzzy information, including relational databases, nested relational databases, and object-oriented databases. In addition, two flexible relational database models for fuzzy and probabilistic information are developed, respectively. Conceptual data models such as ER/EER and IFO are then extended for modeling fuzzy information. The formal methodologies are developed for mapping the extended conceptual data models to the extended database models. At last, two information-modeling tools for engineering applications: IDEF1X and EXPRESS are fuzzily extended, and the issues on database implementation of fuzzy EXPRESS information models are discussed.

2 Logical Database Models with Incomplete Information

The measure of semantic relationship of imprecise and uncertain information is crucial for their representation and processing in relational databases. In relational databases with null values and partial values, only qualitative measures of "*definite*" and "*maybe*" were addressed. These measures are little informative. In fuzzy relational databases, there have been some methods introduced to quantitatively assess the semantic relationship of fuzzy data. However, there are counterintuitive results while

E. Stroulia and S. Matwin (Eds.): AI 2001, LNAI 2056, pp. 349–352, 2001.

applying these methods. So new methodologies of quantitatively measuring the semantic relationships of partial values and fuzzy data are introduced in our research. On the basis, imprecise functional dependencies, fuzzy functional dependencies, fuzzy data redundancy removals, and fuzzy relational operations are defined. Here, functional dependencies can be viewed as one kind of knowledge to be used in approximate reasoning, and relational operations are the means by which query processing can be implemented.

Although fuzzy information and probabilistic information have been introduced into relational databases, they were studied separately. There is no proposal to provide a flexible relational database model that incorporates them simultaneously. In our research, we introduce two kinds of relational databases with hybrid imprecise and uncertain information, i.e., fuzzy attribute-based probabilistic and fuzzy measure-based probabilistic relational databases. The relational operations for the relational databases with hybrid imprecise and uncertain information are developed.

In order to model complex objects for real applications with fuzzy information, we introduce possibility-based fuzzy nested relational databases and develop fuzzy nested relational operations in our research. In addition, little work has been done on fuzzy information modeling in object-oriented databases and their focuses were on fuzzy objects and fuzzy classes. In our research, based on possibility distribution and the semantic measure method of fuzzy data developed, we further investigate fuzzy object relationships and fuzzy inheritances. A generic model for fuzzy object-oriented databases is hereby developed.

3   Fuzzy Conceptual Data Models

Three levels of fuzziness have been introduced into the ER model. Based on fuzzy set theory, the fuzzy extensions of several major EER concepts such as superclass/subclass, generalization/specialization, category, and the subclass with multiple superclasses were introduced. Being one kind of diagrammatic data model, however, the graphical representations of the fuzzy EER have not been developed. In our research, we develop a set of notations to support three levels of fuzziness modeling in a fuzzy EER model.

IFO data model was extended into a formal object model IFO_2 for object-oriented database modeling and design. The extensions of IFO and IFO_2 to model imprecise and uncertain information in object databases were proposed. Their extension mainly focused on the attribute values of the objects and the objects themselves in the object-based data model. However, the fuzzy extensions of some basic notions in IFO such as fragments and ISA relationships are still unclear. Based on fuzzy set theory, a fuzzy extension to IFO data model at the three levels of fuzziness like the fuzzy ER model, denoted by IF_2O, is developed in our research. In addition, the methods of mapping the fuzzy EER model to the FOODBs and mapping the IF_2O model to the fuzzy relational databases are not available in the literature. So, in our research, we develop the formal methods to implement such mappings. It should be particularly emphasized that we extend the IDEF1X data model to describe fuzzy information.

4 Extending EXPRESS for Modeling Fuzzy Information

Product data models can be viewed as a class of semantic models that take into account the needs of engineering data. Some attentions have been paid to modeling information imprecision and uncertainty in semantic data models. However, no attention has been pain for extending EXPRESS, a crucial tool for modeling engineering information.

With the current edition of EXPRESS, null values are permitted in array data types and role names by utilizing the keyword *Optional*. The application of three-valued logic (False, Unknown, and True) is just a result of the null value occurrences. In addition, the select data types define named collections of other types. An attribute or variable could therefore be one of several possible types. In this context, a select data type also defines one kind of imprecise and uncertain data type whose actual type is unknown to us at present. However, further investigations on the issues of the semantics, representation and manipulation of imprecise and uncertain information in EXPRESS are needed.

In our research, we fully extend the EXPRESS language based on fuzzy set and fuzzy logic, including basic elements, various data types, EXPRESS declarations, calculation and operations, and EXPRESS-G. Utilizing the extended EXPRESS, the information model with incomplete information as well as crisp information can be constructed. The extended EXPRESS fully covers the current edition of EXPRESS. In other words, the current edition of EXPRESS should be a proper subset of the extended EXPRESS. When the information has no imprecision and uncertainty, the extended EXPRESS can be reduced the current edition of EXPRESS.

5 Database Implementation of Fuzzy EXPRESS Model

The EXPRESS data modeling language is used to describe a product data model with activities covering the whole product life cycle. Based on such a product data model, product data can be exchanged and shared among different applications. This is the goal of the STEP standard. Generally speaking, the application of STEP is mainly concerned with two aspects. One of the aspects is the establishment of the product information model to represent product data according to information requirements in application environment and the integrated resources in STEP. The other one is the manipulation and management of product data in the product information model. All these are related to the implementation of STEP in database systems.

Utilizing different database models, some mapping operations have been developed in the literature to map EXPRESS to databases. These database models include traditional databases such as network, hierarchical, and (nested) relational databases. Since EXPRESS is semantically richer than traditional database models, the mappings of EXPRESS to object-oriented database model have been investigated. A general mechanism for identifying information loss between data models has been shown in literature. In terms of functions, users define their databases using EXPRESS, manipulate the databases using SDAI, and exchange data with other applications through the database systems. SDAI can thus be viewed as a data access interface. The requirements of SDAI functions are determined by the requirements of the application users. However the SDAI itself is in a state of evolution. This is an indication of the enormity of the task, the difficulty for achieving an agreement as to what functions are to be included, and the viability of implementing the suggestions. Some basic requirements that are needed for manipulating the EXPRESS information model, such as data query, data update, structure query, and validation, have been investigated and their implementation algorithms have been developed.

The formal methods for mapping fuzzy EXPRESS information models to fuzzy nested relational databases and to fuzzy object-oriented databases are developed in our research. According to the feature of incomplete information models, the requirements of SDAI functions are then investigated to manipulate the EXPRESS-defined data in the databases. Depending on different database platforms, the implementation algorithms of these SDAI functions are respectively developed. In addition, the strategies of querying incomplete relational databases are further studied to provide users with power means by which the useful information can be obtained from product model databases with imprecise and uncertain information.

6   Conclusion

Based on the research developed, one could use the following procedure for constructing intelligent engineering information models with imprecision and uncertainty. First, imprecise and uncertain engineering information can be described using EX-PRESS-G, ER/EER, or IFO to form a conceptual data model. According to this conceptual data model that may contain imprecise and uncertain information, an EX-PRESS information model with imprecise and uncertain information can be created. Finally, the EXPRESS information model can be mapped into a database information model based on relational databases, nested relational databases, or object-oriented databases. The manipulations of information model in databases are performed via SDAI operations as well as DBMS. It can be seen that with the modeling methodologies developed in our research and the Application Protocols, the imprecise and uncertain engineering information model can be shared and exchanged between different applications.

Acknowledgements. The authors thank both the NSERC and AECL, Canada and the City University of Hong Kong through a cooperative research and development program.

Incremental Case-Based Reasoning for Classification

Saeed Hashemi

Dalhousie University, Faculty of Computer Science, PhD candidate
Halifax, Canada.
saeed@cs.dal.ca

Abstract. The focus of this paper is on enhancing the incremental learning of case-based reasoning (CBR) systems. CBR systems can accept new cases and therefore learn as they are being used. If some new attributes are to be added to the available classes, however, the similarity calculations are disturbed and some knowledge engineering tasks should be done to let the system learn the new situation. The attempt here is to make this process automatic and design a CBR system that can accept adding new attributes while it is in use. We start with incremental learning and explain why we need continuous validation of the performance for such dynamic systems. The way weights are defined to accommodate incremental learning and how they are refined and verified is explained. The scheduling algorithm that controls the shift from short-term memory to long-term memory is also discussed in detail.

1 Introduction and Motivation

Hybrid case-based reasoning (CBR) systems have many advantages that make them appealing for some machine learning tasks. Flexibility and the ability to learn and enhance the performance of the system over time (incremental learning) are among them. Although CBR is incremental in that new cases can be added to the system, almost nothing has been done in enhancing this capability. In order to let CBR systems stay in use, we often need to make the system accept new attributes for the available classes. For instance, in medical diagnosis, new tests are often introduced to the market that make the diagnosis process more accurate or cheaper; in e-business, everyday manufacturers introduce products with new features. CBR systems that help diagnostic tasks or e-business services can easily become obsolete if they cannot accept new attributes while being used. However, the idea of adding new attributes has not been addressed in the research community. Our approach tries to design and implement an incremental CBR solution for such a dynamic environment in the application area of medical diagnosis.

2 Incremental Learning

A CBR system uses the past experiences from the case library to achieve a solution for the query case. This is done by calculating similarity measures, often using attribute weights, between the query case and the candidate cases in the case library.

E. Stroulia and S. Matwin (Eds.): AI 2001, LNAI 2056, pp. 353-356, 2001.

Machine learning literature, defines incremental (continuous or dynamic) learning, as opposed to one-shot learning, with two characteristics:

1. Learning never finishes. This introduces overfitting problem and the need for a stopping criterion in most machine learning approaches. In CBR, new cases are added to the system after verification and they can be used for future consultations. However, the new cases should have the same number of attributes and fall into one of the pre-specified classes to be understood and classified by the system. We try to expand this limit by letting the system accept new attributes while being used.

2. No complete use of all past examples is allowed which brings up the stability/plasticity dilemma [3]. In conventional CBR systems, once attribute weights are assigned, there will be no learning process other than adding the new verified cases to the case library. However, when we accept new attributes for available classes, the weight assignment process should be done at least for the new combination of attributes. The challenge is how to calculate the new weights so that the system can adopt the changes, keep its stability with respect to the old attributes, and stay in use in a dynamic environment without the help of a knowledge engineer.

Since the system is supposed to be used dynamically, no matter how good the applied algorithms are, the weights estimated by the system must be validated continuously. Otherwise the system may go wrong and cause potential damages. Therefore, we believe that incremental learning should be characterized by three characteristics. In addition to the above two, the third one is indeed a self-validation and online warning scheme to inform the user if the system cannot reach a decision within the acceptable range of validity metrics (accuracy, precision, sensitivity, and specificity). In the following, our approach to these three issues is explained.

3   Learning New Weights Dynamically

Decomposition method (local and overall similarities, calculated by the use of attribute weights) is the most widely used technique for similarity calculations. We use the same technique but to solve the incrementality problem, we define weights as follows.

$$w_i = w_i(a_i, A_j) \qquad (1)$$

Where an attribute weight w_i is considered to be a function of not only its attribute a_i but also the attribute-group A_j it belongs to. This approach can also help in counting the synergic effects among the attributes. A case is also defined as: Case = (time-tag, $a_1...a_n$, A_j, pi) in the case library, where time-tag is the case ID, $a_1...a_n$ are attributes, and pi is the performance index for the self-validation process.

For each attribute group A_j the domain expert gives his preferred weights as an accepted range. The average of this range serves as a starting point in estimating weights. A performance learner does learning the values of weights in the system. When a new A_j is introduced, typically the number of related cases is small. Thus a leave-one-out resampling technique is used for the first time weights are estimated and the corresponding validation. This is done in a batch mode and as the number of cases increases for that A_j, k-fold and finally a simple partitioning method can be used for modification and validation of weights.

Weight correction (in the batch process) is done only when a misclassification occurs. This prevents the system, to some extent, from overfitting problem but can cause a slow convergence of weights. Since we start with the values recommended by the domain expert, the speed of convergence is not critical. The value of change in weights can be determined by taking derivative of the similarity function if it happens to be a smooth function. Otherwise, simpler methods can be used.

4 Batch Validation Scheduling

When to start the batch process for an attribute group is determined by batch validation scheduling algorithm. The idea is basically how to shift the learned weights from short-term to long-term memory and also in opposite direction if the performance of weights is not satisfactory. Fig. 1 shows the general concept of short-term to long-term memory. In short-term memory ideas are more subject to change and show less resistance (R); while in long-term memory the resistance to change is greater and we need much more evidence to change the idea. The purpose of scheduling is to make the system able to differentiate between newly accepted weights and the ones that there have been many cases supporting them. We like the system to be careful and suspicious about the former (sooner batch validation) and feel more relax about the latter (longer periods between two batch validations).

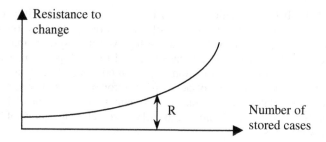

Fig. 1. Short-term and long-term memory

In other words, we try to define a spectrum that begins with the first assigned weights, by the domain expert, (short-term memory) where limited number of cases support the weights and finally ends at long-term memory where many verified cases support the weights. The algorithm that controls this process applies a Fibonacci series to the number of stored cases and also considers the performance of the system since the last validation process. We start the Fibonacci series by $F_0 = 0$ and the next point is when F_1 = some statistically sound number for the number of cases to be validated for their weights (say 30). In other words, any number in the original Fibonacci series is multiplied by this number (30). The rest of the series follows as usual.

$$F_i = F_{i-1} + F_{i-2} \qquad\qquad \text{for } i \geq 2 \qquad\qquad (2)$$

The result of each validation determines *stay, move forward, or move backward* in Fibonacci position (i.e. when to do the next validation). By "when" here we mean the number of stored cases for an attribute group since the last batch validation. If the performance is satisfactory, it steps forward in the Fibonacci series meaning that more cases are stored before initiating the batch process. If the performance is not satisfactory, however, it decides either to step backward or stay in the same position in the series. This process helps the system to react faster when there are valuable things to be learned and, on the other hand, do not keep busy when nothing new is to be learned. It also helps in forgetting what has been learned inappropriately. The algorithm for the batch validation scheduling is as follows.

`P` := acceptable performance (say 85%); given by domain expert

`p` := performance of this period of batch process; based on reliability metrics

Δp := the change in p;   between the last and current periods

$\varepsilon > 0$; significance margin for performance (say 5%) given by domain expert

if $p \geq$ `P` then *move forward;* $(F = F_{i+1})$;

if $(p <$ `P` $\& - \varepsilon \geq \Delta p)$ then *move backward;* $(F = F_{i-1})$ i.e. Δp is worse

if $(p <$ `P` $\& \ |\Delta p| < \varepsilon)$ then *stay;* $(F = F_i)$ i.e. Δp is acceptable but not p

5 Self-Validation Scheme

The role of the batch validation process is to analyze the reliability of the refined weights that are calculated at the end of each period. In addition to the above mentioned batch validation, there is an online warning system that evaluates the performance of the system as every case is added to it. A performance index, pi, is saved for each case after its verification and it can take one of the four possible values (TP, TN, FP, FN). Calculation of accumulators for pi's is done online for each A_j. Using these accumulators, validation metrics, namely accuracy, precision, sensitivity, and specificity, are calculated online and if they are below the threshold (assigned by the user), a warning is issued.

References

1. Aha D.W., Maney T., and Breslow L.A. Supporting dialogue inferencing in conversational case-based reasoning. Technical Report AIC-98-008, Naval Research Laboratory, Navy Center for Applied Research in Artificial Intelligence, Washington, DC, (1998)
2. Althoff K., Wess S., and Traphoner R. 1996. Inreca-A seamless integration of induction and case-based reasoning for decision support tasks. http://citeseer.nj.nec.com April 15, (2000)
3. Grossberg S. Competitive Learning: From interactive activation to adaptive resonance, in: Neural Networks and Natural Intelligence, A Bradford Book, MIT Press, Cambridge, MA. (1988)

Planning Animations Using Cinematography Knowledge

Kevin Kennedy and Robert E. Mercer

Cognitive Engineering Laboratory, Department of Computer Science
The University of Western Ontario, London, Ontario, CANADA
kevink@csd.uwo.ca, mercer@csd.uwo.ca

Abstract. Our research proposes and demonstrates with a prototype system an automated aid for animators in presenting their ideas and intentions using the large range of techniques available in cinematography. An experienced animator can use techniques far more expressive than the simple presentation of spatial arrangements. They can use effects and idioms such as framing, pacing, colour selection, lighting, cuts, pans and zooms to express their ideas. In different contexts, a combination of techniques can create an enhanced effect or lead to conflicting effects. Thus there is a rich environment for automated reasoning and planning about cinematographic knowledge. Our system employs a knowledge base of cinematographic techniques such as lighting, colour choice, framing, and pacing to enhance the expressive power of an animation.

The prototype system does not create animations, but assists in their generation. It is intended to enhance the expressiveness of a possibly inexperienced animator when working in this medium.

1 Related Work

Some computer graphics systems have incorporated cinematographic principles. He *et al.* [3] apply rules of cinematography to generate camera angles and shot transitions in 3D communication situations. Their real-time camera controller uses an hierarchical finite state machine to represent the cinematographic rules. Ridsdale and Calvert [8] have used AI techniques to design animations of interacting characters from scripts and relational constraints. Karp and Feiner [4, 5] approach the problem of organizing a film as a top-down planning problem. Their method concentrates on the structure and sequencing of film segments. Perlin and Goldberg [7] have used AI techniques to develop tools to author the behaviour of interactive virtual actors. Sack and Davis [9] use a GPS model to build image sequences of pre-existing cuts based on cinematographic idioms.

Butz [2] has implemented a tool with similar goals to our own for the purposes of generating animations that explain the function of mechanical devices. The system uses visual effects to convey a communicative goal. The animation scripts are incrementally generated in real time and are presented immediately to the user.

E. Stroulia and S. Matwin (Eds.): AI 2001, LNAI 2056, pp. 357–360, 2001.
© Springer-Verlag Berlin Heidelberg 2001

2   RST Plan Representation

The transformation from animator intent into presentation actions requires some
type of structured methodology to allow implementation. For this purpose we are
employing Rhetorical Structure Theory (RST) [6]. Though RST was envisioned
as a tool for the analysis of text, it also functions in a generative role. Its focus
on communicative goals is useful for modelling the intentions of the author, and
how these intentions control the presentation of the text. This technique is used
by Andre and Rist to design illustrated documents [1].

In our work the author is replaced by an animator and the text is replaced
with images. The communicative acts are not comprised of sentences, but are
assembled from the structure and presentation of the scene.

3   Design Approach

We are using a traditional AI approach: acquire and represent the knowledge,
then build a reasoning system. The source of our knowledge is a traditional
cinematography textbook [10]. The knowledge in this book is general in nature
but has a simple rule-based approach. There are three major components to the
reasoning system: the knowledge base, the planner, and the renderer.

Knowledge Base. The knowledge base is our attempt to capture the "common
sense" of cinematography. Some important concepts represented in the knowledge base are: cameras, camera positions, field of view, lights, colours, scenes,
stage positions, solid objects, spatial relationships, 3D vectors, occlusion, moods,
themes and colour/light effects.

Figure 1 shows an example of some of the knowledge presented in our cinematography reference text in several chapters on scene lighting. In this figure we
have broken down the techniques described into their major classifications ar-
ranging them from left to right according to the visual "energy" they convey. The
terms written below each lighting method are the thematic or emotional effects
that are associated with these techniques. It is these effects that the animator
can select when constructing a scene with our program.

In addition to lighting techniques, the knowledge base represents camera
effects like framing, zooms, and wide-angle or narrow-angle lenses. Colour selections for objects and backgrounds as well as their thematic meanings are also
contained in the knowledge base. These three major techniques (lighting, colour,
and framing) can be used to present a wide variety of effects to the viewer.

We have used a qualitative reasoning approach to representation in our
knowledge base. For instance, a **size** instance is categorized as one-of **tiny**,
small, **medium-size**, **large**, and **very-large** while stage positions consist of
locations like **stage-right** or **stage-left-rear**.

The knowledge base is written in LOOM, a Classification/Subsumption based
language written in LISP. LOOM represents knowledge using Concepts and Relations which are arranged in a classification hierarchy. LOOM's power lies in
its ability to classify concepts into the classification hierarchy automatically.

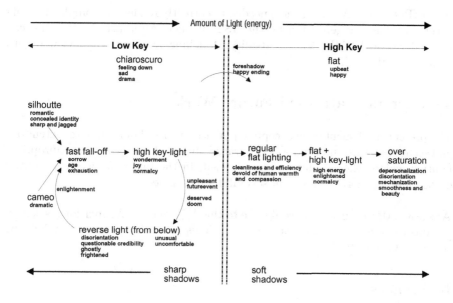

Fig. 1. Semantic Deconstruction of Cinematography Lighting Models

Planner. The planner constructs RST plans which contain cinematographic instructions for presenting animation scenes. The planner is a depth-first forward chainer that actively analyzes the effects of the RST plan steps. While the RST plan is being constructed, the planner searches through the space of all possible RST plans implied by the predefined RST plan steps. The partial RST plan at any point is the "state" of the planner as it searches through possible plans.

As the planner proceeds, a description of the animation shot is created. A Shot concept contains relations (in frame terminology, slots) for characters, light-sets, colour-choices, camera positions, etc. The specifics of a particular Shot are created through a series of constraints and assertions to the knowledge base. This specific Shot is an "instance" of the the Shot "concept". If at any point a Shot instance is found to be inconsistent (for example, it is constrained as both brightly lit and dark at the same time) then this branch fails and the planner backtracks to try another approach.

If a plan succeeds, the resulting shot is presented to the animator. At this point, the animator can evaluate the scene using his or her own criteria and can choose to accept or reject the result. If the animator rejects a shot, the planner is told that the current solution is a failure. The planner then back-tracks to the most recent choice point, and continues to search for another solution.

Renderer. After the planner has found an RST plan for a shot, it can be rendered. The Shot instance for the plan contains all information needed to render the scene visually. For this task we use the Persistence of Vision ray-tracer (POV-ray). A ray-tracer is needed to correctly render the complex lighting effects that can be generated by the RST planner. Alternatively, the shot can be rendered to VRML (Virtual Reality Modelling Language) and viewed with an appropriate tool.

4   Current Status and Future Work

The present implementation accepts input statements about animator intentions and scene structure and produces ray-traced images of the scene with appropriate lighting, colour choice, and framing applied. In the future we will concentrate on assembling short scenes from several distinct shots.

Acknowledgements. We would like to thank Robert E. Webber for his contributions to an earlier version of this paper. This research was funded by NSERC Research Grant 0036853.

References

1. E. Andre and T. Rist. The design of illustrated documents as a planning task. In *Intelligent Multimedia Interfaces*, pages 94–116. American Association for Artificial Intelligence, 1993.
2. A. Butz. Anymation with CATHI. In *Proceedings of the 14th Annual National Conference on Artificial Intelligence (AAAI/IAAI)*, pages 957–962. AAAI Press, 1997.
3. L.-w. He, M. F. Cohen, and D. H. Salesin. The Virtual Cinematographer: A Paradigm for Automatic Real-Time Camera Control and Directing. *Computer Graphics*, pages 217–224, August 1996. SIGGRAPH '96.
4. P. Karp and S. Feiner. Issues in the automated generation of animated presentations. In *Proceedings Graphics Interface '90*, pages 39–48. Canadian Information Processing Society, May 1990.
5. P. Karp and S. Feiner. Automated presentation planning of animation using task decomposition with heuristic reasoning. In *Proceedings Graphics Interface '93*, pages 118–127. Canadian Information Processing Society, May 1993.
6. W. C. Mann and S. A. Thompson. Rhetorical structure theory: Toward a functional theory of text organization. *Text*, 8(13):243–281, 1988.
7. K. Perlin. Real Time Responsive Animation with Personality. *IEEE Transactions on Visualization and Computer Graphics*, 1(1):5–15, March 1995.
8. G. Ridsdale and T. Calvert. Animating microworlds from scripts and relational constraints. In N. Magnenat-Thalmann and D. Thalmann, editors, *Computer Animation '90*, pages 107–118. Springer-Verlag, 1990.
9. W. Sack and M. Davis. IDIC: Assembling Video Sequences from Story Plans and Content Annotations. In *Proceedings International Conference on Multimedia Computers and Systems*, pages 30–36. IEEE Computer Society Press, 1994.
10. H. Zettl. *Sight Sound Motion: Applied Media Aesthetics*. Wadsworth Publishing Company, 1990.

Watching You, Watching Me

Joe MacInnes[1,2], Omid Banyasad[1], and Afzal Upal[1]

[1]Faculty of Computer Science
and
[2]Department of Psychology
Dalhousie University. Halifax, Nova Scotia Canada

Abstract. This paper demonstrates the use of recursive modelling of opponent agents in an adversarial environment. In many adversarial environments, agents need to model their opponents and other environmental objects to predict their actions in order to outperform them. In this work, we use Deterministic Finite Automata (DFA) for modelling agents. We also assume that all the actions performed by agents are regular. Every agent assumes that other agents use the same model as its own but without recursion. The objective of this work is to investigate if recursive modelling allows an agent to outperform its opponents that are using similar models.

1. Introduction

Agents in any environment have a difficult task in modelling the world and their own place in it. Multi-agent environments, particularly with adversarial agents, have the additional problem of the world state being changed by another autonomous entity. In fact, it is the goal of adversarial agents to make it difficult for your agent to succeed. Opponent modelling is a process by which an agent attempts to determine an adversary's most likely actions based on previous observations of that opponent. This can be extended recursively by trying to determine what your opponent thinks of you. We will test this"Recursive Modelling" (you watching me, watching you, watching me...) in a 3-D game environment to determine the optimal depth of this recursion.

2. Environment

We have developed a 3-D "Quake-like" engine to test recursive modelling of autonomous "Quake-Bots" or in our case "Maze-Bots".This environment is ideal for this testing for a number of reasons. 3-D games offer a very rich, dynamic environment in which simulations can be run. The environment can be very easily extended so that the agents compete with and learn from human players with the exact same knowledge, limitations and abilities. Our environment consisted of a maze-like arena with a variety of randomly placed walls for hiding and strategy. The goal of each Maze-Bot was to search for and shoot its opponent, while minimizing the number of times that it was shot. A match ended when one of the agents was shot,

E. Stroulia and S. Matwin (Eds.): AI 2001, LNAI 2056, pp. 361-365, 2001.

causing the defeated agent to be 'spawned' to a new random location and a new match begun. Performance was determined by the number of matches won.

To allow for more interesting strategies, each agent had imperfect knowledge of the world state according to the following guidelines: Agents had perfect knowledge of their own position/state in the world; Agents were only be able to "see" objects in front of them with a 60 degree filed of view; Agents could "feel" when they bumped into an object, or if an agent bumped in to them; Bullets travelled at 10 times the speed of an agent; Agents could not fire a second shot until the first bullet hit an object. Each agent had an unlimited number of bullets in its gun.

3. Agent Model

In this work, we used Deterministic Finite State (DFS) machines to model each agent. The DFS machine used for each player was pre-defined and each agent had knowledge of the other agent's model. In fact, both players used similar models with minor differences. The basic machine used for the first player monitored the state of the world and actions of the other player. Since game theory states that two players are in constant interaction, the output of this model was the action to be taken by the agent *at that moment.* Planning only occurred (implicitly) in the selection of discrete actions. The modelling component added knowledge of the opponent to this decision in an attempt to produce a more successful action. The second player used the same model, differing only in the level of recursion used to predict its opponents next move. To avoid an infinite recursive loop, each agent assumed that the other was not modelling recursively.

In this environment, each agent was in one of two different states: Search state (the default state) occurred whenever an agent was unable to determine the actions of its opponent (player B is not in player A sensors' range). In this state, all the actions of the agent were decided based on the information gathered from the environment. As soon as any sensor provided information about the opponent, the agent entered Fight state. There was also an insignificant End state entered at the end of each match.

The prediction function used in the fight state was at the very heart of the recursive modelling. Unfortunately, it was only possible to estimate (with a fairly high degree of accuracy) where the opponent would be. The algorithm assumed a triangle with vertices being the Agent's current position (A), the opponent's current position (B) and the Opponent's anticipated future position. Substituting the known distance (Dist), the known angle ($\mathcal{H}$) along with the ratio of agent movement to bullet movement(x,5x) to the law of cosines we get:

$(5X)^2 = X^2 + D^2 - 2XD\cos(\mathcal{H})$ or   (1)

$24X^2 + 2XD\cos(\mathcal{H}) - D^2 = 0$ (2)

since X is the only unknown in this polynomial we can solve using the quadratic formula.

$X = (-b +/- \text{sqrt}(b2 - 4ac))/2a$ (3)

Unfortunately this added some uncertainty to our solution since the result of the square root can be positive or negative. In experiment 1, rotations clockwise used the positive result and counterclockwise used the negative. Although this prediction worked for most cases, it was not perfect. Prediction errors occurred when the opponent changes state after the shot was fired, as well as the occasional error from the prediction function itself. For experiment 2, The prediction calculation was fine-tuned; All variables were converted from floating point to double precision, and the estimate of the known angle (B) was improved. After these enhancements, solving for the polynomial was consistently accurate using the positive square root value. The only remaining source of error was from an opponent changing state after the shot was fired.

4. Results and Discussion

Performance of the agents were analysed based on the level of recursive modelling used. Matches were arranged for analysis using a Latin Square design (Each recursive level played all of the others in a best out of 15 round robin) up to a maximum recursion of 4 (R0-3). These results were subjected to a 1-within (recursive level) by 1-between (experiment) repeated Analysis of Variance (ANOVA) and are displayed in figure 2. There was a main significant effect of Recursive level ($F(3,30) = 29.0$, $P < .0001$) and a marginal interaction between recursive level and experiment ($F(3,30) = 2.7$, $P < .07$).

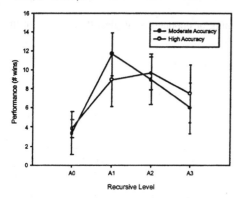

Fig. 1. The effect of recursive level (*R0-4*) on agent performance for both levels of prediction accuracy (*Moderate and High*).

In both experiments, the recursive agents (R1-3) outperformed the non-recursive agent (R0) in every match. The major difference between experiments, was the optimal level of recursion. In experiment 1, R1 agents outperformed all other agents. That they outperformed the non-recursive agent was no surprise, but the fact that they did better than agents with deeper recursion was unexpected. One explanation for this result lies in the errors embedded in the prediction function. Prediction of an opponent's location was prone to errors in rounding, use of the quadratic formula as well as future changes to the opponents state.

It is likely that the decrease in performance was due to these errors compounding as the recursive level increased. Evidence for this theory can be seen in experiment 2, where the prediction function was modified to eliminate rounding and mathematical errors. The only remaining errors would be generated by future changes in state by the opponent agent. In this experiment, the R2 agents have the optimal performance and it is not until R3 that performance drop is noted.

5. Conclusion

Opponent modelling and recursive modelling have been shown to improve performance of agents in a dynamic 'quake-like' environment. The degree of improvement for recursive modelling, however, seems directly linked to the accuracy of the model that agent uses. If there are any errors or assumptions in the model of the opponent, performance will degrade increasingly with the level of recursion used. Errors in prediction compound the more often they are used and the optimal level of recursion depends, at least in part, on the accuracy with which an opponent is modelled.

References

1.   Angluin, D.: Learning regular sets from queries and counterexamples. Information and Computation (1987) 75:87-106.
2.   Carmel, D. and Markovitch, S.: Learning Models of Intelligent Agents, Technical Report CIS9606 (1996).
3.   Gold, E. M.: Complexity of automaton identification from given data, Information and Control (1978) 37:302-320.
4.   Hopcroft, J. E. and Ullma, J. D.: Introduction to Automata Theory, Languages, and Computation. Addison Wesley, Boston (1979).
5.   Hu, J. and Wellman, M. P.: Online Learning about Other Agents in a Dynamic Multiagent System, Second International Conference on Autonomous Agents, (1998) 239-246.
6.   Peterson, G. and Cook, D. J.: DFA learning of opponent strategies, Proceedings of the Florida AI Research Symposium (1998).

Author Index

Lecture Notes in Artificial Intelligence (LNAI)

Lecture Notes in Computer Science